Governance, Democracy and Sustainable Development

Governance, Democracy and Sustainable Development

Moving Beyond the Impasse

Edited by

James Meadowcroft

Professor, School of Public Policy and Administration and Department of Political Science, Carleton University, Canada

Oluf Langhelle

Professor, Faculty of Social Sciences, University of Stavanger, Norway

Audun Ruud

Research Manager on Policy and Governance, SINTEF Energy Research AS, Trondheim, Norway

Edward Elgar

Cheltenham, UK • Northampton, MA, USA

Published by
Edward Elgar Publishing Limited
The Lypiatts
15 Lansdown Road
Cheltenham
Glos GL50 2JA
UK

Edward Elgar Publishing, Inc.
William Pratt House
9 Dewey Court
Northampton
Massachusetts 01060
USA

A catalogue record for this book
is available from the British Library

Library of Congress Control Number: 2012940185

ISBN 978 1 84980 756 2 (cased)

Typeset by Servis Filmsetting Ltd, Stockport, Cheshire
Printed and bound by MPG Books Group, UK

Contents

v

Figures

Tables

Contributors

Carlo Aall is head of the environment research group at the Western Norway Research Institute (WNRI), Sogndal, Norway. Earlier he worked as environmental adviser to the municipality of Ølen. Since 1996 he and his wife have been involved with a farm restaurant specializing in organic and local food (www.henjatunet.no).

Susan Baker is Professor in Environmental Social Sciences, Cardiff School of Social Sciences andLead Academic, Sustainable Places Research Institute, both at Cardiff University, UK. Her research interests relate to the environment and sustainability and she has published widely in this area.

Elizabeth Bomberg is Senior Lecturer in Politics and International Relations at the University of Edinburgh, UK. Her research and teaching focus on environmental politics and policy, especially in Europe and the United States.

Hans T.A. Bressers is Professor of Policy Studies and Environmental Policy at the University of Twente in the Netherlands, and founder of the Centre for Studies in Technology and Sustainable Development (CSTM). He has written widely on environmental policy, particularly in the water management area. Among other public and advisory roles he has served as vice-chairman of the permanent Evaluation Committee of the Environmental Management Act, which advises the Minister on the efficacy of Dutch environmental policy.

Per-Olof Busch is a post-doctoral researcher and lecturer at the Chair of International Organizations and Public Policy at the Faculty of Economics and Social Sciences of the University of Potsdam, Germany. His current research focuses on international institutions and organizations; the role of communication, emulation and learning in international policy coordination; the repercussions of political and economic globalization on national and international politics; and cross-national policy diffusion and policy convergence.

Frans H.J.M. Coenen is Professor at the University of Twente, the Netherlands. He currently heads the Centre for Studies in Technology and Sustainable Development (CSTM) at the university. He specializes in regional environmental policy planning and in public participation for sustainable development.

Katarina Eckerberg is Professor in Political Science, especially Public Administration, Umeå University, Sweden. Her research comprises the field of policy analysis and implementation of environment and sustainable development from the international to the local level, often with a European comparative perspective, including studies of nature conservation, forestry and agricultural policy, environmental policy instruments and Local Agenda 21. She has served on several research boards in Sweden, Norway and the EU as well as high-level advisory bodies in the field of environment and sustainable development.

Helge Jörgens is Senior Lecturer at the Department of Political and Social Sciences of the Freie Universität Berlin,and Managing Director of the Environmental Policy Research Centre (FFU), Berlin, Germany. His main research interests are in the field of comparative environmental politics, the cross-national diffusion and convergence of policies and ideas, and the role of international public administrations in world politics.

William M. Lafferty was until recently Professor of Political Science at the University of Oslo, Norway, and Director of the Programme for Research and Documentation for a Sustainable Society (ProSus) in Norway. He is also Professor Emeritus in Strategic Research for Sustainable Development in Europe at the University of Twente, The Netherlands. He has written widely in the domains of policy-making for the environment and sustainable development.

Oluf Langhelle is Professor of Political Science at the University of Stavanger, Norway. He teaches sustainable development and corporate social responsibility at the University of Stavanger, and his main research interests and publications are in the field of environmental politics and sustainable development.

Lennart J. Lundqvist is Professor of Environmental Policy and Administration at Göteborg University, Sweden. His book *The Hare and the Tortoise: Clean Air Policies in the United States and Sweden* appeared in 1980. Since then, he has published numerous chapters and articles on environmental policy. In 2004, Manchester University Press published his *Sweden and Ecological Governance – Straddling the Fence.*

James Meadowcroft is Professor in the School of Public Policy and Administration, and in the Department of Political Science, at Carleton University, Ottawa, Canada. He holds a Canada Research Chair in

Governance for Sustainable Development. His research focuses on reforms to structures and processes of governance as political systems manage issues of sustainability.

Gerard Mullally is Lecturer in Sociology in the School of Sociology and Philosophy at University College Cork, Ireland. His teaching and research interests include environmental sociology, sustainable development and deliberative democracy. He is currently researching the themes of citizenship and climate change in Ireland.

Michael Narodoslawsky is Professor at the Technical University of Graz, Austria. He has published extensively on sustainability indicators and sustainable regional development. His current research interests include life-cycle analysis of different technologies and products, as well as the synthesis of process networks in renewable resource utilization.

Audun Ruud is Research Manager at SINTEF Energy Research, Trondheim, Norway. He is responsible for activities related to energy policy and governance, but in close dialogue with more technical research on concerns related to production, transmission and consumption of electricity. Ruud is currently particularly concerned with sustainable electricity grid development, planning and public engagement, and how to reconcile energy and environmental concerns in the production of renewable electricity.

Miranda A. Schreurs is Director of the Environmental Policy Research Centre and Professor of Comparative Politics at the Freie Universität Berlin, Germany. Her work focuses on comparative environmental politics and policy in Europe, the US and East Asia. Since 2008 she has served on the German Advisory Council on the Environment.

Preface

This collection of essays has its origins in the 'Oslo Symposium on Democracy, Research Engagement and Sustainable Development', which was held at the Voksenåsen Conference Centre in 2009. The meeting was convened to honour William M. Lafferty, on the occasion of his retirement as Director of the Programme for Research and Documentation for a Sustainable Society (ProSus), a 15-year strategic research initiative supported by the Research Council of Norway. The Symposium generated a lively intellectual exchange around a set of critical issues facing modern societies, and it provided an opportunity for colleagues and collaborators to mark the significance of Lafferty's contributions to research, particularly in the area of the environment and sustainable development.

Lafferty's distinguished academic career spans more than four decades. He held a series of positions, including: Director of Research at the Institute for Social Research, Oslo; Director of Doctoral Studies for the Research Council of Norway at the Faculty of the Social Sciences, University of Oslo; Professor of Political Science at the University of Oslo; and Professor of Strategic Research for Sustainable Development in Europe, Centre for Clean Technology and Environmental Policy (CSTM), University of Twente, in the Netherlands.

Over the years Lafferty has made important contributions to research, education and international collaboration. His research activity can be divided into two basic phases. During the earlier period his work focused on the labour movement, social democracy and the Nordic welfare state (see for example: Lafferty 1971; Lafferty 1975; Lafferty 1981; Lafferty and Hagtvet 1984; Lafferty and Knutsen 1984). During the later period his chief interest shifted to the environment and sustainable development. But a number of threads tie these phases together, including an abiding concern with issues of democracy, equity and citizen influence over centres of economic and political power.

Over the past two decades Lafferty has generated an impressive body of published work relating to the challenge of sustainable development. This includes conceptual analysis of sustainable development (Lafferty 1996; Lafferty and Langhelle 1999), research on national implementation of sustainable development in advanced industrialized countries (Lafferty and Meadowcroft 2000), on local engagement with sustainable development (Lafferty and Eckerberg 1998; Lafferty 2001), on the governance challenges associated with sustainable development (Lafferty 2004), and on renewable energy (Lafferty and Ruud 2008). He was one of the first scholars to insist on the importance of examining exactly what national and local governments were *actually doing* in the name of sustainable development after the idea had been officially endorsed as an international norm at the Rio Earth Summit in 1992 (Lafferty 1996). His work points to the particularities of the governance challenge associated with sustainable development, while also making connections to longer-running issues about democratic self-government (Lafferty and Meadowcroft 1996; Lafferty 2000). His work on 'environmental policy integration' argues that sometimes environmental concerns must trump those of development interests (Lafferty and Hovden 2004). And his invocation of the famous maxim that 'form follows function' in relation to governance for sustainable development is intended to emphasize that significant changes to established governance structures and practices are required if a shift in the current inequitable and environmentally destructive development trajectory is ever to materialize (Lafferty 2004).

With respect to education and training Lafferty devoted substantial effort to raising a young generation of graduate students and to mentoring academics at the early phases of their careers. In the earlier period this work was primarily centred around doctoral training at the Institute for Social Research and University of Oslo, but after he became Director of ProSus this also included a more practically focused orientation.

Lafferty's international contributions include extensive service to international political science associations. He was a founding member of the International Society for Political Psychology (ISPP), and joint Programme Chair of the 10th Anniversary World Congress in San Francisco in 1984. He served four consecutive terms as Norway's representative to the Governing Council of the International Political Science Association (IPSA); was a member of the IPSA Executive Committee between 1995 and 2000; and served as Programme Chair of the 18th World Congress of Political Science in Quebec in 2000. But Lafferty's international contribution was above all realized through his commitment to collaborative comparative research – working with colleagues, especially from European nations, on a series of innovative projects.

On a personal note, the editors would like to acknowledge the support and encouragement which William Lafferty provided to their own work over the years. Meadowcroft and Lafferty met in 1993 as they were scouring the publishers' tables at the Annual General Meeting of the American Political Science Association, searching for new titles on the environment and sustainability. Although that search proved rather fruitless (revealing just a handful of new titles from the 30-odd assembled publishers – which just shows how times have changed), the chance encounter paved the way for a series of subsequent collaborations. Langhelle first encountered Lafferty as a student at the University of Oslo in courses on democracy in 1989. He then had Lafferty as his supervisor both for his master's and PhD theses. Langhelle got his first real job as a research assistant for Lafferty in 1993 and they worked closely together for six years. Ruud first met Lafferty while he was completing his PhD dissertation at the University of Oslo, and from 2000 he worked as senior researcher with ProSus. Ruud has since taken over the leadership of the reconstituted ProSus research unit within SINTEF Energy Research AS in Trondheim and Oslo.

In fact, all the authors included in this volume have worked directly with Lafferty at some point, and view their contributions as a way of honouring his continuing legacy to the environment and sustainable development research enterprise.

In this context, we would like particularly to highlight three important characteristics of William Lafferty's work. First, his deep commitment to intellectual rigour, and to a tradition of political science that acknowledges debts to the classic works of the discipline, and which remains open to insights provided by different methodological approaches and theoretical traditions. Second, he has always advocated an engaged social science, a perspective that is neither obsessed with abstract theory-building nor mired in empiricism, that is not afraid to engage with the big questions confronting modern societies, and believes that intellectuals have a duty of service to the communities in which they live. And, finally, we would like to acknowledge Lafferty's great generosity of spirit and his willingness to offer continuous support and encouragement to his students and collaborators.

James Meadowcroft
Oluf Langhelle
Audun Ruud

WORKS BY WILLIAM M. LAFFERTY CITED IN THE PREFACE

Lafferty, William M. (1971), *Economic Development and the Response of Labor in Scandinavia: A Multi-Level Approach*, Oslo: Oslo University Press.
Lafferty, William M. (1975), 'Participation and democratic theory: reworking the premises for a participatory society', *Scandinavian Political Studies*, 10, 52–70.

Lafferty, William M. (1981), *Participation and Democracy in Norway: The 'Distant Democracy' Revisited,* Oslo: Oslo University Press.

Lafferty, William M. (1984), 'Decision-making involvement in Norway: the nature and scope of citizen access in a social democratic polity', *European Journal of Political Research,* 12, 43–58.

Lafferty, William M. (1996), 'The politics of sustainable development: global norms for national implementation', *Environmental Politics,* 5, 185–208.

Lafferty, William M. (2000), 'Democracy and ecological rationality: new trials for an old ceremony', in Guy Lachapelle and John Trent (eds), *Globalization, Governance and Identity: The Emergence of New Partnerships,* Montreal, QC: Montreal University Press, pp. 39–65.

Lafferty, William M. (ed.) (2001), *Sustainable Communities in Europe,* London: Earthscan.

Lafferty, William M. (ed.) (2004), *Governance for Sustainable Development: The Challenge of Adapting Form to Function,* Cheltenham, UK and Northampton, MA, USA: Edward Elgar.

Lafferty, William M. and Katarina Eckerberg (eds) (1998), *From the Earth Summit to Local Agenda 21: Working towards Sustainable Development,* London: Earthscan.

Lafferty, William M. and Bernt Hagtvet (eds) (1984), *Demokrati og Demokratisering* [*Democracy and Democratization*], Oslo: Aschehoug Forlag.

Lafferty, William M. and Eivind Hovden (2004), 'Environmental policy integration: towards an analytical framework', *Environmental Politics,* 12 (1), 1–22.

Lafferty, William M. and Oddbjørn Knutsen (1984), 'Leftist and rightist ideology in a social democratic state: an analysis of Norway in the midst of the conservative resurgence', *British Journal of Political Science,* 14, 345–67.

Lafferty, William M. and Oluf Langhelle (eds) (1999), *Towards Sustainable Development,* London: Macmillan Publishers.

Lafferty, William M. and James Meadowcroft (eds) (1996), *Democracy and the Environment: Problems and Prospects,* Cheltenham, UK and Brookfield, USA: Edward Elgar.

Lafferty, William M. and James Meadowcroft (eds) (2000) *The Implementation of Sustainable Development in High-Consumption Societies,* Oxford: Oxford University Press.

Lafferty, William M. and Audun Ruud (eds) (2008), *Promoting Sustainable Electricity in Europe: Challenging the Path Dependency of Dominant Energy Systems,* Cheltenham, UK and Northampton, MA, USA: Edward Elgar.

Abbreviations and acronyms

AR4	Fourth Assessment Report of the IPCC
AWM	adaptive water management
BP	British Petroleum
C	Celsius
CA	county administration
CAFOD	Catholic Agency for Overseas Development
CAN Europe	Climate Action Network
CAN-E	Climate Action Network Europe
CCA	climate change adaptation
CCM	climate change mitigation
CD	competitive democracy
CDBs	county development boards
CEIs	chief environmental inspectors
Comhar SDC	Sustainable Development Council
CoP	Conference of Parties
CSD	United Nations Commission on Sustainable Development
DOE	Department of the Environment
DOECLG	Department of the Environment, Community and Local Government (Ireland)
DSB	Directorate for Civil Protection and Emergency Planning (Norway)
EC	European Commission
ECEN	European Christian Environmental Network
EEA	European Environmental Agency
EEAC	European Environment and Sustainable Development Advisory Councils
EENGO	Environmental Ecological NGO
EEB	European Environment Bureau
EEN	Evangelical Environmental Network
ENOVA	Norwegian Agency on Energy Saving
EPI	environmental policy integration
EPIGOV	Coordinated Action on Environmental Policy Integration and Multi-level Governance

ETS	emission trading scheme
EU	European Union
FDI	foreign direct investment
FoE Europe	Friends of the Earth Europe
FoE	Friends of the Earth US
GHG	greenhouse gases
ha	hectare
ICLEI	Local Governments for Sustainability
IEA	International Energy Agency
IEEP	Institute of European Environmental Policy
IEN	Irish Environmental Network
IFN	International Friends of Nature
IPCC	Intergovernmental Panel on Climate Change
IUCN	International Union for the Conservation of Nature
IWM	integrated water management
IWRM	integrated water resources management
km	kilometre
KS	Association of Local and Regional Authorities (Norway)
LA21	Local Agenda 21
LCCA	local climate change adaptation
LIP	Local Investment Programme for Ecologically Sustainable Development
LONA	Swedish Local Nature Conservation Programme
KLIMP	state grants to local climate investment programmes (Sweden)
MENA	Middle East and North African
MIK	Environment in the Municipalities (Norway)
NAE	National Association of Evangelicals
NCPP	National Centre for Partnership and Performance
NEQOs	(Swedish) National Environmental Quality Objectives
NESC	National Economic and Social Council
NESDO	National Economic and Social Development Office
NESF	National Economic and Social Forum
NGOs	non-government organizations
NORADAPT	Community Adaptation and Vulnerability in Norway
NORKLIMA	Norwegian research programme 'Climate Change and Impacts of Norway'
NRDC	Natural Resources Defense Council
NSDS	National Sustainable Development Strategy

OECD	Organisation for Economic Co-operation and Development
ProSus	Programme for Research and Documentation for a Sustainable Society
rNSDS	revised National Sustainable Development Strategy
SCB	Statistics Sweden
SD	sustainable development
SEA	strategic environmental assessment
SEA	Swedish Election Authority
SEPA	Swedish Environmental Protection Agency
SFS	Swedish Code of Statutes
SKL	Swedish Association of Local and Regional Authorities
SNF	Swedish Society for Nature Conservation
SNG	synthetic natural gas
SRES	Special Report on Emission Scenarios
TAED	TransAtlantic Environmental Dialogue
T&E	European Federation of Transport and Environment
UK	United Kingdom
UKCIP	UK Climate Impacts Programme
UNCED	United Nations Conference on Environment and Development
UN	United Nations
USCAN	US Climate Action Network
US	United States
WCED	World Commission on Environment and Development
WCI	World Coal Institute
WFD	Water Framework Directive
WNRI	Western Norway Research Institute
WSSD	World Summit on Sustainable Development
WWF-EPO	World Wildlife Fund (European Policy Office)

1. Governance, democracy and sustainable development: moving beyond the impasse

James Meadowcroft, Oluf Langhelle and Audun Ruud

This volume is concerned with governance of the environment and sustainable development. It considers progress made in addressing environmental problems and explores the difficulties developed countries have experienced in turning more decisively towards sustainability. The individual chapters discuss various dimensions of the governance challenge (political conflicts, policy design, implementation, norms, public attitudes, citizen engagement, steering and measurement, and so on) in relation to a range of environmental problems (climate change, biodiversity/nature protection, water management). Some contributions deal with specific jurisdictions while others have a comparative focus or treat more general issues. But each chapter also says something about the way contemporary democratic systems are coping with the critical challenge of sustainable development.

Notions of sustainability or sustainable development have been central to the evolution of the environmental policy domain in recent decades. Subject to countless definitional wrangles, and continuing argument over their practical implications, these ideas nevertheless point to a critical problem confronting contemporary societies: how to meet continuing societal needs while avoiding damage to local and global ecosystems that could undermine the environmental foundations of long-term welfare. To put it another way, they problematize the current development trajectory: reconsidering the traditional trade-offs between social welfare, economy and environmental protection, and asking us to think about where society is headed, what constitutes genuine social progress, and what sort of world we want to live in.

The 1987 Report of the World Commission on Environment and Development propelled the idea of sustainable development onto the international stage. In a famous passage it characterized sustainable development as 'development that meets the needs of the present without compromising the ability of future generations to meet their own needs' (WCED 1987). Appropriately entitled *Our Common Future*, the report emphasized 'development', a process of societal advance to which all countries – rich and poor, North and South, East and West – could aspire. Development was not just about economic growth, but also about the advance of health, education, science and culture. Sustainable development would respect ecological frontiers while also being more equitable in orientation. The report pointed to vast differences in standards of living and resource consumption in developed and developing countries, arguing that an absolute priority must be placed on meeting the urgent needs of the poor. Yet it also observed that if the whole world adopted the consumption patterns of the rich countries, an impossible burden would be placed on global ecosystems. Since development in the South would ultimately require a greater claim on resources, people in the North must adjust lifestyles, technologies and social organization to dramatically reduce environmental pressures.

The institutions of modern environmental governance are a comparatively recent creation. It was during the late 1960s and early 1970s that the Organisation for Economic Co-operation and Development (OECD) states first established central environmental ministries and agencies, and adopted the framework environmental statutes and national air and water pollution laws, which laid the foundations for the current system of environmental rule (Janicke and Weidner 1997; Hanf and Jansen 1998; Long 2000; Tatenhove et al. 2001). Of course, government had long been active in domains we would today class as 'environmental' – controlling certain industrial emissions, enacting occupational safety legislation and urban sanitary codes, regulating extractive industries (mines, forests, hunting) and managing protected areas. But these activities were typically at the local level, sporadic and fragmented. During the last third of the twentieth century, however, the environment emerged as a significant field of national government activity – as a specialized policy domain, with dedicated legislation, funding and bureaucracies – involving the monitoring and regulation of societal/environmental interactions.

Over time the reach of environmental policy has continued to expand. The scope of the issues with which it is concerned, the range of societal actors with which it must engage and its connections to other policy domains have grown steadily. Key priorities have shifted in response to the identification of new issues, altered economic circumstances, ideological fashions and policy paradigms. From the 1990s the range of policy tools was broadened to include economic instruments (such as emissions trading and green taxation) and negotiated agreements. Greater attention was paid to international coordination; the number of multilateral environmental treaties proliferated; and environmental issues began to be taken more seriously in developing countries. Increased emphasis was placed on engagement with societal stakeholders such as businesses and communities. There was more discussion of 'integrating' environmental considerations into decision-making in key economic sectors and of transforming environmentally destructive patterns of production and consumption. Increasingly there was a realization that environmental policy could not just be about mitigating negative side effects of mainstream economic decision-making (often through 'end-of-pipe measures'), but rather must be concerned with re-orienting development onto lines that avoided excessive environmental pressures.

With the turn towards sustainability, environmental policy was to be 'brought out of itself'. Rather than constituting a specialized ghetto, it was to become a critical dimension of mainstream economic and political decision-making (Meadowcroft 2012). For only by transforming the overall orientation of development policy could the pressures generating environmental destruction be alleviated. This did not, of course, remove the need for specialized institutions in the environmental domain. On the contrary, specialist agencies, monitoring and programmes were needed so that the environment could be successfully integrated into the work of government as a whole.

So, how do things look four decades on from the genesis of modern environmental policy, and some 20 years after the 1992 United Nations Conference on Environment and Development (UNCED) (commonly referred to as the Rio Earth Summit) where world leaders formally endorsed the idea of sustainable development? Certainly there is no shortage of scientific assessments documenting the sorry state of the global environment and the scale of the pressures imposed upon it (IPCC 2007; MEA 2006). And in the run up to the United Nations' Rio+20 conference, official bodies, research institutes and civil society organizations produced countless reports evaluating progress (or the lack thereof) in relation to the economic, social and environmental dimensions of sustainable development.

Focusing on just the environmental side, it is sufficient for our purposes here to note that on the one hand, there have been remarkable successes: air and water quality in developed countries have improved since the 1970s; a variety of toxic substances are more rigorously controlled (heavy metals, persistent organic pollutants, particulates, mercury); protected areas have expanded; and a number of global issues (such as stratospheric ozone depletion) have begun to be addressed. The deployment of renewable energy is expanding in many countries and there are significantly improved practices for managing wastes. Environmental concerns have been integrated into the routines of government and many businesses have internalized environmental management practices. On the other hand, the absolute level of environmental impositions continues to rise globally. And in many domains (for example, greenhouse gas emissions, nitrogen loading, ocean fisheries) burdens are already far beyond what can be sustained over the long term. Some of the environmental gains in the rich countries have been achieved by shifting production overseas. And the environmental conditions in rapidly developing countries have deteriorated.

In short, while we are using the environment more efficiently, degradation is accelerating. There are simply more of us, and more of us are living high-consumption lifestyles – that involve rising material welfare, but which require large inputs of environmental resources and entail generous emission of environmentally pernicious wastes. Although the world has changed considerably since the first Stockholm conference on the Human Environment in 1972, the underlying environmental trends continue unabated.

Over the past five years in particular the political situation has been difficult, with the world economy passing from a boom (with rising resource prices and concerns about shortages) to financial crisis, economic stagnation and fiscal retrenchment. In this context environmental issues have tended to be eclipsed by other concerns, most critically economic regeneration and managing the political fallout from the economic turmoil. International climate negotiations have more or less ground to a standstill. And so long as the US in particular remains unwilling to take action to bring down domestic emissions, other parties will be tempted to equivocate. So even if a climate accord should be concluded, it looks unlikely to represent more than a symbolic effort to engage with the issue. Despite initiatives on some fronts – the promotion of renewable energy in Europe, international negotiations around mercury and the use of stimulus funds in many countries to promote green projects – the overall picture remains sombre. For every advance there is also an apparent defeat. Consider, for example, the recent rapid expansion of more environmentally destructive fossil fuels extraction methods (oil sands, natural gas 'fracking', mountain-top removal coal mining) and rapid moves to exploit the Arctic as the ice retreats with the warming climate.

This raises the question of whether we should conclude that international efforts to promote environmental protection and sustainable development have reached an impasse. Has the forward momentum stalled? Is the path forward blocked? Have the factors militating for and against change reached (at least for now) a stalemate?

Clearly, it is difficult to ground sweeping judgements of this kind. After all, the world is a big place. There is a lot going on, with many currents jostling beneath the surface. Moreover, the environment is not one thing, but an array of interconnected systems operating at different temporal and spatial scales, experienced in different ways by different peoples. Environment and society interact through many channels. Sustainable development may be conceptualized as an overall process of balanced societal change but, if so, it is a process with multiple dimensions, implications at many scales and subject to uncertainties on many levels. The debates around the construction of broadly accepted performance indicators in relation to the environment and sustainable development attest to this complex and contested reality (see for example: Mayer 2008; Langhelle and Ruud, Chapter 9 this volume).

One of the problems with talk of an impasse is that it can give the impression that all forward motion has stopped – when, of course, this may not be the case. There may be progress in some areas and not in others; and there may be barely perceptible changes that may be necessary to pave the way for more rapid transformation in the future. Another difficulty is that reference to an impasse might suggest that we are dealing with one really big obstacle to progress, which accounts for all the difficulties and which, if it could only be removed, would allow the situation to move forward. Yet it seems more likely that there are different types of barriers operative in different contexts, and that overcoming one obstacle may open up movement in some dimension but also reveal other challenges.

Granted these caveats, *impasse* does not appear too strong a word to apply, at least to certain aspects of the current context. For in many respects politics and policy for the environment and sustainable development appear systematically frustrated. Successes are scored on specific issues at particular places and particular times. But on the bigger questions, such as climate change, biodiversity conservation, the sustainable management of land or the oceans, and so on, progress appears blocked. Even issues which seem settled with a positive outcome can subsequently come undone. Pressure grows to open up protected areas as resource shortages threaten; environmentally favourable practices are called into question in lean economic times; and environmental agencies and programmes are cut back due to fiscal retrenchment.

At a broad structural level the themes most often introduced into general discussion of the difficulties contemporary industrialized societies face in coming to terms with environmental issues include: (a) the intrinsically challenging features of environmental problems; (b) the essential character of the dominant economic system; (c) the competitive nature of international relations; and (d) the realities of democratic politics.

The first of these directs attention to the inherent characteristics of environmental problems. It emphasizes the complexity of social/environmental interactions, the uncertainties that discourage action, the difficulty of acquiring scientific knowledge and of using it to inform decision-making, the long-term character of problems (which may accumulate slowly), and the geographic separation of sources and impacts. Environmental problems are by-products of desired activities. Dealing with them requires altering established practices and may threaten entrenched interests. They involve difficult collective action problems and require a break with specific forms of path dependence and technological 'lock-in'. Climate change, for example, displays all of these features. For 200 years economic development has been powered by fossil energy. Established socio-technological regimes, production/consumption patterns, and economic and political elites have evolved in mutual interdependence. So why would we expect change to be initiated by social incumbents – unless catastrophe was more or less imminent *and* obvious?

Each of the three other themes relates to an imperative encouraging society to remain on an environmentally destructive development pathway, generating pressures to expand the absolute scale of material appropriations from nature and to defer engagement with environmental impacts until effects become acute. First, an *accumulation imperative* drives businesses to expand their activities: to compete they must grow, so they stimulate demand for new products and expand commodity relations into new social spheres. Advertising, planned obsolescence, branding and credit expansion contribute to this never-ending drive to sell more goods and services. And as consumption is driven upwards so, too, are negative environmental impacts. Second, in the absence of a genuine world government a *power/security imperative* impels states to look first to their own interests, making collaboration to solve environmental problems difficult. In a turbulent international context states are concerned above all with security, and competition among major powers encourages military and economic expansion, with attendant environmental pressures. Countries resist incurring the costs of addressing global environmental problems because other states may act as free riders. Indeed, the environment itself becomes a locus for competitive interactions, and big power rivalries infect international negotiations (consider recent US and Chinese sparring in the climate talks). Third, in democratic states an *electoral politics imperative* encourages political leaders to defer environmental action and focus on economic and social policies which benefit the electorate more immediately and directly. The perception is that voters want environmental action, but are unwilling to pay the real costs: so party competition drives leaders to reduce their environmental ambitions (to avoid being undercut by another party that promises an extension of the environmental 'free lunch'). Behind the rhetoric, politicians know they must keep the economy growing (no matter how environmentally destructive current practices may be) if they want to have any hope of re-election.

These factors do not indicate that environmental initiatives cannot succeed – otherwise we could not have gotten as far as we have – but rather that there are structural tendencies that make their adoption and implementation difficult. They can be invoked to help explain why there are *limits* to environmental action; or to use the language we have employed here, why on different levels we may currently be facing an impasse. Thus environmental action can achieve much, but in areas where it appears to collide *directly* with the imperatives of accumulation, international power/security, or electoral politics, it will confront an impasse.

Yet even here one must take care. Arguments about accumulation, commodification and the context in which business firms operate do not establish that profits *necessarily* require environmental destruction, or that decoupling environmental burdens from economic activity in a market-mediated and largely privately owned economy is impossible. Indeed, some thinkers have suggested a 'capitalist' economy is entirely compatible with a no-growth or 'steady state' economy (Daly 1992). That international collaboration is difficult, or even that systemic rivalry among major powers is inevitable, does not show that cooperation to resolve global environmental issues is impossible. And, while the difficulty of international coordination may discourage states from acting to address environmental issues, the opposite appears to be even truer: the reluctance of states to take domestic action undermines efforts to build international collaboration. As for the democratic polity, it has typically proven more resilient than its depreciators allow, being able to mobilize surprising resources in times of crisis, and take decisive action when threatened. While building stable political coalitions in favour of a reformed (sustainable) development trajectory is not easy, there is nothing to indicate it cannot be done.

With these caveats in mind, these four factors can be taken as a background against which the essays in this collection are read. To the extent that they are discussed explicitly, it is above all the final element – articulating reform in the context of contemporary representative democratic political systems – that receives attention in this volume. After all, it is the political terrain that could open the door to shift the circumstances operative in the other fields: devising structures and processes that are able to negotiate the complexity of environmental problems; reforming the social economy so that it is compatible with sustainability; and initiating domestic action that can carry forward necessary international processes.

It is possible, however, to approach the idea of *impasse* not at the level of these rather abstract structural features, but rather from the perspective of the specific political and economic forces implicated in particular environment and development problems. This is in fact how most of the essays included in this collection proceed, discussing the circumstances in a particular policy domain, tracing how the current situation emerged, identifying obstacles to further progress, and suggesting how one might move beyond the current context. Thus *impasse* is understood in a more specific or localized manner and the possibilities of overcoming barriers to change are also more concrete. For example, several of the essays explore avenues to move forward action around climate change despite the paralysis at the international level. The concluding essay of this volume returns to the broader theme of impasse, tying together elements raised in earlier contributions.

ORGANIZATION OF THIS VOLUME

As the title of the volume suggests, the essays included in this collection engage with the intersection of three basic themes: governance, democracy and sustainable development. And they should be seen as contributions to the rapidly expanding scholarly literature which strives to understand the complex interactions between practices of democratic governance and emerging environment and development challenges.

In this context *governance* is taken to refer to the range of different ways in which the affairs of contemporary societies are ordered politically, rather than just to the de-centred modes of coordination (such as 'market-based' or 'negotiated' approaches, 'private governance' or 'network governance') which captured attention from the 1990s onwards (Kooiman 2003; Pierre and Peters 2000). *Democracy* is applied in the broad sense of 'popular rule', which in the modern world achieves expression (however imperfectly) in the political arrangements familiar in developed states which include the rule of law, systems of individual and collective rights, periodic elections, competitive party politics and press freedoms. And *sustainable development* is appreciated in political terms, as a normative concept which – like other ideas which structure political argument (such as freedom, justice or rights) – has a definite content, but is subject also to continuous debate and contestation (Lafferty 1996; Meadowcroft 2000). There are, of course, complex linkages among these ideas. Sustainable development is above all about governance: about the deliberate moves societies can take to reorient their development trajectories along more sustainable lines. In the developed countries today governance means democratic governance: not that every governance mode involves demo-cratic mechanisms, but that governments which structure and author-ize governance practices are themselves legitimized through democracy. And while sustainable development is sometimes discussed in relation to countries that do not currently enjoy democratic political systems, strong arguments can be made that sustainable development ultimately implies movement towards political reform.

Over the past decade and a half research on governance of the environ-ment and sustainable development has focused on a variety of specialized themes, including: 'integration' (Lenschow 2002; Nilsson and Eckerberg 2007; Jordan and Lenschow 2008); 'policy instruments' (Dietz and Stern 2002; Fiorino 2006: Cashore et al. 2004); 'participation and partner-ships' (Glasbergen et al. 2007; Huijstee et al. 2007); 'monitoring and assessment' (Mickwitz 2006); 'planning and strategy processes' (Steurer and Martinuzzi 2005); 'local sustainability' (Innes and Booher 2000; Mazmanian and Kraft 2009), 'international agreements' (Miles 2002) and 'transitions' (Geels 2005; Kemp et al. 2007). Climate change has increas-ingly been seen as the paradigmatic sustainable development problem and the issues of sustainable energy and a low carbon-emission society have captured increasing attention. The essays in this collection reflect these trends, engaging with many of these specific areas and contributing to the rich literatures which have grown up around them. But the volume as a whole is intended also to relate to the small but growing body of work that reflects more generally on the conditions required for governance for sustainable development (Lafferty 2004; Voss et al. 2006; Lundqvist 2004; Meadowcroft 2007; Newig et al. 2008; Adger and Jordan 2009).

The chapters in the book are arranged in a sequence that proceeds roughly from the particular to the general. First come chapters which examine specific environment or sustainable development fields (energy, water, nature conservation, climate change), typically in a defined national context. Next come wider comparative pieces. Then there are several con-tributions which approach environment and sustainable development challenges at a more general or conceptual level. Finally, the concluding chapter draws together strands from the proceeding arguments and pro-vides some critical reflection on the challenge of advancing sustainable development in the context of the contemporary democratic polity.

The first contribution is Michael Narodoslawsky's chapter 'A chang-ing energy resource base and the re-invention of the region'. The author takes up the core sustainable development problem of fossil energy dependence and argues that over the coming century a transition towards renewable energy could open the way for regional revitalization. The idea is that a decentralized energy system based on local resources, and a reinvigorated regional economic and political life implementing a sustainable development model, are mutually supportive.

In the next chapter the attention shifts from energy to water, as Frans H.J.M. Coenen and Hans T.A. Bressers explore 'Trends, drivers and dilemmas in the transition towards sustainable water management'. They review efforts at policy 'integration' in the context of Dutch water policy and make a series of cogent observations about policy stability and the challenges of integrative governance practices for sustainability.

Nature protection provides the focus for the next chapter: 'Local participation and learning in nature protection: a Swedish success story'. Here Katarina Eckerberg examines challenges relating to the protection of biodiversity, noting the relative policy stagnation at the national government and EU levels. She presents a study of a successful Swedish conservation initiative, arguing that the involvement of local stakeholders was critical to overcoming obstacles. Eckerberg concludes that 'supporting local initiatives with catalyst funding from the state might therefore be a way forward not only for Sweden but also for other countries'.

Next come three chapters which deal with different dimensions of the politics of climate change. Two of these concentrate explicitly on the local level, exploring the obstacles confronting local authorities in developing programmes of action around climate change. In 'Early experiences of local climate change adaptation in Norwegian society', Carlo Aall focuses on adaptation – examining the way local governments in Norway have engaged with this issue, and analysing barriers to more consequent local involvement with climate adaptation. Swedish municipalities are the focus in Lennart J. Lundqvist's chapter, '"Think globally, act locally!"˸ But what on earth *can* local governments do about global climate change?' The chapter reviews experience to date and emphasizes the distinctive roles that must be fulfilled by *both* local and national governments if climate action is to be effective. The different experiences of climate activists on the two sides of the Atlantic is the focus of Elizabeth Bomberg's chapter, 'Moving beyond the impasse: climate change activism in the US and the EU'. Bomberg explores the different political contexts and institutional constraints faced by the two communities of climate activists and points to the surprising absence of collaboration and systematic learning between the two groups.

One country's experience with implementing sustainable development forms the focus for Gerard Mullally's chapter, 'Governance and participation *for* sustainable development in Ireland: "Not so different after all?"' Here Mullally sets Irish efforts to engage with sustainable development within the broader context of domestic political and social processes, and the boom/bust cycle of Irish economic development. He then raises questions about the current impasse for sustainable development in Ireland, but also more generally.

In 'Measuring what? National interpretations of sustainable development – the case of Norway', Oluf Langhelle and Audun Ruud explore the difficulty of operationalizing the concept of sustainable development and of selecting appropriate indicators to monitor progress towards (or away from) sustainable development. They use the case of Norway to highlight the important political choices which are bound up with understandings of sustainable development, the orientation of policy and the design of indicator sets.

The international character of efforts to manage problems of the environment and sustainable development is brought explicitly to the fore in Miranda Schreurs' contribution, 'Breaking the impasse on global environmental protection'. She suggests that the focus on formal international accords which has pre-occupied decision-makers over the past two or three decades is giving way to new initiatives, including a more 'polyvalent' approach. The international theme is carried forward by Per-Olof Busch and Helge Jörgens in their chapter on 'Governance by diffusion: exploring a new mechanism of international policy coordination'. They argue that governance through policy diffusion – explicitly encouraging international coordination through the voluntary adoption by countries of innovative environmental practices initiated by their neighbours – is an important means for advancing the international environmental effort, particularly at a time when efforts to secure more formal international agreements appear at an impasse.

Another broad theme is taken up by Susan Baker in 'Climate change, the common good and the promotion of sustainable development'. In this chapter Baker argues that a more substantive notion of the 'common good' is required if we are to embrace an ethic of environmental responsibility that can ground more consequent collective action on climate change. In 'Pushing the boundaries: governance for sustainable development and a politics of limits', James Meadowcroft offers a discussion of the importance of 'limits' in environmental politics, and in political thought more generally. He argues that the current impasse in governance for sustainable development is directly related to continuing political resistance to acknowledging the significance of environmental limits.

In the final contribution to the collection – 'Governance for sustainable development: the impasse of dysfunctional democracy' – William M. Lafferty focuses on what he describes as the most critical source of the current impasse in the implementation of sustainable development: 'the Western model of political decision-making' of 'competitive democracy'. In a wide-ranging discussion that draws elements from each of the other chapters in the volume, Lafferty explores the flawed character of the contemporary democratic polity and offers his reflections on possible pathways to reform.

REFERENCES

Adger, N. and A. Jordan (2009), *Governing Sustainability*, Cambridge: Cambridge University Press.

Cashore, B., G. Auld and D. Newsom (2004), *Governing through Markets*, New Haven, CT: Yale University Press.

Daly, H. (1992), *Steady State Economics*, 2nd edn, London: Earthscan.

Dietz, T. and P. Stern (eds) (2002), *New Tools for Environmental Protection*, Washington, DC: National Academy Press.

Fiorino, D. (2006), *The New Environmental Regulation*, Cambridge, MA: MIT Press.

Geels, F. (2005), *Technological Transitions and System Innovations: A Co-evolutionary and Sociotechnical Analysis*, Cheltenham, UK and Northampton, MA, USA: Edward Elgar.

Glasbergen, P., F. Biermann and A. Mol (eds) (2007), *Partnerships, Governance and Sustainable Development: Reflections on Theory and Practice*, Cheltenham, UK and Northampton, MA, USA: Edward Elgar.

Hanf, K. and A. Jansen (eds) (1998), *Governance and Environment in Western Europe: Politics, Policy and Administration*, Harlow: Longman.

Huijstee, M. van, M. Francken and P. Leroy (2007), 'Partnerships for sustainable development: a review of current literature', *Environmental Sciences*, **4** (2), 75–89.

Innes, J. and D. Booher (2000), 'Indicators for sustainable communities', *Planning Theory and Practice*, **1**, 173–86.

Intergovernmental Panel on Climate Change (IPCC) (2007), *Climate Change 2007: Synthesis Report*, Geneva: IPCC.

Janicke, M. and H. Weidner (eds) (1997), *National Environmental Policies: A Comparative Study of Capacity Building*, Berlin: Springer.

Jordan, A. and A. Lenschow (eds) (2008), *Innovation in Environmental Policy? Integrating the Environment for Sustainability*, Cheltenham, UK and Northampton, MA, USA: Edward Elgar.

Kemp, R., D. Loorbach and J. Rotmans (2007), 'Transition management as a model for managing processes of co-evolution towards sustainable development', *International Journal of Sustainable Development and World Ecology*, **14**, 78–91.

Kooiman, J. (2003), *Governing as Governance*, London: Sage.

Lafferty, W. (1996), 'The politics of sustainable development: global norms for national implementation', *Environmental Politics*, **5** (2), 185–208.

Lafferty, W. (ed.) (2004), *Governance for Sustainable Development*, Cheltenham, UK and Northampton, MA, USA: Edward Elgar.

Lenschow, A. (2002), *Environmental Policy Integration: Greening Sectoral Policies in Europe*, London: Earthscan.

Long, B., (2000), *International Environmental Issues and the OECD 1950–2000:*

An Historical Perspective, Paris: Organisation for Economic Co-ordination and Develoment.

Lundqvist, L. (2004), *Sweden and Ecological Governance: Straddling the Fence*, Manchester: Manchester University Press.

Mayer, A. (2008), 'Strengths and weaknesses of common sustainability indices for multidimensional systems', *Environment International*, **34** (2), 277–91.

Mazmanian, D. and M. Kraft (2009), *Towards Sustainable Communities: Transition and Transformations in Environmental Policy*, Cambridge, MA: MIT Press.

Meadowcroft, J. (2000), 'Sustainable development: a new(ish) idea for a new century?', *Political Studies*, **48** (2000), 370–87.

Meadowcroft, J. (2007), 'Who is in charge here? Governance for sustainable development in a complex world', *Journal of Environmental Policy and Planning*, **9** (3–4), 299–314.

Meadowcroft, J. (2012), 'Greening the state', in P. Steinberg and S. Van Deveer (eds), *Comparative Environmental Politics: Advances in Global Change Research*, Boston, MA: MIT Press.

Mickwitz, P. (2006), *Environmental Policy Evaluation: Concepts and Practice*, Helsinki: Finnish Society of Sciences and Letters.

Miles, E. (2002), *Environmental Regime Effectiveness: Confronting Theory with Evidence*, Cambridge, MA: MIT Press.

Millennium Ecosystem Assessment (MEA) (2006), *Ecosystem and Human Well-being: General Synthesis*, Washington, DC: Island Press.

Newig, J., J.-P. Voss and J. Monstadt (2008), *Governance for Sustainable Development: Coping with Ambivalence, Uncertainty and Distributed Power*, London: Routledge.

Nilsson, M. and K. Eckerberg (2007), *Environmental Policy Integration in Practice: Shaping Institutions for Learning*, London: Earthscan.

Pierre, J. and G. Peters (2000), *Governance, Politics and the State*, London: Palgrave.

Steurer, R. and A. Martinuzzi (2005), 'Towards a new pattern of strategy formation in the public sector: first experiences with national strategies for sustainable development in Europe', *Environment and Planning C: Government and Policy*, **23** (3), 455–72.

Tatenhove, J. van, B. Arts and P. Leroy (eds) (2001), *Political Modernisation and the Environment: The Renewal of Environmental Policy Arrangements*, Dordrecht, Netherlands: Kluwer Academic.

Voss, J.-P., D. Bauknecht and R. Kemp (eds) (2006), *Reflexive Governance for Sustainable Development*, Cheltenham, UK and Northampton, MA, USA: Edward Elgar.

World Commission on Environment and Development (WCED) (1987), *Our Common Future*, Oxford: Oxford University Press.

2. A changing energy resource base and the re-invention of the region

Michael Narodoslawsky

The twenty-first century should witness a fundamental shift in the resource base on which human society depends. The brief fossil interlude fuelled first by coal and then by cheap oil and gas will subside due to the double pressure of limited fossil resources and global climate change. Peak Oil (where the production of crude oil reaches its maximum and cannot be increased further) will be the first concrete sign of resource constraints and it is expected within the decade 2010–20 (Schindler and Zittel 2000; IEA 2007). There is a general consensus that Peak Gas (the point where natural gas production reaches its maximum) will follow just two to three decades later (Schindler and Zittel 2000; BP 2005). Coal, however, will remain a relatively abundant resource throughout the twenty-first century (see, for example, WCI 2005).

The fossil fuel end game is linked to severe pressure on society. Markets become increasingly volatile as limitations to a resource's availability loom, as price spikes for crude oil in late 2008 showed, threatening economic development. Frantic efforts to substitute fossil fuel by biofuels pass the tension to other markets, notably the markets for food, threatening the basic needs of the most vulnerable members of society.

There is no doubt that we have to move beyond the impasse by changing the resource base for society. In general terms society is at a crossroads, either intensifying the centralized way of providing energy (by going nuclear) or radically changing the resource base to renewable resources. The decision concerning the energy system on which our society is based is not only formative for technological decisions; it has profound impacts on the basic logistics of industry and the general structure of our economy. As such the decision about the energy system of the future is closely linked to the development of power structures and political systems: the question of which political entities and actors gain more traction and which will end up losing influence is to be decided. The following arguments try to shed some light on this aspect of the resource debate from the particular perspective of renewable resources as a main foundation for human

Table 2.1   Key characteristics of fossil and renewable energy provision

	Non-renewable	Renewable resource based

Resources	Fossil based
	  Coal
	  Crude oil
	  Natural gas
	  Uranium
		Solar radiation
		• Direct
		• Indirect
		  – Hydro power
		  – Wind power
		• Biomass
		Geothermal energy
		Wave/tidal energy

Resource limitation	Limited reserves	Solar radiation: Limited yield per area Others: Availability
Sources	• Point sources • Continuous availability	Solar radiation: • Area sources • Time-dependent availability Others: • Point sources • Continuous (geothermal) • Time dependent (wave/tidal)
Transport characteristics	High transport density No humidity	Low transport density High humidity
Distribution challenge	• Transport to distribution centre • Distribution to periphery • Storage to provide security of provision	• Collection from de-centralized sources • Network to link de-centralized providers with consumers • Storage to cope with divergent consumption and provision profiles

activity in the future. Table 2.1 summarizes key characteristics of fossil and renewable resource-based energy provision.

1.   WHY REGIONS? THE RESOURCE DIMENSION

Although the jury is still out on which way we go, for the sake of argument let us choose the renewable resource pathway. This pathway is inherently linked to profound changes in both the economic and political fibre of society. Renewable resources are ultimately derived from solar radiation (with the notable exception of geothermal and tidal energy forms). However, solar radiation is a de-centralized natural income. No matter what form of renewable resources we utilize, whether solar thermal energy, photovoltaic or biomass in its many expressions, we will need to rethink traditional means of dealing with resource logistics as we have to collect these renewable resources and concentrate them, rather than exploit them and then distribute them. This new approach to renewable resource distribution will in turn exercise an influence on economic and political structures. Global powers that compete to control and exploit centrally available resources will no longer have the same clout in relation to dispersed energy sources that are in the hands of a multitude of owners. Political entities close to resources, in this case regional entities, may become more assertive and use their power as custodians of resources in the political arena.

A close look at the technical and logistical properties of energy provision, distribution and utilization will highlight this argument of profound change in the structure of the economy that will become a major driving force for an increase in the importance of regions. Let us start with considering the distributional characteristics of energy.

In general society does not need energy; rather it needs energy services such as a comfortable indoor climate, access to information, light, mobility or mechanical power. To provide these services at the point of use, some form of energy has to be taken there and must be transformed to provide this service. Energy can be provided either through grids (power, gas or heat) or by storable energy carriers such as heating oil, coal or biomass. In general, distribution via grids itself requires energy, incurs transport losses and requires infrastructure for delivery. Grids can therefore transport energy only over a limited distance with reasonable transport effort: thousands of kilometres for gas, hundreds of kilometres for electrical power and just a few kilometres for heat (and cooling energy).

Every grid has a certain buffering capacity, from the electrical grid's rotating generator masses to the grid hold-up for gas and heat grids. However, grids are not able to store energy. If the dynamics of energy provision and demand differ, storage elements in the grids are necessary. Storage is costly and incurs considerable losses with storage efficiencies in electrical power ranging from 40 per cent for batteries to 85 per cent for hydro reservoir power stations. Thus all grids require back-up, relying on storable material energy carriers such as coal, oil, gas or biomass to match energy provision with energy service demand. Although significant effort is now being invested to make grids smarter (so that demand follows energy provision more closely with the use of sophisticated information technologies to monitor and balance consumer needs and energy supply), there is no doubt that the requirement for energy storage will remain. Summarizing these arguments, it can be stated that gas and electricity grids can provide long-distance energy distribution whereas heat (and cooling energy) grids may only offer distribution at a local level. Furthermore, the energy (and infrastructure) that is required for distribution increases with the distance that must be covered. Storage (based on material energy carriers) is a necessary element of any stable distribution system now and in the future.

The storage aspect becomes even more interesting if we compare existing energy provision technologies with future sustainable energy systems. Currently most energy resources are constantly available (hydro power from rivers, gas, oil and coal from mines and wells, uranium from mines), and most conversion technologies that turn these resources into energy operate continuously. As many technologies are based on (storable) material energy carriers (gas, oil, coal), energy provision can easily be adapted to consumption patterns.

Here we encounter another technical property of energy systems: all technologies that convert material energy carriers into electricity provide heat as well. So whenever we talk about using energy carriers for power provision, we talk about coupling electricity provision and heat generation, with between 40 and 60 per cent of the stored energy turned into heat. That means that we talk about short-distance heat distribution and long-distance power transmission.

Many renewable energy sources, however, are time dependent in their availability. That holds for direct solar energy (photovoltaic, concentrated solar power, solar heat) as well as for wind power. As those sources become more prominent in supplying society's needs, the requirement for smarter grids and more energy storage become more acute. But storing energy as electricity (or heat) is wasteful and expensive. This leaves hydrogen, biomass (and where applicable reservoir hydro power) to stabilize energy delivery to meet society's needs. Hydrogen can mainly be provided by using electricity (for electrolysis), making it a kind of battery system, with roughly the same storage efficiency (around 40–50 per cent). Both hydrogen and biomass may be converted into power only by generating heat as a by-product, again providing roughly 40–60 per cent of the total stored energy as power and the remainder as heat. Increasing the share of solar and wind power in the electricity grid, and factoring in that we will gradually shift energy demand from heat to electricity (as our homes become better insulated and our need for services based on electricity such as information technology and, possibly, even mobility increase) we may face a heat bonanza stemming from conversion technologies for biomass, hydrogen and, for the foreseeable future, also natural gas.

Thus biomass in all its variations (from forest products to agricultural

Table 2.2   Logistical parameters for different biogenic raw materials

Material	Humidity [%w/w]	Calorific value [kWh/kg]	Density [kg/m³]
Straw (grey)	15	4.17	100–135
Wheat	15	4.17	670–750
Rape seed	9	6.83	700
Wood chips	40	2.89	235
Split logs (beech)	20	4.08	400–450
Wood pellets	6	4.90	660
Light fuel oil	*0*	*11.86*	*840*

Source: Narodoslawsky (2010).

by-products such as straw, energy crops and possibly even algae) will not solve our energy needs single-handedly, as biomass's availability is limited and cannot reasonably be expected to meet future global energy needs (see, for example, Wenzel 2009). It will, however, become a crucial element in stabilizing a future renewable-based energy system by providing a major and readily available source of stored energy.

Here we come to a major reason for the pivotal role of regions in a renewable resource-based society. Biomass has a completely different spectrum of logistical properties as compared with fossil resources: it has low transport densities, high humidity and is in many cases perishable.

Table 2.2 shows that between 15 and 40 per cent of any unprocessed biomass is water and that transport densities (based on calorific value per m³ of material) are well below those of fossil fuel (for example, for straw by a factor of 25 as compared with light fuel oil). This means that the transport effort for biomass, especially biomass of lower quality – which is particularly attractive as it does not compete with food provision – is tremendous. To provide a simple example: moving straw 30 km by tractor from a farm to a regional center requires as large a proportion of the energy content of the fuel as does the delivery of crude oil by ship or pipe line 2,500 km from the Middle East to Europe.

An energy system based on renewable resources requires that biomass is either utilized, or transformed into an easily transportable form, close to the location where it is produced. There are many regional technology structures that may achieve this (using biorefineries to produce valuable by-products in addition to energy services and energy carriers), depending on regionally available resources, infrastructure and competences. But all fall into a simple categorization of the possible transformation pathways. Biomass can be transformed into a gas that is fed into a gas grid (biogas plants, synthetic natural gas processes), this requires electrical power and/or heat. Alternatively, biomass can be transformed into liquid energy carriers (and valuable material by-products). This process requires heat, and to a lesser extent power. Biomass can also be converted into (dry) transportable solid energy carriers (for example, pellets). This process consumes large amounts of heat. And biomass can be used to provide heat and power (biomass CHP, Organic Rankin Cycles, biogas CHP, wood gasification). Many of the processes that can either stabilize the energy system (by providing storable energy carriers such as pellets or biofuels), or feed into trans-regional grids, will have to be widely distributed and located close to the land on which the biomass is produced. As heat has to be used locally, an important consideration will be balancing heat-providing and heat-consuming processes to obtain the highest overall revenue from the (limited) resource of productive land. This will become a major determining factor for regional economic success.

A country's various regions will play a more important role than they do now in a future economy based on renewable resources. They will become major providers of renewable energy as this requires a generous land area, regardless of whether we look at wind and hydro power, solar energy technologies or biomass. Regions will assume a more important position in the hierarchy of technology and energy suppliers and they will stabilize energy system components that rely on distribution grids as this will demand biomass as a basic resource.

By optimizing the utilization of heat generated as a by-product of transformation technologies providing electricity, these suppliers will have a marketable resource that may decide their economic success as they develop from (mostly) passive energy-consuming regions into active energy providers that can ensure system stability.

2.   WHAT REGIONS? ENERGY AS A FORMATIVE FACTOR FOR REGIONS

Regions are not merely lines on a map. The conceptualization of a region is saturated with its inhabitants' emotional and psychological identification which is based on its context and its social, cultural and historical characteristics as well as the inhabitants' specific interactions with that region (Lafferty and Narodoslawsky 2003). There is a plethora of reasons why inhabitants of a region form an attachment to where they live that includes their culture and ethnicity, interactions specific to that landscape as well as the region's dominant economic activities. What is interesting is that energy and resource management emerges as one of the most dynamic factors in creating a region. In Austria, for example, the term *Energieregion* is commonly used as a sobriquet for regional development. Some of these regions boast particularly dynamic sustainable development processes, like the region around Güssing (www.eee-info.net/cms/) in the state of Burgenland, and the region of Mureck in Styria (www.seeg.at/). Both are small towns with a few thousand inhabitants that have evolved into pioneering energy regions that boast cutting-edge energy technologies. Others regions, such as the Mühlviertel (www.euregio.at/euregio/) in Upper Austria, and the Vulkanland in Styria (www.vulkan land.at/), link their strategic development closely to resource management processes and long-term energy visions based entirely on renewable resources.

A clear scientific typology of such regions that define themselves via a distinctive approach to energy and resource management is still not available. Looking at examples in the Austrian context, one can discern some interesting trends. Small energy regions and local energy management initiatives (often dating back to the mid-1970s' oil crisis) clearly precede larger regional-scale renewable resource management efforts. A case in point is the development in Mureck that led to the first industrial-scale biodiesel plant worldwide. These local initiatives are almost always technology centred and driven by pioneering individuals. Again Mureck is a pertinent example. In this region there was a small group of farmers, led by a charismatic individual, which concentrated on finding a domestically available alternative for expensive and unreliable diesel for their tractors. Their progress over time as well as their success depended critically on diversifying both their technology and resource base as well as broadening stakeholder engagement within their region. Both Mureck and Güssing illustrate this trend as their initial efforts to pioneer new technologies (biodiesel in the Mureck case and wood gasification in the Güssing case) gradually led to the emergence of a full-blown diversified regional energy system, providing all energy vectors from heat to electricity and fuel. Larger regional entities have almost always embarked on energy and resource management processes as part of an overarching regional development strategy. This is the case for the Vulkanland and the Mühlviertel, which are both larger regional entities (between 100,000 and 250,000 inhabitants) with a long history of regional sustainable development programmes. These processes are resource and economy centred with a general desire to keep money and labour in the region. In many cases, management of regional renewable resources is a potent attraction for bringing together stakeholders from different sectors as well as providing a dynamic element to the whole development process (concentrating on new economic opportunities and green jobs).

3. REGIONS – A SURE BET?

Energy issues are becoming ever more fundamental for regional sustainable development, both as a driving force to start and sustain regional development processes and as a formative subject that defines the discourse between regional stakeholders. However, before we confidently predict a surge in the importance of regions due to the inevitable change of the resource base towards renewables, it is important first to analyse the business case for regions. This is necessary to identify the market opportunities (and hence the bargaining power) for regions in a future economy. First, we will analyse the pathways of grid-bound energy forms, supposing a development that favours renewable resources over other resource systems (such as an increased nuclear option or, at least for this century, clean coal solutions). Following that we will briefly examine the weaknesses of incumbent players in the energy market. Finally, we will present a business case for the regions based on this analysis.

Heat/Cooling Energy

Heat may be provided by any energy grid as all energy forms can be converted into heat. It may be provided by a heat transmission agent such as hot water or steam or by a gas grid (with burners converting gas into heat) or by electricity. Providing heat by means of electricity, however, is becoming less widespread, while district heating grids as well as gas grids providing heat are increasingly relied upon to provide residential heating.

Heat transmitted by heat transmission grids cannot travel over long distances. In general heat grids are viable only in relatively densely populated areas that provide a minimum heat demand per metre of grid length (for example 900 kWh/m.a is the norm in Austria). Consequently, municipalities are the main stakeholders and owners of heat grids.

Heat is the energy form with the lowest quality and is a natural by-product of any energy transformation, especially electricity production in thermal power stations. Besides municipalities, utilities are major stakeholders in heat provision, especially in large urban centres. Large industrial complexes such as oil refineries and waste incineration plants may also act as heat suppliers.

Providing a comfortable climate within a building, however, increasingly requires energy not only for heat but also for cooling. Currently grid-provided cooling is a rare exception, with electricity being the main source for cooling. Given the increasing demand for cooling, this will add further to the already growing electricity demand, all the more so as cooling requires about three times the electrical power compared with the actual cooling energy demand. Although cooling may also be accomplished by using heat as an energy source (via absorption cooling), the application of such technologies is relatively rare, due to the high investment costs for such equipment and the still relatively small differences between electricity and heat prices.

Whenever heat is not provided via a grid, especially in low-density settlements and single-house neighbourhoods, heat generation requires a storable energy carrier such as heating oil, coal, wood logs, pellets or chips. Burning these energy carriers actually transfers high-quality concentrated energy sources to the lowest possible energy form, namely low temperature heat. Technologies that generate electricity besides heat on a small (single-house) level, such as Sterling motors or small combined heat and power plants, are generally inefficient. From the point of view of the efficient utilization of resources, any technology using high-grade energy carriers to provide low-grade heat should be avoided as far as possible. Heat below 100°C should be generated in a flameless way, either by using waste heat (from heat grids) or solar radiation or by means of passive solar house architecture.

Electrical Power

Many of the technological options to generate electrical power from renewable resources are large scale and centralized, and therefore not under the control of regional actors. This applies to large offshore wind power (and to a lesser extent also to onshore wind parks, although these might be part of a regional development process). It applies also to large-scale direct solar energy conversion technologies such as photovoltaic and concentrated solar power plants. Although these technologies require a broad geographic area, they are more likely to be installed in remote regions and deserts that have available land area and abundant solar radiation. This is, for instance, the approach followed by the DESRTEC project which has been proposed by a large consortium of international energy companies. The goal is to supply around 17 per cent of European electrical power by 2050 via imports from Middle East and North African (MENA) states relying on thermal solar power stations in combination with large scale wind farms (DESRTEC 2010). Many regions in Europe lacking a windy coast or very favourable solar yields will not directly generate electricity from large-scale wind or solar installations. As discussed earlier in this chapter, smartening and stabilizing an electricity grid that relies increasingly on wind and solar power may offer opportunities for stakeholders other than large energy companies.

Gas Supply

Although natural gas has a coarser meshed distribution grid than electricity, it has become an indispensable energy form for developed economies and it is increasingly replacing fossil oil in many applications, especially electricity generation and the provision of process energy for industry. Given its more abundant reserves and its clear advantages with respect to greenhouse gas emissions, natural gas may make further inroads into energy services currently provided by fossil oil, especially heating and in particular mobility.

The changes to vehicles and to the fuel distribution logistics involved when switching from oil to gas for transportation are relatively minor when compared with a shift to electric vehicles. Additionally, existing oil companies are also major players in natural gas markets as natural gas accompanies crude oil in most fields. This will remain true, at least for the next few decades until Peak Gas occurs (somewhere between 2040 and 2060), and so natural gas will take over from fossil oil and is likely to compete with electricity in key sectors such as transportation.

There are a number of technologies available to produce methane from bio-resources as biogas may be cleaned and biomass may be gasified and further refined to produce synthetic natural gas (SNG). Given the resources available, however, current demand for natural gas cannot be met by biogenic resources. On the other hand, the methane yield from bio-resources (grass, energy crops and wood) far surpasses that of any other biofuel (methane from biogas and SNG plants gives about three times the mileage per hectare than either biodiesel or bioethanol, see Scandinavian Biogas 2010). The reason for this advantage lies in the fact that bio-methane conversion technologies utilize the whole plant and not just seeds, such as first-generation bioethanol and biodiesel plants. Second-generation biofuel processes that also exploit whole plants to refine liquid biofuels (for example wood gasification with subsequent Fischer-Tropsch synthesis) will show similar yields per hectare, however usually with greater technological effort. This means that biomethane can become an interesting part of the solution for transportation, possibly piggy-backing on the inroads made by natural gas into this sector.

Fossil Oil

Compared with electricity and natural gas, fossil oil has the most coarsely meshed distribution net. It is distributed via ship or pipeline to refineries and relies on truck and rail to reach end consumers. Currently it is the main energy source for road vehicles and it supplies most of the chemical sector with raw material. Its advantage is its high volumetric energy density that allows cars to travel long distances between refuelling and which enables refuelling in a very short time (particularly compared with electricity). It is also a versatile raw material. Its main disadvantages are that reserves are limited, combustion emissions contribute to climate change, and it is associated with a variety of other environmental consequences such as oil spills (for example, the *Exxon Valdez* oil spill in Alaska's Prince William Sound and the BP oil spill in the Gulf of Mexico).

Replacing current and future demand for transport fuel solely through conventional biofuels such as biodiesel and bioethanol is not viable (Wenzel 2009). Part of the solution (especially regarding using automobiles for long-distance transportation) can, however, come from biomethane and possibly from innovative biofuels based on algae.

The demand for raw materials for the chemical sector may easily be addressed by biogenic resources, given the fact that this is only a tiny fraction of the resources consumed by the transportation fuel sector: about 5–10 per cent of crude oil is currently used as chemical feed stock. The technologies to convert bio-resources in to all major chemicals (from biopolymers to solvents and fine chemicals) are already available.

4.   THE BUSINESS CASE FOR REGIONS

The Achilles' Heels of the Behemoths

The energy sector is currently defined by solidly established and large international corporations that control all important means of resource provision, including the technology and distribution networks necessary to fulfil society's energy service demands. The major players are large oil and gas companies as well as energy conglomerates owning power plants and grids. These economic behemoths have deep pockets, operate optimized technologies for energy provision and distribution, and have the technical know-how to develop possible future technologies to perfection.

All these players control the whole value chain of energy provision, from the extraction of basic energy carriers, such as gas and oil wells, coal mines and river dams, to conversion technology used in oil refineries and power plants to the grids and fuel stations that finally serve consumers. From the well or mine to the gas hook-up or electrical socket in your house and the filling pump in your gas station, every step is part of a thoroughly optimized system and in the hands of a very capable and innovative big company. It is within this context that regions have to assert their possible role as an important player for implementing sustainable energy systems.

These companies excel in harnessing fossil fuel resources. This excellence may be their main Achilles' heel, however, as fossil fuel resources originate from centralized sources. So the business models of these companies are very similar, whatever the particular energy with which they deal. They collect energy resources from a few large sources, transport and convert the resources to generate the energy forms necessary to sustain current energy service demands, and distribute and sell to end-use consumers. All of their technologies are optimized to operate in a system that relies on centralized sources and that distributes energy to a mass market via systems designed to flow *from* centre *to* periphery.

In a world that relies on renewable energy, a significant part of these resources, especially all bio-resources, will not be sourced from a centralized location. They grow in fields or forests and are even gathered on house roofs. This alters the geometry of distribution grids and, most importantly, the economic structure of the supply side for a substantial part of the resource market.

The case of the notorious Deep Water Horizon well in the Gulf of Mexico exemplifies this structural mismatch between existing energy companies and the requirements of a future energy system that relies on renewable resources. This well alone spilled between 5,600 and 9,600 tonnes of crude oil a day. The area necessary to provide the same amount of energy using whole corn plants is between 300,000 and 530,000 ha. That is an area 54 km by 54 km to 73 km by 73 km square. It goes without saying that such areas, equal in their productivity to just one well, are not your usual farm size in Europe. This suggests that in order to control the resources to provide feed-stocks for a renewable resource-based energy system, there are two options: either radically alter the ownership structure of agricultural land or de-centralize the supply side, organizing a large number of independent suppliers.

Even if Big Energy succeeds in securing its resource base by controlling large swaths of land, the problem of transportation still remains. The rough calculation above was based on the entire energy content of corn plants. Half the energy, however, is contained in corn stover, a material with a very low transport density. This means that some kind of pre-processing must to be done close to the fields in order either to upgrade this material, or to extract the energy from it and feed it into an appropriate grid. In either case this amounts to a de-centralization of the energy value chain, no matter how the issue of controlling the necessary resources is resolved.

It is not surprising that big energy companies reflexively favour the most centralized options for harnessing renewable resources. These companies pursue projects such as DESERTEC (with a relatively small number of enormous solar thermal plants), or big offshore wind parks, or biofuels from Brazil or the United States, where agro-business comes close to the necessary farm scale to provide a centralized energy system with resources. But these solutions are either inefficient (in the case of biofuels), or require huge investments in infrastructure and transmission grids, or both. None represents a silver bullet that will provide an encompassing solution for an energy system based on renewable sources.

How Regions Can Gain a Foothold

Despite the strong position of the established actors in the energy sector, regions still have an interesting business case in a society that relies on renewable resources. On the side of efficiency improvements, they can help to increase overall societal energy efficiency, mainly by adjusting infrastructure and settlement patterns in a way that reduces overall energy demand (by promoting solar architecture and the use of solar energy for electricity, heat and cooling) and mobility requirements (by denser human settlements and a de-centralized provision of services). Moreover, regions can advance the smartening of grids by raising the awareness of consumers, and they can provide smart mobility and transportation systems that reduce energy demand in the transport sector. Even more importantly, they can act on the supply side, particularly by using bio-resources efficiently. Key in this case is an integrated approach to resource management that guarantees sufficient food provision and utilizes by-products from agriculture and forestry for the production of commodity chemicals as well as energy. Additionally, by-products from conversion processes (ash, biogas manure, and so on) should be recycled in an appropriate way. An integrated resource management system should utilize the heat generated by conversion technologies fully, either for industrial processes, residential heating and cooling, or for conditioning (especially drying) surplus biomass for providing storable energy to stabilize the overall energy system.

As a rule, regions will succeed in such an economy if they can: (a) generate a surplus of grid-distributed energy forms (electricity or gas); (b) provide commodity products (basic chemicals as well as biomass in transportable form such as pellets); (c) maintain the fertility of their land without the import of fossil energy-based fertilizers; and (d) do not waste a single Joule of heat.

5. WHAT REGIONS NEED

Yet this business model has pre-conditions. From the technical side, while there is still room for improvement, many solutions already exist. The most important pre-conditions therefore relate to the performance of key societal and governance functions within the regions.

Strong Identity

As was discussed earlier in this chapter, regions are social constructs. Their main social capital is that they are a common reference point for all actors within the region that is constituted by identification with the region itself. This reference point is the foundation for a feeling of community that in turn serves as the foundation for trust between actors that in turn provides the basis for common action.

The ability to pursue common action on the foundation of a strong common identity is their main advantage as compared with centralized and imposed solutions. While big companies have to control the resource base in order to guarantee their survival, regions may coordinate actors to pursue a common strategy. Coordination, however, needs a context of mutual trust that can grow in the soil prepared by a vibrant and shared regional identity.

Strategic Leadership

Coordination requires a common, long-term plan to give actors in a region a direction with which to align their individual decisions. Almost all decisions necessary to realize the potential success of a region with respect to renewable resource utilization are long term: investments in energy technologies have a time horizon of 10–20 years, and long-term contracts to provide the necessary resources have comparable time horizons. Investment in infrastructure may be on even longer timescales.

In the examples of the Austrian local energy initiatives mentioned earlier, strategic leadership was often provided by charismatic and determined individual leaders who were not part of normal political processes and hence were not subject to the time frames of election cycles. Regions can only be successful if they develop institutions that actors trust to provide the necessary long-term continuity. As actors usually judge on the basis of past experience, any individual or institution pursuing the development of regional sustainable energy systems must have earned their strategic leadership credentials *before* entering this delicate, complex and long-term process. In the Güssing case a successful mayor, together with a competent director of the city administration, provided the necessary leadership. A successful and charismatic farmer started the Mureck process. The Vulkanland energy initiative followed on from a very successful regional sustainable development initiative that established a regional trademark, and was driven by an active regional management association led by a popular local politician. Although energy proves to be a potent generative force for regional development, it may not be the best starting point from which to initiate a development process.

Transparent Strategic Planning Process

Aligning a region with the requirements of the sustainable utilization of its resources involves complex issues. Success depends on convincing actors within the region to submit to coordination. And this can only be achieved by an open and transparent planning process. While external expertise can be called upon in terms of methodology, it is crucial that the planning process be owned by the regional stakeholders. This requires that enough expertise is built up within the region to provide the stakeholders with a solid foundation for their planning discourse. This includes mastering the technicalities of the process as well as providing solidly based scenarios for technology and resource management.

A particularly important point here is the ability to frame the discourse around long-term energy and development planning in an appropriate manner. Strategic questions about responsibilities, and the promotion of the common good of the region as a whole, have to be addressed as well as issues related to the formulation of social, economic and environmental goals. Just starting from a strategy of regional autarky will not lead to optimal and sustainable results. If anything a society based on renewable energy will become more interlinked, not less, as urban centres will have to import energy from rural regions that have enough area to 'catch' solar energy in its various forms. Smart grids will align consumer needs and time-dependent energy provision from technologies such as wind power and photovoltaics. De-centralized energy providers using stored biomass will stabilize electricity and gas grids. De-centralized plants will provide crucial industrial products such as biofuels and base chemicals as a by-product of energy provision. But all of that is only possible if grids evolve from simple nets that distribute centrally provided energy to bi-directional systems, linking distributed providers with consumers, and conveying not only energy but also information. Any strategic planning that ignores these issues will not lead to the full exploitation of the potential within the region.

One particular concern for the strategic planning process within regions will be the management of heat. Heat, as already mentioned, is a natural by-product of all thermal processes that provide electricity. In contrast to all other energy forms, heat cannot be transported over long distances. Effective utilization of heat therefore becomes a prime focus for local and regional integration of economic activity. The regions that develop optimal heat management will use their natural resources most effectively, and so will achieve a comparative advantage over other regions.

Providing Economic Clout

As has already been noted, investments in energy technologies and infra-structure are inherently long term. This means that raising capital for them in conventional markets will be difficult. Currently the single most important impediment to the implementation of renewable resource-based systems is not the lack of technological knowledge but the lack of inves-tors. It does not help that many projects are relatively small, complex and proposed by atypical project proponents such as farmers' associations, communities and SMEs which usually drives up the mark-up calculated by banks to cover the investment risk.

It is therefore necessary to tap into capital from atypical sources. One way is to raise capital within the region itself to realize the investments in the future that offer the possibility to achieve a comparative advantage over other regions. In this case the advantage of increased economic activity within the region and higher security of energy provision will help to convince stakeholders to invest. Moreover, knowledge of the actors, and confidence in their abilities, may lower the risk premium for regional capital.

A positive side effect of raising regional capital is that the more finance comes from actors within the region, the greater are the chances of attracting external funds under favourable terms, which lower the cost for servicing debt. This however requires strong and durable institutions that can distribute risk and bear responsibility. Besides a solid strategic plan-ning process, the ability of regions to provide capital from within will be the most prominent discriminator between success and failure.

6.   POLITICAL ISSUES RAISED BY A MORE PROMINENT ROLE OF REGIONS

The argument presented here has very much centred on (inevitable) changes to the resource base on which human societies draw. It presupposed a pathway that favours renewable resources over other alternatives, although this is by no means a given. Under these circumstances, however, regions as spatial entities with which their citizens identify may play an important role as the existing development path in the energy sector will be broken at least partly by the properties of renewable resources and of the technologies required to harness them.

From the analysis of the pathways of the most important forms of energy provision and the current actors in this sector, a business case for regions was developed. The necessary functions within regions to successfully realize this business case were briefly discussed. If we inspect the functions described above from the point of view of the implications for the political system, we find some interesting, but also somewhat disturbing, dimensions.

A More Democratic Energy Sector?

While today the energy sector is arguably among the least democratic elements in society, a change towards renewable resources will not change that entirely. There will still be large economic entities that control much of this sector as major renewable energy technologies will remain centralized (large wind parks, large solar energy power plants, and so on) and the distribution networks, while becoming smarter, will also be controlled by large interest groups. The increased role of regions will bring decisions closer to the people, but the democratic credentials of such regional development processes, are still to be discussed.

Democratic Regional Development Processes?

The functions described above that are necessary for successful regional development processes that utilize natural and renewable resources clearly point towards the importance of long-term trust in institutions and open planning processes. We encounter here an interesting conundrum of regional development processes. While the success of regions critically depends on the identification of their citizens with these processes, most development processes are actor driven, meaning that they lack representative democratic elements. In fact, one can argue further that most regional development processes are the result of active stakeholders becoming disgruntled with the sluggish progress of representative democratic processes, and taking advantage of the strong affinity of people to their spatial context – that is, their region – to drive development.

In the case of energy regions this implies that important actors who control resources, realize technologies and set up infrastructure will be the major driving forces for these development processes. There is prima facie no necessity for including the representation of all citizens in this process; nor does experience show that this has actually been realized in such processes.

Separating Business and Politics?

Regional sustainable energy systems provide a case for merging, not separating, business and politics. The strategic planning necessary for successful energy regions clearly merges the business interests of particular actors (for example farmers and local industry) with the strategic development of a whole region. While this is not in itself a problem, there is still a lack of clear procedures for balancing these interests against the ambitions of all members of society, as long as regional development processes are based primarily on voluntary participation by active elements.

Taking the Common Good into Consideration?

One of the main problems encountered in regional development is that bottom–up emerging regions do not have exclusive claims to a certain place. We may live in a community that is at the same time part of a certain water region (defined by the catchment of a river), that is also part of a tourism region (defined by a particular landscape feature) and is part of an economic region (defined by a certain cluster of production plants) as well as an energy region relying on a specific set of renewable resources provided in this region. All of these 'regions' may have different shapes, and are the result of different social processes, commanding slightly different identities from their citizens. At the moment we lack basic political theories, as well as real political structures, to mediate the interactions among the regions that are currently emerging. We have to grapple with overlapping, non-hierarchical, problem-oriented spatial entities with ill-defined institutions. As these entities gain more momentum (and the quest for regional sustainable energy systems may accelerate this process) the question arises of how to coordinate these regions in order to achieve overarching societal goals.

7. CONCLUDING REMARKS – OVERCOMING THE IMPASSE

A change from fossil fuels to renewable resources and in particular the implementation of sustainable energy systems is much more than just a challenge for technology. It requires not only a break in the mould of conventional technological paths, but an almost complete rewiring of the software and hardware of the logistics for supplying our global society.

The argument outlined in this chapter points to an intrinsic alliance between advocacy of a switch from fossil fuels and a centralized resource base, to renewable resources and sustainable regional development. As acreage becomes a major limiting resource for sustainable energy provision, and as many biogenic resources have unfavourable logistic properties, dispersed patterns of resource utilization become attractive. At the same time regions become economically, socially and politically active elements. Both development strands may become mutually supportive. Regions as custodians of the area necessary to utilize natural solar income gain bigger economic payoffs as well as political leverage, whereas sustainable energy systems become more prevalent within the whole energy provision structure of society by their regional implementation.

A certain critical mass is required, however, for this mutually supportive function to generate a virtuous cycle. On the one hand, the political issues raised here have to be analysed, addressed and finally resolved. On the other hand, a sufficient number of regions have to follow the business model described here – acquiring a sufficiently robust identity and providing strategic leadership while embarking on transparent strategic planning and accumulating adequate economic clout. It goes without saying that as long as the critical political issues of good sustainable regional governance are not resolved, the barriers for regions to become true and dynamic energy regions remain high. Resolving the problems of regional governance can therefore become a major tool in fighting global climate change. The ball has left the court of the engineering profession and has landed squarely in the court of political science!

REFERENCES

British Petroleum (BP) (2005), 'Putting energy in the spotlight: statistical review of world energy', accessed July 2010 at www.bp.com/liveassets/bp_internet/globalbp/globalbp_uk_english/publications/energy_reviews_2005/STAGING/local_assets/downloads/pdf/statistical_review_of_world_energy_full_report_2005.pdf.

DESERTEC Foundation (2010), 'Homepage of the DESERTEC Foundation', accessed July 2010 at www.desertec.org.

International Energy Agency (IEA) (2007), 'Oil market report', accessed July 2010 at http://online.wsj.com/public/resources/documents/iea20070707.pdf.

Lafferty, W. and M. Narodoslawsky (eds) (2003), *Regional Sustainable Development in Europe – The Challenge of Multi-level, Cross-Sectoral, Co-operative Governance*, Oslo: ProSus.

Narodoslawsky, M. (2010), 'Structural prospects and challenges for bio commodity processes', *Food Technology and Biotechnology*, 48 (3), 270–75.

Scandinavian Biogas (2010), 'Why biogas – Environmental advantages', accessed January 2011 at www.scandinavianbiogas.se/index_why.php?option=displaypage&main=102&subid=102&show=190 .

Schindler, J. and W. Zittel (2000), *Fossile Energiereserven und mögliche Versorgungsengpässe, Studie für den Deutschen Bundestag*, Ottobrun, Germany: LB-Systemtechnik.

Wenzel, H. (2009), 'Biofuels: the good, the bad and the ugly – and the unwise policy', *Clean Technologies and Environmental Policy*, **11** (2), 143–5.

World Coal Institute (WCI) (2005), 'The coal resource', accessed July 2010 at www.worldcoal.org/resources/wci-publications.

3. Trends, drivers and dilemmas in the transition towards sustainable water management

Frans H.J.M. Coenen and Hans T.A. Bressers

In recent years we have heard a lot about 'new' approaches to water management. Opinion leaders have heralded a new water culture (Arrojo et al. 2005), research projects and legislation are labelled as new, as are policy frameworks such as the European Union Water Framework Directive. All this suggests some break with the past, along with a transition from 'old' to 'new' policies and approaches. Yet the question remains whether this change helps us move beyond past obstacles in water management, or whether new interdependencies are fostered which create inertia that is becoming even more difficult to overcome. This is a continuing dilemma in water management. Lafferty (Lafferty and Hovden 2002; Lafferty 2002) argues that integration is key to sustainable development, and integration is exactly what the new water management seeks to promote. But without careful management, integration could also become part of the problem. A resolution can probably be found in adaptive strategies that span sectors and involve multiple actors, promote an enabling rather than a controlling mode of governance and provide enough flexibility for adaptive management (de Boer and Bressers 2011).

Many authors argue that a transition to new governance forms is necessary because of the failures of past approaches, as well as the increased challenges to water management in the future (for instance, due to climate change). An argument against starting from that assumption is that it entails an inherent risk: that the link between means and ends is simply assumed at the outset; and the means may itself become an end. We argue that it is possible to make a transition from a water management approach that is technocratic, expert driven and characterized by a relatively narrow policy perspective with clearly defined problems, towards a much more open, stakeholder-oriented approach that addresses interdependent problems with multiple and possibly partly conflicting goals. This prospective direction for water management is already widely recognized by academics and practitioners. The question as to whether this approach actually works best in practice remains open.

'New' is not always better than 'old'. Many discussions about new water management implicitly assume that new water management also means more sustainable water management. We have to recognize that some changes in water management are made because we want to make water management more sustainable, but other changes are made because we were unsatisfied with the characteristics of the old water management, or because we are simply faced with new challenges such as climate change that require a new approach. A new approach to water management cannot be assumed, by definition, to be more sustainable.

In the next section of this chapter we discuss the broad characteristics of traditional approaches to water management. We then define some general features of what is now called new water management. This new water management is often referred to by the acronym IWM – integrated water management – a term originating a few decades ago which refers mainly to 'internal integration' within the water domain. However, in the last decade there has also been reference to IWRM – integrated water resources management – which directs attention to the 'external integration' of water management with issues beyond water use in mind. Currently the term AWM – adaptive water management – is often used. It takes into consideration the managerial responsibilities inherent in the complexities of both IWM and IWRM as well as in adaptive water management (Lulofs and Bressers 2010, pp. 6–9). Although we recognize developments evident in moving from one of these approaches to the next, we will treat them all as branches of the same tree, as they all emphasize the importance of *integration* rather than of a discrete sectoral approach. Together this line-up of new approaches can be seen as a transition from one management paradigm to another. Although the nature of the change is in line with what transition theorists cite as appropriate governance for 'system transition' towards a more sustainable society (accepting variation, experimentation and uncertainty, spanning scales in space and time, and so on), we deal with it here as essentially a management paradigm transition. And to assess sustainability we cannot simply apply formal criteria, but we must also look at the trends and drivers associated with these new approaches.

Although similar trends can be identified across most of Europe, our essay will concentrate on the developments in the Netherlands over the last 20, and especially the last 10, years. In the Netherlands, an IWM-like vision first appeared in policy white papers in 1985, and in plans and legislation in 1989. In 1995–2000, following high water problems in 1993, 1995 and 1998, the step to more external integration (for instance with land use planning) was made – first in vision, and later in plans and agreements (Kuks 2004). The adaptive water management approach was developed by practitioners and with policy scientists in response to the increased complexity of these integrations. But it is still struggling to gain further acceptance.

Two important questions must be considered: what were the major drivers and trends in this transition, and do these drivers and trends really lead to sustainable water governance? Lafferty has conceptualized sustainable development as an issue of policy integration (for example, Lafferty and Hovden 2002; Lafferty 2002). Sustainable development has to do with integrating environmental, economic and social concerns in decision-making, and it implies a preoccupation with long-term policy effects in addition to the usual short-term concerns. We assess the 'new' water management approach against the perspective of sustainable development as a form of inter-sectoral and inter-temporal integration. We illustrate that the different drivers for the transition in water management can lead to dilemmas in the integration of policies, if we assess them against Lafferty's criteria of *comprehensiveness*, *aggregation* and *consistency*.

1. CHARACTERISTICS OF TRADITIONAL WATER MANAGEMENT

What are supposed to be the characteristics of the old or traditional water management? Of course there is a risk of caricaturing past water management practices. But in general we could say that 'old' water management focused on a technological fix to well-defined problems, typically at a local scale, with a relatively closed governance structure, and a governance style that could best be described as 'command and control' (Bressers et al. 1994, pp. 47–9). Water management was driven by supply concerns (often geared towards agricultural interests) and often approached from the perspective of a single discipline.

Technological Fix for Well-defined Problems

Typically old water management dealt with relatively well-defined problems such as water sanitation in cities, protection against flooding or eutrophication of lakes. These types of problems could often be solved efficiently in a technical way by building infrastructure (dykes, sewage treatment plants), and later by establishing and gradually increasing the technological sophistication of wastewater treatment plants. However, over the past century urban populations have become increasingly concentrated, industrial and agricultural production has intensified and these well-defined problems have become more complex. Because these problems were generally dealt with in isolation, and at a small (urban) scale perspective, potentially undesirable long-term consequences and side effects were often neglected.

Governance by 'Command and Control'

The governance style within the old water management has often been characterized as a command and control approach. Water systems were typically understood to be highly predictable and controllable. The governance was centralized and hierarchical, with minimal stakeholder participation.

Supply-driven Water Management

In the old water management, resource managers and policy-makers were driven to manage and supply water to people for their direct use. The direct and obvious uses were water to drink, to grow and prepare food, and to provide power for domestic and industrial use (Al Radif 1999). This supply-driven water management was characterized by maximizing the volume of water available for direct use. In the same vein, water tables were managed to serve the interests of agriculture and water courses were largely denaturalized.

Single-disciplinary Engineering Approach

Old water management approached water problems mostly from an engineering perspective, which fit with the perception of water problems as well-defined problems that can be solved with technical end-of-pipe solutions and interventions in the water system itself (Bressers and O'Toole 1995). This sectoral approach to water problems meant that problems were considered from one particular discipline at the time.

2.   CHARACTERISTICS OF 'NEW' WATER MANAGEMENT

As summarized in the previous section on old water management, traditionally water problems were dealt with in isolation, from a small (urban) scale perspective, and with a strong engineering focus. Moreover, water management was supply driven. In the past two decades, new approaches to water management have been developed to address the perceived shortcomings of traditional water management. The key word for the new approach is 'integration'. This implies a five-step process which considers the water system as a whole, multiple possible purposes along with a wide range of potential trade-offs, the implications of different scales in space and time, along with potentially undesirable long-term consequences, and side effects affecting other areas. These new approaches also attempt to overcome the shortcomings of the technical end-of-pipe solutions perspective by taking a fourth step, that is a more interdisciplinary view, and a final step that is a non-engineering, multiple-demand-driven perspective on water problems. As a logical consequence of this more inclusive perspective, the style of governance for water management is less hierarchical and more participatory.

System Approach and Uncertainty

Typical of 'new' water management is a recognition that water problems cannot be dealt with in isolation, but that problem-solving has to be done within a water system with different interdependent components. New water management is about influencing system change. The increasing awareness of the complexity of water problems, and of the water system as complex, unpredictable and characterized by unexpected responses to interventions, means that management cannot simply plan and realize, but must engage in continuous learning and adaptation (Arentsen et al. 2000). New approaches to water management use concepts such as 'resilience', 'vulnerability' and 'adaptive capacity' to express this system interdependence and the importance of uncertainty in system change.

Water Governance Structure

The implementation of water management policies in a given river basin must take into account political, economic and social realities, and thus requires a transparent and open discourse between scientists and policy-makers, and a shift towards a more participatory management style (Bressers and Kuks 2004). Governance is therefore less hierarchical with broader stakeholder participation. The coherence of the relationships among various spatial levels and scales, as well as among the actors in the policy network, is seen as crucial for the performance of the governance structure.

Multiple Purposes for Water and Multiple Objectives for Water Management

The new water management approaches recognize that water has different functions for different actors, such as specific water management agencies, governmental and stakeholder groups, and nature itself, and in various geographic regions (whether upstream or downstream), and so on. Given these different functions of water, actors will also have different objectives with respect to water, and will focus on different dimensions. For instance, specific water agencies deal variously with water supply, wastewater and water quality, storm water and flood control, hydropower, navigation, recreation and water for the environment, fish and wildlife. The various aspects include (Mitchell 1990): (i) water dimensions (surface water and groundwater, quantity and quality); (ii) interactions with land and the environment; and (iii) interrelationships with social and economic development.

Geographic Scale of Analysis and Operation

In the old water management the analytical and operational scales were often local or municipal. In the new water management there are multiple scales of analysis and management, stretching from small watersheds to major river basins, encompassing regions or states, or even a global scale. This multi-scalar perspective is logical from the system perspective, where problems at different scale dimensions influence each other.

There is a tendency in the new approaches to take river catchments as the privileged scale of analysis. The necessity of river basin management received positive attention at the Hague Forum, the Bonn Conference and the World Summit on Sustainable Development and is a core principle of the EU Water Framework Directive (WFD). River basin management raises the question of trans-boundary management because rivers cross borders and government jurisdictions (Lulofs and Coenen 2007).

Scale is not just about water. The views of stakeholders at different scales must also be balanced. Examples include conflicts between upstream and downstream stakeholders, differences among stakeholders in the same region and views of stakeholders in a basin of origin versus those in a receiving basin.

Interdisciplinary Perspective

The complexity of water problems requires knowledge from different disciplines. The analysis of water problems in a given water system should not only take into account the natural and technical system but also the political, economic and social systems. Bringing together knowledge from engineering, law, finance, economics, politics, and so on provides valuable knowledge about the possibilities and consequences of water management decisions and actions. For example, engineering knowledge might focus on physical infrastructure, whereas political science or psychology might focus on human behaviour. This interdisciplinary approach enables water management to identify promising alternatives for solving complex problems and to assess the full range of impacts on the natural and human environments instead of focusing only on technical solutions. We also need non-technical policy solutions such as regulation, communication and incentives. The 'science of mud' has had to join in with 'the science of muddling through', precisely because the level of change ambition often surpasses the typical image of incrementalism.

Demand-driven Water Management

In contrast to supply-driven management in the old water approaches stands a demand-driven approach for water allocation and conservation of fresh water supplies (Al Radif 1999). Given the rapid rise in human population globally, including in relatively arid regions, we have unprecedented water demands. We can no longer maximize water supply in terms of the volume of water available for direct use, but have to work on regulating the demand for water.

In countries such as the Netherlands, solutions to make the water system more robust represent a similar change towards more demand-driven management. Interventions more often take the form of integrated multipurpose spatial projects that require extensive consultation among various governments, agencies and other stakeholders (de Boer and Bressers 2011). To realize the full potential of such projects, adaptive management is crucial. In a synthetic approach, many goals are optimized together, making it impossible to focus exclusively on any of them from the outset.

3. SUSTAINABLE DEVELOPMENT AND INTEGRATED WATER MANAGEMENT

Sustainable development and integrated water management are closely linked. In 2002, at the Johannesburg World Summit on Sustainable Development (WSSD), the Technical Advisory Committee of the Global Water Partnership defined integrated water resources management

(IWRM) as: 'a process which promotes the coordinated development and management of water, land and related resources in order to maximize the resultant economic and social welfare in an equitable manner without compromising the sustainability of vital ecosystems' (2005). The Committee also emphasized that water should be managed in a basin-wide context, under the principles of good governance and public participation.

Does integrated water management therefore lead to sustainable development? Another way to frame this question is to ask: to what extent do water policies contribute to sustainable development? Although there are myriad definitions for sustainability, the literature emphasizes a long-term vision. For example, the International Union for the Conservation of Nature refers to sustainable development as achieving a quality of life that can be maintained for many generations (IUCN) (1993). Such a long-term quality of life then can exist because it is socially desirable (fulfilling people's needs in equitable ways), economically successful and maintains the long-term viability of supporting ecosystems.

In essence almost all definitions of sustainable development refer to three dimensions (Denters and Klok 2006): a social perspective (to what extent are social goals such as social cohesion and social equity achieved?); an economic perspective (to what extent are economic goals such as growth and efficiency achieved?); and an ecological perspective (to what extent is the ecosystem's integrity respected and are environmental constraints taken into consideration?).

Analytically there are two approaches to the actual measurement of sustainability. The first approach is based on substantive criteria, which relate to the substance of the policy programmes. Here one might also focus on ultimate effects and outcomes of the policies implemented. But the literature also offers an alternative to a measure based on expected economic, social and ecological effects. William Lafferty (2002) has conceptualized sustainable development as an issue of policy integration. Since sustainable development aims to integrate three major concerns – economic, social and environmental – we can conceive of sustainability as a form of inter-sectoral and inter-temporal integration.

Lafferty suggests three criteria to assess the degree of policy integration: comprehensiveness, aggregation and consistency (2002, pp. 23–4). In the context of sustainable development, the criterion of *comprehensiveness* implies that sectoral policy programmes should reflect environmental, economic and social concerns (cross-sectional comprehensiveness). *Aggregation* refers to the (ex ante) evaluation of the policy from an integrated (cross-sectional) perspective, reflecting the various substantive concerns. Comprehensiveness and aggregation are also furthered by adopting a long-term perspective (involving inter-temporal comprehensiveness and aggregation). Finally, *consistency* pertains to consistency among the different policy components: are the various elements of a comprehensive policy mutually supportive?

Denters and Klok (2006) offer a related approach to measuring sustainable development, employing procedural criteria. As noted earlier, the key question is whether environmental, economic and social concerns are geared to one another. Whereas the concept of integration refers to the substance of a programme and its effects (the results of a policy process), we use the term *coordination* to refer to patterns of involvement in the policy arena. The presumption here is that a higher degree of coordination is achieved when at the political, administrative and policy network levels all three types of concerns (economic, social and ecological) are being represented. In fact, this is the procedural equivalent of comprehensiveness (as a sub-dimension of integration) and can as such be regarded as part of Lafferty's approach.

4. DRIVERS FOR TRANSITION

System Change

The first drivers for the transition to a new way of managing water are changes in the water system itself and pressure on the water system. These changes and pressures lead to more-complex problems and to the intensification of existing problems. Changes in the societal system include urbanization, population rise, economic growth and globalization. Shifts in the physical system are ongoing and additional changes, such as climate change and its negative impact on the environment (such as more irregular rainfall), are expected. These changes in the system make it necessary to make use of integrated water management, because traditional water management has shown in practice that it is unable to address these complex problems. An example is the renaturation of river systems, often undoing earlier interventions in the relatively recent past, such as the last few decades.

Policy and Law

We can ask ourselves whether policies and laws are only the result of the transition in water management or are part of the transition process itself. For instance in the Netherlands the term integrated water management became well known following the publication of the 1985 report *Living with Water: Towards Integral Water Policy* (Ministerie van Verkeer en

Waterstaat (Ministry of Transport and Water Management)). And in 1989, integrated water management became official national policy.

On the broader European level, the Water Framework Directive (WFD, 2000/60/EC) can be seen as an overall framework for integrated management and a driver for the transition in Europe. Integration is a key goal of the WFD. The main purpose of the WFD is to promote sustainable water use in water basins with a good ecological status. Protecting and improving the water environment means achieving an appropriate balance between protection and use. The provisions for protected areas integrate EU nature conservation policy (Natura 2000) into water management. Integration works in two ways because the WFD does not impose fixed objectives for the water environment; rather it provides member states with the flexibility to set objectives that reflect environmental, social and economic priorities.

This flexibility means that the needs and priorities of other policy areas can be taken into account in water management decisions. This has to take place on the European and the member state levels, as well as on the river basin district level. Within water management the WFD framework has to be coordinated with other water uses such as flood defence, hydropower and navigation in setting objectives for the water environment. EU flood defence policy, energy policy and navigation policy also have to accommodate other environmental, social and economic considerations. Conversely, EU agricultural policy and cohesion policy have to take account of water management objectives. Other policy areas have to take into consideration water resource protection, for instance avoiding the need for particular water uses in locations where those water uses would cause environmental deterioration. Another example of such integration is land use planning policies restricting development on floodplains.

International Organizations and Conferences

Efforts of a number of international organizations and a series of conferences led to the evolution of recommendations about integrated water management, and to a growing commitment from governments, stakeholder organizations and donors to the concept of integrated water management.

Already at the United Nations Conference on Water in the Mar del Plata (1977), integrated water management was the recommended approach to reconcile the multiple competing uses of water resources. Although in the 1980s water had for the most part disappeared from the political agenda, the situation changed in the 1990s thanks to the efforts of a number of conferences and international organizations. Events such as the

International Conference on Water and Environment (1992), the Second World Water Forum (2000), the International Conference on Freshwater (2001), the World Summit on Sustainable Development (2002) and the Third World Water Forum (2003) collectively led to breakthroughs that thrust integrated water management onto the political agenda.

5. SUSTAINABILITY OF NEW WATER MANAGEMENT APPROACHES AND ITS DILEMMAS

It is difficult to affirm that new water approaches are by definition more sustainable than the traditional water management. Instead we can ask questions as to how far these new approaches match sustainability criteria, and also attempt to identify the sustainability dilemmas with which they are associated. In this context we should keep in mind two sub-dimensions of sustainability: the concern for long-term policy effects and inter-sectoral and inter-temporal integration.

In the following sections we explore the sustainability of the new water management under five headings: expected sustainability; comprehensiveness; aggregation; consistency; and coordination. Under the first heading we consider whether new water management approaches are likely to contribute to the broad substantive goals of long-term economic prosperity, social welfare and ecological protection. The next sections take up Lafferty's three criteria for integration, asking in turn: (i) whether the new water management approaches consider a broader range of effects on environmental, economic and social concerns (comprehensiveness); (ii) whether the environmental, social and economic consequences of water management are aggregated into the overall evaluation of alternatives (aggregation); and (iii) whether the economic, social and ecological objectives of water management and the instruments for achieving them are in accord (consistency). Under the final heading, we deal with the related issue of 'coordination', considering whether procedural coordination in the new water management leads to a comprehensive representation of interests in water governance processes. Whereas 'integration' refers to the results of the interactions, coordination refers to processes and procedures themselves.

Expected Sustainability

The response to the question, 'Are new water management approaches likely to contribute to long-term economic growth, social welfare and ecological protection?' is that the new water approaches explicitly attempt to integrate multiple objectives, so they are more likely to contribute to different objectives rooted in the three dimensions of sustainable development. A 'command and control' (or 'plan and realize') paradigm requires that system behaviour is highly predictable. A long-term perspective is inherent in a system approach to water problems where we do not think in terms of certainty and control, but rather in terms of uncertainty and unpredictability. For the latter we need a long-term analysis. The WFD is a driver for the transitions in water management and encourages such a long-term perspective.

The purpose of IWRM is to achieve ecological sustainability (Rahaman and Varis 2005). In other words, current water use and maintenance of the water system should be managed in a way that does not prevent future generations from obtaining the same quality of life from the same resource. This is accomplished by achieving an appropriate *balance* between using water for current livelihoods and conserving the resource to sustain its long-term functions and characteristics.

Bressers and Kuks (2004) assume that the sustainable use of water systems requires an optimum distribution of use options among present and future users as well as use functions. An example of the distribution of use options is the distribution between upstream and downstream users. An activity that pollutes water upstream (using a stream to discharge waste water) could interfere with the downstream use of that stream for drinking water supply. Or an upstream weir could impede the downstream flow and impede dependent-use options. Such rivalries not only exist between different (heterogeneous) use types, they may also appear among homogeneous uses (uses of the same type). In arid areas farmers may feel the need to coordinate their water use for irrigation. Or in the field of fisheries, quotas may be used as an instrument to prevent the depletion of fish stocks.

Comprehensiveness

In response to the question, 'Do the new water management approaches lead to an assessment of a broad range of effects of the policy programmes on environmental, economic and social concerns?' new water approaches look at a wider range of problems. A coordinated development and management of water, land and related resources in principle could lead to maximizing the resultant economic and social welfare without compromising the sustainability of the environmental system.

The dilemma is that the need to deal with interdependent problems leads to complex water projects with boundary definition issues and administrative coupling problems. Further integration can create confusion because it defies neat administrative and organizational boundaries. Rivers do not stop at borders, and trans-boundary problems arise with the analysis and management (Lulofs and Coenen 2007). Institutional challenges can restrict the usefulness of integrative management approaches.

The challenges for water management stem from the drivers we mentioned. The complexity of problem pressures, combined with the European Water Framework Directive as a driver, lead to a large number of proposed interventions in the water systems that in turn pose huge demands on the financial and administrative capacity of water managers. A core problem that managers face is the need to combine multiple fields of interest and participation to complete each project, such as: agricultural interests, rural landscape renewal, nature protection, water safety issues and water quality issues. In addition to new resources, all of these fields typically bring in new actors and procedures. This requires water managers to exhibit great skills to merge (or couple) these streams, while remaining aware that a failure in any one of these fields could undermine the basis for an entire project (Lulofs and Bressers 2010).

Aggregation

With respect to the question, 'Are the presumed environmental, social and economic consequences of water management aggregated into the overall evaluation of the water policy alternatives?', there is increasing awareness of the complexity that is a necessary, but not a sufficient, condition for changing water management practices. Whether the environmental, social and economic consequences receive proper attention in the evaluation of water policy alternatives depends on what happens in the hearts and minds of people and whether they really are prepared and able to integrate different concerns (Pahl-Wostl et al. 2007). Many water planners and managers remain focused on opportunities for technical solutions and supply development. As a result, substantial tensions exist between those advocating management solutions designed to increase the efficiency, equity and sustainability of water use and those who still see additional (infrastructure) development as the best solution to water problems (Moench 2003). This tension is related to balancing the quest for control, on the one hand, and the acceptance of a certain degree of uncertainty, on the other hand. Many water managers still think in terms of hierarchy, control and blueprint planning (Lulofs and Coenen 2007), even though the new approach of adaptive management is fashionable and widely supported by analysts from both scientific and practitioner backgrounds.

Consistency

The answer to the question, 'Are the economic and social, economic and ecological, and social and ecological objectives in water management, and the instruments for achieving them, all in accord?' is that there is significant tension between the application of an economic market-oriented approach to water management and the attainment of social goals. The application of economic principles concerns the allocation of water and the development of water services in a more efficient way. However, when water is treated only as a market-oriented commodity, it threatens domestic use for very basic needs (Gunatilake and Gopalakrishnan 2002), particularly for people in extreme poverty. This leads us back to the discussion of whether water is a collective or an economic good. Water is to some extent a basic human need, and access to minimum quantities of safe water (20 litres per person per day) is a basic human right. Lack of access to safe drinking water, sanitation and irrigation is directly related to poverty and poor health (as stipulated in the Millennium Development Goals). As a consequence, water as a human right (a limited amount of water) should be dealt with separately from water as a foundation for economic activity (most water use) (Arrojo et al. 2005).

International water conferences put a lot of emphasis on privatization and public/private partnerships. These concepts were extensively disseminated at water conferences such as the Hague Forum, the Bonn Conference and the WSSD summit. Privatization threatens the ecological system side of water management, however, because it may encourage fragmentation. Privatization of the marketable aspects of water may result in single-purpose planning and management, instead of ecosystem conservation.

Finally, there is a possible tension between water objectives and social goals. It is important that integrated water management not only deals with water supply and wastewater treatment, but combines many other functions, including flood control (safety for people), poverty alleviation, food production and drought management (Rahaman and Varis 2005).

The emphasis of the new water management paradigms on inclusiveness (extent) and coherence might be a remedy for some of these dangers. In a six-country study in Europe which assessed 24 sub-cases, it was shown that as governance became more extensive and coherent, the sustainability of water resources was improved (Bressers and Kuks 2004). Sustainability improvements here were in the first instance evaluated with respect to ecological sustainability and then secondarily in terms of positive (rather than the negative) side effects on the social and economic dimensions. The researchers found that in practice the economic side effects of the observed ecological improvements were largely neutral, while there were substantial positive social side effects (Bressers and Kuks 2004).

Coordination

With respect to the question, 'Does procedural coordination in new water management lead to a comprehensive representation of interests in water management processes at the political, administrative and policy network level?' it is found that coordination is important for integration because water management often involves conflicting objectives and interests. The reason for multiple objectives and interests is a result of competition for water (in arid regions) and space (in high-density regions such as the Netherlands) as well as complex institutional constraints. Coordinating mechanisms can be formal, such as intergovernmental agreements, or informal, such as voluntary local watershed group meetings.

The expansion of the different participants involved in water management who have multiple and potentially conflicting objectives could lead to knowledge claim dilemmas and competing arguments over legitimacy. This is even truer when water management efforts are also externally integrated, that is when they are coupled with efforts from other policy fields that come together in the same projects. When there is an attempt to attain synergies in water projects by having them serve other societal purposes (nature development, recreation, landscape, and so on) various sets of actors and rules have to be combined. At the same time the potential for pooling resources and harvesting multiple dividends can make this approach very worthwhile. This raises the problem of the boundary judgements of the actors involved. It raises the question as to whether they have similar or matching sets of issues, and how they accommodate rules and actors relevant to the project. Modern water management is often characterized as 'boundary spanning' (Bressers and Lulofs 2010).

Accommodating the views of various governments and special interest groups is a challenge for integration because they all have different perspectives. Intergovernmental relationships among government agencies at the same level include regional, state-to-state and interagency issues. Relationships among different levels of government include, for example, state/federal and local/state interactions. Special interest groups range from those advocating resource development to those favouring conservation (or as in the case of the Netherlands, 'renaturation'). In many cases, conflicts arise between the same types of interest groups – for example, between fly fishers and rafters on a stream. Involving many participants often makes the decision-making process lengthy and costly.

While the multipurpose nature of many water policy interventions that stem from integrated water management puts a lot of stress on coordination capacity, this does not imply that they are bound to fail. Probably, like anything else, a sound degree of integration is by definition a matter of balance between too little and too much. Where the balance is precisely located varies according to temporal and spatial contexts, but it is also potentially influenced by learning ever better strategies to cope with dynamics and other forms of complexity (de Boer and Bressers 2011).

6. DISCUSSION: THE DILEMMAS OF INTEGRATION AND CONFLICTING RESPONSES

Many discussions of the new water management assume that new water management automatically implies more sustainable water management. In this chapter we considered the characteristics of old/traditional water management approaches and compared and contrasted these with new water management approaches. Integrated water management is important for sustainability because it brings a long-term perspective to problem-solving and to projects. Additionally, a system perspective is necessary to solve complex issues involving all three dimensions of sustainable development. We acknowledged that integrated water management approaches almost by definition lead towards sustainable development if we define sustainable development in terms of policy integration. But we still face a number of dilemmas. The growing popularity of integrated water management approaches, particularly integrated water resource management (IWRM) that involves both internal and external policy integration, has not occurred without scepticism and criticism.

Although integrated water management can lead to coordinated integrative development of water resources along the lines of all three dimensions of sustainable development (comprehensiveness), it also increases the complexity and dynamic nature of water management processes and projects by adding boundary judgement issues. Additionally, there is the issue of different perceptions of problems, objectives and rules stemming from varying institutional challenges and objectives.

The real integration of the environmental, social and economic consequences of water management aggregated into the overall evaluation of the policy measures (aggregation) depends on the preparedness and ability of water managers and their colleagues from related policy fields to really integrate different concerns and to de-emphasize their reliance on technical solutions.

There are tensions in deploying policy measures to reach the different sustainability dimensions (consistency). This has been found to be true when dealing with competing conceptualizations/objectives of water use such as between the economic (water as an economic good) approach and the social approach (water as a basic need). This is also seen in the conflict between economic (single purpose) and ecological (system perspective) objectives, as well as between social (social functions of water) and ecological objectives.

The expansion of the range of participants in water management (coordination) who have multiple (and potentially conflicting) objectives, can lead to legitimacy and knowledge claim dilemmas in addition to spawning lengthy and costly procedures. This is found especially at the national policy level. Such dilemmas are sometimes seen as a symptom of the Dutch tendency to avoid clear-cut choices and to get stuck in the procedural viscosity of decision-making.

That these dilemmas of integration can ultimately lead to a de-emphasis on integrated water management is illustrated by recent developments in the Netherlands (van Leussen et al. 2007). As we have seen, the Netherlands has been a pioneer in applying integrated water management over the past two decades. Conceptually the approach was developed in national policy documents, best described as 'memoranda' or 'guidance notes' on water management. These were written by the relevant ministries with responsibilities for public works, agriculture/nature and environment/spatial development. These policy documents were discussed and accepted in Parliament. Particularly since the Third National Policy Document on Water Management in the Netherlands in 1989, the concept of integrated water management became very popular. The integrated water management concept was spread to all levels of government: national, provincial, water boards and municipalities.

Although a new integrated water law was adopted in 2006, replacing separate laws on flood defence, quantity, quality, groundwater, and so on, we see clear signs that the political enthusiasm for integrated water management has declined. While the Fourth Policy Note (2008) still explicitly mentions integrated water management as a guiding principle, at the national level recent documents hardly mention it anymore. For instance, in a recent policy note the word 'integrated' is used only once, and the Commission on Integrated Water Management was dissolved and was replaced by the Advisory Commission on Water. Another clear sign of the decline in enthusiasm for this concept is that political attention is mainly directed at specific sectoral policy themes and issues: flooding; space for water (rivers, drainage) and drought, both in relation to possible change in climate and climate variability; water quality/ecology; groundwater, water table assessment; and urban water management.

While the concept of integrated water management is rather fuzzy and does not appeal to some stakeholders, these thematic subjects (flood, drought, pollution) are more easily understood and accepted by stakeholders. On the national level such themes captured the political agenda. The WFD is taking up a lot of time. Climate change reintroduced the issue of flooding on the political agenda. Since the Netherlands is situated in a low-lying delta, the management of water and the struggle against flooding has formed a narrative throughout Dutch history. In a substantial policy programme called WB 21 the focus is on creating space for water by creating retention areas and other measures. However, all of this does not mean that the Netherlands has really abandoned the integrated water management approach.

One could just as well argue that integrated water management concepts have been internalized in water management in the Netherlands, especially at the sub-national level. The main thrust of integrated water management moved from the policy and planning stage at larger geographical scales to the implementation stage at more regional and local levels. Implementing the measures following from focused themes in this densely populated country – where all space already has a clearly designated use – actually boosted the *practice* of integrated water management at the regional level.

Currently the pragmatic necessities of implementing ambitious water management interventions in the context of overlapping spatial claims, and with insufficient financial resources for each separate purpose, make integrated projects unavoidable – even if the concept itself is not overtly stated. This is not restricted to internal integration of the water foci mentioned above. It also encompasses a broad range of other policy fields that are seen as relevant or unavoidable to include, such as nature development, spatial planning, agriculture, rural development, recreation and tourism, urban development, economic diversification, environmental protection, environmental education, and protection of existing nature and cultural history. These, and even more fields, are perceived by water management practitioners (such as water board executives and civil servants) as relevant purposes to be served by spatial interventions in the water system. Most of them also have had extensive experiences with such external integration (van Tilburg et al. 2009).

All of this has led to a rather complicated situation regarding integrated water management in the Netherlands. At the regional and local level, internally and externally, integrated water management is more intensively implemented than ever before. Practitioners have learned to deal more successfully with the complex and dynamic processes that result from such integration. They have learned to use adaptive management strategies that modify the context of the interaction processes that are needed to integrate multipurpose spatial projects into more productive contexts, optimizing the chances for collaboration and finding synergic win-win solutions (de Boer and Bressers 2011). This has a positive outcome for horizontal policy integration (HEPI) (Lafferty and Hovden 2002; Lafferty 2002; Lafferty 2004).

At the same time, top–down support for such integrative and adaptive management action has been waning. Increasingly water management practitioners, and their counterparts from municipalities and other stakeholders, are confronted with senior authorities that replace integrated support schemes and policy guidelines. These authorities choose a direction that unilaterally withdraws essential support for projects (for example, nature linkage zones) or organize the accountability of the measures in such a way that specific goal requirements replace the integrated optimum approach commonly used before. In this way the partial retreat from integrated management at the national and provincial policy levels translates into hindrances for developing really integrated management at ground level in water management projects. This has a negative effect on what is termed vertical policy integration (VEPI) (Lafferty and Hovden 2002; Lafferty 2002; Lafferty 2004).

While the lack of an overall integrated vision can be overcome by creating an integrated vision for regional river basins or even local projects, the top–down fragmented 'quest for control', which is based on distrust, is very difficult to combine with the adaptive management strategies. Building trust among local stakeholders is therefore essential for dealing with the dynamics and complexities of fully integrated water management projects. Making these promising practices more difficult will increase the risk of a negative spiral away from policy integration. The assessment of what makes an appropriate regime to promote sustainable development might therefore be widened not only to include matters of integration, but also matters of flexibility, as well as the degree to which the regime supports and facilitates adaptive strategies, in addition to ensuring that integrated (multi-sectoral) goals and objectives are met (de Boer and Bressers 2011).

Dutch integrated water management has developed from internal integration (IWM), to include external integration (IWRM), and then adaptive water management that allowed it to deal with the dynamics and complexities of integrated approaches. The example of the development of the Dutch water management approach illustrates that overly simplistic solutions cannot deal with complex problems, nor can these problems be addressed by simply fragmenting policy to arrive at a piecemeal solution. Policy integration has proven helpful for sustainable development both at the political and the operational level. This approach has enabled operational-level practitioners to learn how better to deal with the resultant complexities, without reverting to incrementally applying policies and solutions. Such a retreat would prevent attempts to move beyond policy and solution impasses. As Einstein once stated: 'Things should be made as simple as possible, but not any simpler!'

REFERENCES

Al Radif, A. (1999), 'Integrated water resources management (IWRM): an approach to face the challenges of the next century and to avert future crises', *Desalination*, **124**, 145–53.

Arentsen, M., H. Bressers and L. O'Toole (2000), 'Institutional and policy responses to uncertainty in environmental policy: a comparison of Dutch and US styles', *Policy Studies Journal*, **28** (2), 597–611.

Arrojo, P., A. Dionysis, B. Barraque, H. Bressers and C. Estaban (2005), *European Declaration for a New Water Culture*, Madrid: Fundación Nueva Cultura del Aqua.

Bressers, H., D. Huitema and S. Kuks (1994), 'Policy networks in Dutch water policy', in H. Bressers, L.J. O'Toole, Jr. and J. Richardson (eds), 'Networks for water policy: a comparative perspective', *Environmental Politics*, **3**, special issue, 3 (4), 24–52.

Bressers, H. and S. Kuks (eds) (2004), *Integrated Governance and Water Basin Management: Conditions for Regime Change and Sustainability*, London: Kluwer Academic.

Bressers, H. and K. Lulofs (eds). (2010), *Governance and Complexity in Water Management: Creating Cooperation Through Boundary Spanning Strategies*, Cheltenham, UK and Northampton, MA: Edward Elgar.

Bressers, H. and L. O'Toole (1995), 'Networks and water policy: conclusions and implications for research', in Hans Bressers, Laurence O'Toole and Jeremy Richardson (eds), *Networks for Water Policy: A Comparative Perspective*, London: Frank Cass, pp. 197–217.

De Boer, C. and H. Bressers (2011), *Complex and Dynamic Implementation Processes: Analyzing the Renaturalization of the Dutch Regge River*, Enschede, Netherlands and The Hague: University of Twente and Dutch Water Governance Centre.

Denters, S. and Klok, P.-J. (2006), 'Measuring institutional performance in achieving urban sustainability', in H. Heinelt, D. Sweeting, and P. Getimis (eds), *Legitimacy and Urban Governance: A Cross-national Comparative Study*, London: Routledge, pp. 42–58.

European Commission (2000), Water Framework Directive (WFD, 2000/60/EC).

Global Water Partnership (GWP) (2005), *Catalyzing Change: A Handbook for Developing IWRM and Water Efficiency Strategies*, New York: United Nations Department of Economic and Social Affairs.

Gunatilake, H.M. and C. Gopalakrishnan (2002), 'Proposed water policy for Sri Lanka: the policy versus the policy process', *Water Resources Development*, **18** (4), 545–62.

International Union for the Conservation of Nature (IUCN) (1993), *Caring for the Earth*, Gland, Switzerland: IUCN.

Kuks, S. (2004), 'The evolution of the water regime in the Netherlands', in Ingrid

Kissling and Stefan Kuks (eds), *The Evolution of National Water Regimes in Europe*, Dordtrecht, Netherlands: Kluwer Academic Publishers, pp. 87–142.

Lafferty, W. (2002), *From Environmental Protection to Sustainable Development: Environmental Policy Integration as a Challenge for Applied Science*, Enschede, Netherlands: University of Twente.

Lafferty, W. (ed.) (2004), *Governance for Sustainable Development: The Challenge of Adapting Form to Function*, Cheltenham, UK and Northampton, MA: Edward Elgar.

Lafferty, W. and E. Hovden (2002), *Environmental Policy Integration: Towards an Analytical Framework*, ProSus Report, Oslo: University of Oslo.

Lulofs, K. and H. Bressers (2010), 'Innovations in water management requiring boundary spanning: Roots and concepts', in Hans Bressers and Kris Lulofs (eds), *Governance and Complexity in Water Management: Creating Cooperation through Boundary Spanning Strategies*, Cheltenham, UK and Northampton, MA: Edward Elgar, pp. 1–17.

Lulofs, K. and F. Coenen. (2007), 'Cross border cooperation in the Vecht river basin on water quality', in Joris Verwijmeren and Mark Wiering (eds), *Many Rivers to Cross: Cross Border Co-operation in River Management*, Delft, Netherlands: Eburon.

Ministerie van Verkeer en Waterstaat (1985), *Omgaan met Water: Naar een integraal waterbeleid*, The Hague: Dutch Government.

Mitchell, Bruce (1990), 'Integrated water management', in B. Mitchell (ed.), *Integrated Water Management: International Experiences and Perspectives*, London: Belhaven Press.

Moenche, M. (2003), 'Groundwater and poverty: exploring the connections', in R. Llamas and E. Custodio (eds), *Intensive Use of Groundwater: Challenges and Opportunities*, Lisse, The Netherlands: A.A. Bakema.

Nationaal Bestuursakkoord Water (2003) *National Inter-governmental Agreement on Water Policy Implementation*, The Hague: Dutch Government.

Pahl-Wostl, C., J. Sendzimir, P. Jeffrey, J. Aerts, G. Berkamp and K. Cross (2007), 'Managing change toward adaptive water management through social learning', *Ecology and Society*, **12** (2), 30.

Rahaman, M. and O. Varis (2005), 'Integrated water resources management: evolution, prospects and future challenges', *Sustainability: Science, Practice, & Policy*, **1** (1), 15–21, accessed 12 April 2005 at http://ejournal.nbii.org/archives/vol1iss1/0407-03.rahaman.html.

Van Leussen, W., S. Kuks and K. Lulofs (2007), 'Governance of water resources in the Netherlands', in H. Folmer, and S. Reinhard (eds), *Water Problems and Policies in the Netherlands*, Washington, DC: World Bank.

Van Tilburg, M., H. Bressers and F. Coenen (2009), '"Boundary judgments" van waterschapsbestuurders en ambtelijke medewerkers en hun invloed op de rol van kennis', CSTM working paper, Enschede, Netherlands.

4. Local participation and learning in nature protection: a Swedish success story

Katarina Eckerberg

The protection of biological diversity worldwide is increasingly seen as a challenge on par with the quest to remedy the causes and impacts of climate change. The United Nations declared 2010 the International Year of Biological Diversity and this was also the target year (set in 2001) for the European Union (EU) to halt the loss of biodiversity in its territory (EU 2001). Ecosystems provide a number of basic services that are essential for using the Earth's resources sustainably, including provisioning services (food, fibre, water, and so on), supporting services (for example, pollination, primary production), regulating services (climate, pests, flood regulation, and so on) and cultural services (for example recreation, ethical and spiritual values) (Millennium Ecosystem Assessment 2005). Despite ambitious targets, biodiversity is still in decline and land cover changes, including the expansion of urban settlements and the exploitation of natural resources, continue to negatively affect ecosystem services (EEA 2010). Recognizing the urgent need for increased efforts, the European Council endorsed a long-term biodiversity vision for 2050 and set a target to halt the degradation of ecosystem services by 2020, which was also in line with the decisions of the Conference of the Parties (COP) meeting on the Convention of Biological Diversity in Nagoya in October 2010.

The implementation of nature conservation involves multiple levels of government and a range of different methods, including the creation of protected areas of different sizes, specialized management practices, and not least the engagement of local citizens and land owners. However, despite the ambitious targets set at international and national levels, the realization of sustainable methods to protect biological diversity and recreational values is often faced with multiple constraints. When areas are to be set aside from economic activities such as agriculture, forestry or the building of roads and housing estates, in the end priority is typically given to more easily measured and short-term benefits. Moreover, since much of the land is private property, land owners need to be compensated in those cases where economic activities are being restrained, which implies that substantial state funds are required for the protection of biological diversity and amenity values. Conflicts tend to arise, which cannot be resolved unless all parties become convinced of the importance of long-term conservation and the potential benefits to local livelihoods, rather than seeing this as a threat to economic prosperity. Nature conservation policy is not always embraced by all parties at the local level of implementation due to diverging interests.

According to assessments made by the European Environment Bureau, the EU Biodiversity Action Plan has been useful to focus attention on biodiversity, as well as to bring into sharper focus the kind of measures and programmes what would be needed to protect biodiversity. Yet it has largely failed to achieve its goals because of its non-binding character, the low levels of funding and of EU member ownership of the problem, and – perhaps even more critically – the lack of understanding and efforts to address the socioeconomic drivers behind biodiversity loss (EEB 2010, p. 7). When the European Environment Agency discusses the shortcomings of policy responses to date, it identifies some of the main problems to be the poor integration of biodiversity concerns into sector policies affecting the countryside and the environment at large, as well as insufficient public awareness in order to generate political commitment among member states (EEA 2010, pp. 40–43).

How could these challenges of nature conservation policy be met? This chapter presents a case from one EU member state that may serve as inspiration for others to overcome some of the resistance towards implementing measures to protect biodiversity as well as recreational values. In this chapter, I argue that an important key lies in shifting nature conservation policy down to local constituencies, thereby creating legitimacy for action and ownership of the problem and promoting learning among key stakeholders. The argument notes that leaving the definition of what is to be preserved and why to sub-national authorities, and stimulating broader community participation, could overcome some of the inertia in current European biodiversity policy.

The choice of Sweden as an example is justified by two main reasons. First, in international comparison, Swedish local authorities often score high in the promotion of environment protection and sustainable development policy (Lafferty 2001). Thus the country can be regarded as a 'best case' to learn from. Central government leadership and funding programmes have played a major role in such progress, but they have also contributed to a high dependence on investments by state and municipal actors rather than a mobilization of the private sector and local citizens

(Eckerberg 2005; Baker and Eckerberg 2007). Second, the launch of a recent central government investment programme for local nature conservation in Swedish municipalities – the Swedish Local Nature Conservation Programme (LONA) established in 2004 and still ongoing – constitutes an exception to the rule of formulating biodiversity policy in a top–down manner and forcing sub-national authorities to act. The Swedish approach in this programme is to support local initiatives in nature conservation as they emerge from the local social context. The experiences from LONA can therefore be used to shed light on how biodiversity protection can be promoted from the ground up. The question that is posed here is whether – and if so, how – such a policy instrument can help to shift biodiversity policy beyond the impasse.

1. NATURE PROTECTION POLICY ON THE MOVE

As in most other European states, national policy to protect biological diversity in Sweden relies on a three-pronged approach: (1) protecting large-scale nature reserves and national parks; (2) introducing smaller-scale biotope protection within agriculture and forestry; and (3) integrating biodiversity concerns into various sectoral policies, such as road construction, water management and municipal planning. The first types of measures have their background in European biodiversity policy, including the European Commission Habitats Directive and the European Natura 2000 network, and the second and third constitute part of sectoral policies such as the Water Framework Directive and the Environment and Rural Development Policy. Although legislation at the national level in Sweden is subordinated to EU policy since its entry as a European Community member in 1995, Swedish national nature conservation legislation dates back to 1909 when the first 10 national parks and a number of unique natural features were protected by the central government. Since then nature conservation policy has developed in several ways by moving from protecting national cultural heritage and pristine natural areas to including more social concerns, recreational values and biodiversity habitats (Wramner and Nygård 2010).

The introduction of the Swedish National Environmental Quality Objectives (NEQOs) in 1998, with several objectives directly related to nature conservation,[1] along with the policy principle of sector responsibility, implied another shift in emphasis. Increasingly, the substantive contribution of the second and third types of measures for promoting biodiversity has become documented and appreciated (cf. the establishment of the Swedish Species Information Centre in 1991 and the Swedish

Biodiversity Centre in 1994). In parallel, a growing critique of central government policy-making in this area has emerged, in particular from rural communities that voice the concern that excessive protection of lands might threaten livelihoods. Some of this critique also stems from the perception that experts at the Swedish Environmental Protection Agency and in the environment units at the county administrations (CAs) have failed to consult local land owners and residents before plans are made for nature protection. Inadequate communication and long distances between policy-makers and implementing actors contribute to a lack of trust in the establishment of protected areas (Eksvärd et al. 2006). Nature protection policy was perceived by local communities as expert driven and centralized, rather than anchored in local priorities and concerns. The LONA initiative emerged as a response to these debates. It was a direct result of the Swedish Ministry of the Environment communication 2001/02: 173 *A Coherent Nature Protection Policy*, which was presented in the autumn of 2001 and drew on discussions from a number of seminars arranged by the Government with public and private representatives from a wide range of interests, including science. The goal was to de-centralize nature protection policy and engage more local citizens (Olofsson 2001).

The overall aims of the LONA programme are to provide increased engagement in nature protection issues, to facilitate access, to increase local support, to protect more nature in urban areas and to mobilize municipalities for nature protection (Rskr. 2001/02, p. 173; Prop. 2003/04, p. 1; Swedish Environmental Protection Agency 2005). With seed funding from central government, local authorities and organizations were asked to co-finance projects stemming from local priorities. As will be shown in the following discussion, LONA has largely been a success story. In marked contrast to the much larger – and parallel – programme for local investments for ecological sustainability (Local Investment Programme for Ecologically Sustainable Development, or LIP), which lasted from 1998 to 2002 with results that have been contested by various interests (Eckerberg 2005; Baker and Eckerberg 2007), the response from our surveys and interviews of municipal stakeholders and representatives of business and interest groups is clearly positive. The objectives of LONA – to strengthen local support and engagement for nature protection, to raise the number of urban natural areas and increase public access to such areas, and to spur local authorities to protect nature – can be regarded as a success. LONA was also found to contribute substantially both directly and indirectly to the achievement of the relevant NEQOs (WSP 2009). Those positive evaluations have led the current government to continue the programme from 2010 onwards.

The study draws from four investigations of the ways in which LONA was initially designed and managed (Dahlgren and Eckerberg 2006) and how it has contributed to learning processes in relation to environment, nature conservation and outdoor life in schools (Dahlgren et al. 2008), as well as how it promoted local participation and engagement (Dahlgren et al. 2009), and the protection of local nature areas (Nordenstam and Eckerberg 2010). The studies comprise a total of six surveys with county administrations (CAs), municipalities and interest organizations, and almost 100 interviews with key informants representing a wide variety of interests, in addition to analysis of data from the LONA database[2] as well as project documents.

What factors can explain the success of LONA in local mobilizing for nature protection? This chapter investigates the expectations among local authorities and different interest groups. It also evaluates to what extent those expectations were met and finds the answer primarily in the way in which the programme was designed and managed, including the establishment of the criteria and requirements for funding. The legacy of previous local initiatives and established networks of cooperation, as well as national and local policy priorities for recreation and nature protection, are also important explanatory factors to be investigated.

The chapter proceeds as follows: first, the main features of the LONA programme are presented and placed in context of earlier government policy towards catalysing local initiatives towards sustainable development and nature conservation. Second, the findings of the evaluations of LONA, particularly in relation to local participation and engagement, are summarized. This results section also includes a discussion on the effects of LONA on learning processes. Third, these findings are analysed in relation to the procedural and contextual factors that have contributed to those achievements, thus placing the results in a wider frame and comparing them to other similar central funding initiatives. Finally, lessons are drawn for the European inertia in implementing biodiversity policy.

2. DESIGN OF THE LONA PROGRAMME

LONA was established between 2004 and 2006 by the then Social Democratic Government to promote local nature conservation in Swedish municipalities. A total of 300 million Swedish kronor was allocated to 1,530 local projects in 261 municipalities. Most of these projects are now complete. With additional local co-funding provided both through local authorities and voluntary organizations, the total investment came to more than 700 million Swedish kronor over the three years. In 2010 the re-elected Conservative Government decided to continue the LONA programme with an annual state contribution of 50 million Swedish kronor. Compared with the total annual state budget for nature conservation of about 1.7 billion Swedish kronor in 2010 – of which the bulk is directed towards protection and management of nature reserves (of which about 50 per cent is used to secure forested land) – this figure may not appear impressive. However, it is clearly a considerable and novel addition to traditional, central government nature conservation policy.

Even if the funding comes from central government, and the Swedish Environmental Protection Agency (SEPA) guides and monitors the programme, the resources were distributed evenly to the CAs, which were given responsibility for the announcement, selection and final decision of which projects should be approved. Municipalities, NGOs, foundations and individuals could seek support for projects that met the overall criteria of contributing to nature protection and recreation goals. The projects also had to show that they would contribute to one or several of the NEQOs, as well as explain how the project would encourage local participation. Co-funding was required (SFS 2003). This ensured local ownership of the project and could be contributed in the form of voluntary work by NGOs.

In practice the great majority of local authorities (261 out of 290) received funding. The CAs strived to involve as many local authorities as possible, thus applying an equity model rather than a competitive model. In many instances resource-poor local authorities received funding for their projects at the expense of applications from larger local authorities that might have led to more direct nature protection results. Priority was thus given to strengthening the long-term institutional basis rather than short-term benefits for local nature protection. This stood in contrast to some of the earlier government funding towards local sustainable development initiatives.

Almost all CAs had a reference group consisting of their different units from fisheries to regional development to advise on which projects should be financed. About half of the local authorities arranged consultations with their internal units, such as environment and health, planning, culture and leisure, in the planning of the projects and to a somewhat lesser extent in their execution. Most of the projects were carried out with the municipality as prime motor, but there was also much collaboration across municipalities as well as between municipalities, NGOs and farmers. Many schools were involved in projects aimed at knowledge-building, while recreation projects primarily engaged sports and outdoor organizations. A considerable proportion of nature protection associations were initiators of projects, some of which were managed with little involvement of the municipality itself.

3. THE LEGACY OF LOCAL NATURE PROTECTION WORK

Swedish municipalities had a tradition to build upon in nature conservation. They have had the authority to establish protected areas since 1987. This was based initially on delegation by the CAs, but since the Environmental Code of 1999 municipalities can themselves declare nature reserves. About 7 per cent (226) of the total 3,352 nature reserves in Sweden in 2010 have been established by municipalities, which is an increase from 1999 when the municipal proportion was only 4 per cent.[3] But nature conservation policy at the local level has been much more broadly conceived than only protecting nature reserves. In the 1990s, when Local Agenda 21 was at its peak in terms of political attention, Swedish municipalities became very active in efforts to enhance biological diversity and local citizens' access to nature. Local projects towards this end were embraced by more than half of the municipalities as part of their Local Agenda 21 work in the late 1990s. The most common activities were renewable energy and environmental projects in schools and daycare centres (Edström and Eckerberg 2002, p. 11).

Local Agenda 21 activities were carried out with the support of central government funding, but were viewed by the municipalities as a combined top–down and bottom–up initiative. About half of the municipalities equipped with an Agenda 21 coordinator were much more active and also took action to involve their citizens. In 1997 funding for local sustainability initiatives increased dramatically with a new government initiative that lasted until 2002, namely LIP. LIP came about partly as a response to the criticism from the municipalities that the central government had contributed too little to spur locally derived sustainable development action (Eckerberg and Dahlgren 2007). However, even if the LIP contributed substantive new funding and efforts in particular to energy efficiency and renewable energy (one-third of the total funding) and much less to biodiversity projects (6 per cent of the total funding of 6.5 billion kronor over the five years up to 2003), it was clear that the LIP was largely a top–down initiative. The funding was distributed through a competitive mechanism that was largely controlled by the Ministry of Environment, even if the regional CAs became more involved over time. This stood in sharp contrast to the cooperative spirit that characterized the earlier Local Agenda 21 work. There were also limited signs of LIP activities enhancing cooperation across municipalities. And evaluations show little evidence that LIP actually contributed to increased citizen participation. Indeed, communicative measures within the sustainable development agenda were seldom included in the projects it funded (Baker and Eckerberg 2007).

The three central government funding programmes of Local Agenda 21, LIP and LONA share similar characteristics in that they all required matching funding at the local level. However, they were implemented in different ways that had implications for the leverage of local participation beyond the municipality itself. While Local Agenda 21 emerged as a broad initiative, where local organizations outside of the municipality could also receive central funding for sustainability activities, the design of LIP required that the municipality coordinate all action to be funded. As a result few voluntary and business organizations became involved in LIP, as opposed to Local Agenda 21. In LONA, it is possible for voluntary organizations to count their own labour as co-funding, and LONA grants can also be given to local partners. Moreover, the distribution of funding differs between the three programmes. While LIP reached only half of Sweden's 290 municipalities, LONA support has been given to nearly 90 per cent of them. The Local Agenda 21 funds were also shared by a majority of municipalities.

The legacy of the previous Local Agenda 21 and LIP work most likely contributed to raising the awareness about the need to preserve local nature among Swedish municipalities in the 1990s and onwards, and the support by the central government to those local initiatives was highly appreciated at the local level. Local Agenda 21 also catalysed local interest organizations, citizens and some local businesses to become involved, which formed a base for the furthering of nature conservation policy at municipal level.

4.   RESULTS

Content and Environmental Impacts

The LONA nature conservation grants have benefited everything from wetlands to exercise trails, school children, frogs and entire communities through promoting public health, cultural values and recreation. In several cases there are links to a possible boost for the business sector, where nature reserves are regarded as a valuable basis for tourism and local development. In line with set criteria, the majority of projects that were funded targeted information measures, protection and management as well as knowledge-building measures (such as nature schools). Restoration of nature was the fourth largest category, while measures to develop a baseline and initiate processes for establishment of nature reserves were least frequently adopted. The cost distribution followed a similar pattern, although restoration measures were generally more costly than knowledge-building measures. Going into more detailed measures, inventories of biodiversity values of different kinds were by far the most frequent, followed by arranging nature trails, clearing operations and various information campaigns (WSP 2009). The profile of the LONA projects varied in rural (forest-dominated) and urban regions. While projects in rural regions had more connections to regional development and tourism, urban projects were often connected to social and land use planning (Dahlgren et al. 2009, p. 33).

The environmental impacts have been evaluated based on the LONA database, showing that LONA contributed to 10 of the 16 NEQOs, with obvious bias towards those which relate most to nature protection (such as a rich landscape, thriving wetlands, living lakes and watercourses). In addition to the direct effects, LONA also helped indirectly to prepare for further protected areas. As much as half of the measures were judged to give long-term effects rather than direct ones (WSP 2009, p. 24). According to another survey on Swedish municipalities and their work on protected areas, with a 73 per cent response rate, more than half of Sweden's municipalities have created local nature reserves (Nordenstam and Eckerberg 2010). These are primarily aimed to protect green areas for recreational purposes, but they also fulfil important ecological functions. Of those that had created nature reserves, four out of five had also received LONA grants in support of initiating or implementing specific measures in the area, most commonly geared towards providing information to various audiences and enhancing the management plan. This study further indicates that LONA was generally not pivotal to the creation of the protected area, since most municipalities had already started the process before the launch of LONA. But the LONA grant helped to upgrade the political status and the ambitions within the area and speeded up the process considerably. The LONA support also contributed to combining nature protection and outdoor recreation in positive ways. More than one-third of those municipalities that had protected local areas had also utilized the state land access grant, and of those 90 per cent claim that this land access grant was decisive for the establishment of the nature reserve. In total, 60 per cent of the municipalities consider the costs for purchasing land or otherwise compensating land owners to be a major obstacle.

Fulfilment of Expectations

The overall impression from the surveys and interviews is that people are satisfied, or even very satisfied, with the way in which the programme was designed and managed. In our first survey, 70 per cent of respondents of both local authorities and CAs consider the programme to meet local needs well or very well. The vast majority of local authorities are satisfied with the county administrative board as an agent of the state in the programme, and most of the county administrative boards express satisfaction with their role and the distribution of resources between the counties. The only concern that is raised is a wish for the programme to be further extended, and the view is that it should continue as before (Dahlgren and Eckerberg 2006), which is now the case with the reintroduction of LONA in 2010. The most recent government bill on *Sustainable Protection of Nature* reiterates the need to enlarge the constituency for nature conservation and to facilitate the engagement of land owners' biodiversity protection, proposing that dialogues with local interest groups and citizens be intensified through the support of local authorities (Prop 2008/09, p. 214).

Participation and Local Engagement

What effects on local participation and engagement can then be discerned from the LONA initiatives? We combined three surveys to all 21 CAs, a selection of 165 municipalities and 95 representatives of various local organizations as well as six in-depth case studies of LONA projects with different activities and target groups to answer this question (Dahlgren et al. 2009). The results of our research confirm the conclusion from our first study in 2006 that a large number of local stakeholders have become increasingly engaged in local nature protection. In our first survey, 53 per cent of municipalities report that the level of external participation in the projects has been high, or even 100 per cent. Only 3 per cent of the municipalities have had entirely municipality-centred projects. Initiatives for collaboration had been taken in half of the municipalities by both the municipalities and external players, thus suggesting mutual activity and involvement (Dahlgren and Eckerberg 2006). In more than three out of four projects, voluntary organizations contributed directly to the implementation of the projects. Public authorities other than the municipalities contributed together with private individuals in about one-third of the projects. Private stakeholders (other than voluntary organizations) were involved in 14 per cent of the projects. Those were notably private companies and entrepreneurs and some private consultants (Dahlgren et al. 2009, p. 22).

Our more recent surveys show that the participation from NGOs was considerably lower in urban local authorities compared with rural areas. This can be attributed to the fact that urban local authorities enjoy more resources of their own in terms of expertise and finance to be used for nature protection measures. In contrast, rural local authorities must rely on contributions from external forces, such as homestead societies and environmentalists, but also individual farmers and rural develop-ment groups (Dahlgren et al. 2009, pp. 18–23). Also, in the rural forested regions, as many as 42 per cent of the projects involved other public authorities than the municipality itself (compared with 29 per cent on average), which can mostly be attributed to the European Social Fund's, the Public Employment Service's and the Forestry Agency's special ini-tiative between 2004 and 2006 for creating green jobs. The green jobs initiative targeted long-term unemployed people who were paid to carry out projects in culture and nature protection all over the country, and ran parallel to LONA.

Nature protection foundations have also contributed to many LONA initiatives. Examples of such foundations are Upplandsstiftelsen in the county of Uppland, Västkuststiftelsen on the west coast of Sweden, and Hopajola in the county of Örebro with support from the Swedish Society for Conservation of Nature. In the south, Sustainable Skåne (HUT) has activated its membership organizations in LONA projects through assistance from multiple sources of funding, ranging from EU Interreg to municipalities in the area. It was found that those LONA projects that were initiated by these types of foundations and regional organizations tended to be both larger in scope and resources, and to involve more actors at multiple levels of government compared with the average LONA project. Hence, they could build upon both their already established networks and their existing competence in the field of recreation and nature protection.

When representatives from external groups outside of the municipal organization were asked about their relations with the municipality, they were extremely positive: 90 per cent claimed that they felt part of the idea process leading up to the project, 94 per cent that they had major influ-ence in its design, and 90 per cent that the co-management of the project had worked well and they had the opportunity to affect the outcome. These are remarkably high figures when considering the general scepticism about public authorities in other areas of nature protection policy imple-mentation. In particular, the creation of protected areas is often met with protest and the general trust among Swedes in pure state management of such areas scores below 20 per cent (Zachrisson 2008, p. 159). External stakeholders in urban areas were the least content, where one-fifth of them claimed that no collaboration had occurred (Dahlgren et al. 2009, pp. 25–6).

Effects of Local Participation and Engagement

We asked the CA officers, municipalities and external stakeholders about their perceptions of increased networking, collaboration and engagement of multiple interests in the LONA projects. Their response was that LONA has contributed to the building of new contacts and networks that have strengthened, in particular, collaboration between local authorities and external interest organizations. LONA has spurred increased interest and knowledge about nature protection among new actors and societal groups, both within the municipal organization and within the general public, and also among those who by tradition do not tend to use such areas. Further, LONA has stimulated increased use of local nature protection areas. An increased number of visitors is shown in several of the case studies. They also point to greater support for nature conservation and protection of areas for recreation among local politicians, which in turn has resulted in substantial increase of the extent of locally protected areas (ibid., pp. 26–30).

Moreover, according to our respondents, particularly external actors, the competency of municipal officers in nature protection work has increased while their networks have strengthened. And they claim that more municipalities have initiated activities in this field, even in those municipalities where the interest was previously rather low. However, local authorities in rural areas are somewhat more pessimistic about the results, where a larger share of the respondents cannot see any spin-off effects (ibid., p. 27). Possibly, the lower spin-off effects in rural areas can be explained both by the fewer resources due to lower tax revenues and already strained municipal budgets, leading to less potential to take new initiatives in this direction without external funding. However, it could also be that rural communities feel their citizens already have enough access to nature. The representatives from external organizations also point out that their own organization has benefited from the LONA collaboration in that their work has been highlighted, collaboration with others has increased and their own competence in nature protection work has increased. New target groups had become involved in their work for recreation and nature protection and new members recruited. Many of the NGOs also mentioned that an increased interest from the general public in recreation and nature protection issues could be noted (ibid., pp. 27–8). The majority of respondents, both in the surveys and in the case studies, note that LONA would have been even more effective in relation to these aspects if it were a long-term – or even permanent – programme.

Three survey responses are quoted here to express the programme benefits:

> Through LONA, the local authorities were able to kick-start their nature protection work. Those local authorities who were already working with these issues could utilise the opportunities of LONA more directly, but in the later

applications they were joined by local authorities who had not previously been engaged in local nature protection. Of course it takes time to establish working groups, networks etc. so a longer time perspective generally produces better results. (county administration officer)

For us, our LONA project was tremendously fun and rewarding that gave fantastic results in such short time. We would just wish that there would have been an opportunity for follow up as Part 2 of the project. It is also satisfying that the nature trails and the outdoor classroom are used so frequently, and that the demand for recreation education is so great. So we say: thanks for this opportunity! (NGO representative)

LONA is viewed as a very good initiative that has produced local effects in terms of changing attitudes to nature protection and environmental work. Since we have a development perspective on our projects, we see this as socially very rewarding as it has contributed to lowering the tensions and conflicting attitudes between nature protection/environment on the one side and development/growth on the other. That is, the projects have helped create a vision that a good environment and nature protection supports a positive development. (local authority representative in rural (forest) area)

The study also shows that the ways in which LONA has been administered at the CA as well as among local authorities has contributed to increased participation. Various reference groups and dialogues have been created between the public authorities and a range of NGOs and voluntary groups. Representatives from external groups outside of the municipal organization think that the collaboration has worked well in that they have really felt involved and had the opportunity to affect the outcome of the LONA projects.

The most important factor is, however, that voluntary work was counted as co-funding to the projects. Hence, in contrast to many other state initiatives, where municipalities were also asked to provide co-financing for the projects to materialize, local NGOs felt that their contribution was more valued. As a result LONA has given local stakeholders opportunities to realize a range of new ideas and to connect municipal work to nature protection and recreation.

Learning for and about Nature Protection

To what extent and how have the LONA projects contributed to learning processes? This question was analysed in one of our studies that focused on those LONA projects that were classified as relating to schools (Dahlgren et al. 2008). In the following discussion a review of the main results are made as the issue of learning is an important ingredient in mobilizing interest and legitimizing the need for local nature protection. We specifically studied the ways in which LONA projects could contribute to knowledge-building, broad engagement for recreation and nature protection, and to stimulate physical activities in nature areas. Such measures to stimulate knowledge and interest about nature can be more effective when targeting children and youth, as these groups are more receptive than older generations. Also, these issues are part of a global discussion about methods for learning about sustainable development and how younger generations should be involved (SOU 2004, p. 104; Wickenberg et al. 2004).

In total, 282 projects were classified as relating to schools' activities in the LONA database. In our survey of all of these projects, we received 171 individual answers from 157 projects (Dahlgren et al. 2008, p. 10). The respondents testified that the LONA projects had been used primarily to foster knowledge of the local natural and cultural environment (86 per cent) and of a holistic perspective on socioecological relationships (67 per cent). The projects had helped to introduce innovative pedagogical methods for learning about the environment (80 per cent) and to promote public health (57 per cent). These activities are directly connected with one of the objectives of the programme, namely to contribute to the spreading of knowledge about nature conservation as an important part of sustainable development (Rskr 2001/02, p. 173).

The direct effects reported in the survey are that students spend more time outdoors and that their interest in nature conservation and outdoor life has increased. The four case studies also show an increased interest among the students and signs of new learning processes on these issues (Dahlgren et al. 2008). This implies that the projects have had a real impact and have served the educational purpose mentioned above. It further shows that the relationship between nature conservation and outdoor life and public health was manifested in a concrete manner.

According to the survey, the initiative in the school-related projects was distributed among different categories, with the local authorities as the major initiators in most cases (87 per cent), followed by NGOs (61 per cent) and representatives of schools (40 per cent). Partly or completely new networks had been used in either planning or implementation in two-thirds of the cases, indicating that the projects had a direct impact on cooperation between local stakeholders (ibid.). The projects were stimulated by a variety of new learning perspectives and activities. It is difficult to measure transfer of knowledge and learning in single projects or project activities. Nonetheless, learning is a central factor in changing lifestyles and behavioural patterns, as well as in achieving societal change (cf. Milbrath 1990). Knowledge-promoting activities as well as efficient learning processes and local participation are increasingly seen as prerequisites for sustainable development. Building of environmental awareness and promotion of interest in nature conservation should also be directed towards children from an early age, when they are most receptive. This should occur in a playful manner and through practical observation and action (Dahlgren and Szczepanski 1997).

From our case studies, it was found that learning had occurred over time among those project leaders who were responsible for participatory activities aiming to encourage increased engagement from new groups. These project leaders point to the need to adjust the information for targeting immigrants as well as for involving land owners and other local groups on their own premises. The most successful projects in this regard were those with local stakeholders outside of the municipal organization who felt that they had great influence on the design process.

The study shows that it is possible to combine nature protection and outdoor recreation in positive ways. Nature trails, nature schools and other informational activities connected to actions for increased accessibility provide opportunity for more people of different ages – not least children and the elderly – to gain knowledge about nature and the need to protect it, at the same time as this benefits public health. There is great potential to engage private companies and commercial interests in different forms of recreational and public health activities within local nature protection areas, which could be further promoted in the future.

It has already been noted that these positive results have been acknowledged at higher levels by the Government, which has decided to continue with the LONA programme. Learning therefore has also taken place at the central political level. The lessons from the earlier and higher financial support from LIP were that the sharing of experiences did not work well when municipalities had to compete with each other for funding. LONA was therefore designed as a broader programme targeting also those municipalities that lacked resources to formulate advanced proposals. In LONA, municipalities were assisted by the CAs to develop their nature conservation projects in line with local priorities but taking into account the funding criteria. This contributed to the development of local projects that could combine local and regional priorities for recreation and regional development, including tourism, with the protection of biodiversity values. It also implied a much broader engagement of local stakeholders as compared with LIP.

5. DISCUSSION

The LONA initiative is perceived by various authorities, special interest organizations and private stakeholders as a great success. The reasons for this can be attributed to a combination of factors. First, LONA was designed to take the local priorities and resource context into account, thereby combining centrally established criteria for funding with generous appreciation of local possibilities and constraints. Since the CAs were delegated the task of encouraging applications and also selecting the parties to receive funding, their procedures in this process became central to the outcome. In practice the CAs chose to consult widely among their different units, and prioritized those projects that would support long-term local recreation and nature protection work and that were well anchored in the local community. Local authorities, for their part, gave priority to applications that were supported by NGOs, which further enhanced broad participation in the projects. They largely built on already established networks that had been used in previous work in pursuit of sustainable development, such as Local Agenda 21 and LIP projects related to nature protection. The success of LONA therefore also builds upon the existence of previous competence and experience with public/private partnerships in similar local initiatives.

Smaller municipalities, notably those in rural areas, have not benefited as much as large municipalities. The problem of 'rebound effects' – where other environmental work must be abandoned in favour of the latest programmatic funding source – is apparent in such municipalities, and can be noted also in LONA, albeit less so than in the earlier LIP initiative. In small municipalities, expertise and resources are scarce, and new initiatives for nature conservation are less anchored among politicians. Therefore engagement from various stakeholders external to the local authority becomes a necessary condition for activity. When the municipalities have left more responsibility to the external stakeholders for initiation and management of projects, the result was that external stakeholders have felt really involved. However, it has also put pressure on the external stakeholders to mobilize labour and/or funding, which sometimes has been perceived as a problem for long-term engagement.

The possibility of counting voluntary labour as part of the co-funding for the projects has been pivotal to the intense activity of NGOs in the LONA projects. For the local authorities, it meant that they could benefit from NGO support not only by way of spreading the responsibilities for the different stages of the projects' implementation, but also they could save on their own resource inputs. NGOs could also save their own limited financial resources for other purposes and instead mobilize their members to work in the projects to gain appreciation and credibility in their local community.

There are many similarities between the central funding given to LA21 projects in the early 1990s and that allocated under LONA. However, the funding for LA21 was distributed by SEPA at central level, while LONA funding was allocated at the county level. The local knowledge of the situation within each county could therefore be included in the decision-making process. However, both the LA21 funding and LONA were different from the LIP programme in terms of spurring broad mobilization. LIP funding was distributed through a politicized process as a joint endeavour between the Ministry of Environment and each local authority involving negotiations in which the CAs were consulted. In LIP, the municipality had to apply for the funding, while in LA21 and LONA there was room for applications from other local stakeholders as well. Thus the LIP projects became largely dominated by the local authority itself, and few external interests were involved in the projects. In contrast, both the LA21 projects of the early 1990s and the LONA projects are characterized by a high degree of public-private participation. Moreover, the distribution of the funds was highly competitive in the LIP, with only about half of the local authorities receiving grants (although almost all applied), while LONA funding was widely spread to almost all local authorities. In this regard, LONA came out as a de-centralized design, guided by an interest to spread competencies and resources in an equal fashion by the CAs. In contrast, LIP was a highly centralized design aiming at efficiency rather than democratic ideals.

The LONA initiative succeeded in bridging the inherent conflicts between recreation and nature protection in local communities. The combination of measures to increase knowledge and facilitate access to nature areas, together with measures to also restore natural values, was central to the programme. It helped to create legitimacy for the projects among local politicians and the general public. It also spurred new interest in preserving local nature. Hence, protection of nature is not necessarily in conflict with the objective that more people should enjoy and have access to nature. Nature trails, nature schools and other informational activities can give both older and younger generations a renewed interest for nature itself, as well as greater understanding of why it is important to take care and preserve biological diversity and other environmentally related values for the future. The many LONA projects that involved schools and children contributed greatly in this respect. As an added value, nature experiences can also be combined with physical exercise, thus contributing to improved public health. In conclusion, LONA has played an important role in catalysing the municipalities' work towards locally protected areas and has contributed to increased local political interest and engagement in nature protection.

Lessons Learned for Moving beyond the Impasse

This study of the implementation of the Swedish LONA programme shows that there are important lessons to be learned for other European and non-European industrialized countries with similar problems in reaching ambitious targets for biodiversity protection. The observation by the EEB and the EEA that low levels of funding and insufficient public awareness are major problems for biodiversity policy was mentioned in the introduction. Their assessments point out that many politicians have little interest and give low priority to biodiversity concerns in practice, even if the policies are formally in place. The same low level of interest is often ascribed to private landowners. Competing goals for economic development and for the protection of nature are prevalent and constitute a major challenge to moving ahead in taking new nature conservation initiatives at the local level. However, the experience from LONA tells us that, even with rather limited funding, central government can provide political salience to the issue of biodiversity protection merely by offering the technical and state budget support to local action. Both LONA itself and the state grants for land purchasing have been pivotal to changing priorities in a large number of municipalities and helped them to secure urban nature areas and broaden the accessibility to, and information about, those areas. They have also extended this engagement to schools and daycare centres and thus to younger generations who will become voters and politicians in the not-too-distant future. Local support for nature conservation among interest groups, including landowners, has substantially increased as a result. Additionally, institutional competence has risen, which may lead to spin-off effects not only in further local initiatives but also in improved understanding of the necessity to protect biodiversity by other means, including those of the three-pronged approach mentioned in the introduction. The state protection of large-scale nature reserves and national parks, small-scale biotope protection in agriculture and forestry, and the integration of biodiversity concerns into sectoral policies all depend heavily on the political support of constituencies. With more people engaging in nature conservation from the ground up and formulating their own projects, the likelihood that important biodiversity values will be attended to will also increase. Supporting local initiatives with catalyst funding from the state might therefore be a way forward, not only for Sweden but also for other countries.

NOTES

1. Of the 16 Environmental Quality Objectives to be achieved by 2020, ten are relevant for nature conservation, including: a non-toxic environment; flourishing lakes and streams; good-quality groundwater; a balanced marine environment and flourishing coastal areas and archipelagos; thriving wetlands; sustainable forests; a varied agricultural landscape;

a magnificent mountain landscape; a good built environment; and a rich diversity of plant and animal species.
2. The LONA register includes information from all funded projects, see http://swenviro. naturvardsverket.se/dokument/epi/lona/start.php
3. SCB (2010) – it should be noted that the percentage refers to the number of reserves and not the total area.

REFERENCES

Baker, S. and K. Eckerberg (2007), 'Governance for sustainable development in Sweden: the experience of the local investment programme', *Local Environment: The International Journal of Justice and Sustainability*, **12** (4), 325–42.
Dahlgren, K. and K. Eckerberg (2005), *Status för Lokal Agenda 21 – en enkätundersökning 2004*, Umeå, Sweden: Hållbarhetsrådet.
Dahlgren, K. and K. Eckerberg (2006), *Erfarenheter av lokala naturvårdsbidrag (LONA) i processperspektiv*, Report 5605, Stockholm: Swedish Environmental Protection Agency.
Dahlgren, K., K. Eckerberg and Å. Swartling (2008), *Lärande i lokala naturvårdsprojekt (LONA)*, Report 5811, Stockholm: Swedish Environmental Protection Agency.
Dahlgren, K., K. Eckerberg and E. Mineur (2009), *Effekter av delaktighet i lokala naturvårdsprojekt (LONA)*, Report 5923, Stockholm: Swedish Environmental Protection Agency.
Dahlgren, L-O. and A. Szczepanski (1997), *Utomhuspedagogik. Boklig bildning och sinnlig erfarenhet – ett försök till bestämning av utomhuspedagogikens natur,* Skapande Vetande nr 31, Linköping, Sweden: Linköping University.
Eckerberg, K. (ed.) (2005), *Understanding LIP in Context: Central Government, Business and Comparative Perspectives*, Report 5454, Stockholm: Swedish Environmental Protection Agency.
Eckerberg, K. and K. Dahlgren (2007), 'Project or process? Fifteen years' experience with Local Agenda 21 in Sweden', in special issue Desarrollo sostenibilie y Agenda 21 Local, *Economiaz: Revista Vasca de Economia*, **64**, 124–41.
Edström, C. and K. Eckerberg (2002), *Inför Johannesburg: Svenska kommuners arbete med Agenda 21 – en jämförelse över tid*, Nationalkommittén för Agenda 21 och Habitat, Ministry of the Environment, Stockholm: Temo tryck.
Eksvärd, K., L. Hallgren, G. Lönngren, T. Norrby, A. Tivell, L. Westberg and M. Byström (2006), *Gå en mil i mina skor på väg mot samförvaltning*, Department of Rural Development and Agro-ecology working paper no 8, Uppsala, Sweden: Swedish University of Agricultural Sciences and Biodiversity Centre.
European Environment Agency (EEA) (2009), *Progress Towards the European 2010 Biodiversity Target*, EEA report no 4, Copenhagen: EEA.
European Environment Agency (EEA) (2010), *The European Environment: State and Outlook 2010*, Copenhagen: European Environment Agency.
European Environmental Bureau (EEB) (2010), *Biodiversity Protection After 2010: Time to Launch the Ultimate Rescue Plan*, Brussels: European Environment Bureau.
European Union (2001), Communication from the Commission to the Council and the European Parliament – Biodiversity Action Plans in the Areas of

Conservation of Natural Resources, Agriculture, Fisheries, and Development and Economic Co-operation COM/2001/0162, Brussels: European Union.

Forsberg, B. (2005), *I skuggan av lokala investeringsprogrammet – kommunerna som inte beviljades stöd samt synen på staten i LIP:s efterföljd,* Umeå Centre for Evaluation Research report no 16, Umeå, Sweden: Umeå University.

Lafferty, W.M. (ed.) (2001), *Sustainable Communities in Europe,* London: Earthscan.

Milbrath, L. (1990), *Envisioning a Sustainable Society: Learning Our Way Out,* New York: State University of New York Press.

Millennium Ecosystem Assessment (MEA) (2005), *Ecosystems and Human Wellbeing: Synthesis,* Washington DC: Island Press, accessed 8 November 2011 at www.maweb.org/en/index.aspx.

Ministry of the Environment (2001-02), Rskr (2001/02), Government communication 2001/02:173. *En samlad naturvårdspolitik.* Stockholm.

Ministry of the Environment (2008/09), Prop (2008/09), Government bill 2008/09:214, Hållbart skydd av naturområden, Stockholm.

Ministry of Finance (2003/04), Prop (2003/04), Government bill 2003/04:1, *Budgetproposition för 2004,* Stockholm.

Nordenstam, A. and K. Eckerberg (2010), *Kommunalt naturskydd i lokala naturvårdssatsningen (LONA),* Report 6397, Stockholm: Swedish Environmental Protection Agency.

Olofsson, J-O. (2001), *Naturvården alltför lågprioriterad?!* IEH ekologiskt, Nyhetsbrev nr 3.

Statens Offentliga Utredningar (SOU) (2004), SOU 2004: 104, *Att lära för hållbar utveckling,* betänkande av Kommittén för utbildning för hållbar utveckling, Stockholm: Ministry of Education, Committee for Education for Sustainable Development.

Statistiska Centralbyrån (2010), *Skyddad natur 31 december 2009,* Statistiska meddelanden, MI SM 1001, Stockholm: Swedish Environmental Protection Agency and Statistics Sweden.

Swedish Environmental Protection Agency (SEPA) (2005), *Naturvård Sverige runt. Exempel på lokala naturvårdsprojekt 2004–2005,* Stockholm: Swedish Environmental Protection Agency.

SFS (2003), 2003: 598, *Förordning om statliga bidrag till lokala naturvårdsprojekt.* Swedish Statute Book.

Wickenberg, P. et al. (eds) (2004), *Learning to Change Our World?: Swedish Research on Education for Sustainable Development,* Lund, Sweden: Studentlitteratur.

Wramner, P. and O. Nygård (2010), *Från naturskydd till bevarande av biologisk mångfald. Utvecklingen av naturvårdsarbetet i Sverige med särskild inriktning på områdesskyddet,* COMREC Studies in Environment and Development no 2, Stockholm: Södertörn University College.

WSP (2009), *Den lokala naturvårdssatsningens (LONAs) bidrag till uppfyllelse av miljömålen,* Report 5922, Stockholm: Swedish Environmental Protection Agency.

Zachrisson, A. (2008), 'Who should manage protected areas in the Swedish mountain region? A survey approach to co-management', *Journal of Environmental Management,* **87,** 154–64.

5. Early experiences of local climate change adaptation in Norwegian society

Carlo Aall

This chapter is based on findings from a number of joint research projects between the Western Norway Research Institute (WNRI) and ProSus dating back to 1996. This cooperation started with a project on assessing the status of local environmental policy and Local Agenda 21 (LA21) in Norway (Lafferty et al. 1998), followed up by an evaluation of the first government-funded project on promoting the implementation of LA21 in Norway (Aall et al. 1999). Parallel to these two projects, ProSus had developed a combined research effort through a European Union project on LA21, which led to two volumes comparing LA21 in a number of European countries (Lafferty and Eckerberg 1998; Lafferty 2001). In both of these books the contribution on Norway was produced by WNRI. The joint research efforts on LA21 also resulted in the publication of two co-edited scientific books on LA21 in Norwegian (Aall et al. 2002a; Lafferty et al. 2006). This cooperation also included several reports on local environmental policy and LA21. Over time it was expanded to include research on local climate change mitigation policy (Lindseth 2006; Aall et al. 2007) and local climate change adaptation (Aall and Norland 2003; Næss et al. 2006).

Since the start of this cooperation the environmental policy agenda has changed, and the topic that has succeeded LA21 as the hottest local issue is climate policy, in which local climate change adaptation (LCCA) is the latest addition to this process. In this chapter I examine this latest entrant to the local environmental policy agenda and assess the early experiences of LCCA in Norway. In doing so I refer to insights gained from the many previous studies by ProSus and WNRI on local environment policy and LA21. This chapter is based on findings from several studies, many of them still ongoing, ranging from national surveys to qualitative case studies. The main reference point for this chapter is a four-year research project called 'Community Adaptation and Vulnerability in

Norway' (NORADAPT) financed by the Norwegian research programme 'Climate Change and Impacts of Norway' (NORKLIMA) and carried out jointly by the WNRI, CICERO, the Eastern Norway Research Institute, the Norwegian Meteorological Institute and eight municipalities (Nesseby, Hammerfest, Høylandet, Flora, Voss, Bergen, Stavanger and Fredrikstad).

In the following discussion I address six questions: (1) How was the policy issue of climate change adaptation (CCA) put on the agenda at the local level of government?; (2) What has been the policy content of LCCA in Norway?; (3) How is CCA framed in local policy-making?; (4) What types of management systems and tools are used in LCCA?; (5) What has been the role of local government as compared with the national government in CCA?; and (6) What seems to be the main precondition for local government to take up an active role in CCA? These questions are inspired by an evaluation research approach developed on the basis of Sabatier (1986) and applied in many projects at WNRI and ProSus to implementation of LA21 and other dimensions of sustainable development (see Aall et al. 1999 for an early application of this approach).

1.   SETTING THE POLICY AGENDA ON CLIMATE CHANGE ADAPTATION

It seems fair to say that CCA is a late entrant to the climate policy agenda in Norway (Swart et al. 2009). None of the four government white papers on climate policy (1995, 1998, 2001 and 2007) have identified CCA as a relevant task for policy-making in Norway. In fact, the first three government white papers on climate change described the possible effects of climate change in Norway as negligible. The most recent of the four white papers was the first to present any specific policies on CCA: specifically, to support research on the possible effects of climate change in Norway (Miljøverndepartementet 2007, p. 58), and to increase institutional capacity on CCA in Norwegian development aid (Miljøverndepartementet 2007, p. 44). However, this situation recently changed. In 2008 a Public Committee on Climate Change Adaptation was established with a mandate to prepare a government green paper, which was duly presented in the autumn of 2010 (NOU 2010). In addition to assessing Norway's vulnerabilities with regard to climate change, this report also recommended a number of policy measures. These include integrating CCA in all aspects of public planning, increasing the knowledge base for CCA, and raising the capacity and competence of the public administration to address what the government green paper described as an infrastructure 'adaptation deficit' (NOU 2010). This term refers to the inadequacy of current efforts to maintain the country's physical infrastructure.

In Norway, the emergence of CCA on both the local and national agenda has to a large extent been *research* driven (Dannevig et al. 2011). An initial effort was begun in 1997 with a programme called RegClim, which made it possible a decade later to launch a free, web-based service to downscale climate change scenarios.[1] Parallel to this natural-science-based research effort, the Research Council of Norway funded a minor programme on assessing the potential consequences of climate change for Norwegian society, which was undertaken by CICERO, ProSus and WNRI (Aall and Norland 2003; Næss et al. 2006). This then paved the way for a major 10-year research programme, NORKLIMA (Climate change and impacts in Norway 2004–13). It includes local adaptation and vulnerability studies with social science perspectives and an emphasis on collaboration with communities and analysis of barriers to adaptation. In Norway, there is thus a strong research focus that has the potential to create direct links between climate researchers and local actors.

The main catalyst for bringing CCA onto the *national* policy agenda has been the civil protection bureaucracy, in particular the Directorate for Civil Protection and Emergency Planning (DSB) (Groven et al. 2012). DSB's interest has in part been related to defining a new role for the agency in the post-Cold War era by focusing on civil rather than military protection. The focus on adaptation was also the result of work by idealists within DSB who had concerns about severe natural hazards in the 1990s (Husabø 2008). The New Year's Day storm (in Norwegian, *Nyttårsorkanen*) in 1992 and the Vetleofsen flood in 1995 are commonly referred to as milestones in the awareness within the civil protection sector of extreme weather vulnerability. By 2003 directorate officials were already drawing attention to the importance of adaptation (Justis- og politidepartementet 2004), in contrast to the rather complacent attitude expressed in the Norwegian Government's white papers on climate policy that climate change consequences would be insignificant or could be managed in virtue of Norway's alleged high adaptive capacity. However, cooperation with officials in the Ministry of Environment sympathetic to the idea of putting CCA on the policy agenda eventually secured government backing for a CCA strategy. In May 2006 the Ministry of Environment formally established a cross-ministerial working group on CCA. Moreover, a secretariat placed within the DSB was given the mandate to implement the Norwegian Climate Change Adaptation Programme. In May 2008 the Government issued a brief statement on CCA[2] and proceeded to appoint a commission of experts to review the aforementioned Public Committee on Climate Change Adaptation. Later in 2008 a web portal was launched[3] presenting examples of CCA in Norway along with advice on how to develop CCA strategies and means.

In 2008, before any national CCA strategy was starting to evolve, a large government-funded project called Cities of the Future was set up involving the 13 largest cities in Norway to develop combined climate change mitigation (CCM) and CCA strategies. Prior to this initiative several research projects on CCA were initiated focusing explicitly at the local level of government. The first of these projects was initiated in 2006 by the small coastal city of Flora in cooperation with WNRI.[4] This was the very first example of a Norwegian public body explicitly putting CCA on their policy agenda. The following year, in the spring of 2007, the Association of Local and Regional Authorities (KS) initiated a major project to assess the possible effects climate change would have on the duties of local authorities whose responsibility was to deal with natural hazards; a project that was assigned to WNRI in cooperation with the Eastern Norway Research Institute; the University of Stavanger; the Norwegian Geotechnical Institute; and seven municipalities (Groven et al. 2008). Soon to follow in 2007 and in 2009 were a number of larger projects funded by the Norwegian research council and their research programme NORKLIMA. In the winter of 2008 the Congress of KS adopted a two-page declaration on climate policy, which included the following statements: 'There seems to be general agreement that there is a need to both mitigate and adapt to climate change. . . . Local authorities should develop CCA strategies and plans' (our translation).[5] In 2009 DSB presented figures from their annual survey on the state of civil defence at the local level of government in which 14 per cent of the municipalities stated that they had done a formal risk assessment on the issue of climate change at least once during the years 2004–8 (DSB 2009). In 2010 KS produced a handbook on CCA[6] that presented examples of CCA means and strategies from ten municipalities.[7] That year KS also initiated their second major project on CCA, this time to analyse the consequences of climate change on physical infrastructure. The project was completed in February 2011, presenting recommendations very much in line with that of the government green paper on CCA mentioned above, but moving one step further on the 'adaptation deficit' by suggesting a moratorium on the construction of new public buildings and roads until the maintenance backlog had been eradicated (Aall 2011). The question remains open, however, as to whether the government white paper will be followed up by a formal strategy (for example, in the form of a corresponding government white paper) and what role will be assigned local government in such a strategy if it does materialize.

2. POLICY CONTENT: WHAT IS *CLIMATE CHANGE ADAPTATION*?

How is climate change adaptation understood and conceptualized by local authorities? No studies have been conducted that can fully answer this question. However, participating in different projects involving the municipalities – especially the NORADAPT project – reading local policy documents on CCA, and having direct communication with representatives of municipalities that have placed CCA on their policy agenda does allow for two general reflections on this question.

The first reflection is that, as in earlier experiences with local environmental policy-making in Norway, there can be a difference between a *locally* and a *globally* oriented policy approach. In analysing the outcome of a national government-initiated reform called 'Environment in the Municipalities' (abbreviated MIK in Norwegian) initiated in 1991, Jon Naustdalslid (1994, p. 33) noted a difference between where environmental problems are generated (concentrated or diffuse) and where their effects are manifest (concentrated or diffuse). By means of this typology Naustdalslid identifies four categories of environmental problems: the combination 'concentrated/concentrated' constitutes what he denotes as genuinely *local* environmental problems, while the combination 'diffuse/ diffuse' constitutes genuinely *global* environmental problems. On the basis of this typology he formulated a hypothesis suggesting that the local level will primarily relate to local problems (for example pollution of a local watercourse from municipal sewage). According to Naustdalslid, the assessment of the MIK reform has corroborated this hypothesis. He observes that 'local management bodies in the first place hardly can function as activators in the work with more superior, global environment problems . . . the municipalities give priority to issues which lead to visible local gains' (Naustdalslid 1994, pp. 22–3). And he continues, 'if one wants the municipalities to give priority to global environmental issues, there is a need for national co-ordination of local environmental policy'. He claims that '[such] an environmental-political U-turn presupposes changes in people's values and priorities' (Naustdalslid, p. 25). In-depth case studies of front-runner municipalities' environmental policies indicate that municipalities *can* give priority to what Naustdalslid calls genuinely global environmental problems if there is local will to move from merely acting as a structure for implementing central government environmental policy into that of being a policy actor by defining policy goals and means independently of national environmental policies (Aall 2000).

The following is a typology of CCA inspired by Naustdalslid's analysis. Instead of using the concentrated/diffuse dichotomy, however, I have used the local/global distinction. For the case of *problem-generation* local/ global refers to the geographical scale at which climate change is assessed, illustrated by the maps generated from models for downscaling, that is localizing, climate change scenarios. To establish the manifestation of *effects*, the term local means within, and global means outside of, the municipality. Thus we can distinguish between four main categories of problems which CCA policies should address:

- local/local: direct local CCA problems, defined as adaptation to the local effects of local climate change;
- local/global: indirect local CCA problems, defined as adapting to the local effects of climate change taking place outside of the border of the municipality;
- global/local: external (non-indigenous or non-native) local CCA problems defined as actors located outside of the municipality in question that have to adapt to problems originating from the municipality in question; for example an increase in local precipitation, which also creates river flooding problems for municipalities situated along the river and downstream from the municipality in question;
- global/global: global problems manifested as sum effects on a global scale, an example of which would be a weakening of global food security or a general increase in the global number of climate refugees.

To date local/local seems to be the dominant approach in local CCA policy-making processes. Furthermore, all existing guidance provided by the national government falls within this approach, and so does most of the Norwegian research on CCA. The basic concept is to provide information on how changes in the local climate conditions may affect localities (for example, rivers, biodiversity in defined localities, and so on) or local interests (for example municipalities), and how to adapt to such eventual effects. However, NORADAPT is one of the few ongoing Norwegian research projects that specifically focus on the local/global relationship. One of the municipalities participating in NORADAPT, the city of Fredrikstad, commissioned a report in 2009 from WNRI on this specific approach (Sælensminde et al. 2010). In this report a number of CCA issues were identified as relevant for the Norwegian municipalities within a local/ global context. The basic idea for identifying these issues is to analyse all the possible streams linking a community with the rest of the world. Three main categories or streams were identified: people and companies; economic resources; and non-economic resources. Each of these streams may

Table 5.1   A typology for climate change adaptation policy approaches

		Problem generation	
		Local	Global
Manifestation of effects	Local	(1) Direct local effects of climate change	(2) Indirect local effects of climate change
	Global	(3) Proliferation problems	(4) Problems of the commons

occur in two directions: external (non-indigenous) and internal (indigenous or native). Two of the most well-known issues embedded in this approach are the increased value of local farmed land as a consequence of reduced global food security and the possibility of increased immigration due to an increase in the global numbers of climate refugees.

The second reflection on the content of CCA relates to the idea of applying what we might denote as a two-dimensional approach to analysing climate change vulnerabilities. The two dimensions are *climate change* and *societal change*. The Intergovernmental Panel on Climate Change (IPCC) has in its Fourth Assessment Report (AR4) presented the following conclusion regarding advances in knowledge and future research needs (Parry et al. 2007, p. 77): '[Since the IPCC Third Assessment] there has been little advance on impacts under different assumptions about how the world will evolve in the future – societies, governance, technology and economic development.' Even though the IPCC has developed very sophisticated methods for analysing changes in societies, governance, technology and economic development – the SRES scenarios (named after the Special Report on Emission Scenarios prepared for the Third Assessment Report in 2001) – these methods are only used to analyse possible future development in GHG emissions; they do not assess how vulnerabilities to climate-induced incidents and processes may develop (Table 5.1). Even so, societal change has long been recognized, at least in the academic discourse, as having fundamental importance in determining climate change vulnerability (see for instance Tol 1998). Thus several attempts have been made to produce guidance notes on how to apply the use of societal scenarios to analyse the relationship between changes in society and the shaping of vulnerabilities towards climate change as seen, for example, in the UK (UKCIP 2001) and in Finland (Kaivo-Oja et al. 2004). But still climate change vulnerabilities are generally analysed on the basis of a one-dimensional approach – even in the case of the UK, which was a pioneering country in promoting this approach towards local authorities.

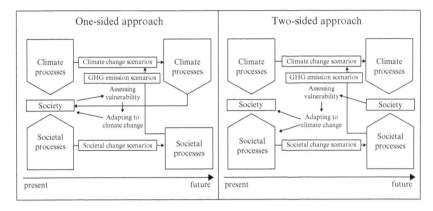

*Figure 5.1   Two approaches to analysing climate change vulnerabilities
and developing adaptation policies*

The idea of adding a second dimension by using societal scenarios
was first presented in Norway in 2008 in a project commissioned by KS
(Groven et al. 2008). The model developed in that project was based on
three distinctions: (1) that climate change vulnerability is a sum effect of
climatic change (changes in pressures from climate) and societal change
(changes in exposure to pressure from climate); (2) that expectations on
future climate-change-related risks should be applied to expectations on
what society might be in the future, not on what society is today (which
tends to be the case in many climate change vulnerability assessments)
(Heiberg et al. 2009); and (3) that by including societal change as a separate
dimension when assessing climate change vulnerabilities, a better understanding of the need to apply a combination of effect-oriented adaptation
measures (reducing natural vulnerabilities) and cause-oriented adaptation
measures (reducing societal vulnerabilities) is facilitated (see Figure 5.1).
The model incorporates three modes of climate change vulnerabilities
(Groven et al. 2008):

- *natural* vulnerability: climate change and the expected effects on
  changes in nature (for example increased precipitation and increased
  risks of flooding);
- *socioeconomic* vulnerability: societal change and the expected
  effects on changes in exposure to pressure from the climate (for
  example changes in land-use patterns increasing building of new
  residential houses close to the rivers thus increasing exposure to
  flooding);

- *institutional* vulnerability: societal change and the expected effects on changes in the institutional capacity to adapt to climate change (for example downsizing of the administrative capacity for land-use planning in local authorities).

In order to assess *natural vulnerability*, standard methods for down-scaling climate change models were used (see for instance, www.senorge. no and click on the climate button for an example of a free-of-charge, Internet information resource). In order to assess *societal vulnerability*, a scenario about societal change was developed (Selstad 2010). This model also allowed for downscaling (localizing), although this is very different from the quantitative downscaling used in climate change scenarios. The downscaling of the societal change scenario was a combination of quali-tative data on demographic development with more qualitative assess-ments of how commercial structure, physical infrastructure, mobility and perception may develop (Selstad 2010).

Inspired by Dessai and Hulme (2003), we applied a combined top–down and bottom–up approach in assessing both the natural and societal vulnerabilities to climate change. In the case of natural vulnerability, an important part of the bottom–up process was requests from the munici-palities for downscaling specific climate parameters believed to be of special relevance for each municipality in question. In the case of societal vulnerability, local stakeholders were invited to comment on a first draft of the local scenario. In addition, local policy documents were used as input for making the scenarios. However, the most important part of the bottom–up process was the merging of the natural and societal perspec-tives into an assessment of total climate change vulnerability. This was done more or less entirely by the local actors.

3.   POLICY FRAMING: WHERE SHOULD CLIMATE CHANGE ADAPTATION *BELONG?*

In the case of any specific policy issue we can raise the question of whether CCA should be integrated into all policy areas or should be developed into a policy area in and of itself. This is far from being settled and is one of the important questions to be addressed in the ongoing follow-up of the Norwegian green paper on CCA mentioned above. So far, we can see signs of both possibilities mentioned above.

At the *national* level the establishment of the cross-ministerial working group on CCA has had as one of its main tasks the promotion and coor-dination of the development of CCA within all ministries. At the *local* and *regional* level of government we see signs of several alternatives for designating CCA to a specific sector or section of local government.

Civil defence is the government department that so far has made the most of putting CCA on its policy agenda and implementing CCA in its policy processes and strategies. This was seen, for example, in 2008 when the Directorate for Civil Protection and Emergency Planning (DSB) included questions on CCA in their annual survey, which evaluates how municipalities are working with civil defence (DSB 2007). Second, in 2009, the civil defence department at the County Governor, a Norwegian government agency, was instructed to start checking whether or not local land-use plans included risk assessments on climate change and natural hazards (Husabø 2010).

Norway's planning and building act has recently been revised and new regulations addressing CCA are included. As of 2010 it was mandatory for Norwegian municipalities to make a risk assessment as part of land-use planning and this assessment has to include the issue of climate change. Furthermore, municipalities are now allowed to define caution zones in their land-use plans, in which they can impose restrictions on land use out of concern for climate-change-induced risks.

CCA is often presented as the policy twin to CCM. The latter has eventually established itself as an accepted policy area to be addressed by most local authorities. In 2007 the Government introduced earmarked funding (50,000 NOK) for each municipality to produce a local climate and energy plan, which was followed up by issuing two handbooks on making such plans.[8] In 2009 the Ministry of Environment set a deadline of 1 June 2010 for all Norwegian municipalities to make a climate and energy plan. At that time an assessment made by the Norwegian Agency on Energy Saving (ENOVA) showed that 41 per cent of Norwegian municipalities had adopted such a plan, and that 57 per cent were still working on it, while 2 per cent had not started implementation. However, CCA has not been part of these initiatives and local processes. The latest national guidelines on local climate policy planning issued in the autumn of 2009 did not mention CCA.[9] Additionally, the environmental department at the County Governor, which has a defined role in advising municipalities on matters of CCM, has so far been silent on the matters of CCA – whereas the civil defence department has been highly active (Husabø 2010).

My own intuition is that, more or less independently of how CCA is eventually approached by national government, at the local level it will be framed in different ways according to local conditions. Examples of such conditions may be: the dominant concern (for example, extreme weather events or drought problems in agriculture), the extent to which (and where in the municipal organization) there is sufficient institutional capacity (knowledge, interest and available work hours) to allow the uptake of new tasks (for example the planning department, civil defence department, environment department or climate department). To date, front-runner municipalities on CCA can be divided into two main categories as to how CCA has been framed:

- a new element in local *civil defence*: those municipalities recently hit by extreme weather events (for example Bergen and the case of a landslide – the Hatlestad terrace slide incident in 2005 that resulted in four casualties (Groven 2012));
- as an extension of existing *CCM policy*: those municipalities that have not been hit recently by extreme weather events, but have a history of being front-runner municipalities on CCM, such as Stavanger and Fredrikstad (Aall et al. 2007).

Common to both of these categories is that they also are among the few remaining municipalities that still, after the termination of the arrangement with earmarked funding for applying a local environmental officer in 1997, have a full-time environmental officer in place. They also often have in common that they were among the most active Norwegian municipalities working with LA21.

4. MANAGEMENT SYSTEMS AND TOOLS: SOME LIKE IT HOT AND SOME LIKE IT COLD

The history of working with local environmental policy and LA21 has entailed a great deal of movement in developing new environmental planning and management methods and tools such as handbooks (Miljøverndepartementet and KS 1988; Aall et al. 1996); a national criteria for LA21 (Miljøverndepartementet and KS 1999); and a national system of local sustainability indicators (Aall et al. 2002b).[10] Most of this activity has been focused on developing these systems and tools while less effort has been put into promoting the actual use of such systems and tools – and even less on assessing these systems' and tools' effectiveness (Høyer and Aall 2002). It is perhaps not surprising that studies have indicated only a limited use of such systems and tools. In 2000 only 8 per cent of Norwegian municipalities reported that they had adopted formal environmental management systems or environmental indicators (Bjørnæs and Lafferty 2000). Still, both the municipalities themselves, and the Ministry of Environment and KS, often point to the need to develop new and more sophisticated environmental planning and management systems and tools.

Terje Kleven has discussed the paradox of the strong support for using these kinds of rational public management steering instruments and what he describes as overwhelming scientific evidence that such instruments do not actually work (Kleven 1990). To explain this paradox Kleven (1993) differentiates between a 'Sunday' and an 'everyday' ideology. When applying a Sunday ideology, Kleven states, organizations act like their official policy goals represent real steering signals and they produce data and indicators that seemingly support goal achievements. However, below the surface of the Sunday ideology is the real-life ideology – the everyday ideology in which other and far less rational rules govern the outcome of the decision-making process.

Research on sustainability indicators has tried to bridge the gap between these two worlds of ideology by introducing the concepts of 'hot', 'warm' and 'cold' indicators (MacGillivray and Zadek 1995). The notion of cold refers to high scientific quality information (for example an indicator system) that might be difficult for the layperson to understand and is used as a basis for decision-making, whereas the notion of hot refers to information that is easily understood and is easy to relate to decision-making, but is not necessarily of high scientific quality. Examples of cold indicators are expert systems such as the pressure-state-response model developed by the OECD (1994), whereas the many local sustainability indicator systems developed through broad participatory processes under the heading of LA21 are an example of hot indicators (Høyer and Aall 2002). The challenge according to MacGillivray and Zadek (1995) is to develop warm information systems that represent an optimal balance between hot and cold.

The requests from local government representatives for advanced management systems and tools are just as important for the case of CCA as for local environment policy in general (Heiberg et al. 2009). The most prominent example, in the context of CCA, are the different systems developed for the purpose of downscaling global climate change scenarios. A number of European countries have established some sort of downscaling service,[11] with many of them offering free-of-charge web-based services, and there seems to be a common opinion in both the research and policy-making communities that the way to proceed on providing such services is to develop more sophisticated models allowing for more specified downscaling with higher geographical resolution (Aall et al. 2009). This approach seems to be driven by a belief that uncertainty is a major hindrance in CCA and that this uncertainty is linked with an absence of accurate models for downscaling global climate change scenarios. However, examples from the NORADAPT project suggest that this might not always be the case and that this approach may lead to producing too cold information. Still, we find examples of representatives of local government that tend to have the beliefs outlined above – typically those working within infrastructure departments handling issues such as water management. From people within planning departments working with land-use planning and economic development, however, we often get a different opinion such that the uncertainties relating to CCA are not greater than uncertainties in other policy areas. In their view trying to allow for more accurate downscaling of global climate scenarios (thus producing more 'cold' indicators) is not necessarily the best way to proceed.

Furthermore, there appears to be no one-to-one relationship between the success rate in developing CCA strategies and the level of sophistication in services of downscaling global climate change scenarios. We may find examples where municipalities (for example Flora) and counties (for example Sogn og Fjordane) have developed quite specific CCA strategies and measures as a response to very general descriptions about how climate change may develop within their geographical area (Groven et al. 2007; Sogn og Fjordane fylkeskommune 2009). Just as in developing local sustainable indicators, it seems important to develop warm – not too cold and not too hot – ways of communicating how climate change may affect local communities.

5. THE ROLE OF LOCAL AUTHORITIES: FRONT-RUNNERS FOR NATIONAL GOVERNMENT ACTION?

The rationale for the Ministry of Environment putting through the MIK reform was to strengthen the ability of local authorities to implement national environmental policies (Jansen 1991; Naustdalslid and Hovik 1994). Local authorities were thus first of all looked upon as policy *structures* for implementing national environmental policies. However, as the local institutional capacity for environmental policy increased, some of the municipalities started to act independently of national policy signals and took on policy tasks outside existing national environmental policies, thus assuming an additional role as policy *actors* (Aall 2000).

An important role in widening the policy agenda from traditional local environmental policy to sustainable development and LA21 has been played by front-runner municipalities, which have served as 'guinea pigs' for developing new policy areas, for example in the area of sustainable consumption (Aall 2001). By means of the project Sustainable Local

Communities, which took place from 1995 to 1999, seven municipalities were given earmarked funding to assist the national government in raising sustainable consumption onto the international policy agenda within the work of the United Nations Commission on Sustainable Development (CSD). The idea was to use local action in Norwegian test municipalities to demonstrate how the work on sustainable consumption could be done (Aall et al. 1999). However, one of the main findings from the evaluation of this project was that national government itself was very reluctant to accommodate suggestions from the municipalities about changes to national policies that might overcome existing hindrances to sustainable consumption (such as increasing taxes on energy use and promoting public transportation) (Aall 2001).

Based on experiences from previous work with local environmental policy and LA21, we may identify at least three possible roles for local government in CCA:

- assuming the role of a guinea pig for developing more concrete national approaches to, and strategies for, CCA;
- creating a policy structure for implementing national CCA policies;
- becoming a policy actor to develop local approaches and strategies more or less independent of prevailing national policies.

A fourth alternative is also possible, namely a situation in which islands of front-runner municipalities are surrounded by a sea of business-as-usual practitioners, and the front-runners serve to distract attention from a more or less passive national policy. This is a situation so nicely described by Bulkeley (2000) with respect to the mitigation dimension of climate policy.

6. THE ACHILLES' HEEL OF LOCAL CLIMATE CHANGE ADAPTATION: LACK OF CONTINUITY AND SUPPORT

Experiences from local CCA in Norway illustrate that there are a number of important impasses to overcome in order to achieve effective local adaptation to climate change. In a 2007 survey of all Norwegian municipalities, 90 per cent of the respondents stated that they would like to have clearer guidelines from the national level on CCA (Amundsen et al. 2010). However, a more recent study indicates that in some cases relevant government information and guidance actually do exist, but the local authorities do not know about them. A 2010 study done by the Office of

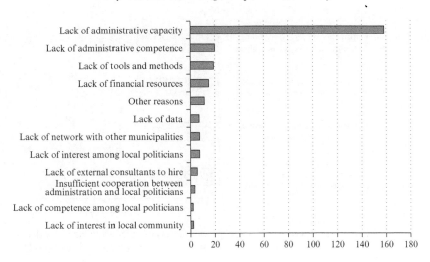

Source: Aall et al. (2009).

Figure 5.2   *Number of informants stating what they feel is among the three most important hindrances when working with local environmental policy*

the Auditor General of Norway showed that a majority (56 out of 106) of the municipalities for which maps on geohazards had been produced did not know of these maps – even if they had been informed by official emails, and the maps were available free of charge on the national website for geohazard assessments since 2007[12] (Riksrevisjonen 2010). So perhaps it is a lack of administrative capacity at the local level to make use of existing government information and guidance that is the real problem. Two different studies support this assumption. The first is an assessment of the government-funded programme 'Viable Communities'.[13] This is a follow-up to the MIK reform and the national support for LA21 – more or less working along the same lines by means of funding local government network activities in support of local knowledge-building related to sustainable development. A survey on what the local actors involved in these activities found were the main hindrances to promoting sustainable development showed that a lack of administrative capacity was the leading hindrance, more so than other defined categories of hindrances (see Figure 5.2).

Furthermore, a national survey done by DSB in 2007 was analysed in a project that WNRI carried out for the Ministry of Environment in 2009. In this survey 14 questions on different aspects of CCA were divided into four

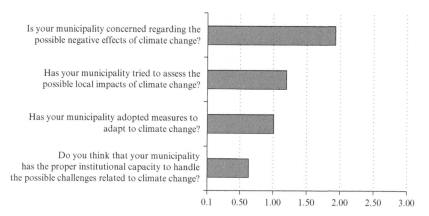

Note: 14 questions grouped into four groups with the answers made into indexes with 0 = not at all; 1 = to very little extent; 2 = to some extent; 3 = to a large extent. Response rate of 72 per cent.

Source: Aall et al. (2009).

Figure 5.3   Index of how DSB survey respondents evaluate their work on climate change adaptation

sub-groups of questions (the four questions stated in Figure 5.3) and the answers were made into indexes with the following values: 0 = not at all; 1 = to very little extent; 2 = to some extent; 3 = to a large extent. The response rate was 72 per cent out of all Norwegian municipalities. Figure 5.3 shows a somewhat disturbing mismatch between the extent to which the informants consider climate change to be a serious threat and how they assess whether their administrative capacity is adequate to handle the threat.

The experience from the NORADAPT project further supports the mismatched responses illustrated in Figures 5.3 and 5.4. During the period from 2007 to 2010 many municipalities lost their environmental officers, consequently the work on CCA very quickly dropped down to zero (a situation which has proven to be the case for the CCA front-runner municipality of Flora). In contrast, the most successful municipalities (in the sense that they have managed to produce a CCA strategy document during the NORADAPT project period) were those that were able to maintain the position of an environmental officer over a long period of time with the same individual holding the position (see for example the municipalities of Voss, Stavanger and Fredrikstad).

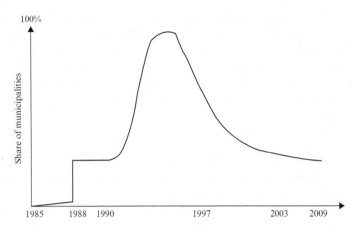

Source: Aall (2008).

Figure 5.4 *Number of Norwegian municipalities with at least one position as a full-time environmental officer*

7. THE PROSPECTS FOR LOCAL CLIMATE CHANGE ADAPTATION

Christensen (1996) adopts the term 'formative period' from Rothstein (1992) in order to describe the emergence of Nordic environmental political institutions during the late 1960s and early 1970s. The concept of formative relates to the potential of inducing radical changes in existing political institutions and thus creating something totally new. During this period existing political institutions become dysfunctional in the handling of environmental crises and emergencies, but at a crucial moment in the process participants actually manage to change the political agenda. However, one of Christensen's main conclusions is that the Nordic countries experienced a formative period, but the formative moment did not materialize. Thus, despite numerous initiatives in the late 1960s and early 1970s – several of them quite radical – the institutionalization of environmental politics and policy in the Nordic countries largely followed existing norms for public management.

This conclusion has also been applied to the reform period in Norway that took place at the local level of government during the late 1980s and 1990s (Aall 2000). It can probably be applied to the other Nordic countries as well. In the case of Norway, local government proved to be dysfunctional during the late 1980s with regard to handling environmental crises and emergencies such as increasing pollution problems relating to waste and sewage treatment, the algal bloom in the North Sea and radioactive pollution in parts of Norway due to the Chernobyl disaster. For the case of local environmental policy it is not only a question of the formative moment never having materialized; it is also a question of de-institutionalization after an initial period of institutionalization (see Figure 5.4).

If it is true that the MIK reform has not really led to a lasting institutionalization of the work with environmental policy and sustainable development at the local government level, one is then left with the question: 'What is then the prospect of introducing a new policy area, such as CCA, on the local environment policy agenda?'

Given that the dominant approach to CCA will continue to be limited to the direct local effects of climate change (category 1, local/local, presented in Table 5.1) I am relatively optimistic with respect to the possibility of this area being placed on the local agenda, at least for those municipalities still having a minimum of administrative capacity in environmental policy. However, I still fear the possibility of negative consequences. My fear is that this may provoke a political backlash to climate change mitigation initiatives and perhaps to environmental policy more generally. The reason for this is the mismatch between the descriptions provided by the IPCC of the potentially catastrophic consequences on society if we do not dramatically reduce GHG emissions, and what seems to come out of the local climate change vulnerability assessments done within the local/local approach, as illustrated in Table 5.1.

The well-known (but controversial) climatologist Dr James E. Hanson was awarded the Sophie Prize in 2010. The prize, established in 1998 by the Norwegian international bestselling author Jostein Gaarder, recognizes the international contributions of individuals or organizations to the environment and sustainable development. In his speech at the award ceremony Hanson gave the following description of the current challenge of climate change:

> Our planet today is close to climate tipping points. Ice is melting in the Arctic, on Greenland and Antarctica, and on mountain glaciers worldwide. Many species are stressed by environmental destruction and climate change. Continuing fossil fuel emissions, if unabated, will cause sea level rise and species extinction accelerating out of humanity's control. Increasing atmospheric water vapour is already magnifying climate extremes, increasing overall precipitation, causing greater floods and stronger storms.[14]

In contrast to this description of the very challenging situation facing society are the perspectives presented in a recent major study summing up existing research on climate change vulnerabilities for the case of Norway done for the Norwegian Public Committee on Climate Change. One of their main conclusions was as follows: '. . . if society manages to limit the global temperature increase to a maximum of 2 degrees, the chances are good that the socio-economic and social consequences of climate change might be moderate [in Norway]' (Aaheim et al. 2009, p. 8, my translation). A central reference point for this conclusion is a previous study commissioned by the Nordic Council and carried out by CICERO and the consultancy firm COWI. One of their main conclusions was that 'due to the many uncertainties linked with assessing climate change vulnerability it is hard to say if a global temperature increase of 2 degrees centigrade will, all in all, have negative or positive effect on Nordic society' (CICERO 2008, p. 12, my translation).

Professor Marianne Ryghaug (2010) at the Norwegian Technical University in Trondheim has noted another potential area where perceptions could militate against action. Based on focus group interviews of ordinary people and individual interviews with climate scientists, elected representatives and representatives of public government and private business, she concludes that the increasing mismatch between the climate change challenges outlined by the scientists and the lack of serious policy action to address these problems may lead to increased climate scepticism. According to Ryghaug, the public seems to believe that they have understood the message from the climate scientists, but they feel that climate change cannot be that dangerous because they don't see anyone taking serious measures to deal with the problem.

Hence, it seems important to develop additional means to assess possible consequences of climate change and communicate this in a more concrete manner. One option could be to include assessments of the local consequences of climate change taking place in other countries, as was done for the case of Fredrikstad in the NORADAPT project (Sælendsminde et al. 2010). A second option could be to include assessments of the local consequences of climate change mitigation policies. This is an option that has come up in local discussions in the Interreg project Climate Change – Adapting to the Impacts, by Communities in Northern Peripheral Regions (Clim-ATIC).[15] Aall and Høyer (2005) have termed these two perspectives on climate change vulnerabilities as 'double climate vulnerability'.

These two options could be considered as a sort of missing link in local climate change vulnerability assessments (see Figure 5.5). Including this missing link would imply developing and improving methodological approaches that can more convincingly illustrate the links among the local environment, local community and the global environmental effects of climate vulnerability. If this is not done, I fear that pushing for more

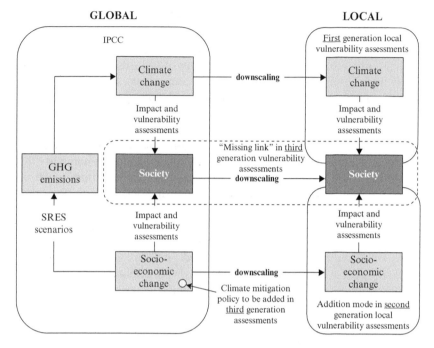

Figure 5.5   Suggested merging of existing climate vulnerability assessment approaches (first and second generation) into a new approach (third generation)

local as well as sector-specific climate change vulnerability assessments (resulting for example from a more ambitious national policy on climate change adaptation) may lead to a serious political backlash against climate policy.

NOTES

1. See: http://www.senorge.no/mappage.aspx, 'Climate' (in English).
2. See: http://www.regjeringen.no/upload/MD/Vedlegg/Klima/Klimatilpasning/ Klimatil pasning_redegjorelse150508.pdf (in Norwegian).
3. See English version: http://www.regjeringen.no/en/dep/md/kampanjer/engelsk-forside-for-klimatilpasning/on-climate-change-adaptation-in-norway.html?id=540010
4. See: http://www.regjeringen.no/en/dep/md/kampanjer/engelsk-forside-for-klimatilpas ning/library/cases/Flora-Municipality-adapting-to-climate-change.html?id=542726 (in English).
5. See: http://www.ks.no/PageFiles/949/VedtakKlima.pdf (in Norwegian).
6. See: http://www.ks.no/PageFiles/11077/KS_klimatilpasningshefte_2010_litenfil.pdf (in Norwegian).

7. The municipalities are: Fredrikstad, Sogndal, Hammerfest, Ski, Stavanger, Flora, Oslo, Bergen and the counties of Sogn og Fjordane and Buskerud.
8. See: http://naring.enova.no/sitepageview.aspx?sitePageID=1286 and http://naring.eno va.no/ sitepageview.aspx?sitePageID=1287
9. See: http://www.regjeringen.no/nb/dep/md/dok/lover_regler/retningslinjer/2009/planre tningslinje-klima-energi.html?id=575764
10. Later to be developed to a full-scale and official web-based system: http://livskraftig. bedrekommune.no/more/reports/
11. See for example http://www.senorge.no/mappage.aspx, 'Climate' (in English) for the case of Norway.
12. See: www.skrednett.no
13. In Norwegian: Livskraftige kommuner: www.livskraftigekommuner.no
14. See: http://www.sofieprisen.no/Articles/514.html
15. See: www.clim-ATIC.org

REFERENCES

Aaheim, A., H. Dannevig, T. Ericsson, B. van Oort, L. Innbjør, T. Rauken, H. Vennemo, H. Johansen, M. Tofteng, C. Aall, C. Groven and E. Heiberg (2009), *Konsekvenser av klimaendringer, tilpasning og sårbarhet i Norge, Rapport til Klimatilpasningutvalget*, Rapport 2009:4, Oslo: CICERO.

Aall, C. (2000), 'When is change change? From nature conservation to sustainable development in Norwegian municipalities', PhD thesis, University of Aalborg, Aalborg, Denmark.

Aall, C. (2001), 'Local Agenda 21 as means of interpreting and introducing the new policy issue of sustainable production and consumption – experiences from seven Norwegian municipalities', in W. Lafferty (ed.), *Sustainable Communities in Europe*, London: Earthscan Publishers, pp. 82–104.

Aall, C. (ed.), (2008), *Kartlegging og analyse av kommunenes miljø og plan-leggingskompetanse. Presentasjon av resultater fra en analyse utført på oppdrag fra Miljøverndepartementet*, VF-notat 2008:12, Sogndal, Norway: Vestlandsforsking.

Aall, C. (ed.) (2011), *Klimaendringenes konsekvenser for kommunal og fylkeskom-munal infrastruktur*, Sluttrapport, VF-Rapport 2011:3, Sogndal, Norway: Vestlandsforsking.

Aall, C. and K. Høyer (2005), 'Tourism and climate change adaptation – the Norwegian case', in C.M. Hall and J. Higham (eds) *Tourism, Recreation and Climate Change*, London: Channelview Press, pp. 209–23.

Aall, C. and I. Norland (2003), *Indikatorer for vurdering av lokal klimasårbarhet*, Rapport 2003:15, Sogndal/Oslo, Norway: Vestlandsforsking/ProSus.

Aall, C., E. Erstad and S. Vestby (1996), *Håndbok i kommunal miljørevisjon*, Oslo: Kommuneforlaget.

Aall, C., W. Lafferty and T. Bjørnæs (1999), *Kartlegging av hindringer i pros-jekt Bærekraftige lokalsamfunn: hovedrapport*, Rapport 1999:01, Oslo: Statens forurensingstilsyn- TA 1607.

Aall, C., K. Høyer and W. Lafferty (eds) (2002a), *Fra miljøvern til bærekraftig utvikling i kommunene. Erfaringer med Lokal Agenda 21*, Oslo: Gyldendal akademisk.

Aall, C., K. Breisnes, J. Hille and K. Høyer (2002b), *Bærekraftige kommuner i praksis. Omtale av et styringssystem for integrering og konkretisering av bærekraftig praksis i kommunen*, Rapport 2002:17, Sogndal, Norway: Vestlandsforsking.

Aall, C., K. Groven and G. Lindseth (2007), 'The scope of action for local climate policy: the case of Norway', *Global Environmental Politics*, **7** (2), 83–102.

Aall, C., L. Halvorsen, E. Heiberg and A. Tønnesen (2009a), *Følgeevaluering av Livskraftige kommuner og Grønne energikommuner. Sluttrapport*, VF-Rapport 2009:7, Sogndal, Norway: Vestlandsforsking.

Amundsen, H., F. Berglund and H. Westskog (2010), 'Overcoming barriers to climate change adaptation – a question of multilevel governance?', *Environment and Planning C: Government and Policy*, **28** (2), 276–89.

Bjørnæs, T. and W. Lafferty (2000), *Miljøvernlederstillinger og Lokal Agenda 21. Hva er status? Basert på en spørreundersøkelse i norske kommuner våren 2000*, Rapport 2000:1, Oslo: ProSus.

Bulkeley, H. (2000), 'Down to Earth local government and greenhouse policy in Australia', *Australian Geographer*, **31** (3), 289–308.

Christensen, P. (ed.) (1996), *Governing the Environment: Politics, Policy, and Organization in the Nordic Countries*, Copenhagen: The Nordic Council of Ministers (Nord 1996:5).

CICERO (2008), *Betydningen for Norden av 2 grader global oppvarming*, Nordisk Ministerråd Rapport 2008.

Dannevig, H., T. Rauken and G. Hovelsrud (2011), 'Implementing adaptation to climate change at the local level', submitted to *Local Environment*.

Dessai, S. and M. Hulme (2003), *Does Climate Policy Need Probabilities?* University of East Anglia Tyndall Centre working paper 34, Norwich.

Direktoratet for samfunnssikkerhet og beredskap (DSB) (2007), *Klimatilpasning 2007. Klimatilpasning i kommuner, fylkeskommuner og blant fylkesmenn*, Rapport, Tønsberg Direktoratet for samfunnssikkerhet og beredskap.

Direktoratet for samfunnssikkerhet og beredskap (DSB) (2009), *Nasjonal sårbarhets- og beredskapsrapport (NSBR) 2009. Et nasjonalt risiko-, trussel- og sårbarhetsbilde. Risiko, sårbarhet og beredskap i nordområdene*, Tønsberg, Norway: Direktoratet for samfunnssikkerhet og beredskap.

Groven, K., K. Holden and C. Aall (2007), *Klimagassutslipp og klimatilpassing i Sogn og Fjordane 1991–2005*, VF-Rapport 2007:4, Sogndal, Norway: Vestlandsforsking.

Groven, K., H. Leivestad and C. Aall (2008), *Naturskade i kommunene – Sluttrapport fra prosjekt for KS*, VF-Rapport 2008:4, Sogndal, Norway: Vestlandsforsking.

Groven, K., C. Aall, M. van den Berg, A. Kanyama and F. Coenen (2011), 'Civil protection and climate change adaptation. Comparing lessons learned from three coastal cities in Norway, Sweden and the Netherlands', *Local Environment on Local Climate Change Adaptation*, DOI: 10.1080/13549839.20 12.665859.

Heiberg, E., C. Aall, F. Ekström and H. Storm (2009), *Lokal sårbarhet for klimaendringer. Demonstrasjon av metoder for kartlegging av den institusjonelle sårbarheten for klimaendringer*, VF-Rapport 2009:6, Sogndal, Norway: Vestlandsforsking.

Høyer, K. and C. Aall (2002), 'Lokale indikatorer for bærekraftig utvikling. Bærekraftindikatorenes teori og historie – men med hvilken framtid?', in C. Aall, K.G. Høyer and W. Lafferty (eds), *Fra miljøvern til bærekraftig utvikling i kommunene. Erfaringer med Lokal Agenda 21*, Oslo: Gyldendal akademisk, pp. 200–243.

Husabø, I. (2008), 'Exit war, enter climate? Institutional change and the introduction of climate adaptation in Norway's public system of civil protection', WNRI Report 2008:9, Sogndal, Norway: Western Norway Research Institute (Vestlandsforsking).

Husabø, I. (2010), *Ekstremvêrhendingar. Erfaringsgrunnlag for klimatilpassing hos Fylkesmannen*, VF-Rapport 2010:4, Sogndal, Norway: Vestlandsforsking.

Jansen, A. (1991), *Reform og resultater. Evaluering av forsøksprogrammet Miljøvern i kommunene*, Oslo: NORAS.

Justis- og politidepartementet. (2004), *Samfunnssikkerhet og sivilt-militært samarbeid, Stortingsmelding,* Rapport 2003–2004:39, Oslo: Justis- og politidepartementet.

Kaivo-Oja, J., J. Luukanen and M. Wilenius (2004), 'Defining alternative national-scale socio-economic and technological futures up to 2100: SRES scenarios for the case of Finland', *Boreal Environment Research*, **9**, 109–25.

Kleven, T. (1990), *". . . det rullerer og det går . . .", Studie av et forsøk med resultatorientert kommunal planlegging"*, Rapport 1990:23, Oslo: Norsk institutt for by- og regionforskning.

Kleven, T. (1993), *'Sørensens konklusjoner'. Et essay om forskning og målstyring,* Rapport 1993:23, Oslo: Norsk institutt for by- og regionforskning.

Lafferty, W. (ed.) (2001), *Sustainable Communities in Europe*, London: Earthscan Publishers.

Lafferty, W. and K. Eckerberg (eds) (1998), *From the Earth Summit to Local Agenda 21. Working Towards Sustainable Development*, London: Earthscan.

Lafferty, W., C. Aall and Ø. Seippel (1998), *Fra miljøvern til bærekraftig utvikling i norske kommuner*, Rapport 1998:2, Oslo: ProSus.

Lafferty, W., C. Aall, G. Lindseth and I. Norland (eds) (2006), *Lokal Agenda 21 I Norge: Så mye hadde vi – så mye ga vi bort – så mye har vi igjen*, Oslo: Unipub.

Lindseth, G. (2006), *Political Discourse and Climate Change: The Challenge of Reconciling Scale of Impact with Level of Governance*, PhD dissertation, VF-Report 2006:6, Trondheim, Norway: Norges teknisk-naturvitenskapelige universitet i Trondheim.

MacGillivray, A. and S. Zadek (eds) (1995), *Accounting for Change. Papers from an International Seminar*, Toynbee Hall, London, October 1994, London: New Economics Foundation.

Miljøverndepartementet (2007), *Norsk klimapolitikk*, Stortingsmelding Rapport 2006–2007:34, Oslo, Norway: Miljøverndepartementet.

Miljøverndepartementet and KS (1988), *Håndbok – Kommunalt miljøvern*, Oslo: Kommuneforlaget.

Miljøverndepartementet and KS (1999), *Bærekraftige kommuner. Er vi på rett kurs? Veiledende kriterier for Lokal Agenda 21-arbeidet*, Oslo: Miljøverndepartementet.

Næss, L., I. Norland, W. Lafferty and C. Aall (2006), 'Data and processes linking vulnerability assessment to adaptation decision-making on climate change in Norway', *Global Environmental Change*, **16** (2), 221–33.

Naustdalslid, J. (1994), 'Globale miljøproblem – locale løysingar', in J. Naustdalslid and S. Hovik (eds), *Lokalt Miljøvern*, Oslo: Tano, pp. 13–16.

Naustdalslid, J. and S. Hovik (eds) (1994), *Lokalt Miljøvern*, Oslo: TANO/NIBR.

Noregs offentlege utgreiingar (NOU) (2010), 'Tilpassing til eit klima i endring.

Samfunnet si sårbarheit og behov for tilpassing til konsekvensar av klimaendringane', NOU 2010: 10, Oslo: Miljøverndepartementet.
Organisation for Economic Co-operation and Development (OECD) (1994), *Environmental Indicators. OECD Core Set*, Paris: OECD.
Parry, M., O. Canziani and J. Palutikof (2007), *Technical Summary. Climate Change 2007: Impacts, Adaptation and Vulnerability. Contribution of Working Group II to the Fourth Assessment Report of the Intergovernmental Panel on Climate Change*, Cambridge: Cambridge University Press.
Riksrevisjonen (2007), *Riksrevisjonens undersøkelse av bærekraftig arealplanlegging og areal – disponering i Norge*, Oslo: Riksrevisjonen.
Riksrevisjonen (2010), *Riksrevisjonens undersøkelse av måloppnåelse og styring i jordbruket*, dokument 3:12 (2009-2010), Oslo: Riksrevisjonen.
Rothstein, B. (1992), *Den korporativa staten*, Stockholm: Nordstedts.
Ryghaug, M. (2010), 'Moderating the drama of global warming: public engagement with media's accounts of climate change', submitted to *Public Understanding of Science*.
Sabatier, P. (1986), 'Top-down and bottom-up approaches to implementation research: a critical analysis and suggested synthesis', *Journal of Public Policy*, **6** (1), 21–48.
Sælensminde, I., C. Aall and H.O. Hygen (2010), Klimatilpasning i Fredrikstad. Faglige innspill til Fredrikstad kommunes arbeid med en plan for tilpasning til klimaendringer, Vestlandsforsking-rapport 3/2010, Sogndal, Norway: Vestlandsforsking
Selstad, T. (2010), *Lokalsamfunn og klimatilpasning – et framtidsperspektiv*, ØF Rapport 2010:7, Lillehammer, Norway: Østlandsforsking.
Sogn og Fjordane fylkeskommune (2009), *Fylkesdelplan for klima og miljø*, Leikanger, Norway: Sogn og Fjordane fylkeskommune.
Swart, R., G. Biesbroek, S. Binnerup, T. Carter, C. Cowan, T. Henrichs, S. Loquen, H. Mela, M. Morecroft, M. Reese and D. Rey (2009), *Europe Adapts to Climate Change: Comparing National Adaptation Strategies*, Helsinki: Partnership for European Environmental Research (PEER).
Tol, R. (1998), 'Socio-economic scenarios', in J. Feenstra, I. Burton, J. Smith and R. Tol (eds), *UNEP Handbook on Methods for Climate Change Impact Assessment and Adaptation Studies*, Amsterdam: United Nations Environment Programme and Institute for Environmental Studies, Vrije Universiteit Amsterdam.
UK Climate Impacts Programme (UKCIP) (2001), *Socio-economic Scenarios for Climate Change Assessment: A Guide to Their Use in the UK Climate Impacts Programme*, Oxford: Climate Impacts Programme.

6. 'Think globally, act locally!' But what on earth *can* local governments do about global climate change?

Lennart J. Lundqvist

Assessing the pros and cons of taking climate action presents local decision-makers with a political dilemma. To take the slogan 'think globally, act locally!' seriously implies that although the effects of climate change are globally shared, 'the physical scale of the human impact on the non-human natural world has reached a point where not just local or regional, but truly global ecological processes are being effected' (Meadowcroft 2002, p. 176). If this is seen as postulating that an effective climate strategy must simultaneously address the individual and global scales together, local actors should never forget that economic and social activities within their cities and municipalities do contribute to climate change far beyond their local jurisdictions. But at the same time as these activities are necessary for developing and sustaining local welfare, the specific contribution – and thus responsibility – of one local community to global climate change may remain unclear to its decision-makers.

In a pessimistic scenario this could lead to an impasse. When local climate action is seen as jeopardizing local economic and social development, local governments may resort to minimalist modes of governing climate change and may even opt for a free ride on the issue of climate change. In an optimistic scenario the competition among local governments to mobilize resources may lead some to view actions on climate change as an opportunity to enhance local identity and thus, in the long run, to attract and develop new resources (see Zannakis 2010; Schreurs 2008; ICLEI 2010).

In a comparative perspective, there are good reasons for examining how Swedish local governments navigate between the scenarios of impasse and opportunity. Regardless of political stripe, Swedish national governments have made strong political commitments to bring down GHG emissions by 2020 (and even 2050) well beyond the objectives set by the EU. They have also set aside considerable financial resources to stimulate local sustainability and climate-related activities (for an exhaustive evaluation see Baker and Eckerberg 2007). Additionally, Swedish municipalities: (1) enjoy generous constitutional latitude in tending to the 'common interests' of the municipality and its constituents; (2) have the authority to levy income taxes on local citizens; and (3) enjoy formidable powers in physical planning. However, one should also note that Swedish municipalities have powers to influence directly only a limited range of sectors contributing to GHG emissions, such as public heat and electricity production, and energy use in housing and waste management, which constitute only about 18 per cent of the 64 million tonnes of CO_2 emitted in 2008 (SEPA 2010, p. 32).

Given the particular mix of institutional incentives and disincentives for local action on global climate change further outlined in the next section, the following questions arise. Do Swedish local governments engage in *specific modes* and patterns of climate governance similar to, or different from, those found in other countries? Does the Network of Climate Municipalities (see below, p. 114ff) exhibit patterns of climate governance different from Swedish municipalities in general? Can the observed patterns be explained by the fact that municipalities differ in terms of internal resources and capacities for responding to similar contextual incentives and constraints? Finally, how should the patterns in modes of governing be evaluated in light of the two scenarios of climate governance – impasse and opportunity?

To answer these questions, I begin by outlining further the contextual incentives and disincentives facing Swedish local governments contemplating climate actions. I then present a conceptual framework for analysing modes of governing regarding climate change, followed by a discussion of methods and data. I next analyse what Swedish municipalities actually do about climate change, based on nationwide surveys from 2007 and 2009. Finally, I discuss my findings in light of the possibilities of moving beyond the impasse implied by the political dilemma facing local climate action.

But let me first return to the issue of impasse and opportunity. Even the most optimistic scenario must not obscure the question of what local governments actually *can* do. On the one hand, constitutional and jurisdictional distributions of power and authority do seem to level the playing field of local governments in a country. On the other, this also makes them into enclosures on the global commons. Their authority to act on climate change is constrained through past and present 'interplay among scale-dependent environmental and resource regimes' (Young 2006, p. 27). Lines of authority between national, regional and local governments provide a challenging mix of incentives and disincentives for local governments contemplating climate action (Lundqvist and von Borgstede 2008). The nation-state circumscribes the range of local climate initiatives through binding decisions on, for example, large infrastructure investments as well as through such policy instruments as vehicle emission standards or emission taxes. National climate policy also prescribes local responsibility for certain actions, thus making it difficult for local governments to opt out of local action on climate change. At the same time, national governments may empower local governments – for instance by affording them rights to impose taxes and make development plans for their territories, as well as by providing special climate-related economic incentives.

These institutionally enclosed local governments need political support and guidance as well as more resources and incentives if they are to play a significant role in climate protection. A crucial thing is that they actually do so to differing degrees. Local governments enter climate politics with varied amounts of power and resources to assume responsibility and choose specific climate actions. Objective and interrelated factors such as municipal size and administrative capacity are important. With large size comes a large and diversified municipal administration with higher 'response capacity' to deal with complex socioeconomic and ecological problems such as climate change, and a wider 'response space', that is, a richer economic and technological potential for attacking and solving those problems (Tompkins and Adger, 2005). Local action on global climate change remains crucially dependent on contextual institutional incentives 'to solve the significant governance dilemmas that often make decisions to invest in natural resource governance quite costly' (Andersson and Ostrom, 2008, p. 80). This not only concerns support from above; there is also the question of local support. Different levels of public support for climate-related actions, as well as different degrees of dependency on specific types of industries, may enhance or reduce local governments' room for manoeuvre.

1. GLOBAL COMMITMENTS, NATIONAL POLICY AND MUNICIPAL COMPETENCE: THE ACTUAL 'ENCLOSURE' OF SWEDISH LOCAL CLIMATE ACTION

Sweden's current climate objective is to reduce national emissions of greenhouse gases by at least 4 per cent on average from 1990 levels between the years 2008 and 2012. This goes beyond the reduction demanded by the EU as Sweden's contribution to the implementation of the European climate strategy. For the period up to 2020, the objective for Swedish national reductions of GHG emissions is set at 40 per cent. For the longer term, Sweden has adopted reduced climate impact as one of its

16 inter-generational National Environmental Objectives. The Climate Bill of March 2009 envisions that net GHG emissions from Sweden to the atmosphere 'will be zero by 2050' (Ministry of Environment 2008/9, p. 162).

These goals and visions mean a growth in national ambition. The 2002 Climate Bill only aimed to reduce GHG emissions by 50 per cent by 2050. But the philosophy remains the same. Climate policy objectives are to be reached by close cooperation throughout Swedish society; the realization of the 'zero vision' rests on everybody's participation and engagement (Ministry of Environment 2008/9, p. 162). Just as in 2002, local government is given a key role here. The 2009 Bill enumerates several locally available instruments that can be classified under the 'modes of governing' presented below: energy conversion in public buildings and public housing, use of authority under environmental and planning legislation, as well as the provision of services and use of enabling strategies (Ministry of Environment 2008/9, p. 162).

The Swedish constitutional framework of local self-governance provides both opportunities and obstacles to local climate action. The power of the 290 popularly elected municipal councils in Sweden to levy income taxes on their citizens enables them to carry out several mandatory municipal tasks of relevance to climate policy, such as infrastructure development, environmental and public health protection, waste management, water and sewage treatment, and emergency services. Of particular importance is local governments' monopoly on physical planning. The Planning and Building Act updated in 2010 empowers individual municipalities to seek their own developmental paths within the framework of national legislation, such as the 1998 Environmental Code. The Master Plans (*översikts-planer*) – which are formally revised every five years – have become a more or less continuous exercise in which municipalities lay out visions and plans for the use of land and eco-services to develop infrastructure and built environments (see Ministry of Finance 2004).

Still, 'local action is not well suited to regulating mobile global conduct yielding a global externality' (Wiener 2007, p. 1962). Major national traffic arteries passing through local communities are a national responsibility, as are the technical emission performance standards for vehicles on the roads and highways. To date only the large cities in Sweden have the power to issue local 'environmental zone' ordinances regulating what types of lorries and vans should be allowed in the inner city (SFS 1998b, p.1276). Constituting 30 per cent of total Swedish GHG emissions (SEPA 2010, p. 32), the transport sector is thus literally out of the control of municipalities. Add to this that inter-municipal and regional/local cooperation in such fields as energy, transport and regional infrastructure planning is still mostly unregulated. However, the 2009 Cabinet Bill fore-sees a stronger role for the state regional boards (*länsstyrelserna*) to initiate and coordinate such intensified cross-level and cross-scale cooperation (Ministry of Environment 2008/9, p. 162). As for large industrial and infrastructural facilities emitting greenhouse gases, municipalities are just one party in the court-like procedures under the Environmental Code that decide if and under what conditions such facilities should be permitted. These environmental court decisions mean that municipal environmental inspectors cannot introduce more exacting standards (SFS 1998a, p. 808). The development of international emission trading schemes means that Sweden's local governments have lost earlier powers to regulate large companies now engaged in emissions trading. All of this implies that local politicians and administrators may ask themselves how far they should go in assuming responsibility for a problem they can see is not fully theirs (Langlais 2009, p. 264).

2. TAKING CLIMATE ACTION: A TYPOLOGY OF 'MODES OF GOVERNING'

In a comparative study of local climate strategies in Great Britain and Germany, the authors suggest that rather than focusing on 'either govern-ment or governance', attention should be paid to analysing what they call 'multiple modes of governing' (Bulkeley and Kern 2006, p. 2238). They argue that 'the recognition of multiple modes of governing enhances our understanding of the ways in which climate change is being governed locally and the fundamental challenges encountered' (ibid.). To more 'fruitfully examine the modes of governing which are deployed with respect to climate protection', Bulkeley and Kern suggest a typology of four major governing modes:

- *self-governing*: the capacity of local government to govern its own activities;
- *governing by provision*: the shaping of practice through the delivery of particular forms of service and resources;
- *governing by authority*: the use of traditional forms of authority such as regulation and direction;
- *governing through enabling*: the role of local government in facili-tating, coordinating and encouraging action through partnership with private and voluntary sector agencies, and to various forms of community engagement (Bulkeley and Kern 2006, p. 2242; italics mine).

This typology addresses both the formal 'government' aspect, that is, the distribution of power and authority to the local level, and the 'governance' capacity. The authors point out that 'each mode is distinct in terms of the type of governing capacity brought to bear'. Self-governing relies on organizational management processes, and governing by provision uses practical, material and infrastructural means. To govern by authority implies the use of sanctions, whereas governing through enabling works through persuasion, argument and incentives (Bulkeley and Kern 2006, p. 2242).

3. POLITICIANS, ADMINISTRATORS AND THE PROSPECTS FOR LOCAL CLIMATE ACTION

To find out what local Swedish actors foresee in terms of possibilities and obstacles for local climate action, I draw on survey and interview data from the years 2002–4. The questions in the 2002 survey targeted 756 selected decision-makers in the Västra Götaland region, half of them within local government and the other half in private trade and industry. The response rate was 51 per cent and the analyses are based on 356 usable questionnaires (von Borgstede and Lundqvist 2006). In 2004 semi-structured, follow-up interviews were held with 18 elected local councillors and appointed top administrators in four local governments in the Greater Gothenburg area: Gothenburg, Stenungsund, Härryda and Öckerö (see Lundqvist and von Borgstede 2008). The analysis also uses climate-related responses from the 2004 survey of the chief environmental inspectors (CEIs) in the 290 Swedish municipalities.

The 2002 COPE survey asked who 'has' and who 'should have' responsibility for actions on climate change. Respondents ranked national government, international organizations and regional administrations as the top three among ten alternatives. Most notably, both public and private sector respondents ranked private and public companies higher than local government on both actual and preferred responsibility. Local government came out sixth or seventh on actual reponsibility, and only slightly higher in terms of preferred allocation of reponsibility. Local actors were not satisfied with the amount of resources for action on climate change. More than 75 per cent of the 2002 respondents found time, manpower and material resources lacking or insufficient. Knowledge was found lacking or unsatisfactory by 66 per cent of the respondents (COPE 2002). Responses to the 2004 CEI survey indicate that about 40 per cent of the CEIs thought local governments lacked the capacity and resources necessary for environmental action, and about 75 per cent saw national support as decisive for local environmental capacity. CEIs even judged local municipal councillors and the council board as less important for *local* environmental action than national government or the European Union (CEI Survey 2004).

Responses to face-to-face interviews in 2004 with actors in four local governments in the Gothenburg region further reveal the intricate relationship between local capacity and dependence on national government for climate action. At first, they defend the local level's existing scope and strength of authority and recognize both the local contribution to the political dilemma of climate change and the need for more local action. But then the differences in size, capacity and resources clearly come to the fore. The views of the respondents from Gothenburg (a city equal in size to the Nordic capitals of Oslo and Helsinki) oozed confidence in the city government's political and administrative capacity to take climate action. The Head of the City Office's Infrastructure Group, Leif Johansson, stated, 'There is no limit to what Gothenburg City can do in its different sectors . . . it is the state that puts on the brakes actually.' The City Environmental Councillor, Kia Andreasson, even contended that the National Road and Railway Administrations sometimes block the more comprehensive transport solutions offered by the city.

On the other hand, smaller municipalities find it impossible to meet increasing national government demands for local climate engagement without matching resource inputs from the state. The environmental inspector from the tiny island municipality of Öckerö, Malin Innala, commented, 'Generally speaking, too much responsibility is laid down on local governments without any resources to go with it.' Summing up his discussion on local climate capacity, the chief environmental inspector in Stenungsund, Lars Wilke, complained that resources 'are so scarce that in practice, it is difficult for the municipality to play any role whatsoever'. Bengt Anders Nordwall, the Härryda Head of Infrastructure Development, succinctly summarized the opportunities and obstacles facing local governments in this field:

> Generally speaking, it's good to have as much as possible done at the local level. However, the big problem is that a lot of responsibility is put on local government without allocating adequate resources; money is just too scarce. I would like to see a strategy of transferring responsibility down to the municipal level *together* with supportive resources.

Moreover, what locals consider they *can* do about climate change is closely linked to their evaluation of climate policy instruments. Respondents in the 2002 COPE survey were asked about their willingness to accept five different climate policy instruments related to transport, energy,

technology and greenhouse gas emissions. The answers ranged from (1)
'certainly oppose' to (5) 'certainly accept'. Factor analysis of the instruments provided two broad categories. Information, subsidies and regulations seem more acceptable to local actors (mean values >3.4), whereas
taxes and emission trading seem less acceptable (mean values ≤3.4) (von
Borgstede and Lundqvist 2006). The answers indicate that local actors
value climate policy measures very much in accordance with the existing
distribution of power and authority between global, national and local
levels. They see regulation and information as within the realm of local
modes for governing climate change, while climate-related taxes and
emission trading schemes are not within those modes.

4.   SWEDISH MUNICIPALITIES AND THE RECORD OF LOCAL CLIMATE ACTION

Nationwide surveys performed in 2006–7 and 2009 provide data on what
local governments say they *do* to address climate change. The 2007 survey
from the Swedish Association of Local Authorities and Regions (SKL)
was directed at the chairpersons of the municipal boards of councillors.
The 2007 survey from the Swedish Society for Nature Conservation
(SNF) contained almost the same questions but was directed at a broader
spectrum of local administrators in the environmental sector. The SNF
data are used to corroborate the patterns emerging from the SKL survey.
Patterns of governing modes among the 23 members of the Climate
Municipalities Network can be derived from those two surveys. The
2009 SKL survey concerned how local governments address issues of
climate adaptation in physical planning. Finally, the 2006 Swedish Energy
Authority's (*Energimyndigheten*) survey of municipal energy planners
asked about local government activities in energy planning and how they
relate to local climate action. That survey found that 75 per cent of the
municipalities that had adopted local energy strategies by 2006 gave the
attainment of *locally* adopted *climate* objectives as their prime motive
(Energimyndigheten 2006). The nationwide SKL and SNF 2007 surveys
revealed that four out of five local governments either had adopted or
were about to adopt local climate objectives and action plans (SKL 2007;
SNF 2007). The reader should note that the following analysis of governing modes is based on the 'large degree' frequencies from Table 6.1; the
'some extent' category is too broad and diffuse to lend itself to meaningful
analysis.

The most favoured mode is *self-governing* in the energy sector. This
reflects the tendency towards picking low-hanging fruit, that is, to focus

Table 6.1 Swedish local governments and modes of governing climate change

Modes of governing/activity	Share of local governments' responses in percentage							
	Yes, to a large degree		Yes, to some extent		No, not at all		Don't know, N.A.	
	All*	'Climate municipalities'	All	'Climate municipalities'	All	'Climate municipalities'	All	'Climate municipalities'
Self-governing/energy efficiency and conversion to renewable energy								
• in own facilities	68	75	27	25	2		3	
• in public housing	57	75	30	25	4	–	9	–
Self-governing/local government's own travel and transport								
• car-pooling	40	65	37	15	20	15	3	5
• performance demands on municipal vehicle fleet	38	80	42	20	10	–	10	–
• travel/conference policy	29	65	45	30	21	5	5	
• bikes for use on duty	18	45	67	50	13	5	2	
• eco-driving education	16	40	60	55	21	5	3	
• route planning	13	10	43	50	19	10	25	30
Provision/climate performance demands on:								
• publicly paid transport (school, elderly, ill)	16	35	41	45	21	15	22	5
• delivery of goods	8	10	38	60	36	25	18	5

Table 6.1 (continued)

	Share of local governments' responses in percentage							
	Yes, to a large degree		Yes, to some extent		No, not at all		Don't know, N.A.	
Modes of governing/activity	All	'Climate municipalities'**	All	'Climate municipalities'	All	'Climate municipalities'	All	'Climate municipalities'
Enabling/Climate-related:								
• information/engagement of local citizens	20	65	61	35	17	–	**	–
• cooperation with local business	13	40	65	60	15	–	**	–
*Authority/*Physical planning used as a means to reduce GHG emissions	15	35	73	65	8	–	4	–

Notes:
* Members of the Climate Municipalities Network are identified from www.klimatkommunerna.infomacms.com/?page=start
** SNF figures collapse 'don't know and 'no answer' into one item.
Author's remark: Since the two surveys were answered by close to the same number of local governments, they are here collapsed into one mean percentage in each column.

Source: SKL (2007); SNF (2007).

on actions potentially achieving large emission reductions with limited up-front government expenditures and not confronting other barriers (see Vandenbergh et al. 2008). More than two-thirds of responding Swedish local governments say they work to increase energy efficiency and speed up conversion to renewable energy in municipal facilities and on public housing estates. This strategy is also visible in transportation when local governments decide on municipal travel and the composition of their vehicle fleets. About 40 per cent of Sweden's local governments have made significant efforts to institute car-pooling and put demands on vehicles in terms of environmental performance and climate effects. About one-third of local governments actively adapt their travel and conference policy to climate objectives. Fewer than one out of five local governments have worked more actively to provide bikes for use on duty as a climate-related activity and the same holds for offering eco-driving education to municipal employees. Somewhat surprisingly, only 13 per cent of the municipalities institutionalize route planning to a large degree in services such as care for the elderly.

As for governing by *provision*, that is, influencing practices of consumption to limit greenhouse gas emissions, close to 40 per cent say they frequently use measures to increase inhabitants' walking, bicycling and use of collective transport. Fifteen per cent of local governments, to a large degree, pursue strategies to increase the use of alternative fuels in collective transport. While research on Germany and the UK points to increasing local use of *enabling* modes of governing (Bulkeley and Kern 2006), only 20 per cent of Sweden's local governments very actively engage in strategies to inform their citizens about climate problems and to involve them in climate-saving activities. Only 13 per cent of Sweden's local governments say they are quite active in seeking climate-related cooperation with local business. This is amazing since the Swedish political culture is strongly characterized by cooperation and consensus (Goldsmith and Larsen 2004). Since municipalities enjoy a monopoly over physical planning within their territory, and this could be used as a means to reduce greenhouse gas emissions, there is ample room for using *authority* as a governing mode in local climate politics. However, only a minority of responding local governments (15 per cent) use their planning monopoly to a large degree as a measure to affect climate change.

5. SWEDISH LOCAL CLIMATE ACTION: NOT READY FOR EVERY MODE OF GOVERNING?

'Think globally – act locally!' is a popular saying. However, there is a great leap from sentiment to action. First of all, there is the political dilemma.

Why should local governments engage in climate action on their own and risk becoming disadvantaged, while others less bent on making such efforts may reap the benefits (see Vohs et al. 2007)? Elected local politicians are hard pressed to mobilize economic and other resources to enhance the growth potential, or halt a possible decline, in their municipalities. This they do under the competitive logic of mobilizing resources. To embark on a strategy of local climate action that risks seeing businesses locate in other municipalities may make local politicians think twice before taking tough climate action (see Lundqvist 1998). Second, we have seen that local governments are enmeshed in a multi-scale institutional structure of incentives and disincentives both directing and limiting their scope for climate action. National policies allocate authority and responsibility and they use economic measures to constrain, condition and orient local spending. From the local angle, the auspices for climate action going beyond demands of national policy or local horizons may thus seem obscure (Aall et al. 2007). A third factor is the local configuration of public demand and support. Being heavily dependent on large climate-affecting industries, local politicians would reasonably need strong local support for local climate measures. Bo Pettersson, the municipal board chairman of a local municipality, interviewed in 2004, stated:

> As I see it, we could have done things of extreme importance for the climate, but then we would not have gotten the support of our citizens. Such a strategy would hurt the climate issue. The question is how do I get strong citizen support for positive climate measures?

The chairman could of course rely on certain enabling factors in the institutional setting, particularly the power of Swedish local governments to levy income taxes on their inhabitants and to make use of the strong authority to physically plan and shape the use of their territory. He could also point to the local government responsibilities spelled out in national policy documents. Furthermore, he could make use of the national programmes to support local initiatives for sustainability and climate-related investment. Finally, public opinion seems increasingly favourable to climate action. A 2007 survey from the Swedish Environmental Protection Agency (SEPA) reported that as many as 88 per cent said 'we in Sweden' *can* do something to limit climate change. National climate-related subsidies and taxes (!) were seen as 'good' or 'fairly good' measures by 88 per cent and 64 per cent, respectively (SEPA 2007).

Against this mix of contextual and local factors, one could reasonably expect a greater use of authority through local governments' strong planning monopoly, as well as a more extensive use of provision and enabling as an effect of generous state subsidy programmes and widespread public support for climate action. However, the results do not show such patterns. Just as in Germany and the UK, a self-governing mode is dominant. Swedish municipalities in general tend to opt for climate-related measures over which they have the fullest control themselves. Prime examples include energy provision, energy consumption and conversion to renewable sources in municipally owned facilities and public housing. Local governments are furthermore fairly active in taking measures to make their own travel policies and means of transportation more climate friendly, including climate performance standards when renewing local vehicle fleets.

Most notable is the limited recourse to the governing modes of enabling and authority among local governments in general. With high nationwide public support for climate governance (SEPA 2007), it is surprising that no more than 20 per cent of all municipalities use information to engage local citizens and interest organizations in climate action. And despite Sweden's political culture of cooperation and consensus, only 13 per cent of all municipalities report significant levels of cooperation with local business. Given the strong authority of Swedish local governments to physically plan and shape the use of their territory, it is astonishing that climate issues find their way into the physical planning process in a substantial way in only 15 per cent of all municipalities.

The dominance of the self-governing mode clearly reflects what rational local decision-makers see as the politically most easily adopted strategy and may preclude climate governing guided by actors' thinking globally about climate change. Our interviews indicate that motives are primarily economic. Savings on municipal energy have positive effects for the budget and thus – indirectly – for all local taxpayers, all of which can be exchanged for increased political support. The energy adviser of Stenungsund, Bengt Nilsson, succinctly captured what drives energy efficiency investments:

> It's the money. The climate issue only comes in second. It's nice to inform about bio-fuel since it is so much cheaper which means that economic and climate motives support each other. This is really the grand opening for us energy advisers!

Swedish local governments in general seem reluctant to use the modes of provision, enabling and authority despite comparatively generous national support and encouragement. National grant programmes to induce local investments for sustainability and climate actions encouraged local governments to compete with one another for state support for local investments for sustainable development – the LIP programme – and climate-related investments – the KLIMP programme (Swedish state grants to local climate investment programmes) (Baker and Eckerberg 2007; see also Forsberg 2007; SEPA 2008). Evaluations of these programmes imply a clash between national programme design and local capacity for climate action: '[A]llocation was skewed towards environmental leader municipalities and LIP was never fully integrated into other sustainable development initiatives. Further, few public/private partnerships were developed' (Baker and Eckerberg 2007, p. 325). The KLIMP grants to local climate investment programmes had limited budgets and placed strong demands on local governments to present a competitive application, thus discriminating against smaller and less resource-endowed local governments (Forsberg 2007).

With respect to enabling modes of governing, local decision-makers in the Gothenburg area revealed how incentives work here. First, projects with national economic support encourage collaboration on issues such as district heating because such projects imply win-win situations for all involved. Second, even when actors recognize the local relevance of global climate change, they seem hesitant to go beyond their jurisdictional responsibility and competence except when state money is forthcoming. Patterns of climate cooperation in Gothenburg city are telling; cooperation projects were mainly driven by national KLIMP grants since, as Ann-Marie Ramnerö has noted, they provided 'a very visible carrot for *inter-bureau* cooperation' (my italics).

Neither the historic record of Swedish climate information campaigns nor the local incentive structure seems to promote local efforts to inform and engage the citizens. The three-year National Swedish Climate Campaign launched in 2002 was to be carried out through cross-scale cooperation among the Swedish Environmental Protection Agency (SEPA), local governments and national NGOs. With a three-year budget of 90 million Swedish kronor (€10 million) up to 2004, Swedes would be subjected to a trickle of information at an annual cost of only 3 Swedish kronor (roughly €0.30) per capita. The first campaign round happened to be launched when harsh wintry conditions seemed to profoundly contradict the campaign's global warming message. As a result, national funding was withdrawn for the campaign's final year, thus aborting the last step including local activities (Ministry of Environment 2005).

No wonder that local government actors judge information to be a troublesome option. It is seen as less efficient than other measures, and thus a waste of time and money. The Head of Traffic and Planning within Gothenburg City's Environmental Administration, Ann-Marie Ramnerö, said that there 'must be a willingness among the public to receive the information if it's going to work at all'.

Despite holding formidable powers in physical planning and land use, there are some strong incentives for rational local actors not to use authority as a governing mode for climate action. Putting restrictions on land and resource use for climate reasons might be seen as limiting freedom of trade and freedom of movement and possibly clashing with objectives of economic and social development. Second, taking strong climate action risks creating a disadvantage vis-à-vis other local governments with respect to the municipality's ability to attract new business and new jobs. This was evidenced by a top officer in Gothenburg City, Leif Johansson. After saying that increased consciousness will help everyone acknowledge responsibility for our common climate, he added a reminder of the city's crucial dependence on the car and truck industry (read *Volvo*, now owned by the Chinese company Geely):

> [W]e must all be rational . . . We must not act so as to create competitive disadvantages for industries. One cannot make fewer cars in Sweden at the same time as car imports increase.

6.   HEADING FOR AN IMPASSE?

All of this gives the impression that by 2007 Swedish local governments were heading towards an impasse with respect to climate governance. The prevailing incentive structures did not exactly help municipalities to bypass the political dilemma they were facing when deciding whether or not to go for strong action on climate change. Were they to opt for such a course, they faced the risk of being outdone in the competition for new industries, businesses and jobs by other local governments less concerned with the future effects of climate change. Even interviewees in the large and very resourceful city of Gothenburg aired such worries. Admittedly, the local governments' monopoly on physical planning is supposed to strike a long-term balance between economic and social development, on the one hand, and a sustainable use of natural resources, on the other. It is, however, fair to say that the planning process is strongly guided by the logic of resource mobilization. Attracting new business in order to land more jobs in the municipality functions as the first commandment even among the most 'climate friendly' local governments (see Forsberg 2007, p. 30).

Thus it is not surprising that local governments hesitate to move beyond the low-hanging fruit strategy of self-governing in municipal housing and transport. This provides quickly recognizable economic gains which can be translated into public support, while using wider means to reach a sustainable climate may lead to less tangible benefits sometime in the future.

Locals lament national government loading local governments with more and more responsibilities for climate action, but not following this up with financial support. This may seem surprising in view of the unique Swedish LIP and KLIMP programmes supporting local sustainability and climate investment. But as already pointed out, the formal provision of equal opportunities for all local governments to get financial support was thwarted by the competitive structure of those programmes. This structure in effect hindered the development of inter-municipal cooperation to combat climate change, which is the most suitable local organizational response in view of the cross-boundary character of the climate issue.

As evidenced by our interviews, insufficient local public support can be used as a reason for not going too far in local climate action. This is where enabling modes of governing should come to the fore, but local actors may conclude that steering through information is an uphill battle. An evaluation of the Swedish Radio's Climate Fever campaign in the spring of 2007 found that while listeners came to see the climate issue as more important than before, they also tended to judge themselves less personally affected by it. Over the week-long campaign, there were signs of information saturation, as the view of the climate issue's importance began to go down (Jagers et al. 2009, p. 93).

The reader might compare this account of local climate governance as similar to travelling along a one-way street where national and local road signs point towards an impasse as overly pessimistic. Should we not rather see the situation in 2007 as one where the local governments had reached a certain stage, from which they would be able to launch a reordering of the modes of governing climate change? Indeed, there are signs of such movement.

7. MOVING BEYOND THE IMPASSE: LOCAL NETWORKING AND PLANNING FOR CLIMATE ADAPTATION

Returning to Table 6.1, we find that the 23 members of the Swedish Climate Municipalities Network use some modes of governing – provision, enabling and authority – to a remarkably greater extent than other local governments. This they do despite being subjected to the same incentive structure from above as all 290 Swedish municipalities. One might interpret this as a result of internal similarities among the network members. However, they exhibit considerable differences in terms of size and capacity, from Stockholm City with 810,000 inhabitants to municipalities with fewer than 13,000 inhabitants (SCB 2009). Nor is there any clear political pattern among network members: for example, in terms of strong Green Party representation that could mean increased political pressure for local climate action (SEA 2009).

The Climate Network municipalities' most distinguishing feature compared with Swedish municipalities in general is their uptake of the national LIP and KLIMP grant programmes. More than three-quarters of the network members have received grants from both of these programmes, compared with 55 per cent (LIP) and 24 per cent (KLIMP) for all Swedish local governments. Furthermore, most of the network members received several grants from the KLIMP programme (SEPA 2008).

The network's foremost characteristic is as a 'learning centre' and a catalyst for ideas and inspiration by continuously pointing to opportunities for local climate action and diffusing information and experiences from such action (see Kern and Bulkeley 2009, p. 319). One example of this clearinghouse function is the Network Manual for starting up and implementing a local climate action programme. The network also engages in international cooperation to improve contacts and stimulate learning from similar networks in other countries. Since 2009, the network functions as a support structure to the EU Covenant of Mayors, giving it an increased capacity to gather and diffuse information about local climate strategies. From 2006 to 2009, the network used funding from the Swedish Environment Protection Agency for climate coaching to help 23 small municipalities establishing climate strategies. Since 2007, the network has published a monthly newsletter with information on activities, experiences and examples from network members and other local governments around Sweden, as well as about upcoming national and international climate conferences (Klimatkommunerna 2009).

It thus comes as no surprise that network members are keener to adopt a broad range of self-governing strategies in local travel and transport as well as to inform citizens and engage local business in their climate strategies (see Table 6.1). Neither is it surprising that the 23 network members fare quite well in climate rankings and in getting disproportionate shares of new national grants for local climate action. In the SNF ranking of 2005, six network members were among the top 10. In 2007, seven ranked among the top 12 (SNF 2007). At the end of 2009, seven network members raked in 70 per cent of the investment or planning grants awarded from the national Delegation for Sustainable Cities (Klimatkommunerna 2009).

However, it is not only the members of the Network of Climate Municipalities that show signs of moving beyond the impasse indicated by the patterns of governing modes found up to 2007. The 2009 survey done by the Swedish Association of Local and Regional Authorities (SKL) indicates that climate issues are coming to the fore also in municipal planning

Table 6.2   Swedish local governments and the use of planning authority for climate mitigation and adaptation, 2007 and 2009

Swedish municipal planning activities directed at climate change	Percentage of municipalities (figures include activities performed to a 'large degree' as well as 'to some extent')	
	2007	2009
Mitigation		
• localization for decreased transport needs	57	75
• localization of wind power	51	77
• localization of housing for expanded district heating	48	70
• localization of shopping malls	22	43
• energy demands for buildings on municipal property	23	40
• voluntary energy performance agreements on private property	9	22
Adaptation	To a large	To some
(*Note:* figures only concern 2009)	degree	extent
• incorporated in master planning	32	57
• incorporated in detail planning	34	51
• incorporated in risk and vulnerability analyses	19	58
• incorporated in establishing building guidelines	18	53
• cooperation with neighbour municipalities on flooding, erosion, landslides	36	58

Source: SKL (2009); SKL (2010).

with respect to both mitigation and adaption. Nearly 60 per cent of all Swedish local governments have now placed the overall responsibility for climate action at the centre of local politics, that is, in the politically elected municipal council board. Close to one-third have also adopted comprehensive, cross-sectoral climate strategies (SKL 2009, p. 2).

Even more interesting from the perspective of modes of governing, more local governments are now using their authority in planning. This is true with respect to both 'mitigation, that is planning for building a low carbon society, and adaptation, that is planning focused on living in a warmer world' (I owe this expression of the dichotomy to James Meadowcroft). Table 6.2 shows that by 2009, a majority of Swedish municipalities reported that they include climate mitigation to some extent in their master and detailed plans for localizing GHG-producing facilities and activities. Two-fifths of the municipalities include such considerations when planning for new shopping malls, as well as specifying energy performance demands for buildings on municipal property.

Aspects of climate adaptation also seem to be rapidly coming to the fore in municipal master and detail planning. By 2009, one-third of all municipalities reported that they include adaptation aspects in both types of planning. This is twice the share from 2007 and equals the level exhibited by the Climate Municipalities Network in that year (see Table 6.1). Local governments are increasingly incorporating adaptation measures when establishing building guidelines, and making risk and vulnerability analyses in their planning. At the same time, however, between half and three-quarters of the municipalities say they lack data for analysing local risks of flooding and landslides, as well as tools for creating climate scenarios and using cost–benefit analyses in local planning (SKL 2009). This underscores the demands of the SKL position paper on energy and climate from 2008:

> National government must freely provide premises for planning and tools for analysis adapted to local governments so they can make adequate decisions and take their responsibility for decreasing the climate effects of local physical planning. (SKL 2008, p. 17)

8. CONCLUSION

The findings above at first imply a looming impasse. Local decision-makers place much of the responsibility for actions on climate on higher levels of government. What they *do* take responsibility for is what most easily lends itself to self-governing given the structural enclosures on autonomy and authority imposed by those other levels. These structural limitations, in turn, imply ideational constraints on alternative modes of climate governance. Institutionalized logics of competition – whether it concerns physical planning, seeking national financial support, or getting to the top of environmental and climate ranking lists (see, for example, Hugo 2010) – seems to make local governments both think and act locally before invoking their strong planning authority for unilateral climate action. Experiences with earlier climate information campaigns discourage local actors from efforts to get the general public to look beyond the potential costs of early action on climate change and to accept municipal climate activism. Altogether, structural as well as ideational factors point to a need for change if acting locally is to become more influenced by thinking globally.

Findings from the most recent data indicate a possible path beyond this looming impasse. Members of the Climate Municipalities Network are more knowledgeable and more innovative when opting for different modes of governing in their climate strategies. Their major strategy is learning; the Network Secretariat is actively gathering and freely disseminating information and knowledge among network members and from other local governments, both nationally and internationally. The contact persons in the member municipalities fill several functions; they promote new projects, coordinate and monitor the processes of climate action, and run their own projects (Lamppa 2010). But even if 'key actors play a critical role in driving change', local administrations must possess a strong coordinating capacity for 'more sustainable and integrated adaptation' (Storbjörk and Hedrén 2011, p. 271), in view of the conflicting local objectives and mandates revealed by our interviewees. No local governments, not even the network members, can break out of the dependence and enclosure patterns created by national and international actors. However important local climate action may be, this built-in tension implies that it can be 'no substitute for national, federal, or supranational action' (Schreurs 2008, p. 353).

However, if local governments are to break out of structurally imposed and now dominant 'think and act locally' climate strategies, they must look for support from national government. Indeed, the 2008 call from the Association of Local and Regional Authorities for national support and guidance has not gone unheeded. The 2008 Climate Bill calls for more integration in physical planning through increased cooperation among actors on local, regional and national levels. It also gives the state regional boards (*länsstyrelserna*) authority to change local master plans that do not assess climate effects. These boards can now also initiate and bring about inter-municipal regional master planning for climate action (Ministry of Environment 2008/9, p. 162). However, the Bill also does exactly what local actors most hate; it places more responsibilities on municipalities without providing money to go with them.

To paraphrase William M. Lafferty, our findings indicate that the challenges of climate change are 'demonstrably altering political processes, alliances and outcomes'. They also indicate that in order to know how the phrase 'Think globally, act locally!' is to 'be realized most effectively', we must know 'which forces appear to either foster or retard its implementation' (Lafferty 1999, p. 126). We have found that to get beyond the impasse there is need for strengthened top–down authority to ensure the integration of nationwide and even global climate aspects into local and inter-municipal master and detail planning. But there is also a need for strengthening horizontal and bottom–up processes for learning and diffusion of knowledge to enable local actors to deliver accordingly.

REFERENCES

Interviewees Cited

Gothenburg City
Andréasson, Kia, elected City Councillor, and Environmental Commissioner on the City Council Board.
Johansson, Leif, Head of Infrastructure Group at City Office.
Ramnerö, Ann-Marie, Head of Planning and Traffic Bureau, City Environmental Administration.

Härryda municipality
Nordwall, Bengt Anders, Head of Infrastructure and Planning Administration.

Stenungsund municipality
Nilsson, Bengt, Municipal Energy Adviser.
Pettersson, Bo, elected Municipal Councillor, Chairman of Municipal Council Board
Wilke, Lars, Chief Environmental Inspector.

Öckerö municipality
Innala, Malin, Chief Environmental Inspector.
Network of Climate Municipalities
Lamppa, Andreas, Secretariat.

Publications

Aall, C., K. Groven and G. Lindseth (2007), 'The scope of action for local climate policy: the case of Norway', *Global Environmental Politics*, **7**, 83–101.
Andersson, K. and E. Ostrom (2008), 'Analyzing decentralized resource regimes from a polycentric perspective', *Policy Sciences*, **41**, 71–93.
Baker, S. and K. Eckerberg (2007), 'Governance for sustainable development in Sweden: the experience of the local investment programme', *Local Environment: The International Journal of Justice and Sustainability*, **12**, 325–42.
Bulkeley, H. and K. Kern (2006), 'Local government and the governing of climate change in Germany and the UK', *Urban Studies*, **43**, 2237–59.
CEI Survey (2004), *Chief Environmental Inspector Survey 2004*, Gothenburg, Sweden: University of Gothenburg Department of Political Science and School of Public Administration.
Communication, Organisation, Policy Instruments, Effectiveness/Efficiency (COPE) (2002), *Klimatenkät 2002* [*Climate Survey 2002*)], Gothenburg, Sweden: University of Gothenberg/Faculty of Social Sciences, Communication, Organisation, Policy Instruments, Effectiveness/Efficiency (COPE).
Energimyndigheten (Swedish Energy Agency) (2006), *Kommunal energiplanering*

En enkätundersökning av Sveriges kommuner (*Municipal Energy Planning. A survey of Sweden's municipalities*). Eskilstuna, Sweden: Energimyndigheten, accessed August 2011 at www.swedishenergyagency.se/web/biblshop.nsf/FilAtkomst/ER2006_40w.pdf/$FILE/ER2006_40w.pdf?OpenElement.

Forsberg, B. (2007), *Med sikte på klimatmålet lokalt? En utvärdering av framkant-skommuner i klimatpolitiken* [*Local Aim at Climate Targets? An Evaluation of Frontrunner Municipalities in Climate Policy*], Umeå, Sweden: UCER (Centre for Evaluation Research).

Goldsmith, M. and H. Larsen (2004), 'Local political leadership: Nordic style', *International Journal of Urban and Regional Research*, **28**, 121–33.

Hugo, L. (2010), 'Hård fajt om listplaceringar' ['Tough fights over ranking list positions'], in *Miljö & Klimat* [*Environment & Climate*], appendix to *Dagens Samhälle* #32/2010, pp. 4–9.

ICLEI (Local Governments for Sustainability) (2010), *Cities for Climate Protection* (CCP), accessed August 2011 at www.iclei.org/index.php?id=10829.

Jagers, S., J. Martinsson and A. Nilsson (2009), *Kan vi påverka folks miljöattityder genom information? En analys av radiosatsningen 'Klimatfeber'* [*Can People's Attitudes be Influenced through Information? An Analysis of Swedish Radio's 'Climate Fever' Campaign*], Stockholm: Ministry of Finance, EMS report 4.

Kern, K. and H. Bulkeley (2009), 'Cities, Europeanization and multi-level govern-ance: governing climate change through transnational municipal networks', *Journal of Common Market Studies*, **47**, 309–32.

Klimatkommunerna (Climate Municipalities Network) (2009), *Presentation. Klimatstrategier; [Climate Strategies]. Klimatcoachning; [Climate Coaching]. Nyhetsbrev [Newsletters]*, accessed August 2011 at www.klimatkommunerna.infomacms.com/.

Lafferty, W. (1999), 'Introduction: The pursuit of sustainable development – concepts, policies and arenas', *International Political Science Review*, **20** (2), 123–8.

Langlais, R. (2009), 'A climate of planning. Swedish municipal responses to climate change', in S. Davoudi, J. Crawford and A. Mehmood (eds), *Planning for Climate Change. Strategies for Mitigation and Adaptation for Spatial Planners*, London: Earthscan, pp. 262–71.

Lundqvist, L. (1998), 'Local-to-local partnerships among Swedish municipali-ties: why and how neighbours join to alleviate resource constraints', in J. Pierre (ed.), *Partnerships in Urban Governance. European and American Experiences*, London: Macmillan, 93–111.

Lundqvist, L. and C. von Borgstede (2008), 'Whose responsibility? Swedish local decision makers and the scale of climate change abatement', *Urban Affairs Review*, **43**, 299–324.

Meadowcroft, J. (2002), 'Politics and scale: some implications for environmental governance', *Landscape and Urban Planning*, **61** (2–4), 169–79.

Ministry of Environment, Sweden (2005), *Sweden's Fourth National Communication on Climate Change – Under the United Nations Framework Convention on Climate Change*, Stockholm: MoE Ds 2005#55.

Ministry of Environment, Sweden (2008/09:162), *En sammanhållen klimat – och energipolitik – Klimat* [*A Coherent Climate and Energy Policy – Climate*], accessed August 2011 at www.regeringen.se/content/1/c6/12/27/78/4ce86514.pdf.

Ministry of Finance, Sweden (2004), *Local Government in Sweden – Organisation,*

Activities and Finance. Stockholm: MoF Report Fi 2004:43, accessed August 2011 at www.regeringen.se/content/1/c6/03/91/67/b5d68d50.pdf.

SCB (Statistics Sweden) (2009), *Population in the Country, Counties and Municipalities on 31/12/2008 and Population Change in 2008*, accessed August 2011 at www.scb.se/Pages/TableAndChart 262455.aspx.

Schreurs, M. (2008), 'From the bottom up: Local and subnational climate change politics', *The Journal of Environment and Development*, 17, 343–55.

SEA (Swedish Election Authority) (2009), *Valresultat allmänna val: kommunval 17 september 2006*, accessed August 2011 at www.val.se/val/val2006/slutlig/K/rike/delar.html.

SEPA (Swedish Environmental Protection Agency) (2007), *Allmänheten och klimatförändringen (The Public and Climate Change)*, Stockholm: SEPA Report 5760.

SEPA (2008), *Effekter av investeringsprogrammen LIP och Klimp [Effects of the Investment Programs LIP and Klimp]*, Stockholm: SEPA Report 5861.

SEPA (2010), *National Inventory Report 2010 Sweden*, submitted under the United Nations Framework Convention on Climate Change and the Kyoto Protocol, Stockholm: SEPA.

SFS (Swedish Code of Statutes) (1998a), *Miljöbalken [Environmental Code]* 1998:808, accessed August 2011 at www.notisum.se/rnp/SLS/lag/19980808.htm.

SFS (1998b), *Trafikförordning [Traffic Ordinance]* 1998:1276, accessed August 2011 at www.notisum.se/rnp/SLS/lag/19981276.htm.

SKL (Swedish Association of Local and Regional Authorities) (2007), *Klimatarbetet i kommuner, landsting och regioner [Climate Action in Municipalities, Counties and Regions]*, Stockholm: SKL, accessed August 2011 at http://brs.skl.se/brsbibl/kata_documents/doc39141_1.pdf.

SKL (2008), *Energi och klimat – Positionspapper [Energy and Climate – Position Paper]*, Stockholm: SKL, accessed August 2011 at www.skl.se/web/klimat_2.aspx.

SKL (2009), *Läget i landet – en enkätundersökning om klimatanpassning i den fysiska planeringen [The Lay of the Land – A Survey on Climate Adaptation in Local Physical Planning]*, Stockholm: SKL, accessed August 2011 at www.skl.se/web/laget-i-landet.aspx.

SKL (2010), *Fysisk planering i kommunerna för minska klimatpåverkan [Municipal Physical Planning for Reduced Climate Impact]*, Stockholm: SKL, accessed August 2011 at http://brs.skl.se/brsbibl/kata_documents/doc39698_1.pdf.

SNF (Swedish Society for Nature Conservation) (2007), *Klimatindex för kommuner 2007 [Climate Index for Local Governments 2007]*, Stockholm: SNF, accessed August 2011 at www.naturskyddsforeningen.se/upload/Foreningsdokument/Rapporter/rapport_klimatindex.pdf.

Storbjörk, S. and J. Hedrén (2011), 'Institutional capacity-building for targeting sea level rise in the climate adaptation of Swedish coastal zone management. Lessons from Coastby', *Ocean and Coastal Management*, 54, 265–73.

Tompkins, E. and W. Adger (2005), 'Defining response capacity to enhance climate change policy', *Environmental Science and Policy*, 8, 562–71.

Vandenbergh, M.P., J. Barkenbus and J. Gilligan (2008), 'Individual carbon emissions: the low-hanging fruit', *UCLA Law Review*, 55, 1701–58.

Vohs, K., R. Baumeister and J. Chin (2007), 'Feeling duped: emotional, motivational, and cognitive aspects of being exploited by others', *Review of General Psychology*, 11, 127–41.

von Borgstede, C. and L. Lundqvist (2006), 'Organizational culture, professional role conceptions and Swedish local decision-makers' views on climate policy instruments', *Journal of Environmental Policy and Planning*, **8**, 279–82.

Wiener, J. (2007), 'Think globally, act locally: the limits of local climate policies', *University of Pennsylvania Law Review*, **155**, 1961–79.

Young, O. (2006), 'Vertical interplay among scale-dependent environmental and resource regimes', *Ecology and Society*, **11**, accessed August 2011 at www.ecologyandsociety.org/vol11/iss1/art27/.

Zannakis, M. (2010), *Climate Policy as a Window of Opportunity. Sweden and Global Climate Change,* doctoral dissertation, Gothenburg, Sweden:University of Gothenburg Department of Political Science.

7. Moving beyond the impasse: climate change activism in the US and the EU

Elizabeth Bomberg

This volume is dedicated to William Lafferty's work on democracy and sustainable development governance. It pays particular attention to Lafferty's desire to move beyond the impasse and to discover ways to enact effective environmental policy. This chapter seeks to engage with this theme by examining environmental activism (defined here as concerted, active engagement with an environmental issue or campaign intended to bring about political or social change) in two liberal pluralist democracies: the United States (US) and the European Union (EU). The chapter compares how societal actors – mainly environmental NGOs but also other actors engaged with environmental themes – have responded to the challenges presented by climate change and the governance issues it raises. In particular it seeks to identify the institutional constraints blocking effective mobilization and activists' efforts to overcome them.

The impetus for a focus on activism arises in great part from questions raised by Lafferty and his colleagues' work on democracy and sustainable development governance (Lafferty 1996; 2004a; 2004b; 2004c; Lundquist 2004; Meadowcroft 2004). Following Lafferty, the term governance is defined here as established patterns of rules and norms steering a polity in a stipulated direction. Lafferty suggests that some of the greatest challenges of modern governance are related to the nature of contemporary democracy itself. He is concerned above all with how democratic values and democratic decision-making can be maintained while pursuing a goal (such as sustainable development) characterized by compelling urgency, devilish complexity and long-term commitment (Lafferty 2004b, p. 20ff). I suggest here the same imperatives apply to the challenge of climate change and efforts to address it.[1] More generally I argue that insights from Lafferty's study of sustainable development governance – especially its transformative character – can help us probe challenges and prospects of climate change governance. Recent policy and media discussions about the need to shift to a low-carbon economy, the need to decouple economic growth and carbon emissions, or a renewed emphasis on policy integration (Giddens 2009; Stern 2009) are all transformative challenges anticipated by Lafferty's work on sustainable development.

The focus of this chapter – activism or engaged participation – is only one small component of governance, but it is crucial and deserves closer treatment. Meadowcroft (2004), for instance, notes the centrality of participation to successful sustainable development governance and how different traditions may shape that contribution. While this chapter is inspired by both Lafferty's and Meadowcroft's conceptual explorations, it seeks a more specific empirical aim: to explore comparatively how institutional constraints and multilevel dynamics shape participation, and how activists have sought to navigate those dynamics. To do so, this chapter compares three different dimensions of activism – framing, alliance-building and mobilization – in the EU and the US. It first identifies the institutional constraints and multilevel dynamics shaping activism and suggests how activists have sought to overcome the impasse hindering effective action.

Institutional constraints refer here both to formal institutions (for example legislative structures, voting rules, federal/quasi-federal structures) and informal institutions – behavioural norms such as adversarialism, incrementalism, fragmentation, competition and cooperation that shape actors' political behaviour. Institutionalists suggest such structures and norms operating in the EU or US constrain policy action in powerful ways (Weaver and Rockman 1993; Nivola and Jones 2008). Institutionalists, for instance, demonstrate how in fragmented multilevel or federal systems it is often difficult to form winning coalitions for policy proposals because decisions are easily blocked and veto points are many (Peterson and Bomberg 1999, p. 17; Scharpf 1998). Further they suggest how previous policy decisions constrain current and future policy choices (Pierson 1996; Jordan et al. 2010, p. 15; Peterson and Bomberg 1999, p. 21). Both the EU's and the US's political systems are 'deliberately designed to restrain the scale and pace of change' (Nivola and Jones 2008, p. 13). In the US the design was more deliberate: it features bicameralism with staggered terms for elected officials and an independent judiciary. But in the EU, too, power is widely dispersed across levels of governance and institutions (Peterson and Shackleton 2006). These institutional constraints mean that activists with ambitious plans must work across levels of government and across institutions to shift policy in a particular direction. This chapter identifies as particularly important the existence or lack of mobilization networks able to overcome institutional constraints and steer polities towards particular goals.

Before we begin, several caveats are in order. First, the scope of the

chapter is necessarily limited. I focus primarily on climate change mitigation rather than adaptation. I do not, in this chapter, assess directly
the impact of activism, although findings from this analysis might well
contribute to such a future study. Second, the structural and constitutional differences between the US and EU are significant; political, historical and cultural variations make comparison additionally challenging
(see Bomberg 2009). But understanding the differences and similarities
between the EU and US environmental and climate change activism
matters empirically and conceptually. The US and EU are two powerful
polities with a potentially tremendous impact on global policies related
to climate change and sustainability. We can also gain greater conceptual
understanding of the nature of activism by comparing these two major
polities who share similarities (high consumption, liberal democracies) but
also key institutional differences.

The chapter begins with an examination of framing, followed by an
exploration of alliance-building and mobilization around the issue of
climate change.[2] It concludes with a brief discussion of the links between
activism and governance and suggests how insights from Lafferty's governance work can inform and animate future research on climate change
activism and governance.

1.   FRAMING[3]

For the purposes of this study framing can be understood as the process of
defining, selecting and emphasizing particular aspects of an issue according to an overarching set of underlying assumptions (Daviter 2007; Miller
2000, p. 211). The definition suggests issues are not predefined, rather their
definition is constructed and often highly contested. Similarly, literature
on agenda-setting (Baumgartner and Jones 1993; Princen 2007) focuses
on the construction of an image that associates a given policy issue with
certain values and symbols. Proponents of a framing approach claim that
how an issue is framed can shape significantly policy decisions and success.
This chapter does not refute that claim. How activists frame their message
and how salient that message is to the general public and to policy-makers
is of key importance in shaping the success or otherwise of climate change
activism (see Schlosberg and Bomberg 2008, p. 189). But rather than focus
on the policy-shaping properties of framing, I direct attention here to
the institutional factors which may drive such framing in the first place.
Drawing on an analysis of major NGOs' published texts,[4] I argue that
how issues are framed on both sides of the Atlantic is a result of activists'
attempts to respond to, or overcome, institutional imperatives. Activists in

both the US and EU face the challenge of framing an issue such as climate change which is simultaneously long term and urgent, complex and uncertain, and is only indirectly visible.[5] But we can also discern differences in how activists on both sides of the Atlantic frame climate change and the shifting nature of those frames.

The United States

US environmentalists have traditionally secured their most visible successes through lobbying and legislative battles (Bosso 2005). By the early 2000s, however, environmental activists faced a hostile Republican administration, an inactive Congress and unsympathetic courts. While the election of Barack Obama promised a new era for environmental and especially climate legislation, legislative success in Congress has remained stalled with congressional–presidential relations gridlocked and presidential attention thinly spread. Those institutional barriers – gridlock, stagnation and institutional competition – have stymied effective environmental action and compelled environmental activists to consider shifting their energies away from legislative battles and towards broader goals of persuading the wider public and shaping public discourse on climate change.

Initially environmentalists struggled to frame climate change in terms suitably attractive to the wider population. Bryner, for instance, notes that in the 1980s and 1990s environmental groups framed climate change as principally an issue of emissions reduction and especially regulation of power plant emissions (2008, p. 323). Framing climate change as a pollution problem meant primarily focusing on legislative measures rather than a more general problem of lifestyle requiring a transformative political response (Bryner 2008, p. 326). Comfortable with well-trodden avenues of lobbying, environmentalists therefore placed little emphasis on educating the public on the long-term impact of climate change and the fundamental energy and lifestyle questions it raised. Meanwhile, Meyer (2008) suggests the tone and discourse of large professional Washington, DC-based environmental groups has often been paternalistic, especially in the late 1990s and early 2000s. Groups adopting a paternalistic frame assumed climate change was too complex to be understood by the uninitiated masses, which were viewed as an obstacle to effective action to combat climate change. This narrow, paternalistic approach and its perceived inability to bring about significant change on climate change was a key plank of Shellenberger and Nordhaus's (2004) contentious and provocative 'death of environmentalism' claim. Shellenberger and Nordhaus argued that the old-fashioned environmentalism was to blame for the lack of success on climate change. They maintained further that old environmentalism

should be allowed to die so as to make room for a new, more imagina-
tive and progressive approach to climate change – especially one involving frames that could more effectively engage the public in transforming
society (see Schlosberg and Bomberg 2008).

Brick and Cawley (2008) suggest, however, that environmentalists
have begun to shift from ledger politics (tallying up legislative victories
and failures) to a broader, more inclusive frame, using climate change
as a discursive bridge to connect a wide variety of ideas and events that
were not previously understood as connected. Certainly some broadening of frames has occurred. First, US groups are increasingly likely to
frame climate change as a core economic issue. A major NGO network,
the US Climate Action Network (USCAN), insists it is leading the way
in 'framing the environmental and economic urgency of global warming'
(USCAN 2010a). More striking is the emphasis on energy independence
and energy security. Both FoE and USCAN endorse stronger domestic
legislation on climate change primarily as a means to strengthen national
security (USCAN 2010b; FoE 2010). Illustrative is a warning repeated by
Carl Pope, Executive Director of the Sierra Club, of the 'imperative' to
diversify the nation's energy supplies and 'reduce our foreign dependence,
especially on oil from the Middle East, which imperils our national security' (quoted in Pope 2009). This frame is double-edged. If the problem is
framed primarily in terms of energy security, the answer may be opening
up or securing more domestic sources – including coal, nuclear and offshore drilling – even if, in the wake of the devastating 2010 Gulf of Mexico
oil spill, the risks of such exploitation have proven to be profound.

Similarly, the need to bypass existing ledger politics and engage the
broader public has also led American climate change groups to frame
climate change in increasingly dramatic terms. For instance, several
American groups (both grassroots and more professional NGOs) now
often begin climate change discussions with adjectives such as 'catastrophic', 'chaotic' or 'irreversible' and focus heavily on extreme weather
events.[6] Such framing can alter the public discourse around climate
change (Hulme 2009) but it, too, is a double-edged sword. A scary weather
frame is effective in grabbing the public's attention but the result may be
that citizens feel they cannot prevent or change the weather, rather they
merely prepare for it, adjust to it or move away from it (Roberts 2006).
The focus on extreme consequences has also provided grist for the mill of
opponents of climate change action who repeatedly frame climate change
concerns not only as unfounded – whatever the majority of scientists may
say – but alarmingly alarmist. Recent polls suggest a growing percentage
of Americans believe the threat to be over-rated (Gallup 2010).

Thus by expanding the climate frame from one of emissions to an urgent, all-encompassing issue in need of lifestyle change, American environmentalists have sought to move beyond the incremental reform inherent in ledger politics. But in so doing they may have raised new barriers to action: a population either overwhelmed by an insurmountable challenge or increasingly sceptical of environmentalists' message.

The European Union

By comparison the climate change frame in the EU appears softer, almost de-radicalized. Climate change is still depicted as a dangerous problem in need of urgent action (see CAN Europe 2009). But in their demands EU-wide umbrella groups such as the European Environmental Bureau and the 'Green 10' (made up of the 10 largest environmental NGOs in Europe'[7]) tend to frame climate change in less dramatic terms, even if their national chapters remain more radical. At the EU level climate change is framed less in terms of catastrophe and more in terms of a greater need for energy efficiency, responsibility and competence. Both CAN Europe and the Green 10 have focused on modifying the EU's emission trading scheme (ETS) or reforming EU budget priorities by incorporating sustainability and new technologies.

These differences (especially in the level of emotion, intensity and radicalism) are due in part to different public perceptions of the problem. European citizens (publics) demonstrate a higher awareness of, and concern about, climate change than do Americans.[8] But differences in public perceptions alone cannot explain differences between NGO strategies. NGOs on both sides of the Atlantic undeniably share a view of climate change as a serious problem requiring urgent action. Thus the differences in NGO framing may be due less to NGOs' different perceptions and more to different strategic and multilevel institutional imperatives that favour some frames over others. Following years of inaction by policy-makers in both the executive and legislature, American groups have sought to supplement traditional lobbying by securing wider media attention and public support. Framing an issue as a security imperative or as catastrophically urgent is in part a campaign device meant to overcome institutional barriers to action by galvanizing the public.

EU groups face a different institutional architecture. There is still no coherent 'European public' to which they might appeal, but rather a collection of national publics, each with its own variation in the way climate change is perceived (see Vogler 2009). Nor is there a meaningful Europe-wide media that would privilege European over national groups. Indeed, media coverage of EU-wide environmental activism is notably sparse. So EU-wide groups primarily directly target their own member groups (for example national chapters) and, especially, EU policy-makers. But EU policy-making relies heavily on technocratic arguments and consensus-building (Bomberg et al. 2008; Peterson and Shackleton 2006). Targeting the latter can thus encourage a contraction of conflict (Princen 2007), a de-escalation or even de-radicalizing of the climate change issue, by making it more technocratic and more amenable to the functional or incrementalist arguments familiar to EU policy-making (Peterson and Bomberg 1999). In sum, in both the EU and the US activists operate within an institutional framework that is more favourable to some frames than to others.

2. ALLIANCE-BUILDING

Framing has implications for alliance-building, the second dimension of activism explored here. Alliance-building refers to how activists form and sustain coalitions of like-minded actors or stakeholders bound together through social interaction. Sabatier (1988) refers to these as 'advocacy coalitions'. In the US and EU different alliances are the product of different historical and cultural trajectories, but they are also shaped by institutional dynamics. More specifically, prevalent institutional norms and patterns tend to facilitate some alliances and hinder others.

The United States

In the US we find a recent shift in alliance-building strategies. The putative failure of US environmental groups to engage with other interests affected by climate change was one of the key critiques of the 'death of environmentalism' thesis mentioned above. By framing climate change narrowly as a pollution problem, environmental groups failed to engage (and indeed often alienated) other constituencies such as organized labour, businesses, social or environmental justice movements. Discussion of how climate change affects jobs, international trade and development and social justice were largely absent. But in the last few years intriguing, if sometimes awkward, coalitions have emerged. The very institutional dynamics that have stymied traditional Washington, DC-based environmental activism (partisanship, separation of powers, hostile executive) have opened up new opportunities for alliance-building.

First, we see renewed and intensified climate change action from grassroots movements involved with women's rights, social justice or sustainability. For instance Schlosberg and Bomberg (2008, p. 195) note how government inaction on climate change has galvanized a range of environmental justice movements and discourses with deep ties to human rights, social justice and sustainability. Similarly DiChiro (2008) examines the linkage of environmental and women's concerns, tracking how groups came together under a shared understanding of the threat to everyday life and the functioning of the community. Other civil rights and community activists have sought to link poverty with green jobs on the community level in an attempt to shake up Washington (see Kolbert 2009).

Less likely alliances are also emerging. One is the link between environmental activists and security supporters keen to limit US reliance on unstable energy sources (Friedman 2008). Another is that between traditional environmental activists and a new breed of evangelicals concerned with climate change. A cohort of mainly younger Christian evangelicals within the National Association of Evangelicals (NAE) have developed the idea of creation care – a bible-based duty to care for God's creation (Wardekker et al. 2009).[9] The NAE's call for action on climate change was directed specifically at institutional gridlock characterizing American policy-making (see NAE 2006). The adoption is important first because of the high proportion of Americans who identify themselves as evangelical Christians and second because it suggests intriguing coalition possibilities between traditional environmentalists and new partners. Of course such an alliance is fragile. It is preceded by decades of mutual mistrust, and significant opposition to climate change action among evangelical right-wing groups persists. Yet an issue such as climate change which is urgent, encompassing and complex may well create odd alliances (see Bomberg and Schlosberg 2008).

All of these alliances remain fledging and tentative. On the one hand, they have been given succour and support from the highest office. A key underlying theme in Obama's climate change pronouncements continues to be the need to link green jobs, security and climate change (see Bomberg and Super 2009; Obama 2010).[10] Yet on the other hand, an engaged executive – especially one that can eventually convince Congress to share its enthusiasm – also removes some of the key drivers that created these alliances in the first place. It was precisely the mounting frustration with a hostile Congress and administration, the apparent neglect of linkages between security, prosperity and environment as well as the dominance of a conservative Christianity dismissive of global problems that encouraged these varied activists to look beyond traditional allies. Recent battles over climate change legislation in Congress have seen splits amongst traditional environmentalists as well as new coalitions; some environmental groups were far more enthusiastic about possible legislation and the inevitable compromise it entailed.[11] Institutional change under the current administration will certainly continue to affect alliance-building, but precisely what the effect will be is uncertain.

The European Union

Alliance-building in the EU has taken on different forms. Environmental activists in the EU have a longer history of liaising and working with a broad range of stakeholders, including social NGOs, businesses, think-tanks and experts. Both on the national and EU level European environmental activists have traditionally been more comfortable forming alliances with these groups. The institutional norm of adversarialism noted above is important here. EU environmental NGOs' greater inclination to form alliances with these groups, including businesses and labour, contrasts with the more adversarial, single-issue dynamic defining (until recently) environmental activism in the US. That difference derives in part from different historical trajectories. European green groups grew largely out of a leftist social movement milieu and tended to combine post-materialist issues with wider New Left agenda concerns of class and inequality (Doherty and Doyle 2006, pp. 706–7). Left-wing and green alliance-building was both necessitated and nurtured by the development of green parties which, in their most successful manifestations, explicitly brought together new Left and green advocates in Europe. American environmental groups, in contrast, emerged not out of the Left but parallel to it; they were concerned primarily with apolitical post-materialist concerns and shied away from green-red alliances (Bomberg and Schlosberg 2008).

Today we thus see a variety of comparatively comfortable alliances amongst different activists in the EU. These include close ties between the Green 10 and development NGOs such as Oxfam International (see Oxfam 2009) in addition to poverty and church groups such as CAFOD or the European Christian Environmental Network (ECEN 2008). Importantly, we also see institutionalized means for cementing these alliances. For instance, a resource-poor European Commission welcomes input from groups and favours those that are both trans-national and cross-cutting (Greenwood 2011). Regular European summits or G8 summits also serve as focal points where alliances of social development, environmental and other activists concerned with climate change can converge (for an example of such alliances see CAN Europe 2007). The more general point is that participation in general, and alliance-building in particular, plays out differently on either side of the Atlantic. American activists – partly in response to frustration with Congress and closed points of institutional access – have only recently built bridges with other social groups; in the EU such alliances are historically grounded and institutionally encouraged.

3.   MOBILIZATION

Activism involves not just framing issues and forging alliances but mobilizing key actors – across different constituencies, institutions and levels of government – who can take concerted political action to mitigate climate change. In structure/agency terms the template of inertia or inaction in federal or quasi-federal systems is such that an agency of some kind is needed that transcends institutions, interest groups and levels of government (Bomberg 2009). Adapting Klandermans' (1997) notion of mobilization as a process facilitating, motivating and galvanizing individuals to actively participate, this chapter examines how activists, allies and stakeholders are galvanized, motivated and facilitated in their efforts to shape climate change policy and overcome barriers to action.

A useful way to capture this mobilization dynamic is to combine insights from stakeholder perspectives of participation (Meadowcroft 2004) and policy network analysis. In his comparison of different participation traditions, Meadowcroft argues that effective participation means moving beyond mobilization of noble citizens or an engaged community and focusing instead on interaction among representatives of organized interests already enmeshed in environmental problems (2004, p. 162). Network analysis also focuses on stakeholders and the exchange of resources among them.[12] Networks are more than the alliances or advocacy coalitions described above. Whereas alliances and advocacy coalitions include like-minded actors sharing the same goals and (usually) means, a mobilization network includes a wider range of stakeholders, each with different aims, but all with resources with which to bargain. A mobilization network therefore involves core activists reaching beyond traditional alliance partners to other stakeholders with whom they may bargain even if they do not share the same core priorities or values. This section compares mobilization of EU and US activism across interests, institutions and levels of governance and investigates the extent to which networks are able to overcome institutional barriers hindering effective mobilization.

The United States

The potential for climate change mobilization is great. A prerequisite of mobilization is the ability to expand an issue to increasingly wider circles of participants (Klandermans 1997; Baumgartner and Jones 1993). The alliance-building described above suggests an undeniable expansion of activists and advocates. Other actors who may not yet have formed alliances may also be ripe for mobilization. The last decade has witnessed amongst US corporate groups a growing receptiveness to the seriousness of climate change and the need to reduce emissions. A typical example is Walmart's shift towards sustainability and carbon neutrality, not just because its CEO desires to reduce the company's carbon footprint, but because doing so makes financial sense (Schlosberg and Rinfret 2008).

Yet despite these prerequisites of alliance-building, there is less evidence of successful mobilization across various interests in the US. These different interests are not yet successfully integrated or working together. A potential key lead mobilizer might be the large professional environmental groups, but they have thus far failed to launch a 'coordinated, united, effective strategy to address climate change' (Bryner 2008, p. 327). Without such coordination there is no visible sign of the exchange of resources, bargaining, prolonged interaction or trust necessary to create and sustain a mobilization network. One particular stumbling block is the legacy of adversarialism that has made building of networks – especially those involving stakeholders with different priorities – enormously difficult. Environmental NGOs remain distrustful of corporate overtures, however well intentioned they may be (Meadowcroft 2004, p. 171; Bomberg and Schlosberg 2008, pp. 344–5).

Successful mobilization needs to transcend not just different interests but also different institutions. In the US institutional fragmentation and competition has constrained mobilization in potent ways (see O'Toole 2004, p. 35ff). Building support for climate change measures to be passed by the US Congress, in particular, has been stymied by an entrenched partisan divide. In stark contrast to the relatively bipartisan embrace of climate change in European countries, US Republicans and Democrats remain sharply divided on this issue (see Dunlap and McCright 2008; Krosnick 2010). Obama's proposals for a cap and trade scheme to limit greenhouse emissions and subsequent congressional bills have met with fierce opposition from Republicans reluctant to reach across the aisle on this issue.[13]

Finally, mobilization may take place at only one level of governance or may successfully span different levels of governance. One feature of climate change activism in the Bush era was the remarkable mobilization at the sub-national level. Activists were, in this case, able to exploit the multilevel nature of the American political system. While American federal efforts to reduce emissions remained stagnant at best, activism at the state level blossomed. The many and varied state initiatives are well documented (Rabe 2004, 2007; Knigge and Bausch 2006; Moser 2007). This mobilization has resulted in a plethora of state-level efforts to reduce greenhouse emissions through measures such as greenhouse gas registries and action plans as well as emission caps for power stations. Particularly striking in comparative terms is the extent to which these measures are a result of stakeholders bargaining and working together. In his comprehensive study Rabe (2004) suggests that, in contrast to federal-level stagnation, the state experience in climate change initiatives has generally been bipartisan and consensual.

Under the Bush administration these state networks were actively prevented from uploading policies and initiatives to the federal level. Particularly notable here is the Bush administration's quashing of California's attempt to regulate carbon emissions from automobiles (see Rabe 2007). These legal and institutional constraints from above encouraged Californian activists to look beyond the federal level to regional and even transatlantic cooperation.[14] Action by the Obama administration early in his term suggested there might be far more coordination across levels. During his campaign Obama had stressed that efforts to combat climate change 'demand integration among different agencies, cooperation between federal, state and local governments and partnership with the private sector' (Obama 2008). Once elected he explicitly encouraged state climate change action and ambition by, for instance, establishing a new Office of Energy and Climate Change Policy charged with facilitating climate change efforts across levels of government. Yet stalled efforts in the early years of his administration suggest such integration is difficult in a country with such fragmented and partisan institutional norms. Mobilization is not impossible in the US, but it will prove enormously difficult.

The European Union

Compared with the US, an examination of climate change activism in the EU reveals a more developed mobilization network – a confluence of shared interests, a willingness to negotiate and a fruitful exchange of resources among key stakeholders across interests, institutions and levels.[15] First, there is evidence of a network spanning interests or constituencies. The mobilization network in the EU includes representatives from key EU institutions and NGOs as well as scientific experts, think-tanks and industry groups. Some of the most interesting advice, initiatives and ideas on concerted action to address climate change have emerged from just this sort of collaboration among different actors (see IEEP 2009). Of particular importance – especially in contrast to the US – is the EU's climate change mobilization network's privileging of business actors that has encouraged engagement of groups who might otherwise block political action on climate change.

Industry federations remain closely involved in elaboration and practice of EU and national climate change policies (see Keleman and Vogel 2010). These firms are by no means viewed uncritically by European NGOs. They are subject to close scrutiny and often trenchant critique. But the underlying relationship between the two sectors allows for a level of dialogue missing in the US (see Wälti 2009). Nor is it defined by the same level of profound mistrust as often found in Washington, DC. EU norms on consensus facilitate that interaction and even institutionalize it to a certain extent (Trenz 2008). An example is the European Commission's stakeholder conferences that are designed to provide 'an opportunity for citizens, businesses, policy makers, NGOs, authorities, scientists and others to contribute to the debate on the future of global climate policy' (European Commission 2004).

Mobilization needs to span governmental institutions as well as interests. Climate change activism (as long as it is not too radical or disruptive) is welcomed by a number of EU institutions, several of which are populated by key actors who are keenly engaged with climate change policies. Of course, enthusiasm for climate change action varies across institutions and that affects trans-institutional mobilization (see Bomberg 2004, p. 78ff). But the general point is that the embrace of climate change has served EU institutions very well. It has provided a highly visible and salient issue demanding common action and task expansion (Zito 1999). More importantly, it is one of the few areas commanding broad and deep public support that in turn helps ensure a level of much sought after legitimacy for EU institutions. Finally, it has allowed the EU to play a widely recognized role as global leader (Oberthür and Kelly 2008; Vogler and Hannes 2007). Whether or not that leadership extends beyond the rhetorical, the benefits to EU legitimacy and global role are clear. Activists hoping to mobilize on climate change across institutions are to a certain extent pushing at an open door; each of the EU institutions has clear incentives for seizing this issue.[16]

Finally, let us examine how well this mobilization network brings together activists from different levels of governance. The EU's multilevel structure – which disperses power and authority across multiple levels – not only encourages but requires mobilization and interaction across levels of governance. However, the impact on activism is complex. Activists unsatisfied with climate change action or policies on the national level can and do enjoy an alternative venue for activism and mobilization. A key finding of the multilevel governance school (Hoohge and Marks 2001) as well as more specific research on EU environmental movements (Fairbrass and Jordan 2001; Poloni-Staudinger 2008) suggest that activists can bypass or at least supplement an unresponsive national level and mobilize action on the EU level. Alternatively, as discussed above, uploading environmental demands onto the EU level often results in a dilution of demands, a contraction of conflict as mobilization becomes more complex and players far more varied and numerous. EU climate change activists thus can and do build networks steering policy in a particular direction, but that direction is determined only after considerable compromise and negotiation.

In sum, both US and EU activists face institutional constraints to mobilization. But this preliminary examination suggests activists in the EU have been better able to overcome such constraints by building networks that span institutions, interests and levels.

4. CONCLUSION: IMPLICATIONS FOR GOVERNANCE

This chapter has sought to underscore the weight of institutional and multilevel dynamics shaping US and EU climate change activism, especially those institutional norms – adversarialism, fragmentation and partisanship – constraining mobilization and attempts by activists to overcome them. These comparative findings on activism – especially the institutional factors shaping it – have implications for broader issues of climate change governance. Climate change represents a mega-challenge similar to sustainability: addressing it requires not just discrete policies but a change in economic and political governance. Moreover, combating climate change will challenge existing democratic norms and patterns of participation and mobilization (Lafferty 2004b, p. 21). This final section therefore applies conclusions from this comparative study to broader insights from Lafferty's seminal work on sustainable development governance. More specifically, it identifies three areas of Lafferty's research that are crucial to understanding activism and wider issues of governance.

Focus on Actors: the 'Steerers'

Lafferty's work on sustainable development highlights not just processes and structures but also the actors 'steering' a community – the governments, institutions and civil society members able to surmount institutional barriers to action. This chapter has sought to highlight the challenge that activists face when addressing questions of how best to overcome the continuing institutional barriers to concerted, far-sighted action and the related need to work above, below and beyond the state. The discussion of mobilization and especially mobilization networks suggests that such transcendence is possible, but it is neither easy nor foreordained. Further research that focuses on 'steerers' and the prospects for their success, especially practical, policy-informed research of the type in which Lafferty excels,[17] is needed.

Focus on Substance: Complexity, Holism and Linkages

Lafferty's work makes clear the complex, intertwined nature of sustainable development governance that includes environmental, economic and democratic elements. Like sustainable development, addressing climate change requires major changes to the economy but also 'clearly implies a challenge to existing norms and procedures' (2004b, pp. 21–2). The recent and increasingly urgent discussions of a necessary move to a low-carbon economy (Antholis and Talbott 2010; Milne 2009; Stern 2010); a new emphasis on incorporating climate change into government and business strategies; and a call for greater business, citizen and stakeholder involvement (McKibben 2010), parallels very closely the dynamic outlined earlier by Lafferty's (and colleagues') sustainable development scholarship (see Lafferty but also Lundquist 2004; Meadowcroft 2004; Ruud 2004). The substantive challenges Lafferty outlines are directly relevant to activists: whatever their differences outlined here, activists on both sides of the Atlantic (and beyond) share certain imperatives. These include the need to address (and not just frame) linkages among environment, energy and security interests in addition to the necessity for urgent global action they entail.

Focus on Mechanisms: Policy Learning

Finally, Lafferty's work on governance pays particular attention to learning mechanisms available for 'influencing social change in preordained directions' (2004b, p. 5). He gives a particularly prominent role to the social learning needed to adapt existing governance forms, and the cooperation such tools may require. Like sustainable development, the uncertainty, complexity and ambitious demands of climate change not only invite, but arguably require, an open and learning-oriented system (Lafferty 2004b; O'Toole 2004; Bomberg 2004). That requirement is broad indeed but can include the notion of policy learning across constituencies, states and polities.

This chapter compared activism within the US and EU but also notes a relative lack of cooperation or learning between them. The shared challenges outlined above make the relative lack of concerted transatlantic activist cooperation striking. There are some limited signs of such collaboration.[18] The German Marshall Fund has sponsored a series of transatlantic dialogues for non-state stakeholders (Paterson 2009,

p. 146) and think-tanks such as the Institute of European Environmental Policy (IEEP) have joined with American environmental groups such as the Natural Resources Defense Council (NRDC) to launch a series of seminars and discussions (see IEEP 2009). But to ensure future concerted cooperation, the next stage in climate change activism needs to involve not just mobilization of stakeholders within the US or within the EU, but between them. 'Lafferty-like' analysis – rich, enlightened, theoretically informed and policy relevant – can help both understand and further that cooperation.

NOTES

1. I do not maintain that sustainable development and climate change are the same, only that addressing either requires a fundamental shift in economics, politics and society.
2. While I examine these three dimensions in a particular order, all are interconnected and their progression is probably circular rather than sequential. So, framing shapes alliance-building, but the inverse is also true. Mobilization may lead to new sets of frames and so on.
3. This section draws from a wider study on climate change activism, part of which appears in Bomberg 2012.
4. The research draws on simple content analysis of the websites and key documents of several major NGO groups, including: Climate Action Network (CAN) Europe; CAN US; Friends of the Earth (FoE) US, and FoE Europe as well as several umbrella organizations. For each group 10 key documents relating to that group's climate change goals, assessments and recommendations for policy-makers were manually coded to identify key themes, phrases and words. The results were then used to make inferences about the messages within the text. The purpose was to gain a general idea of key themes and priorities of the groups and how they compared. The author wishes to thank Madeleine Scarlett-Smith for her assistance in this analysis. A full breakdown of coding or list of websites is available from the author.
5. These challenges are very similar to those faced by advocates of sustainable development; see Meadowcroft (2004), p. 174.
6. See, for instance, US Climate Action Network's *Burning Beds* video http://www.usclimatenetwork.org/policy/road-to-copenhagen or Greenpeace's warning of '...more severe storms that wreak havoc on our homes and communities, and all kinds of changing cycles in the natural world' at http://www.greenpeace.org/usa/campaigns/global-warming-and-energy
7. Members of Green 10 are: Birdlife International (European Community Office); CEE Bankwatch Network; Climate Action Network Europe (CAN-E); European Environment Bureau (EEB); European Federation for Transport and Environment (T&E); EPHA Environment Network (EEN); Friends of the Earth Europe (FoEE); Greenpeace EC-Unit; International Friends of Nature (IFN); WWF European Policy Office (WWF-EPO).
8. A Pew Research Center (2009) survey indicates higher levels of concern among EU publics than amongst the US public. However, both publics hold remarkably similar views on whether the environment should be protected even if that protection entails economic costs. For other similarities see also Adelle and Withana (2008).
9. The Evangelical Environmental Network (EEN)'s creation care aim is to educate, inspire and mobilize Christians in their effort to care for God's creation (see Bomberg and Schlosberg 2008).

10. In a press statement on 15 June 2010, President Obama explained that his efforts to pass comprehensive energy and climate legislation were designed 'to protect our nation from the serious economic and strategic risks associated with our reliance on foreign oil, to create jobs, and to cut down on the carbon pollution that contributes to the destabilizing effects of climate change' (Obama 2010).

11. For instance, some environmental NGOs – such as NRDC – fully endorsed the American Clean Energy and Security Act that passed the American House of Representatives in June 2009, while others felt it did not go far enough. (An equivalent Senate bill floundered and was sidelined completely following Republican gains in the November 2010 congressional elections.)

12. Although usually used to explain policy outcomes (Marsh 1998), this chapter adapts the idea of networks to help explain mobilization rather than its outputs.

13. The House bill (Waxman Markey) passed in June 2009 broadly along party lines, even though eight Republicans supported it. The non-compromising stance of Republicans is evident in John Boehner's (then the House Republican leader) heated claim that proposed cap and trade 'will increase taxes on all Americans who drive a car, who have a job, who turn on a light switch, pure and simple' (quoted in *The Economist* 7 March 2009, p. 48). The bill languished in the Senate and was withdrawn by summer 2011.

14. Former California Governor Schwarzenegger was lobbied heavily to discuss with then UK Prime Minister Tony Blair the possible cooperation on climate change. Note also the subsequent development of a UK-California partnership designed to facilitate such cooperation (see Rabe 2007; Paterson 2009; Climate Group 2006).

15. Here I draw on earlier studies of sustainable development networks in Bomberg (2004, 2009).

16. Focusing on interests (economic gain, global leadership, legitimacy) and institutions offers a challenge or at least qualification to the notion that the EU's lead role on climate change is primarily the result of moral superiority or greener values (Krämer 2004; Schreuers and Tiberghien 2007).

17. The introduction to Lafferty's (2004c) edited volume on sustainable development governance makes clear his 'hope of building better communicative bridges between the efforts of strategic and academic research' (p. 8). Earlier he made the point more bluntly: 'The world has use of political scientists only in so far as political scientists can help us to make a better world' (Lafferty 1996, p. 186).

18. It should be noted, however, that earlier efforts at cooperation have not been successful. For instance, formalized attempts in 1999 to build bridges between NGO communities in Washington and Brussels through the TransAtlantic Environmental Dialogue (TAED) could not successfully establish itself and by 2001 the TAED had failed (see Steffenson and Peterson 2009).

REFERENCES

Adelle, C. and S. Withana (2008), 'EU and US public perceptions of environmental, climate change and energy issues', Institute for European Environmental Policy (IEEP), available at: http://www.ieep.eu/publications/pdfs/t_page/eu_us_public_perceptions.pdf.

Antholis, W. and S. Talbott (2010), *Fast Forward. Ethics and Politics in the Age of Global Warming*, Washington, DC: Brookings Institution Press.

Baumgartner, R. and B. Jones (1993), *Agendas and Instability in American Politics*, Chicago, IL: University of Chicago Press.

Bomberg, E. (2004), 'Adapting form to function? From economic to sustainable development governance in the European Union', in Lafferty, W. (ed.), *Governance for Sustainable Development. The Challenge of Adapting Form to*

Function, Cheltenham, UK and Northampton, MA, USA: Edward Elgar, pp. 61–94.

Bomberg, E. (2009), 'Governance for sustainable development: The US and EU compared', in M. Schreurs, H. Selin and S. Van Deveer, (eds), *Transatlantic Environmental and Energy Politics*, Farnham, UK and Burlington, VT: Ashgate Publishing, pp. 21–40.

Bomberg, E. (2012), 'Mind the (mobilization) gap: comparing climate activism in the United States and European Union', *Review of Policy Research*, **29** (3), 411–33.

Bomberg, E., J. Peterson, and A. Stubbs (eds) (2008), *The European Union: How Does It Work?*, 2nd edn, Oxford, UK: Oxford University Press.

Bomberg, E. and D. Schlosberg (2008), 'US environmentalism in comparative perspective', *Environmental Politics*, **17** (2), 337–48.

Bomberg, E. and B. Super (2009), 'The 2008 US presidential election: Obama and the environment', *Environmental Politics*, **18** (3), 424–30.

Bosso, C. (2005), *Environment Inc.: From Grassroots to Beltway*, Lawrence, KS: University of Kansas Press.

Brick, P. and M. Cawley (2008), 'Producing political climate change: the hidden life of US environmentalism', *Environmental Politics*, **17** (2), 200–18.

Bryner, G. (2008), 'Failure and opportunity: environmental groups in US climate change policy', *Environmental Politics*, **17** (2), 319–36.

CAFOD (Catholic Agency for Overseas Development) (2008), 'G8 falls short on climate change', *Independent Catholic News*, 8 August. accessed 4 August 2011 at www.indcatholicnews.com/news.php?viewStory=5821.

CAN Europe (Climate Action Network Europe) (2007), 'Joint NGO EU Climate and Energy Policy Statement', accessed 4 August 2011 at www.climnet.org/pubs/01NGOletter_Briefing_0307.pdf.

CAN Europe (2009), accessed 4 August 2011 at www.climnet.org/.

CAN Europe (2010), 'CAN-E Letter to members of the European Council March 2010', accessed 4 August 2011 at www.climnet.org/policywork/un-climate-negotiations/206-something-resembling-progress-in-bonn.html.

Climate Group (2006), 'Blair and Schwarzenegger join international business leaders for energy roundtable', available at www.theclimategroup.org/our-news/news/2007/6/26/blair-and-schwarzenegger-meet-business-leaders-to-accelerate-climate-change-solutions/

Daviter, F. (2007), 'Policy framing in the European Union', *Journal of European Public Policy*, **14** (4), 654–66.

DiChiro, G. (2008), 'Living environmentalisms: coalition politics, social reproduction and environmental justice', *Environmental Politics*, **17** (2), 276–98.

Doherty, B. and T. Doyle (2006), 'Beyond borders: transnational politics, social movements and modern environmentalisms', *Environmental Politics*, **15** (5), 697–712.

Dunlap, R. and A. McCright (2008), 'A widening gap: Republican and Democratic views on climate change', *Environment*, **50** (5), 26–35.

ECEN (European Christian Environmental Network) (2008), 'Climate justice now', accessed 4 August 2011 at www.ecen.org/content/climate-justice-now.

European Commission (2004), 'Post-2012 climate policy for the EU', stakeholder conference, 22 November 2004, accessed 4 August 2011 at http://ec.europa.eu/environment/climat/stakeholder_conf.htm.

Fairbrass, J. and A. Jordan (2001), 'Protecting biodiversity in the European Union: national barriers and European opportunities', *Journal of European Public Policy*, **8**, 499–518.

FoE (Friends of the Earth US) (2010), 'The path to an international climate agreement in Copenhagen', accessed 4 August 2011 at www.foe.org/inter national-work/international-climate-negotiations.

Friedman, T. (2008), *Hot, Flat and Crowded: Why We Need a Green Revolution – and How It Can Renew America*, New York: Farrar, Straus and Giroux.

Gallup Organization (2010), 'Americans' global warming concerns continue to drop', Frank Newport Report, available at www.gallup.com/poll/126560/ americans-global-warming-concerns-continue-drop.aspx.

Giddens, A. (2009), *The Politics of Climate Change*, Cambridge: Polity Press.

Greenwood, J. (2011), *Interest Representation in the European Union*, 3rd edn, Basingstoke: Palgrave Macmillan.

Hooghe, L. and G. Marks (2001), *Multi-level Governance and European Integration*, Langham, MD: Rowman and Littlefield.

Hulme, M. (2009), *Why We Disagree About Climate Change: Understanding Controversy, Inaction and Opportunity*, Cambridge: Cambridge University Press

IEEP (Institute of European Environmental Policy) (2009), 'IEEP and NRDC's transatlantic platform for action on the global environment (T-PAGE)', available at www.ieep.eu/projectminisites/t-page/index.php.

Jordan, A., D. Huitema, H. van Asselt, T. Rayner and F. Berkhout (eds) (2010), *Climate Change Policy in the European Union. Confronting the Dilemmas of Mitigation and Adaptation?* Cambridge: Cambridge University Press.

Keleman, D. and D. Vogel (2010), 'Trading places: the role of the United States and the European Union in international environmental politics', *Comparative Political Studies*, **43** (4), 427–56.

Klandermans, B. (1997), *The Social Psychology of Protest*, Oxford: Blackwell.

Knigge, M. and C. Bausch (2006), 'Climate change policies at the US subnational level – evidence and implications', ecologic discussion chapter, Berlin, available at www.ecologic.de.

Kolbert, E. (2009), 'The political scene: greening the ghetto', *The New Yorker*, 12 January, available at www.newyorker.com/reporting/2009/01/12/090112fa_ fact_kolbert.

Krämer, L. (2004), 'The roots of divergence: a European perspective', in N. Vig and M. Faure (eds), *Green Giants? Environmental Policies of the United States and the European Union*, Cambridge, MA and London: MIT Press, pp. 53–72.

Krosnick, J. (2010), 'The climate majority', *The New York Times*, 8 June.

Lafferty, W. (1996), 'The politics of sustainable development: global norms for national implementation', *Environmental Politics*, **5** (2), 185–208.

Lafferty, W. (2004a), 'From environmental protection to sustainable development: The challenge of decoupling through sectoral integration', in W. Lafferty (ed.), *Governance for Sustainable Development. The Challenge of Adapting Form to Function*. Cheltenham, UK and Northampton, MA, USA: Edward Elgar, pp. 191–220.

Lafferty, W. (2004b), 'Introduction', in W. Lafferty (ed.) *Governance for Sustainable Development. The Challenge of Adapting Form to Function*, Cheltenham, UK and Northampton, MA, USA: Edward Elgar, pp. 1–31.

Lafferty, W. (ed.) (2004c), *Governance for Sustainable Development. The Challenge of Adapting Form to Function*, Cheltenham, UK and Northampton, MA, USA: Edward Elgar.

Lundquist, L. (2004), 'Management by objectives and results: a comparison of Dutch, Swedish and EU strategies for realizing sustainable development', in W. Lafferty (ed.), *Governance for Sustainable Development. The Challenge of Adapting Form to Function*, Cheltenham, UK and Northampton, MA, USA: Edward Elgar, pp. 95–127.

Marsh, D. (ed.) (1998), *Comparing Policy Networks*, Buckingham: Open University Press.

McKibben, B. (2010), *Earth. Making a Life on a Tough New Planet*, New York: Times Books.

McKinsey Global Institute (2008), 'The carbon productivity challenge: curbing climate change and sustaining economic growth', available at www.mckinsey.com/mgi/publications/Carbon_Productivity/index.asp.

Meadowcroft, J. (2004), 'Participation and sustainable development: modes of citizen, community and organisational involvement', in W. Lafferty (ed.), *Governance for Sustainable Development. The Challenge of Adapting Form to Function*, Cheltenham, UK and Northampton, MA, USA: Edward Elgar, pp. 162–90.

Meyer, J. (2008), 'Populism, paternalism and the state of environmentalism in the US', *Environmental Politics*, **17** (2), 200–18.

Miller, C. (2000), 'The dynamics of framing environmental values and policy: four models of societal processes', *Environmental Values*, **9**, 211–33.

Milne, R. (2009), 'How to grow in a low-carbon future', *The Financial Times*, 21 April, p. 14.

Moser, S. (2007), 'In the long shadows of inaction: the quiet building of a climate protection movement in the United States', *Global Environmental Politics*, **7** (2), 124–44.

NAE (National Association of Evangelicals) (2006), 'Climate change. An evangelical call for action', available at www.christiansandclimate.org/statement.

Nivola, P. and C.O. Jones (2008), '"Change" or plus ça change . . .? Pondering presidential politics and policy after Bush', *Issues in Governance Studies*, paper 20, available at www.brookings.edu/papers/2008/09_change_nivola_jones.aspx.

Obama, B. (2008), 'Remarks of President-Elect Barack Obama: announcement of Energy and Environment Team', 15 December. accessed 4 August 2011 at http://change.gov/newsroom/entry/the_energy_and_environment_team/.

Obama, B. (2010), Press statement 'Energy and environment. A new foundation', available at www.whitehouse.gov/issues/energy-and-environment.

Oberthür, S. and C. Kelly (2008), 'EU leadership in international climate policy: achievements and challenge', *The International Spectator*, **43** (3), 35–50, available at www.iai.it/pdf/articles/oberthur_roche-kelly.pdf.

O'Toole, L. (2004), 'Implementation theory and the challenge of sustainable development: the transformative role of learning', in W. Lafferty (ed.), *Governance for Sustainable Development. The Challenge of Adapting Form to Function*, Cheltenham, UK and Northampton, MA, USA: Edward Elgar, pp. 32–60.

Oxfam International (2009), 'Climate change campaign', available at www.oxfam.org/en/climatechange.

Paterson, M. (2009), 'Post-hegeomonic climate change?', *British Journal of Politics and International Relations*, **11** (1), 140–58.

Peterson, J. and E. Bomberg (1999), *Decision-making in the European Union*, London: Palgrave.

Peterson, J. and M. Shackleton (2006), *The Institutions of the European Union*, 2nd edn, Oxford: Oxford University Press.

Pew Research Center (2009), 'Global warming seen as a major problem around the world', *Pew Global Attitudes Survey*, 2 December, available at http://pewresearch.org/pubs/1427/global-warming-major-problem-around-world-americans-less-concerned.

Pierson, C. (1996), 'The path to European integration: a historical institutionalist analysis', *Comparative Political Studies*, **29** (2), 123–63.

Princen, S. (2007), 'Agenda-setting in the European Union: a theoretical exploration and agenda for research', *Journal of European Public Policy*, **14** (1), 21–38.

Poloni-Staudinger, L. (2008), 'The domestic opportunity structure and supranational activity', *European Union Politics*, **9** (4), 531–58.

Pope, C. (2009), 'Start your engines', *Huffington Post*, 31 March, available at www.huffingtonpost.com/carl-pope/start-your-engines_b_181300.html.

Rabe, B. (2004), *Statehouse and Greenhouse. The Merging Politics of American Climate Change Policy*, Washington, DC: Brookings Institution Press.

Rabe, B. (2007), 'Environmental policy and the Bush era: the collision between the administrative presidency and state experimentation', *Publius: The Journal of Federalism*, **37**, 413–31.

Roberts, D. (2006), 'Framing climate change', available at http://gristmill.grist.org/story/2006/5/20/212741/461.

Ruud, A. (2004), 'Partners for progress? The role of business in transcending business as usual', in W. Lafferty (ed.), *Governance for Sustainable Development. The Challenge of Adapting Form to Function*, Cheltenham, UK and Northampton, MA, USA: Edward Elgar, pp. 221–45.

Sabatier, P. (1988), 'An advocacy coalition framework of policy change and the role of policy-oriented learning therein', *Policy Sciences*, **21** (2), 129–68.

Scharpf, F. (1998), 'The joint-decision trap: lesson from German federalism and European integration', *Public Administration*, **66** (3), 239–78.

Schlosberg, D. and E. Bomberg (2008), 'Perspectives on American environmentalism', *Environmental Politics*, **17** (2), 187–200.

Schlosberg, D. and S. Rinfret (2008), 'Ecological modernization – American style', *Environmental Politics*, **17** (2), 254–75.

Schreuers, M. and Y. Tiberghien (2007), 'Multi-level reinforcement: explaining European Union leadership in climate change mitigation', *Global Environmental Politics*, **7** (4), 19–46.

Shellenberger, M. and T. Nordhaus (2004), 'The death of environmentalism: global warming politics in a post-environmental world', available at www.grist.org/news/maindish/2005/01/13/doe-reprint/index.html.

Steffenson, B. and J. Peterson (2009), 'Transatlantic institutions: can partnership be engineered?', *British Journal of Politics and International Relations*, **11** (1), 25–45.

Stern, N. (2009), *A Blueprint for a Safer Planet*, London: The Bodley Head.

Stern, N. (2010), 'Climate: what you need to know', *The New York Review of Books*, 24 June.

Trenz, H.J. (2008), European civil society between participation, representation and discourse', in H.J. Trenz and U. Liebert (eds), *Reconstituting Democracy from Below*, Oslo: RECON, pp. 53–67.

USCAN (US Climate Action Network) (2010a), 'Achievements' ('About us' home page), available at www.usclimatenetwork.org/about-us/achievements-1.

USCAN (2010b), 'Dirty air act vote tests Senate's direction on climate, clean energy', available at www.usclimatenetwork.org/policy/dirty-air-act amendment.

Vogler, J. (2009), 'Climate change and EU foreign policy: the negotiation of burden sharing', *International Politics*, **46** (3), 469–90.

Vogler, J. and S. Hannes (2007), 'The European Union in global environmental governance: leadership in the making?', *International Environmental Agreements*, **7**, 389–413.

Wälti, S. (2009), 'Intergovernmental management of environmental policy in the United States and the EU', in M. Schreurs, H. Selin and S. Van Deever (eds), *Transatlantic Environment and Energy Politics. Comparative and International Perspectives*, Farnham: Ashgate, pp. 41–54.

Wardekker, A., A. Petersen and J. van der Sluijs (2009), 'Ethics and public perception of climate change: exploring the Christian voices in the US public debate', *Global Environmental Change*, **19** (4), 512–21.

Weaver, R.K. and A. Rockman (eds) (1993), *Do Institutions Matter? Government Capabilities in the United States and Abroad*, Washington, DC: Brookings Institution Press.

Zito, A. (1999), 'Task expansion: a theoretical overview', *Environmental and Planning C: Government and Policy*, **17** (1), 19–36.

8. Governance and participation *for* sustainable development in Ireland: 'Not so different after all?'

Gerard Mullally

The differentness of sustainable development from other modes of national development, for example market liberalism, social-democratic liberalism and ecological modernization requires 'political initiatives to ameliorate the negative impacts on life-support systems of over- and under-development within an ethical context of global and intergenerational equity' (Lafferty 2004, p. 17). Lafferty identifies five main characteristics of sustainable development: it is an exogenous outside-in programme; it is a trans-border, supra-national programme; it is a transformative programme; it is a holistic, interdependent and contingent programme; and, it is a normative long-term programme (Lafferty 2004, pp. 17–22). Accepting these key characteristics as the basis of any further discussion regarding governance for sustainable development, my specific point of departure is a question posed by Lafferty in the conclusion to *Governance for Sustainable Development*:

> how the sustainable development programme – with its very clear logic of goal formation, strategic planning and multi-level, multi-sector implementation – can develop learning mechanisms that pragmatically address the challenge of converting 'ideas' to 'outcomes' in, and particularly across, institutionalized arenas. (2004, p. 341)

A number of recent evaluations of sustainable development in Ireland (OECD 2010; NESC 2010), while acknowledging some progress, have remarked on the loss of momentum in the implementation of the National Strategy for Sustainable Development; the lack of integration of environmental considerations into sectoral policies and practices (for example land-use planning, agriculture and transport); and, the need to enhance implementation capacity at the local level (OECD 2010, p. 15). Furthermore, there is a strong suggestion that the strategy has 'influenced policy only to a certain extent' (NESC 2010, p. 140). The Organisation for Economic Co-operation and Development (OECD), National Economic and Social Council (NESC) and the recent government consultation paper on Rio+20 (DOECLG 2011), all highlight the need to revitalize sustainable development in Ireland. NESC, in particular, emphasizes the need for 'more sustained participation in the process' and the need for reflexivity within the domestic policy system through 'indicators, monitoring and refashioning policy in light of learning obtained' (NESC 2010, pp. 140–1). In keeping with the theme of moving beyond the impasse, this chapter examines the experience of governance for sustainable development in light of the recent crises affecting Irish society.

Until recently a central part of the narrative of Irish development is that of a shift which successfully negotiated the transition from 'a crisis ridden economy' (Van Dyk 2009, p. 81) to a European success story, owing its genesis in part to: the importance of foreign direct investment; favourable corporation tax rates; access to European markets (OECD 2010); net transfers from Europe predominantly in the form of structural funds; and to the central role of social partnership in generating a consensus on the direction of national development (Kirby 2010). The global financial crisis has been compounded in Ireland by a series of interlocking crises that precipitated the demise of the Celtic Tiger economy in late 2008. The NESC has identified five dimensions of the Irish crisis making it *different* from crisis found elsewhere, that is: a banking crisis; a fiscal crisis; an economic crisis of competitiveness and job losses; a social crisis of unemployment; and a reputational crisis (NESC 2009, p. 3).

Ireland is at the end of an 'unfulfilled decade' (NESC 2010, p. 175). The narrative of success has become one of failure. Discourses of retrenchment and reform have come to the fore as a response, and sustainability has become a prefix for the management of public finances and the debt crisis. The following framing is a case in point:

> The adjustment process must be sustained until Ireland comes through the crisis, must yield a sustainable public finance approach and should, *as far as possible*, put Ireland on a path that is sustainable – economically, socially and environmentally. (NESC 2009, p. 24 [my italics])

In light of these trends a number of questions regarding governance for sustainable development come into focus: what is the nature of the governance impasse in Ireland? What configuration of institutional and ideational factors impedes change towards sustainable development? Are impediments to sustainable development temporary or are there more serious structural barriers to further innovation? Is the space for meaningful reform expanding or contracting? And what, if any, are the general lessons for governance for sustainable development stemming from the Irish case?

Given the fact that my own collaboration with William Lafferty began with research on the Irish dimensions of Local Agenda 21 in a European context, it is perhaps appropriate that my contribution to *Governance, Democracy and Sustainable Development* revisits this theme in engaging with these questions.

Drawing on research on the role of public participation in promoting local sustainable development in Ireland (Mullally et al. 2009),[1] this chapter first sketches the contours of the debate on sustainability governance, focusing in particular on the idea that governance for sustainable development requires both horizontal and vertical integration and that it involves strategic learning processes and, as well, that such participation requires an ongoing process of capacity-building. The chapter then turns to a core aspect of the debate on governance and sustainable development, that is, the procedural emphasis on the participation of civil society. The specific focus is on deliberative democracy in stakeholder governance for sustainable development and the disjuncture between legitimacy and effectiveness identified at a global level (Bäckstrand 2006a, 2006b). In addition to developing adequate institutional pre-conditions for achieving desired outcomes, governance processes must also address issues of deliberative quality (Petschow et al. 2005). From more general theoretical and contextual considerations we then move on to consider the specific adaptation of Irish governance for sustainable development. In this section we examine the empirical and contextual conditions for the interpretation and implementation of sustainable development and the emerging pattern of governance. Here we explore the idea that a unique combination of an exogenous stimulus, that is, sustainable development, and indigenous path dependence, that is, social partnership, have both contributed to the impasse that is a central theme of this volume. The theoretical, contextual and empirical strands are then drawn together in a case study of *local* governance for sustainable development to demonstrate how the combination of the intrinsic challenges of stakeholder governance (bridging the gap between inputs and outputs), with the exigencies of contextual institutional conditions (the limiting horizon of the existing structure of governance), are compounded by crises and profound social change. Against this background we then assess the specific nature of the governance impasse and the potential lessons of the Irish experience.

1. GOVERNANCE *FOR* SUSTAINABLE DEVELOPMENT

In its broadest sense governance 'refers to the intersection of power, politics and institutions' (Leach et al. 2010, p. 65). A governance perspective moves beyond a singular focus on institutional actors to encompass 'the complex relationships, networks and processes by which policy is framed and acted upon' (Connaughton et al. 2008, p. 146).

State-centric approaches stress the importance of institutional designs that increase both the self-regulating capacity of governance networks *and* the coordination capacity of the state (Sørensen and Torfing 2008, p. 174). We are not simply looking at the decoupling of power and authority of the state, but we are also looking at active and deliberate attempts at recoupling in newer societal formations and through new institutional designs. This does not imply the abandonment of regulatory power; indeed, it remains central to policy-making (Jänicke 2006, p. 6), but it is now one among a mix of policy instruments and steering mechanisms employed in governing sustainable development (Lafferty 2004; Voß et al. 2007).

The specific model for sustainable development considered here is the Rio model of governance that emerged from the Earth Summit in 1992 (Jänicke 2006, p. 1). This is a knowledge-based model of steering rather than one based solely on power and legal obligation, essentially a voluntary process of policy innovation, lesson-drawing and policy diffusion (Jänicke 2006, p. 4). In essence it is a multi-actor, multi-sector, multilevel system of governance (Jänicke 2006). Partnerships have become an intrinsic part of governance for sustainable development 'since political power has become dispersed among a variety of public and private actors' (Glasbergen 2011, p. 9). Glasbergen questions whether partnerships represent a fundamental shift in the pattern of governance in liberal-democratic societies and whether they are able to institutionalize a new sense of collective responsibility for sustainable development (Glasbergen 2011, p. 9). My focus is far more context specific, but may have more general implications.

Governance as an Integrative Process

Lafferty (2004) conceives of governance for sustainable development as referring to vertical environmental policy integration, which is found across levels of governance, and horizontal environmental policy integration, which is located across sectors. In a similar vein, we might distinguish between *horizontal* and *vertical governance* where the horizontal level includes 'the relevant actors in decision-making processes within a defined geographical or functional segment' (for example community, region, nation), and the vertical level that describes the links between the segments, such as the institutional relationships between the local, regional and state levels (Renn 2008, p. 9). The governance of *local* sustainable development, as such, does not exist in a vacuum and must take account of the influence of multiple levels of governance. A key problem is that integration, in the context of sustainable development, requires new and different forms of governing which have to contend with a range of interests embedded within existing structures of governance (Atkinson and Klausen 2011, p. 233).

Governance as a Strategic Learning Process

Sustainable development problems often involve the complex interaction between very different elements from the domains of society, technology and nature (Voß et al. 2007, p. 197). The structuring of these interactions is important because feedback loops and the emergent dynamics of systems can make interventions risky (ibid.). Sustainability as an orientation for development delivers ambiguous goals (Voß and Kemp 2006, p. 15) and consequently governance has to contend with *ambivalence* and *conflict* (Voß et al. 2007, p. 194). Institutional designs for the governance of sustainable development cannot afford to be self-referential. They must also be able 'to generate sufficient knowledge and power through learning, if they are to survive in complex and ever more contingent circumstances' (Crozier 2007, p. 12).

The growing complexity and intensified uncertainty of contemporary society increases the demand for knowledge in decision-making. In this context there is also a growing demand from society for inclusion in decision-making (Crozier 2007, p. 4). The consequence is a shift from the relatively closed networks of experts and decision-makers to more open, multilateral knowledge networks as inputs to policy-making and deliberation (ibid.). Knowledge here is concerned with 'processes of sense making, improving the capacity for action and decision-making' and is always related 'to social processes of communicative interpretation' (Atkinson and Klausen 2011, p. 234). Governance for sustainable development is concerned not *only* with the design and implementation of government policy, but *also* with collective processes of monitoring, reflection, debate and decision that establish the orientation for policy (Meadowcroft et al. 2005, p. 5). Governance for sustainable development is interactive, but 'not just in the instrumental sense that societal inputs can facilitate progress towards known objectives, but also in the deeper sense that the objectives themselves must be collectively defined, refined and re-defined' (Meadowcroft and Bregha 2009, p. 4).

Governance as a Capacity-Building Process

When referring to strategies for sustainable development, Jänicke argues that 'ambitious strategies need adequate capacities' wherein capacity can be defined by the limits of possible action within a given context (Jänicke 2006, p. 7). Adequate capacities refer to the requirement for the state to develop its 'integrative capacity' as well as 'capacity for strategic action' in addition to its 'participative capacity' (Jänicke 1997, cited in Meadowcroft 2004, p. 164). Capacities to influence societal change in the direction of sustainable development are distributed between different levels of governance (EU, national, local) as well as between different functional domains and the actors within these domains (Voß and Kemp 2006, p. 16). In an extensive study of Local Agenda 21 in Europe, Evans et al. (2006) highlight the importance of capacity-building measures at the local level. They stress the importance of the relationship between the institutional capacity of local governments and the broader social capacity of their communities.

The OECD defines social capital as 'networks together with shared norms, values and understandings that facilitate cooperation within and between groups' (Keeley 2007, p. 103). Social capital is essential to sustainable development because 'the reconciliation of the three imperatives [economic, environmental and social] can only occur through collective action, and collective action will not occur unless there is an adequate stock of social capital' (Dale and Onyx 2005, p. 7). Key elements of institutional design within local governance are crucial for the creation and mobilization of social capital (Evans et al. 2006, p. 854). These elements are: the relationship between local government and the voluntary sector; the presence of opportunities for citizen participation; responsiveness of decision-making to policy inputs and preferences; and the capacity to listen to and channel demands (Evans et al. 2006, pp. 855–6). Attention to these elements can provide a bridge between local governments and local communities (Newman and Dale 2007, p. 82). However, the need to deliver on policy goals means 'the process of bridging has to be more selective, focused and instrumental' (Rydin and Holman 2004, p. 124). 'Bracing social capital' is primarily concerned with 'strengthening links across and between scales and sectors, but only operates within a limited set of actors[. It] provides a kind of social scaffolding' (Evans et al. 2006, p. 853) for strengthening local capacities for sustainable development. Its function is developing the capacity 'to leverage resources, ideas and information from formal institutions' beyond the local level (Lehtonen 2004, p. 205).

Although they are useful, distinctions between different types of social capital are less central than their implications for capacity-building. The ability to turn social capital into action for sustainable development denotes 'the capacity of persons to transform existing states of affairs, the capacity to plan and initiate action, and the ability to respond to events outside of one's immediate sphere of influence to produce a desired effect' (Newman and Dale 2007, pp. 81–2). This is closely aligned with the idea of social power, that is, 'the ability to influence the outcome of societal processes relevant for the solution of public issues' (Glasbergen 2011, p. 9). However, strengthening societal capacity is not just a matter of building new participative institutions, that is, input conditions, it is also about ensuring that such institutions are designed to maximize the prospects for effectively steering change towards sustainable development, meaning output conditions. The prospects for embedding designs that institutionalize a sense of collective responsibility for sustainable development are contingent on existing 'institutional conditions' (Van Dyk 2009, p. 80). Institutional conditions can act as filters, resulting in place, context and actor-related combinations of knowledge, which are then strategically mobilized in selecting the knowledge that is relevant to choosing a course of action to shape a specific outcome (Atkinson and Klausen 2011, p. 233).

2. PARTICIPATION AND SUSTAINABLE DEVELOPMENT

The 1992 Earth Summit in Rio heralded the participative turn in the governance of sustainable development, as the emphasis on the participation and involvement of major groups from civil society emerged as a cornerstone of the Rio Accords and Agenda 21 (Bäckstrand 2006a, p. 470). The emphasis on participation was reiterated at the World Summit on Sustainable Development (WSSD) held in Johannesburg in 2002. The Johannesburg Declaration on Sustainable Development recognizes that 'sustainable development requires a long-term perspective and broad-based participation in decision-making and implementation at all levels'. It goes on to state that 'as social partners, we will continue to work for stable partnerships, with all major groups, respecting the independent, important roles of each of them' (United Nations 2002, section 26).

Participation and Deliberation

In spite of a wide range of theoretical models and empirical modes of participation that are available, there has been a tendency to converge, albeit for different reasons, around *deliberative* approaches to participation (Renn 2008). In the context of the present discussion, 'one of the main messages of Agenda 21 was that the building up of deliberative capabilities of societies forms an indisputable part of their sustainable development' (Glasbergen 2007, p 3).

Participatory processes, if they are to contribute effectively to sustainable development, must encourage 'adequate representation of implicated interests and openness to public scrutiny; deliberative engagement among the implicated parties; the application and integration of different types of knowledge to decision-making; and the promotion of societal learning' (Meadowcroft 2004, p. 165). Meadowcroft is talking here about mechanisms for *enhanced* participation in public decision-making and implementation – above and beyond well-established modes of electoral representation, public debate, political organization, pluralist bargaining or corporatist interaction. He is talking about deliberation.

Typically we can identify three main types of participation, namely citizen participation, community-centred participation and participation by stakeholder organizations. *Citizens* as individuals can participate in public life through a variety of mechanisms; for example, joining a political party, becoming active in a social movement or associational life in civil society or by contributing to public debate. In the context of the discussion here, mechanisms such as public consultation, public enquiries, referenda and citizen juries are potential mechanisms for structuring *citizen participation* (Meadowcroft 2004).

Community-centred approaches emphasize local communities as the locus of participation, where groups are brought more actively into problem-solving processes. While it can be directed through mechanisms such as consultation and enquiries, it is generally more targeted towards consultation with organizations and groups in the community and voluntary sector that make up local civil society. In the context of sustainable development this often means directly targeting typically excluded groups, for example women, youth and non-nationals.

Stakeholder approaches allow for established groups, organized interests and peak organizations to engage in focused interactions in a particular policy domain through the participation of their representatives. These approaches are typically focused on the interaction of a limited set of actors through partnerships: 'institutional designs for collaboration [that] offer flexibility and stakeholder engagement, but are loosely coupled to representative democratic systems' (Skelcher et al. 2005, p. 573). In practice many processes involve compound participation combining some or all of the above (Meadowcroft 2004, p. 180).

Deliberation, Legitimacy and Effectiveness

Deliberation in theoretical terms refers to an account of democratic politics 'in which reasoning and exchange of viewpoints provide a way of understanding the values of democracy and the sources of political legitimacy' (Weale 2007, p. 79). While the concept of sustainable development indicates the kinds of issues that should be of concern, it is subject to democratic *legitimacy* since 'its practical bearing cannot be established independent of the concrete life circumstances of a particular society and the needs, interests, values and aspirations of its members' (Meadowcroft 2007b, p. 161). A key challenge for sustainable development is that the sites of governance are multiple and power is diffused among many actors (Bäckstrand 2006b, p. 295). In order to be effective, 'various social sectors, strata and organizations must be involved because the knowledge required to establish pathways to sustainability is dispersed throughout society' (Meadowcroft 2007a, p. 161). As a result of the encompassing nature of sustainable development, enhanced participation 'can promote the integration of knowledge and the adaptation of governance to diverse cross cutting contexts relevant to its achievement' (Meadowcroft 2007a, p. 166). Furthermore, it can help 'to promote adaptive management and knowledge acquisition by societal partners' (Meadowcroft 2007a, p. 166).

In theory deliberation also evokes a sense of 'agency, intention and change' where actors reflect not only on environment and development problems, but also upon 'the approaches, structures and systems that reproduce them' (Hendriks and Grin 2007, p. 335). This suggests that participation is not simply a question of legitimacy; there is also some expectation of *effectiveness*. Bäckstrand has noted a qualitative shift in the understanding of the relationship between participation and sustainable development in the Johannesburg debate since 'more participation was not enough; it had to be structured to encourage deliberation and collaboration of disparate actors with a stake in the implementation of Agenda 21' (2006a, p. 470).

Bäckstrand distinguishes between input and output legitimacy as standards for evaluation of deliberative institutional forms (2006a, 2006b) 'legitimacy stems from a procedural logic (that rules are predictable and determined by legitimate actors) and a consequential logic (that rules and institutions lead to collective problem solving)' (2006b, p. 294). Input legitimacy concerns procedural demands such as: representation from different stakeholder groups; forums for deliberation; and issues around transparency, access and accountability (Bäckstrand 2006a, p. 477). The issue of deliberative quality is important here since it is not simply an issue of *gaining access to decision-making*, but also of the ability to *influence* norms and values as well as to shape discourse (Petschow et al. 2005, p. 11). Output legitimacy concerns the effectiveness of new modes of governance in relation to their problem-solving and implementation capacity (ibid., pp. 478–9). Bäckstrand makes a very important distinction between 'outcome effectiveness', or the ability to solve problems, and 'institutional effectiveness', the extent to which adequate institutional frameworks for measuring, monitoring and review are in place as a precondition of achieving desired sustainable development outcomes (Bäckstrand 2006a, p. 477). Evaluation of the type advocated by Bäckstrand is not about absolutes or tight classification, rather it generates insights into degrees and continuums of legitimacy and is very much in keeping with recent evaluative approaches elucidated by Renn (2008) and Fung (2006).

3.   ADAPTING IRISH GOVERNANCE *FOR* SUSTAINABLE DEVELOPMENT?

The nature of governance and the pathways to sustainable development are intertwined: 'which pathways are introduced and which are not are in large part a question of governance: a politics of narratives and pathways shaped by power relations and institutions' (Leach et al. 2010, p. 65). The 'past shapes the present, and thus the deliberate process of [path] creation, may be constrained such that existing institutional arrangements are reproduced in a new context', along with their limitations and weaknesses (Skelcher et al. 2005, p. 576).

The cycle of innovation for sustainable development in Ireland tends to peak in preparation for global sustainable development summits and in response to elaborations of EU policy (Mullally et al. 2009). Equally, the emergence of institutional arrangements of governance for sustainable development is broadly contiguous with periods of economic recovery and boom in the 1990s and in the early part of the twenty-first century. During this period a distinctive model for the governance of national development – Irish Social Partnership – has provided the template for most forms of collaborative or participative institutions, including institutions for sustainable development. Therefore, it is worthwhile exploring how the interplay of exogenous and endogenous drivers has enabled and constrained pathways to a *different* model of development, involving a *different* model of participation.

The *Differentness* of Sustainable Development in Ireland

Most Irish analysts of sustainable development vacillate on a continuum between business as usual and ecological modernization when evaluating the Irish experience, usually converging around the idea that it is a weak form of ecological modernization. *Sustainable Development: A Strategy for Ireland* (DOE 1997), although currently under revision, remains the pre-eminent statement of sustainable development policies in Ireland. The impetus for developing the National Sustainable Development Strategy (NSDS) was to respond to the United Nations Conference on Environment and Development (UNCED) process and obligations under Agenda 21. The primary focus of the strategy was on the integration of the environment into various policy sectors (agriculture, forestry, marine resources, energy, transport, tourism and trade) while providing a rebalancing of the previous situation where environmental concerns were generally not well integrated into national policy. It also provided the foundation for purpose-built and adapted stakeholder institutions for sustainable development at national and local levels.

An interim review of the strategy outlined the policy objectives of sustainable development as: eco-efficiency, meaning a more efficient production with less environmental impact and a progressive decoupling of economic activity and environmental degradation; quality of life, meaning an increased environmental quality for present and future generations coupled with greater opportunities for participation in decision-making and in community life more generally; and social policy, involving reducing consistent poverty, building an inclusive society, developing social capital and eliminating long-term unemployment (DOELG 2002, pp. 92–4). The review also detailed the emerging mix of policy instruments, with 'voluntary and participative instruments operating in conjunction with instruments to improve existing regulatory measures' (DOELG 2002, pp. 97–8).

The revised National Sustainable Development Strategy (rNSDS), originally due for publication in 2007, is currently in preparation and will form part of Ireland's contribution to the Rio+20 Summit in 2012. Referencing the *Renewed EU Strategy for Sustainable Development*, the following priorities are identified: the need to decouple natural resource use and economic growth; economic resilience and fiscal sustainability; climate change and energy; sustainable transport; social inclusion; food security; public health and global poverty (DOECLG 2011, p. 6).

The OECD confirms that sustainable development has made some headway up to the period of the current crisis, between 2000 and the second half of 2008:

> Ireland made progress in decoupling environmental pressures from economic trends, especially for trans-boundary air pollutants; CO_2 emissions increased, but at a lower rate than GDP (relative decoupling). Energy intensity was considerably reduced and is now the lowest in the OECD. Material intensity also steadily decreased, reaching the OECD average. These changes were closely linked with restructuring the economy towards sectors with low energy intensity and high added value. (OECD 2010, p. 15).

The report goes on to state that 'governance for sustainable development was consolidated', noting that Comhar Sustainable Development Council (SDC) has served as a multi-stakeholder forum providing independent advice to government and that mechanisms such as Strategic Environmental Assessment (SEA) and regulatory impact assessment have been used to integrate environmental decision-making at both macro and micro levels (OECD 2010, p. 10). There are also several shortcomings in relation to governance for sustainable development that have been picked up and elaborated by NESC (2010, p. 140).

The *integrative dimension of governance for sustainable development* is regarded as being particularly problematic in terms of vertical integration 'with no intensive coordination between the national and sub-national [sustainable development] processes' (NESC 2010, p. 140). Governance *as a strategic learning process* has been enhanced by the creation of key stakeholder institutions at the national level, through Comhar SDC (originally established in 1999, as the National Sustainable Development Partnership) and its participation in the EEAC (European Environment and Sustainable Development Advisory Councils) and at the local level, through the embedding of Local Agenda 21 in local government reform (DOECLG 2010, p. 6). Since its inception, Comhar SDC has been instrumental in providing support for local sustainable development in the form of networking resources, case studies of best practices and a forum for stakeholder deliberation at the national level. It has been, however, characterized as a marginal entity in the architecture of governance nationally, 'even if its contribution has been laudable' (Flynn 2007, p. 178). A noted weakness of the Irish approach is the lack of indicators for the implementation of the NSDS, which has hampered strategic learning and resulted in a lack of progress (NESC 2010, pp. 140–1). The conclusion is that this has contributed to a loss of momentum and a limited impact on policy-making (ibid.). There is perhaps a more fundamental problem, namely 'the Irish interpretation of sustainable development remains largely focused on economic factors and discourse as opposed to guidance from the NSDS' (Connaughton et al. 2008. p. 165).

While the integrative and strategic capacities of governance are important conditioning factors for moving beyond the impasse, the *participative capacities* of governance are also a key factor in what is supposed to be different about sustainable development. Two distinct categories of collective actors are relevant to consideration of civil society participation: the community and voluntary sector as well as the environmental sector. In the early to mid-1990s, the community and voluntary sector gained entry to, and consolidated a position in, national social partnership (see below). This sector is a cluster of representative groups loosely bound together by a common interest in social inclusion, but characterized by an expansive and diversified composition making strategic action difficult to coordinate (Adshead and Tonge 2009, p. 135). The historically weak participation of environmental NGOs in decision-making is a potential impediment to the way in which environmental sustainability is addressed in Irish development planning at national level (OECD 2010, p. 16). In terms of EU environmental policy, there is a notable tendency towards responsiveness to social concerns at the initiation stage, with a decline in effective civil participation until the implementation stage, which is then often adversarial in character (Connaughton et al. 2008). The reconfiguration of the Irish environmental sector began in 2001 with the creation of the EENGO (Environmental Ecological NGO) Fund by central government (Flynn 2007). In 2009 this was consolidated through the creation of the Irish Environmental Network (IEN) with a secretariat provided by the Department of the Environment, Heritage and Local Government (now Environment, Community and Local Government). The creation of the IEN provided the organizational basis for the inclusion of the environment pillar in Irish social partnership in April 2009. The integration of the environment pillar, however, seems to have coincided with the swansong of social partnership.

The *Differentness* of Participation in Ireland

One of the key features of the Irish model of social partnership, distinguishing it from other European neo-corporatist variants, is the scope of its inclusion. In addition to the usual tripartite membership of employers, trade unions and government, the Irish model also includes civil society associations that articulate the interests of the community and voluntary sector (Teague and Donaghey 2009, p. 50). Although the composition of Irish social partnership is relevant to our discussion here, the claim that it has embedded deliberation within the Irish democratic system is more immediately interesting. It has been suggested that the Irish model of social partnership differs from its European counterparts because it conjoins negotiation, problem-solving and consensus-seeking governance in deliberative democratic forms (Adshead 2006).

The adaptation of the social partnership model seemed to provide fertile institutional conditions in which to implant a deliberative approach to governance for sustainable development in Ireland. Sustainable development partnerships were ultimately constructed and conducted at a remove from the mainstream social partnership process (Flynn 2007), but were nevertheless subsumed within its core logic.

Although there was a consistent stream of policy initiatives during the social partnership era, often guided by deliberative democracy, they have not amounted to a radically new system of governance and their outcomes have been limited (Teague and Donaghey 2009, p. 65). Coordination between social partnership and representative democracy at a peak level has functioned more effectively than the links between deliberative experiments and those at lower levels (Teague and Donaghey 2009, p. 65). The fact that both the narratives and pathways of sustainability governance have been embedded in institutional conditions characterized by social partnership has arguably proved to be a barrier to its progression. The recent debate on *resilience, vulnerability* and the *limits to deliberation* in Irish social partnership is instructive for understanding the prospects for governance for sustainable development in Ireland.

Throughout the Celtic Tiger period, social partnership proved to be 'remarkably resilient', surviving several changes in the composition of government through the 1990s (Baccoro and Simoni 2004, p. 2). It became an indisputable part of the narrative of the success of the Irish model of development. Prior to its disintegration in the years 2009 to 2010, there was a period of consolidation with the integration of several key social partnership institutions (the National Economic and Social Council (NESC), the National Economic and Social Forum (NESF), and the National Centre for Partnership and Performance (NCPP)) in the new National Economic and Social Development Office (NESDO) in 2006. While NESDO and the NESC remain in place, other key social partnership institutions (NESF, NCPP) fell victim to retrenchment and were dissolved in April 2010. The withdrawal of political support and the creation of a social climate that viewed it as part of the problem and not part of the solution prompted the reframing of social partnership as a model for better times. The dramatic shift in economic, political, social and institutional conditions has led to a context that is far less accommodating of deliberative approaches to governance. However, the impasse in governance for sustainable development did not originate in the current crisis.

The nature of the consensus on Irish development, mediated and sustained by social partnership, has recently been identified as a source of vulnerability and is therefore a threat to resilience in the face of crises (Kirby 2010, p. 50). Furthermore, it seems to have inhibited rather than cultivated deliberative democracy. Kirby defines vulnerability as a 'state of high exposure to certain risks and uncertainties, in combination with a reduced ability to protect and defend against those risks and uncertainties and cope with their negative consequences' (ibid.). He instances the vulnerabilities of the global financial system and climate change as key challenges to contemporary society. As far as social partnership is concerned, the nature of the consensus forged was not a shared consensus about the costs of rapid economic change. Rather it was a narrow consensus about the dependence of the Irish growth model on multinational companies and 'deliberations were limited to doing nothing to undermine the conditions that were seen to attract high levels of multi-national investment' (Kirby 2010, p. 54). This narrow consensus effectively neglected consideration of the vulnerability of the Irish model of development, with 'high levels of dependence on global flows and its weak mechanisms to build resilience' (ibid.). Gaynor reaches similar conclusions and points out that the scope of deliberation was considerably constricted since 'the strict focus on problem solving rather than problem framing forecloses the possibilities for structural debates; with problem solving addressing symptoms rather than root causes' (2009, p. 313). It was possible for new collective actors to be incorporated in Irish social partnership, 'particularly those who could obstruct the future implementation of public policy' (Ó Broin 2011) and to create facsimile institutions for sustainable development without fundamentally challenging the prevailing narrative, norms, values and understandings at the core of the Irish development model. By far the most sombre assessment comes from within the institutional core of social partnership itself. The NESC concludes that while it appeared that the Irish approach to governing was developing in tandem with the EU governance regime, 'the expected evolution of disciplined policy development and review, focused on problem-solving with social partners and others, and nourished by international benchmarking, did not happen' (2010, p. 198).

4. GOVERNANCE FOR *LOCAL* SUSTAINABLE DEVELOPMENT

As the level of governance closest to the people, local authorities play a vital role 'in educating, mobilizing and responding to the public to promote local sustainable development (Local Agenda 21 cited in Lafferty 2001, p. 1). LA21 is simultaneously committed to two goals, namely: the procedural goal of enhancing public participation in local decision-making and the substantive goal of sustainable development as it is promulgated in the UNCED process (Feichtinger and Pregernig 2005, p. 212). Local Agenda 21 in Ireland has undoubtedly contributed to stimulating democratic experimentalism through projects and initiatives often involving partnerships between local authorities and local communities for sustainable development (Mullally et al. 2009). The Irish Government has acknowledged its ongoing importance, noting 'much progress has been made under Local Agenda 21, but there is still need for greater awareness and capacity building to further advance sustainable development issues' (DOECLG 2011, p. 6).

Local government in Ireland is often regarded as another forum for national politics, rather than as 'a political and civic space in its own right' (Adshead and Tonge 2009, p. 171). Nevertheless, the lifecycle of Local Agenda 21 in Ireland is bound up with the reform of local governance and attempts to reinvigorate local democracy (Mullally et al. 2009). The introduction of 'new structures established under local government reform offered the potential for linking Local Agenda 21 to local governance through the City and County Development Boards (CDBs)'. The primary function of the CDBs is *not* sustainable development, rather they were introduced to redress the growing divergence between local government and local socioeconomic development partnerships (for example LEADER, a European Union initiative for rural development) identified by central government and the OECD (Mullally et al. 2009). CDBs were introduced in 2000, in an attempt to build consensual problem-solving institutions with strategic intentions at the local level of governance in Ireland. The primary function of CDBs is the integration of local government and local development systems. CDBs are networking and strategic planning organizations linked to, but separate from, local government under the auspices of a director of community and enterprise within the local authority (Mullally et al. 2009). They are responsible for formulating and reviewing a 10-year strategy for local economic, social and cultural development, but have no executive authority. It was intended from the outset that the CDB process would localize the NSDS and act as a vehicle for local sustainable development; specifically Local Agenda 21 (Mullally et al. 2009). The CDBs are *substantively* considered vehicles for the integration of sustainable development at local level; *procedurally* intended as the localization of the Irish social partnership; and have a *reflexive* dimension since they emerged from structured consultation processes; encompass agreed visions, goals, objectives and actions; and have built-in mechanisms for monitoring, review and revision.

Co-ordinating Distributed Capacities at the Local Level?

In theory, the coordinative and communicative dimensions of the CDB process could contribute to building integrative, participative and strategic learning capacities for sustainable development at the local level.

(i) Building integrative capacities?
Although there is some variation in the labelling of elements of strategies, the discourse and principles of sustainable development have been

integrated into their texts. In terms of the interpretations and understandings of the stakeholders involved, sustainable development is 'secondary to the functional requirement of inter-organizational/inter-agency strategic coordination' (Mullally et al. 2009, p. 39). Local Agenda 21 is less prominent in the texts of strategies nationwide and it has declined even further since 2005 (Mullally et al. 2009, p. 39). The integration of the economic, social and environmental dimensions of sustainable development in the process is skewed towards social inclusion measures. In the years 2002–5, 18.5 per cent of all actions progressed related to social inclusion measures, whereas approximately 10 per cent of actions took place in the areas of economic development and environment respectively. In terms of environmental initiatives, the most common clusters of activity emphasized biodiversity/nature/heritage, waste management and renewable energy. Following the interim review, there was a slight rebalancing of priorities with environment-related measures increasing to nearly 16 per cent, with some evidence of an increase in climate change initiatives within those measures. At the outset of the process, it was projected that the CDBs would move up the 'integration ladder' from network/ information exchange through coordination (altering activities) and by cooperation (shared resources) and through collaboration (joint activities) (Fitzpatrick/ERM 2002, pp. 76–9). In terms of environmental policy integration and the distribution of implementation capacities, the process has not moved much beyond the first rung.

Meanwhile, activities at sub-national level, such as housing development, have contradicted the principles of sustainable development (OECD 2010; NESC 2010; Kitchin et al. 2010) and there has also been an increased incidence of conflict between communities and the state in relation to environmental quality and quality of life in the context of major infrastructural projects and developments (Leonard 2009, p. 291). Although public expenditure on the environment increased significantly between 2000 and 2008, it accounts for a small share of GDP (OECD 2010, p. 8). A large portion of this expenditure is at the local level, but local government has traditionally had limited fiscal autonomy. The Irish economic crisis, debt burden, budget deficit and consequent retrenchment process impose 'serious constraints on [local] government action and put at risk Ireland's ability to meet its environmental commitments' (OECD 2010, p. 8).

(ii)   Building participative capacities?
The CDBs comprise elected representatives (local government), local socioeconomic development agencies and partnerships (for example LEADER) and area-based partnerships (local development); state

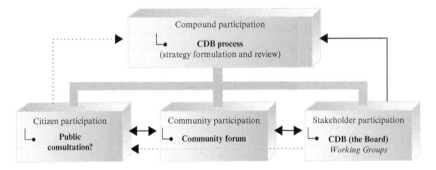

Source: Mullally et al. (2009, p. 42).

Figure 8.1 *Types of participation in the CDB process*

agencies; and social partners, for example business representative organizations as well as the community and voluntary sector. The participation of the community and voluntary sector is dependent on being organized in a community forum: a city or countywide structure to channel participation and feedback among community and voluntary organizations. The CDB process represents a compound type of participation, which includes a mixture of stakeholder and community-centred participation. The original development of the strategies provided for public consultation, that is, strategies that are publicly available and open to scrutiny and have largely indirect feedback mechanisms. Apart from structured representation via the community forum and through stakeholder participation in the CDB, citizen participation is passive.

The CDB process was designed to foster participation, deliberation and a consensus on integrated local development (Mullally et al. 2009). The process mixes several approaches: consultation in the initial stages; active participation in the case of the working groups and reviews; and deliberation at the level of the plenary. The nature of the consensus generated through the process is largely restricted to those inside the process and the participation of the wider community is limited. An equally fundamental weakness is a lack of integration of the CDB process in wider statutory processes with the power to influence outcomes (land-use planning, development planning, transportation, and so on), and poorly articulated linkages with decision-making at national level. While horizontal forms of communication may be suitable for building bridges, they are less successful when it comes to scaling ladders of (vertical) integration.

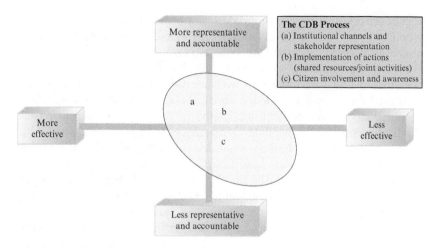

More representative and accountable

The CDB Process
(a) Institutional channels and
    stakeholder representation
(b) Implementation of actions
    (shared resources/joint activities)
(c) Citizen involvement and awareness

a
b

More
effective

Less
effective

c

Less representative
and accountable

Source: Mullally et al. (2009, p. 43).

Figure 8.2   The legitimacy of the CDB process

(iii)   Building strategic learning capacity?

On the surface the CDB process appears to have design features that have the potential for enhancing strategic learning, approximating 'reflexive governance for sustainable development' (Voß and Kemp 2006, pp. 4–7). Equally, the conditions for institutional effectiveness are also present to some extent.

The institutional link to the local authority (a), through the participation both of elected representatives and local authority officials, provides direct access and inputs to policy-framing by stakeholders, but CDBs are not decision-making bodies per se. Local government remains primarily responsible for the implementation of local sustainable development. Responsibility for taking the lead on different initiatives under the strategies is distributed among different stakeholders (b) with clear differences in terms of decision-making capacity, power and discretion over resources. While monitoring and review does allow for a learning process to take place, the lack of a direct link back to local citizens (c) is a weakness. The gap between stakeholder participation and citizen participation has been acknowledged by central government, noting 'structures do not have a universal reach [and therefore] it may be necessary for local government to creatively and proactively seek new avenues of direct participation' (DOEHLG 2007, p. 79).

While attention to the design features of the process is important, the (deliberative) quality of the process is fundamental to understanding whether it is different from other forms of governance. Both the local authority officials and the stakeholders involved value the process as a context for communication and learning, but there is also some frustration that it lacks the power to translate this into action. Stakeholders identified 'increasing knowledge about plans and projects taking place, defining gaps in the general application of resources, and reducing the duplication of effort' in local development as key learning outcomes of the process (Mullally et al. 2009, p. 36). Local authority officials, on the other hand, noted that multi-stakeholder participation of this type is recent and insufficiently embedded in the political culture and therefore a learning process in its own right (Mullally et al. 2009, p. 33). A key factor limiting the deliberative quality of the CDB process, however, is that while it has increased access to decision-makers (thus exerting a communicative influence), there is very little sense that it is influential in terms of shaping outcomes (Mullally et al. 2009, p. 39). This limitation has also been noted by independent evaluations of the process (Indecon 2008; O'Riordan 2008). Although the design features of the process provide the basis for institutional effectiveness, this is heavily circumscribed by the structural limits of existing institutional conditions.

In terms of local governance, 'even when local autonomy and partnership approaches are promoted by central government this is typically offset by countervailing trends towards the centralisation of power' (Larragy and Bartley 2007, p. 207). Rather than representing transformation, new institutional structures simply 'constitute an accretion to prevailing arrangements' (Larragy and Bartley 2007, p. 207). In terms of governance for sustainable development, local-level engagement remains structured by the low degree of autonomy granted by national government to sub-national government (Baker and Eckerberg 2008).

5.   SUMMARY AND CONCLUSIONS

Almost 20 years on, the Rio model of governance has contributed to the formation of a substantial amount of policy development, institutional innovation and democratic experimentation in Ireland, albeit with variable success. For much of that time, William Lafferty has been at the vanguard of attempts to understand and clarify the relationship between democracy and sustainable development internationally. The defining characteristic of his work has been, and is, the consistency of a normative-pragmatic commitment to sustainable development, an insistence on the importance of cross-national and contextual comparison with, above all, a championing of collaborative research engagement. Although *governance for sustainable development* is not a term invented by Lafferty, it has certainly gained definition under his tutelage through strategic collaboration, careful theorizing and rigorous empirical testing over the last decade or more. Lafferty has gainfully employed the device of specifying national storylines or narratives of sustainable development as a means of structuring a comparative research programme. At the very core of his methodological approach has been the deceptively simple, but decidedly effective, telling of stories about sustainable development.

The story of Irish development over the last two decades, the one we tell ourselves and others, is that we are *exceptional*: exceptionally innovative, enterprising and successful in the case of the Celtic Tiger, and exceptionally unfortunate that the global financial and economic crisis converged with indigenous crises to bring it all to a crashing halt. Although social partnership has now been jettisoned as vigorously as it was once embraced, adherence to the narrative of Irish development remains otherwise remarkably intact (Kitchin et al. 2010; Kirby 2010). Governance for sustainable development has to contend with this narrative and compete for space within it. The progression of sustainable development and stakeholder participation, during a prolonged period of economic expansion and growth, never fundamentally altered Ireland's development path. While ecological modernization appears to have been integrated in the narrative of recovery, sustainable development will, it seems, have to wait for the return of better times.

Sustainable development has helped to accelerate the diffusion of new environmental policy instruments, mechanisms and institutional designs in Ireland. This has been part of a process to negotiate coherence and narrative consistency within the context of a multi-actor, multi-sector, multilevel system of governance for sustainable development. The complex multilevel nature of EU, national and sub-national governance structures in which environmental policy instruments are implemented places limits on what other policies, processes or actors can be taken into account (Atkinson and Klausen 2011, p. 246). While the EU has played a significant role in modernizing Irish environmental policy, there has not been a corresponding institutional overhaul that would allow for the sufficient embedding of sustainable development (Flynn 2007, p. 177). The Irish system of environmental governance needs to be reviewed and reformed to enhance the prospects of more effective governance for sustainable development (EPARG 2011, p. 79). In keeping with the experience elsewhere, pre-existing ways of working and thinking have structured processes and outcomes; therefore sustainable development has been (re)interpreted to fit with pre-existing modes of governing/governance (Atkinson and

Klausen 2011, p. 247). It is difficult to challenge the conclusion that the Irish approach 'is more aligned to development that has to be sustained and a blurred acceptance of ecological modernisation rather than a strong ideological commitment to sustainable development' (Connaughton et al. 2008, pp. 147–8).

Existing institutional conditions and path dependency have also shaped the development of the integrative, strategic learning and participative capacities of governance for sustainable development. The coupling of stakeholder participation and social partnership has imposed contextual constraints on the integration of deliberation and therefore *differentness* into Irish governance for sustainable development. The creation of stakeholder institutions to steer strategic integrated local development that once promised to give Local Agenda 21 an institutional anchorage at the sub-national level appears instead to have sublimated it to other priorities. The CDB process explored here has arguably been more about fostering social trust than sustainable development and less about integration than institutional accommodation at a remove from real influence (Mullally et al. 2009). If capacity is conditioned by the limits of possible action in a given context, structural limitations to both horizontal and vertical integration have a profoundly dampening effect on the possibility for strategic learning and action. The diagnosis of the need for more capacity-building in the Irish case is perceptive, though pointless without corresponding measures to adapt the structural conditions that would actually allow it to take place, as much as is possible in a globalized world.

Governance for sustainable development, for many of the reasons explored here (and others), has emphasized stakeholder participation and partnership as a steering mechanism to convert ideas to outcomes (Lafferty 2004). In spite of global crises, the more general contextual conditions that precipitated the evolution of governance remain relevant. To coin a phrase: 'just as functional diversity is critical to the resiliency of eco-systems, it appears equally critical to the development' of governance capacity (Newman and Dale 2007, p. 88). While the story told here has a pronounced Irish accent, there are, of course, more general structural limitations on governance for sustainable development. These structural problems attenuate, and sometimes amplify, the weakness of country-specific institutionalized settings and narratives. These are best expressed in the conventional language of *necessity* and *sufficiency*.

Governance is a necessary, though not a sufficient, condition for steering social change in the direction of sustainable development. Governance is only one dimension of a multifaceted approach that also requires a combination of legal, regulatory and market-based instruments (Mullally et al. 2009, p. 44). Stakeholder models for steering still, therefore, depend on the responsibility and integrative capacities of governments for successful implementation (Jänicke 2006; Lafferty 2004).

Participation is a necessary, but not sufficient, condition for sustainable development. What is critical is whether a country's policy system, including its participative or partnership element, is geared to review and learning (NESC 2010), as well as to implementing that learning. While it is evident from Irish analyses that there is a deficit when it comes to strategic learning in Ireland, this is not merely a parochial problem. Evaluations of global stakeholder governance (Bäckstrand 2006a, 2006b) and partnerships for sustainable development (Glasbergen 2011) have identified the gap between inputs, outputs and outcomes as a key structural limitation to governance for sustainable development. While acknowledging the contextual limits to the institutional capacity of local governance in Ireland, it is difficult to ignore comparative European studies that were unable to find a *causal* connection between the 'pursuit of sustainable development and the emergence of new institutional practices' at the sub-national level (Baker and Eckerberg 2008, p. 226).

We might also conclude that deliberation is also a necessary, but not sufficient, condition of governance for sustainable development. While acknowledging the contextual limits to deliberation in Ireland, there are wider structural limits to deliberative governance for sustainable development. The first is that it often downplays the diverse and dynamic political landscape in which deliberative institutions must actually operate (Hendriks and Grin 2007) and the contingent uncertainty of the relationship between a governance process and the existing democratic context. The second problem is the instrumentalizing of civil society participation (Hendriks and Grin 2007). Participation in reforming practices and structures that fall far short of realizing fundamental change undermines, rather than reinforces, societal capacity. Finally, the tendency to focus *primarily* on the existence of deliberative structures risks overlooking the asymmetry of political and social power, within and outside, those structures. This effectively reproduces existing power relations and knowledge, undermining any transformative potential and limits the development of governance for sustainable development.

The story of governance and participation for sustainable development in Ireland is certainly distinctive: but is it merely a variation on a theme?

NOTE

1. The author gratefully acknowledges that research presented in this chapter was conducted as part of the Environmental Research and Technological Innovation Programme. This

programme was financed by the Irish Government under the National Development Plan, from the years 2000 to 2006. It is administered on behalf of the Department of the Environment, Heritage and Local Government by the Environmental Protection Agency.

REFERENCES

Adshead, M. (2006), 'New modes of governance and the Irish vase: finding evidence for explanations of social partnership', *Economic and Social Review*, **37** (3), 319–42.

Adshead, M. and J. Tonge (2009), *Politics in Ireland: Convergence and Divergence in a Two Polity Island*, Hampshire, MA and New York: Palgrave Macmillan.

Atkinson, R. and J. Klausen (2011), 'Understanding sustainability policy: governance, knowledge and the search for integration', *Journal of Environmental Policy and Planning*, **13** (3), 231–51.

Baccoro, L. and M. Simoni (2004), 'The Irish Social Partnership and the "Celtic Tiger" Phenomenon', International Institute For Labour Studies discussion paper, DP/154/2004, Geneva.

Bäckstrand, K. (2006a), 'Democratising global environmental governance? Stakeholder democracy after the World Summit on Sustainable Development', *European Journal of International Relations*, **12** (4), 467–98.

Bäckstrand, K. (2006b), 'Multi-stakeholder partnerships for sustainable development: rethinking legitimacy, accountability and effectiveness', *European Environment*, **16** (5), 290–306.

Baker, S. and K. Eckerberg (eds) (2008), *In Pursuit of Sustainable Development: New Governance Practices at Sub-national Level in Europe*, Oxford: New York: Routledge.

Connaughton, B., B. Quinn and N. Rees (2008), 'Rhetoric or reality? Responding to the challenge of sustainable development and new governance patterns in Ireland', in Susan Baker and Katarina Eckerberg (eds), *In Pursuit of Sustainable Development: New Governance Practices at the Sub-national Level in Europe*, Routledge/EPCR Studies in European Political Science, Oxford: New York: Routledge, pp. 145–68.

Crozier, M. (2007), 'Recursive governance: contemporary political communication and public policy', *Political Communication*, **24** (1), pp. 1–18.

Dale, A. and J. Onyx (eds) (2005), *A Dynamic Balance: Social Capital and Sustainable Community*, Vancouver, BC: UBC Press.

Department of the Environment (DOE) (1997), *Sustainable Development: A Strategy for Ireland*, Dublin: DOE.

Department of the Environment and Local Government (DOELG) (2002), *Making Ireland's Development Sustainable: Review Assessment Future Action*, Dublin: DOELG.

DOEHLG (2007), *Stronger Local Democracy – Options for Change*, Dublin: DOEHLG.

DOECLG (2011), *Rio+20: Towards the Green Economy and Better Governance*, Consultation Document (July), Dublin: DOECLG.

Environmental Protection Agency Review Group (EPARG) (2011), *A Review of the Environmental Protection Agency*, Dublin: EPARG.

Evans, B., M. Joas, S. Sundback and K. Theobald (2006), 'Governing local sustainability', *Journal of Environmental Planning and Management*, **49** (6), 849–67.

Feichtinger, J. and M. Pregernig (2005), 'Participation and/or/versus sustainability? Tensions between procedural and substantive goals in two Local Agenda 21 processes in Sweden and Austria', *European Environment*, **15** (4), 212–57.

Fitzpatrick/ERM (2002), *Review of the County/City Development Board Strategies*, Dublin: Department of the Environment and Local Government.

Flynn, B. (2007), *The Blame Game: Rethinking Ireland's Sustainable Development and Environmental Performance*, Dublin and Portland, OR: Irish Academic Press.

Fung, A. (2006), 'Varieties of participation in complex governance', *Public Administration Review*, **66** (Supplement s1), 66–75.

Gaynor, N. (2009), 'Deepening democracy within Irish social partnership', *Irish Political Studies*, **24** (4), 303–19.

Glasbergen, P. (2007), 'Setting the scene: the partnership paradigm in the making', in Pieter Glasbergen, Frank Biermann and Arthur Mol (eds), *Partnerships, Governance and Sustainable Development: Reflections on Theory and Practice*, Cheltenham, UK and Northampton, MA, USA: Edward Elgar, pp. 1–28.

Glasbergen, P. (2011), 'Understanding partnerships for sustainable development analytically: the ladder of partnership activity as a methodological tool', *Environmental Policy and Governance*, **21** (1), pp. 1–13.

Hendriks, C. and J. Grin (2007), 'Contextualising reflexive governance: the politics of Dutch transitions to sustainability', *Journal of Environmental Policy and Planning*, **9** (3), 333–50.

Indecon (2008), *Review of the City and County Development Board Strategic Reviews and Proposals for Strengthening and Developing the Boards*, Dublin: Indecon International Environmental Consultants.

Jänicke, M. (2006), *The 'Rio Model' of Environmental Governance – A General Evaluation*, FFU-Report 2006-03, Berlin: Forschungsstelle Für Umweltpolitik [Environmental Policy Research Centre], Freie Universitat Berlin.

Keeley, B. (2007), *Human Capital: How You Know What Shapes Your Life*, OECD Insights, Paris: OECD.

Kirby, P. (2010), 'Lessons from the Irish collapse: taking an international political economy approach', *Irish Studies in International Affairs*, **21**, 43–55.

Kitchin, R., J. Gleeson, K. Keaveney and C. O'Callaghan (2010), *A Haunted Landscape: Housing and Ghost Estates in Post-Celtic Tiger Ireland*, National Institute for Regional and Spatial Analysis (NIRSA) working paper 59, Maynooth, Ireland: NIRSA, NUI Maynooth.

Lafferty, W. (ed.) (2001), *Sustainable Communities in Europe*, London and Sterling, VA: Earthscan Publishers.

Lafferty, W. (ed.) (2004), *Governance for Sustainable Development: The Challenge of Adapting Form to Function*, Cheltenham, UK and Northampton, MA, USA: Edward Elgar.

Larragy, J. and B. Bartley (2007), 'Transformations in governance', in Brendan Bartley and Rob Kitchin (eds), *Understanding Contemporary Ireland*, Dublin, Ann Arbor, MI and London: Pluto Press, pp. 197–207.

Leach, M., I. Scoones and A. Stirling (2010), *Dynamic Sustainabilities: Technology, Environment, Social Justice*, London and Washington, DC: Earthscan Publishers.

Lehtonen, M. (2004), 'The environmental-social interface of sustainable development: capabilities, social capital, institutions', *Ecological Economics*, **49** (2), 199–214.

Leonard, L. (2009), 'Social partnership's boiling point: environmental issues and social responses to neo-liberal policy in Ireland', *Critical Social Policy*, **29** (2): 279–93.

Meadowcroft, J. (2004), 'Participation and sustainable development: modes of citizen, community and organisational involvement', in William Lafferty (ed.) *Governance for Sustainable Development: The Challenge of Adapting Form to Function*, Cheltenham, UK and Northampton, MA, USA: Edward Elgar, pp. 162–90.

Meadowcroft, J. (2007a), 'Who is in charge here? Governance for sustainable development in a complex world', *Journal of Environmental Policy and Planning*, **9** (3), 299–314.

Meadowcroft, J. (2007b), 'National sustainable development strategies: features, challenges and reflexivity', *European Environment*, **17** (3), 152–63.

Meadowcroft, J. and F. Bregha (2009), *Governance for Sustainable Development: Meeting the Challenges Ahead*, Policy Research Initiative research paper, Ottawa, CA: Policy Research Initiative.

Meadowcroft, J., N. Farrell and J. Spangenberg (2005), 'Developing a framework for sustainability governance in the European Union', *International Journal for Sustainable Development*, **8** (1&2), 3–11.

Mullally, G., A. Henry, B. Motherway, J. O'Mahony and G. Weyman (2009), *Sustainable Participation? Evaluating the Role of City and County Development Boards in Promoting Public Participation in Local Sustainable Development*, EPA STRIVE report 41, Wexford, Ireland: Environmental Protection Agency.

National Economic and Social Council (NESC) (2009), *Next Steps in Addressing Ireland's Five Part Crisis: Combining Retrenchment with Reform*, NESC no. 129, Dublin: NESC.

NESC (2010), *Re-Finding Success in Europe: Challenges for Irish Institutions and Policies*, NESC no. 122, Dublin: NESC.

Newman, L. and A. Dale (2007), 'Homophily and agency: creating effective sustainable development networks', *Environment, Development and Sustainability*, **9** (1), 79–90.

Ó Broin, D. (2011), 'Deliberation for participatory Democrats: lessons from social partnership in Ireland', *Irish Journal of Public Policy*, **3** (1), accessed 14 September at http://publish.ucc.ie/ijpp/2011/01.

O'Riordan, S. (2008), *Briefing Paper: County and City Development Boards Role and Composition of Proposed New Environment Sub-Committees*, prepared for Comhar National Sustainable Development Council, Dublin: Sean O' Riordan and Associates.

Organisation for Economic Co-operation and Development (OECD) (2010), *Environmental Performance Reviews: Ireland*, Paris: OECD.

Petschow, U., J. Rosenau and E. Von Weizsäcker (2005), 'Introduction', in Ulrich Petschow, James Rosenau and Ernest Ulrich von Weizsäcker (eds), *Governance and Sustainability: New Challenges for States, Companies and Civil Society*, Sheffield: Greenleaf Publishing, pp. 9–18.

Renn, O. (2008), *Risk Governance: Coping with Uncertainty in a Complex World*, London and Sterling, VA: Earthscan Publishing.

Rydin, Y. and N. Holman (2004), 'Re-evaluating the contribution of social capital in achieving sustainable development', *Local Environment*, **9** (2), 117–33.

Skelcher, C., M. Navdeep and M. Smith (2005), 'The public governance of collaborative spaces: discourse, design and democracy', *Public Administration*, **83** (3), 573–96.

Sørensen, E. and J. Torfing (2008), 'Theoretical approaches to metagoverance', in Eva Sørensen and Jacob Torfing (eds), *Theories of Democratic Network Governance*, Basingstoke: Palgrave Macmillan, pp. 169–82.

Teague, P. and J. Donaghey (2009), 'Social partnership and democratic legitimacy in Ireland', *New Political Economy*, **14** (1), 49–69.

United Nations Department of Economic and Social Affairs, Division for Sustainable Development (2002), *Johannesburg Declaration on Sustainable Development*, New York: United Nations.

Van Dyk, S. (2009), 'From peripherality to consensus-based success? Applying a Foucaulidan perspective on power and discourse to the Irish model of social partnership', *Irish Journal of Sociology*, **17** (1), 75–94.

Voß, J.-P. and R. Kemp (2006), 'Sustainability and reflexive governance: introduction', in Jan-Peter Voß, Dierk Bauknecht and Rene Kemp (eds), *Reflexive Governance for Sustainable Development*, Cheltenham, UK and Northampton, MA, USA: Edward Elgar, pp. 3–28.

Voß, J.-P., J. Newig, B. Kastens, J. Monstadt and B. Nölting (2007), 'Steering for sustainable development: A typology of problems and strategies with respect to ambivalence, uncertainty and distributed power', *Journal of Environmental Policy and Planning*, **9** (3), 919–23.

Weale, A. (2007), *Democracy*, 2nd edn, Basingstoke and New York: Palgrave Macmillan.

World Commission on Environment and Development (WCED) (1987), *Our Common Future*, Oxford: Oxford University Press.

9. Measuring what? National interpretations of sustainable development – the case of Norway

Oluf Langhelle and Audun Ruud

The concept of sustainable development was proposed by the World Commission on Environment and Development (WCED) as a guiding principle to steer *global* development (Lafferty 1996). Global concerns, however, have to be *translated* into regional, national and local settings. To be able to draw actual policy implications from sustainable development at the national level, there are a number of issues that must be (pre)determined.

First of all these issues concern the question of what to translate. It is necessary to determine what sustainable development means, what should be included in the concept, and how different dimensions of sustainable development are to be measured and weighed. During the past two decades various political efforts have been undertaken to promote, measure and operationalize sustainable development. Numerous challenges still remain and there is as yet no common measure of sustainable development. This is hardly surprising. As a report issued by the UNECE/ OECD/Eurostat Working Group on Statistics for sustainable development (United Nations 2008, p. 13) has argued, sustainable development is 'difficult to define with precision and, therefore, difficult to measure'. Moreover, there is no agreement on how to measure global sustainable development. Stiglitz et al. (2009, p. 234) argue that 'no indicator emerges as consensual, even among those that try to rely on a well-defined concept of global sustainability. Such a situation is obviously a source of perplexity. . .'.[1] Therefore one of the major challenges of sustainable development remains at the conceptual level, concerning what it is and how it should be measured.

Even if we agreed on a definition, the dimensions that should be included in the concept of sustainable development would still have to be translated to the national level. The issue of climate change is a good example. Although it is first and foremost conceived as a global problem, it has regional and local impacts, and efforts at many political/administrative scales will be required to mitigate climate change. However, there is no agreement on how this translation should be done and what it implies. What is the appropriate national share of global greenhouse gas (GHG) reductions? The second challenge of sustainable development is the lack of political agreement on global goals and targets and how to transform these into practical measures and operational targets at the national level. Without a global agreement, this translation process is far from easy, and as we shall argue, the translation process from the global to the national can become messy and complicated. There is also the question of how these two concerns interact. On the one hand, what sustainability is seen to be at the global level could (and should) be strongly linked to its operationalization at the national level, and how you actually measure sustainable development. On the other hand, such a linkage may not be present in actual day-to-day politics.

In the following discussion we will use the report *Our Common Future* (1987), authored by the World Commission on Environment and Development (WCED), as the point of departure. We will use the concept presented by the WCED to explore how the global concerns of sustainable development are translated into actual policies in Norway. Two cases are used to illustrate the complexity of this translation. The first case explores the Norwegian set of national indicators for sustainable development and its relatively strong emphasis on national wealth. The second case discusses Norwegian national climate change policy. It is argued that there is a considerable gap between the global political framing of sustainable development and actual policy, and that this gap partly is explained by the *translation* process from the global to the national level, given the preference of continuing the production of oil and gas in Norway.

1. THE POINT OF DEPARTURE: DEFINING SUSTAINABLE DEVELOPMENT

The World Commission on Environment and Development (WCED) was led by a former prime minister of Norway, Gro Harlem Brundtland. Sustainable development, as articulated in *Our Common Future* (1987), is first and foremost an ethical theory or a developmental goal where sustainable development is defined as 'development that meets the needs of the present without compromising the ability of future generations to meet their own needs'. According to the report, this definition embodies two key concepts:

- the concept of needs, in particular the essential needs of the world's poor to which overriding priority should be given;
- the idea of limitations imposed by the state of technology and social organization on the environment's ability to meet present and future needs (WCED 1987, p. 43).

Social justice, physical sustainability and the global dimension are crucial parts of this framework for sustainable development. However, to some extent the definition conceals all three dimensions and their (inter-) relationship. The relationship(s) between social justice and sustainable development are nonetheless part of the conceptualization of sustainable development. In light of the definition and the first key concept, the satisfaction of human needs must be seen as the primary objective of development (WCED 1987, p. 43). Malnes (1990, p. 3) calls this the *goal of development*. It could also be seen as the answer to what is to be sustained and for whom: the ability to meet human needs today and in the future. The qualification that this development must also be sustainable is a constraint placed on this goal, meaning that each generation is permitted to pursue its interests so long as they do not undermine the ability of future generations to meet their own needs. Malnes (1990, p. 3) calls this the *proviso of sustainability*. Since the sustainability constraint is a necessary condition for future need satisfaction, which is part of what sustainable development is supposed to secure, the proviso of sustainability becomes a necessary part of the goal of development, thus providing the state of interdependency in the concept (Lafferty and Langhelle 1999). As Malnes notes, 'the proviso is entailed by the very goal whose pursuit it constrains' (Malnes 1990, p. 7).

Arguably *Our Common Future* places social justice at the core of sustainable development and as such the relationship is not, as Dobson (1998) contends, first and foremost 'empirical' or 'functional'. Social justice is *the* primary development goal of sustainable development. Of course, Dobson (1998) is right in pointing out that *Our Common Future* strongly argues that there are empirical and functional relationships between social justice and sustainable development. Poverty is seen as a 'major cause and effect of global environmental problems' (WCED 1987, p. 44) and the 'reduction of poverty itself [is seen as a] precondition for environmentally sound development' (WCED 1987, p. 69).

Yet the priority given to the world's poor is also *independent* of the poverty-environment thesis (Lafferty and Langhelle 1999). That is, even if the thesis is proved wrong, and there is no clear dependency between poverty and environmental degradation, the underlying framework of *Our Common Future* would still lead to a prioritization of the essential needs of the world's poor in the name of social justice (and sustainable development). As stated in the report, poverty is 'an evil in itself' (WCED 1987, p. 8). Sustainable development requires meeting the basic needs of *all*, thus extending to all the opportunity to fulfil aspirations for a better life (WCED 1987, p. 8) and 'an adequate livelihood base and equitable access to resources' (WCED 1987, p. 39). The equal opportunity principle should thus be seen as an inherent part of the concept of sustainable development (Lafferty and Langhelle 1999; Langhelle 1999).

There is no doubt that intra-generational justice – understood here as need satisfaction and equal opportunity – is the first priority of sustainable development. It constitutes the first part of the definition – 'development that meets the needs of the present [. . .]' (WCED 1987, p. 43) – and it is seen as the primary concern both within and between countries. As such, sustainable development entails a strong commitment to redistribution between rich and poor, both nationally and globally. As Adams (1990, p. 59) points out: '*Our Common Future* starts with people' and accordingly intragenerational justice becomes the first objective of sustainable development policy, but within the constraints of inter-generational justice and physical sustainability. There is therefore some truth in Jacobs' (1999, p. 30) argument that environmental protection is 'without doubt the central idea' of sustainable development. It is true in the following sense: without the environmental challenges, the concept might not be needed at all; a good notion of development would be sufficient.

Accordingly, the fundamental goal of the WCED was to *reconcile* physical sustainability, need satisfaction and equal opportunities within and between generations. Sustainable development is what defines this reconciliation. Whether they succeeded or not is disputed. Our claim is that this was the primary goal, or intention, of sustainable development. The need for this reconciliation is based on a conflict between intra- and inter-generational justice in the sense that there is no neat and easy functionality between social justice within our generation and physical sustainability as a precondition for intergenerational justice. An accelerating *ecological* interdependence, historical inequality in past resource use and the 'the growth of limits' are further assumptions which lie behind the very construction of sustainable development (Langhelle 2000a, p. 309). It is thus the combination of social justice (especially between the developing and developed countries, but also between generations) and global environmental problems (threats to physical sustainability) that creates the special challenge of sustainable development.

To move from here to indicators and policy implications, however, one is in need of additional information. What are the key threats to physical sustainability? What does intra-generational justice entail? What does inter-generational justice require? When these parameters are established at the outset, it is possible to draw policy implications with some precision and to argue that sustainable development has important consequences for the goals, priorities and strategies that follow from the concept (or more precisely, the *conception*) of sustainable development. Unfortunately, there is no real agreement on what represents excessive pressure on the world's ecosystems. The report *Our Common Future* described climate change (and the energy issue) and threats towards biological diversity as acute and pressing problems (Langhelle 2000b). If these assumptions are changed, it is obvious that the implications that follow from sustainable development also change.

2. FROM THE GLOBAL TO THE NATIONAL

Since *Our Common Future* was published, a number of approaches have been suggested to operationalize and measure sustainable development, or certain aspects of sustainable development, at the global and national level. These include 'factor 4/factor 10', 'environmental space', 'ecological footprint', 'adjusted net savings' (ANS), and 'green GDP', to mention just a few. In the following discussion we will focus on the capital approach. There are two reasons for this. First, the capital approach has been at the core of the foremost expression of economic interpretations of sustainable development. Part of the issue turns on understandings of 'very weak', 'weak', 'strong' and 'very strong' concepts of sustainability, which has been extensively debated (see for example the disputes among Beckerman 1994, 1995; Daly 1995; Jacobs 1995; Skolimowski 1995; Serafy 1996; and Common 1996). Second, the capital approach is widely used and seems to have become the basic operationalization of sustainable development in many countries, including Norway.

The capital approach was also at the core of the joint UNECE/Eurostat/ OECD Working Group established in 2005, which was tasked with identifying 'good concepts and practices to assist national governments and international organizations in the design of sustainable development indicator sets' (United Nations 2008, p. iii). The mandate of the group was to develop a 'broad conceptual framework for measuring sustainable development with the concept of capital at its centre' (United Nations 2008, p. iii). The group consisted of members from 48 countries and international organizations. In the capital approach, sustainable development is defined as non-declining per capita wealth over time.

The report includes a thorough discussion of the concept of sustainable development. It also points to an unresolved fault line within the Working

Group, relating to intra- and inter-generational justice. The integrated view follows the Brundtland report and argues for the need to reconcile present and future needs. This view balances two forms of distributional justice – the inter-generational and the intra-generational – defined in the following manner:

> The former, justice between generations, is about securing freedom and options to exist and develop for the generations to come. The latter, justice within a generation, is about securing freedom and options to exist and evolve for today's world population. One is not to be achieved at the detriment of the other (United Nations 2008, p. 21).

The other perspective is called the 'future-oriented view' of sustainable development and it limits the scope of sustainable development to future well-being (United Nations 2008) and eschews the reconciliation of intra- and inter-generational justice altogether, arguing that only by limiting the scope 'can the concept offer focused policy direction' (United Nations 2008, p. 21). There was no attempt by the Working Group to resolve the debate, but it was acknowledged and discussed. Given that there are many commonalities between the approaches, the Working Group hoped 'that a single set of sustainable development indicators can be found to satisfy both views' (United Nations 2008).[2]

3. NORWAY'S TRANSLATION OF GLOBAL SUSTAINABILITY

Norway has followed an integrated view of sustainable development. Norway has also been a driver internationally in the OECD and other bodies (including the above Working Group) to develop analytically coherent and internationally accepted indicators. In Norway the need for more specific sustainable development indicators gradually emerged as part of the first national action plan for sustainable development, presented in the national budget for 2004. An indicator set was prepared by a government-appointed commission which conducted several open hearings and established a reference group of academics and NGO representatives. This resulted in an expert panel report issued in 2005 (MoF 2005; NOU 2005, p. 5; Danielson et al. 2007). The indicator set was first presented as part of the national budget in 2006, although a number of changes were introduced in the 2008 national budget. Since then there have been no further changes to the indicator set; however, the Norwegian Government is currently working on a revision of the national sustainable development strategy due in 2012.

Table 9.1   Norway's national indicator set for sustainable development

Issue area	Indicators	Actual development (from state budget 2011) Positive (+)/ unchanged (~)/negative (-)
International cooperation for sustainable development and combating poverty	1. Norwegian official development assistance, in NOK, and as percentage of gross national income	~
	2. Imports from least developed countries and from all developing countries	+
Climate, ozone and long-range air pollution	3. Norwegian emissions of greenhouse gases compared with the Kyoto Protocol target	+
	4. Emissions of NO_x, NH_3, SO_2 and NMVOC	+
Biodiversity and cultural heritage	5. Bird population index – population trends for breeding bird species in terrestrial ecosystems	~
	6. Proportion of inland water bodies classified as 'clearly not at risk'	+
	7. Proportion of coastal waters classified as 'clearly not at risk'	~
	8. Trends in standards of maintenance of protected buildings	~
Natural resources	9. Energy use per unit of GDP	+
	10. Size of spawning stock of Norwegian Northeast Arctic cod and Norwegian spring-spawning herring, compared with the precautionary reference points	~
	11. Irreversible losses of biologically productive areas	~
Hazardous chemicals	12. Potential exposure to hazardous substances	~
Sustainable economic and social development	13. Net national income per capita by sources of income	+
	14. Trends in income distribution	+
	15. Generational accounts: Need to tighten public sector finances as a share of GDP	+

Table 9.1 (continued)

Issue area	Indicators	Actual development (from state budget 2011) Positive (+)/ unchanged (~)/negative (-)
Sustainable economic and social development	16. Population by highest level of educational attainment	+
	17. Disability pensioners and long-term unemployed persons as a percentage of the population	~
	18. Life expectancy at birth	+

Source: Brunvoll and Smith (2010) (translation); 5/Ministry of Finance (MoF) 2010–11, p. 171 (actual development).

The indicator set strongly reflects the conceptual logic of Norway's system of national accounts and different types of capital. It is not, however, a pure capital approach. It also includes policy-based indicators that are supposed to meet the information needs of the national sustainable development strategy and that can also be presented as a 'dashboard' of indicators (Stiglitz et al. 2009, p. 235). The indicators are intended to serve as 'a tool for monitoring whether development is becoming more sustainable over time' (Brunvoll et al. 2008, p. 17). The set is designed to cover six issue areas: (1) climate, ozone and long-range trans-boundary air pollution; (2) biodiversity and cultural change; (3) natural resources; (4) hazardous substances; (5) sustainable economic development; and (6) social issues (MoF 2005).[3] Including some minor amendments, there are now 18 indicators used to evaluate the follow-up of the SD strategic objectives. These indicators are listed in Table 9.1.

Statistics Norway (SSB) is responsible for updating and interpreting changes in the indicators. In the national budget for the years 2010 to 2011, each of the indicators is discussed and summarized according to whether its development was negative, positive or unchanged. Of the 18 indicators, ten showed positive evolution, eight were unchanged, and none showed a negative trend. Sounds good. But is Norway really on a sustainable development path?

The above indicators are state oriented. Analysis does provide some information on pressures driving change in the indicators, but there is very limited feedback concerning the necessary responses. There is a weak relationship, therefore, between socioeconomic drivers and the adjustments necessary to alter negative trends. So the indicator system does not follow the pressure-state-response approach championed by the OECD (OECD 1993, 1997). The monitoring and evaluation of sustainable development in Norway remains relatively descriptive and static, with a focus on the presentation of incremental changes in the SD indicators in the annual state budget and on the bi-annual reports from the MoE on the state of the environment. Responses are to be dealt with in other policy documents.

While this gap between status and responses may be problematic, there are more fundamental questions that can be raised about the indicators. One can ask whether or not these indicators are good measures of a development trajectory towards sustainable development. To be indicators of a sustainable development trajectory they would have to address the fundamentals of sustainable development – the core issues that the concept of sustainable development is supposed to address at the global level. They should be adapted and translated to a national context and they should be linked to national measures, goals and targets that try to say something about the long-term goals or the end-state that would constitute the basis of a sustainable society.

The basic assumption on which the indicators are based is the understanding of sustainable development as 'developments where the level of welfare, or living standards broadly defined, are not deteriorating over time' (MoF 2005, p. 6). This implies that 'the assessment of whether or not a given development may be called sustainable, depends on whether our overall wealth broadly defined increases or decreases' (MoF 2005, p. 8). While the expert commission argued that national wealth should be 'a central indicator in the area of sustainable development, they nonetheless argued that this could be insufficient to ensure sustainability' and they also argued that '. . . we do not argue that a favourable development of our overall national wealth guarantees that sustainable development in fact will take place. Maintenance of our national wealth is therefore only a necessary, but not a sufficient, condition for sustainable development' (MoF 2005, pp. 10, 9). The national wealth approach should therefore be seen as a necessary but not sufficient condition for capturing sustainable development. The composition of national wealth is presented in Figure 9.1.

Figure 9.1 shows that in Norway the most valuable resource is human capital. In second place are non-renewable resources. In the case of Norway, this refers primarily to income from petroleum resources. The value of renewable resources seems a bit odder. Despite the fact that Norway is the second largest exporter of fish and fish products worldwide, the net national income from renewable natural resources is negative in

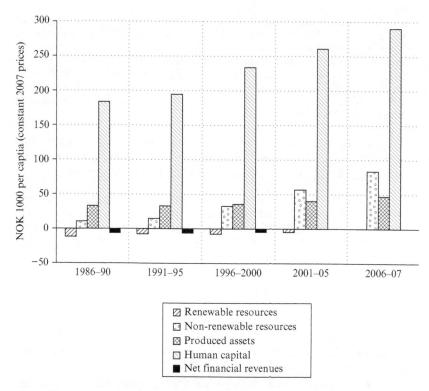

Note: Shown by decomposing average net national income per capita for each period.

Source: Statistics Norway (SSB) (2008, p. 38).

Figure 9.1   Net national income in NOK 1000 per capita, by sources of income, 1986–2007 (constant 2007 prices)

four out of five periods. The reason is the following: agricultural subsidies outweigh or equal the income from other renewable natural resources, making the total income from natural resources negative or marginal.

What else can be read from the capital approach component of the indicator set? The government-appointed commission that established the basics of the indicators gave four arguments or reservations leading to a conclusion that the national wealth approach is a necessary but not sufficient condition for sustainable development. The first argument was the existence of critical resources. This argument addressed the longstanding debate between advocates of weak and strong sustainability on the issue of substitutability, but defined it as a political issue and not a technical issue:

... if one wealth component declines, e.g. petroleum wealth, is this being offset by growth of other components such as human capital? This last question touches on a difficult point of whether, and to what extent, the various wealth components can be expected to substitute for each other as far as welfare effects are concerned. On this point, opinions may differ, and in the last instance the political authorities will have to decide. In other words, we argue that the question of 'weak' versus 'strong' sustainability is a political, and not a technical one. (MoF 2005, p. 9)

By doing this the expert commission, to some extent, avoided the issue of substitutability altogether. It did, however, acknowledge that national wealth components are not necessarily replaceable with each other:

it is not so that for instance the services we receive from the environment, which may be considered as dividends of our environmental capital, without difficulty can be replaced by increased income, i.e. the dividend of other wealth components such as financial, real, natural resource or human capital. As an example one may consider a fundamental asset such as a reasonably stable climate. If the climate is destabilized by increased global warming, the basis for our civilization in the long run may be threatened in a fundamental sense, almost irrespective of our material wealth. (MoF 2005, p. 9)

Similar arguments were made about biological diversity, suggesting that the individual components would also have to be maintained 'at certain minimum levels' in order to secure sustainable development (MoF 2005, p. 10).

The second reservation was the possibility that other ethical considerations could limit the exploitation of nature and environment beyond the perspective of national wealth. This was not further explored; however, eco-centric, or non-anthropocentric, ethics is probably what they had in mind. The third reservation was 'system complexity' (MoF 2005, p. 10). Here, it was argued that we have 'limited understanding of how economic activity depends on and influences environment and social relations' (MoF 2005, p. 10). The last reservation was labelled 'practical problems' (MoF 2005, p. 10), and was first and foremost linked to the problem of finding a common unit of measurement:

In order to add the various components of national wealth, they have to be expressed in a common unit of measurement, usually in the form of money. Ideally, the value of a unit of national wealth should reflect how a unit of the relevant element could contribute to our welfare. However, it is difficult to estimate these so-called shadow prices, especially if the services are not traded in perfectly functioning markets. Again, certain individual environmental services provide good examples of services that are not traded in the markets. Thus, estimates of national wealth are usually incomplete. The complex nature of the systems referred to above makes it difficult to find correct prices of several wealth components. (MoF 2005, p. 10)

Despite these reservations, the expert commission argued strongly in favour of the national wealth approach:

> ... a stable or growing national wealth suggests rather strongly that such a development may be taking place. Conversely, a negative development of national wealth suggests that sustainable development is threatened. National wealth should therefore be a central concept and central indicator in the area of sustainable development. Ideally, it may indicate whether – yes or no – conditions lend themselves to such a development in the longer term. (MoF 2005, pp. 8–9)

The expert commission also reviewed other attempts to measure the sustainability of development, including measures proposed by the UN Commission on Sustainable Development, the OECD, the World Bank, Daly and Cobb (Index of Sustainable Economic Welfare), and Rees and Wackernagel (Ecological Footprint). However, none of these was judged particularly successful:

> none of the approximate measures listed above can be said to have been successful as indicators of sustainable development on the basis of their influence on practical policy. This may in some cases be due to the fact that rather large numbers of indicators, often representing measurements without theory, have been developed which only to a limited extent have been able to focus on issues of critical importance for the sustainability of developments. Instead, attempts have been made to measure almost all aspects of developments. On the other hand, the construction of single aggregate indicators has often made it difficult to judge how individual areas of importance for sustainability have been weighted and aggregated, reducing the confidence in and thus the usefulness of such aggregate indicators; it often leads to discussion of methodology rather than substance. (MoF 2005, p. 12)

From this critique of other measures of sustainable development, some core purposes of the national indicator set can be spelled out. The indicators should: measure sustainable development understood as non-declining welfare over time; take into account the environmental, social and economic dimensions of sustainability; be designed such that they have an influence on practical policy; be theory driven; and avoid weighted and aggregated indicators. They should also maintain 'a sharp focus on matters that are or may be of great political and practical importance for policies to enhance the sustainability of future developments' (MoF 2005, p. 13). This was what the national indicator set should achieve.

4. CAPTURING THE GLOBAL AGENDA

The national indicator set undoubtedly captures some crucial elements of sustainable development as outlined in *Our Common Future*. Its main aim is to function as an aid to policies to enhance sustainable development in Norway. However, the core indicator also somewhat obscures what sustainable development is, and how it should be measured. International cooperation for sustainable development, combating global poverty, climate change, biodiversity, and so on, are core sustainable development issues regardless of whether one belongs to the weak or strong sustainability camps. And yet there are a number of questions that can be raised regarding the 18 indicators. Here we will discuss the system of indicators, singling out a few of them for particular comment.

The first question that can be raised concerns the assumption that sustainable development necessarily implies non-declining welfare over time. There is no necessary logical link between this assumption and the standard definition where sustainable development is defined as development that meets the needs of the present without compromising the ability of future generations to meet their own needs (WCED 1987, p. 43). Meeting needs is not necessarily equivalent to welfare. Serafy points out 'weak sustainability' is not the same as 'sustainable development' and neither is 'strong sustainability' (1996, p. 76). Instead 'weak' and 'strong' sustainability should be seen as 'rules' for how sustainable development could or should be attained (Asheim 1999, p. 164). It is therefore quite easy to imagine that under given circumstances a decline in welfare could be better for achieving sustainable development than increased welfare. The following argument from the expert commission gives some substance to such an image:

> There is probably widespread agreement that a main threat to global sustainable development can be found in the uneven distribution of resources between rich and poor countries and between rich and poor populations and the conflicts that these inequalities create. Unless the needs of the poor over the longer term are better met than today, we may ask whether sustainable development can be achieved. Key challenges are poverty and global environmental problems. (MoF 2005, p. 7)

Sustainability, according to the expert commission, is further assumed to rest on three pillars: economic, social and environmental. The claim, which the commission attributes to the Brundtland Commission, is that 'without satisfactory developments in all three areas, society as a whole could not achieve sustainable development' (MoF 2005, p. 6). The three pillars of sustainability, however, were not formulated explicitly by the Brundtland Commission, although these pillars – or dimensions – can be identified in the report.

The categorization of dimensions of sustainability has led to an analytical approach where different dimensions have to be seen together, not only

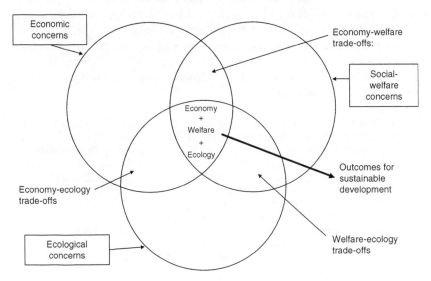

Figure 9.2   Three widely used dimensions of sustainable development

at the state level but also at business and industry levels. The argument for this approach is that there are economic concerns that must be balanced with social-welfare concerns. While increased *production* is understood as a measure of achieving economic growth, it is important that the outcome of the production process also satisfies social welfare concerns for those involved in, and affected by, the process. At the same time there may be adverse ecological impacts of production in terms of pollution. Too much of a focus on ecological concerns may, however, challenge the profitability of the production process. As a consequence economic and social welfare concerns may be hampered by ecological requirements. While this may appear to be a difficult task to implement in practice, it is nonetheless a necessary exercise if both nature conservation and poverty eradication are to be promoted. It is argued that we should remain focused on economic, welfare and ecological concerns, as illustrated in the centre of Figure 9.2. Figure 9.2 summarizes the challenge of promoting sustainable development as that of resolving trade-offs between economic, social welfare and ecological concerns.

While this makes intuitive sense, it nonetheless conceals one of the basic assumptions behind sustainable development as envisaged by the

Brundtland Commission – *the global partnership*. The basic assumption here is that sustainable development leads to different priorities in developed and developing countries. For developed countries, sustainable development cannot be about development in the traditional sense. Developed countries are already developed. Arguably the sustainable development challenges for a rich country such as Norway are first and foremost *environmental*. The following quote from John Dryzek encapsulates this perspective:

> The core story line of sustainable development begins with a recognition that the legitimate developmental aspirations of the world's peoples cannot be met by all countries following the growth path already taken by the industrialized countries, for *such action would over-burden the world's ecosystems*. Yet economic growth is necessary to satisfy the legitimate needs of the world's poor. ... Economic growth should therefore be promoted but guided in ways that are both environmentally benign and socially just. Justice here refers not only to distribution within the present generation, but also to distribution across future generations. Sustainable development is not just a strategy for the future of developing societies, but *also for industrialized societies, which must reduce the excessive stress their past economic growth has imposed upon the earth*. (Dryzek 1997, p. 129)[4]

An understanding of sustainable development as primarily environmental for developed countries does not imply that there are no trade-offs among the social, economic and environmental dimensions involved, but it imposes a hierarchy of obligations and priorities on which sustainable development goals receive the most emphasis. In Figure 9.2, the circle representing 'ecological concerns' should be at least twice as big as the other two (representing economic and social welfare concerns), and the core should be largely environmental. Understanding the challenges of sustainable development as primarily environmental for developed countries has, to some extent, become part of the rhetoric of Norwegian politics, but not of its practice.

5.   'TWO OUT OF THREE AIN'T BAD'

The second question that can be raised concerns the assumption that growing national wealth indicates that sustainable development is being achieved. Is this really the implication? If not, how central should the concept of national wealth be? In the reports from Statistics Norway reviewing progress on each of the indicators, the national wealth approach leads to some rather absurd conclusions. The main message on indicator 13 is formulated as follows: 'Net national income is increasing. It indicates that the Norwegian economy is on *a sustainable course'* (Brunvoll et al. 2008, p. 63).[5] A major reason for this is the 'extraction of non-renewable natural resources, i.e. oil and gas for the most part, is an important source of income for Norway. The significance of this source has increased from yielding 5 per cent of our income in the first period to 20 per cent in the last period' (Brunvoll et al. 2008, p. 11).

To say that the Norwegian economy is on a *sustainable course,* however, is not only misleading but is also highly questionable. As acknowledged by the authors of the report from Statistics Norway, it is not possible from this position to argue 'that the development is sustainable from a holistic perspective' since 'the value of access to national parks/untouched nature, the value of biological diversity and a stable climate is left out' (Brunvoll et al. 2008, p. 66). But then it does not make sense to claim that the Norwegian economy is on a sustainable course either. Sustainable would then imply and refer to something else other than sustainable development, which it does not. The same conclusion with the same reservations were presented in the report for 2010 on the indicators. Development in Norway is sustainable when it comes to 'economic sustainability' (Brunvoll and Smith 2010, p. 778).

Unfortunately the direct linkage to environmental problems through physical sustainability has by and large disappeared in the economic conceptions of sustainability. There are two main reasons for this. Consistent with the economic view of *natural capital* is that natural capital 'does not consist of the actual physical items themselves, the "physical stock", but the realised or realisable value of that stock' (Holland 1999, p. 58). According to Holland (1999), this implies that if more value is realized or realizable from less physical stock, the capital value could be sustained and the level of natural capital must accordingly be held to remain no lower than what it was before, despite a real degradation of the environment. Under the notion of 'natural capital', therefore, environmental degradation need not be *'identified as a "running down" of natural capital at all'* (Holland 1999, p. 59).

The second point relates to what Norton refers to as the 'Grand Simplification', which is 'an implausibly strong, even extreme, statement of the ignorance problem', which suggests that we cannot know anything about the preferences of future generations (Norton 1999, p. 127). Instead, the only thing we can do is to maintain a non-diminishing stock of capital. Hence, sustainable development is operationalized as non-declining welfare over time, what Holland (1999, p. 119) refers to as the 'utility comparison' (UC) approach. The problem with this is that it ignores the effects of current actions on future generations, and it also obscures our moral obligations to future generations. In effect, the UC approach argues that as 'long as the future is richer, the future will have no right to complain that they have been treated unfairly' (Holland, 1999, p. 124). Thus, the main threats to physical sustainability identified in *Our Common Future* (1987) – climate change, loss of biological diversity, pollution, food security – more or less vanish in natural capital and the Grand Simplification.

Seen from this perspective, the system of indicators seems unable to answer the two most important questions they are supposedly meant to address. This is also acknowledged in the report from Statistics Norway:

> *First:* Are we using up too much of the world's resources thereby preventing future generations from maintaining the same level of welfare? Are we practicing good housekeeping so that we can leave the earth in an equally good condition for future generations? *Next:* What resources are the most critical – is it the case for example that dwindling natural resources to a marked degree can be replaced by human knowledge? One example can help to throw light on this problem: Knowledge and technological insight can result in the same benefit being achieved with less consumption of, for example energy resources, but does the increase in knowledge help to reduce the energy consumption or is the consumption increased due to new goods steadily being available? (Brunvoll et al. 2008, p. 9)

The indicator set's impotence is further illustrated by the weak indicators in the two areas that may be seen as the core global environmental sustainability problems: biological diversity and climate change. On the issue of biological diversity, the following comment summarizes the current status of this indicator:

> There is currently no systematic, nationwide monitoring of the condition of any of the indicators in this area. The figures that are presented are therefore encumbered with a large degree of uncertainty. The development of bird populations in farmland, forests and mountains is uncertain. A comprehensive assessment of inland and coastal waters shows that the poorest quality of freshwater is south of Møre og Romsdal and the poorest quality of sea water is along the coast and fjords from the Swedish border to Rogaland. (Brunvoll et al. 2008, p. 10)

The description of climate change was not much better:

> Greenhouse gas emissions in Norway in 2007 were five million tonnes higher than the Kyoto target for the year preceding entry into the agreement period (2008–2012). The level has never been so high. The increase was 3.0 per cent from 2006. Norway's emission quota is 1 per cent higher than the level in 1990. In order to meet the obligation, substantial purchases of discharge permits from abroad may be needed. (Brunvoll et al. 2008, p. 10)[6]

Three remarks should be made regarding the indicator on climate change. First, given the fact that climate change is *the* sustainability challenge of the twenty-first century, it should not be lumped together with ozone and long-range air pollution. Rather, it deserves its own heading. Second, with respect to indicator 3, Norwegian emissions related to the Kyoto target seem grossly inadequate as an indicator for any notion of sustainability. It should at least be supplemented with the national long-term targets that the Norwegian Parliament agreed to in 2008 in what is termed *Klimaforliket* (the climate settlement). These targets would therefore include: being *carbon neutral* by 2050 (or by 2030 if there is substantial progress in the international negotiations); significantly reducing its own greenhouse gas emissions and offsetting the remaining through the purchase of emission reductions worldwide; to over-fulfilling the Kyoto Protocol commitments for emission cuts by 10 per cent, corresponding to 5 million tonnes of CO_2 equivalents annually in the period 2008–12; cutting a further 10 million tonnes of CO_2 by 2020; reducing emissions of greenhouse gases by 30 per cent or more by 2020 compared with 1990 levels, and taking two-thirds of the reductions at home (although not explicitly stated in the compromise, the new target was officially interpreted to imply that). Third, it could be argued that a pure CO_2 target would be a better indicator of a sustainability trajectory for the Norwegian economy than a comprehensive coverage of greenhouse gases. As a gas, CO_2 is by far the most difficult to address and is therefore of greater strategic importance. This raises the question of the purpose(s) of the indicators chosen. Is it to provide strategic information for a sustainable development transition, or is it designed to make one look good?

Seen together, both the economic and social indicators show a positive development (with the exception of indicator 17). Although this is not stated, one could, within the paradigm of national wealth, draw the conclusion that social development in Norway is also on *a sustainable course*. Both economically and socially Norway is on a sustainable trajectory, despite increasing GHG emissions and increasing energy and material consumption. Since 'two out of three ain't bad', the mockery of sustainable development would be complete. The national translation of sustainable development thus captures some core elements but is unable to say anything about priorities, weighting or whether or not developments are in fact sustainable when seen together, thus begging the question of the value of the capital approach.

6.   LINKING THE GLOBAL AND THE NATIONAL: CLIMATE CHANGE

The second case that illustrates the challenge of moving from the global concept of sustainable development to national policies is climate change. Officer-in-Charge at the UNFCCC, Richard Kinley, has argued that the 'greatest challenge in this 20 year odyssey is posed by global climate change' (Kinley 2006, p. 1). Moreover, climate change 'has traditionally been characterised as an environmental issue. I feel that this is a fundamental misperception. Rather, climate change is the ultimate sustainable development issue' (Kinley 2006, p. 1). The reason is of course that climate change historically has been intrinsically linked to development and it is the largest market failure yet discovered. In terms of climate change, traditional development crashes with the environment. Climate change may threaten human need satisfaction both today and in the future. It also endangers the natural systems that support life on Earth.

Climate change implies the potential for human activities to alter the Earth's climate to an extent unprecedented in human history with severe but also unpredictable consequences for humans and ecosystems. The dilemma is that given the first priority of sustainable development (meeting the essential needs of the world's poor, to which overriding priority should be given), as well as expected population growth rates, 'a five- to tenfold increase in manufacturing output will be needed just in order to raise developing-world consumption of manufactured goods to industrialised world levels by the time population growth rates level off next century' (WCED 1987, p. 15). Climate change therefore represents a tremendous challenge for a global community with billions of poor people, and growing global GHG emissions. Unfortunately, the 'future-oriented view of sustainable development' is unable to capture these linkages between intra- and inter-generational justice, which ultimately makes the task of achieving sustainability even harder.

As we have seen, climate change has not been given any special status in the Norwegian national indicator set for sustainable development as it is just one of 18 indicators. How then should the global problem of climate change be translated into national goals and targets? What constitute appropriate national targets? And, finally, how should they be achieved? These issues are complex, and the appropriate translation of the *global* has been highly controversial in Norway. Hovden and Lindseth (2004) argue that there have been two dominant climate-related political discourses in Norway: the *national action* (NA) discourse and the *thinking globally* (TG) discourse. These can be seen as two different translations of the global. According to Hovden and Lindseth, there was a broad political consensus in Norway in the late 1980s and early 1990s where 'climate change was viewed as a serious environmental problem where national action for reducting CO_2 emissions was required'. During the mid-1990s, however, and within a short period of three to four years, this was replaced with an 'equally' committed focus on the so-called Kyoto mechanisms and, more generally, the supposed positive international climate effects of the Norwegian petroleum industry' (Hovden and Lindseth 2004, p. 64).

Hovden and Lindseth (2004, p. 64) refer to this as a 'change in focus from "national action" to "thinking globally"'. They further define the *national action* (NA) discourse as emphasizing 'a national climate policy based on reductions in domestic GHG emissions in order to fulfil an international obligation and to demonstrate willingness to be an environmental pioneer'. The *thinking globally* (TG) discourse 'emphasises the need to think globally and to help secure the internationally most cost-effective reductions in GHG emissions' (Hovden and Lindseth 2004, p. 66). The report from the expert commission on indicators blends these two framings of climate change in Norway:

> The focus of the Commission has therefore been to develop indicators regarding the sustainability of national development. However, it may be asked how useful it is to assess national sustainability in isolation. Can Norway as a nation ever be said to be sustainable if international developments clearly fall short of a sustainable development? . . . However, we agree that national policies and action plans make sense because if developments and policies in each OECD country are sustainable, it will make important contributions to sustainable development globally. Many policy measures should in any event be taken by nation states, and in e.g. the realization of the Kyoto protocol – a global agreement – national action in addition to international permit trading is needed. And unless developed nations take the lead, one may not expect developing nations to follow suit. (MoF 2005, pp. 6–7)

The first part of this statement reflects the importance of the global dimension of sustainable development, which has frequently been used as a justification for global action and global solutions rather than national ones. The second part reflects the importance of national action, not for moral but for instrumental reasons: it is needed to get the developing countries on board. The argument that Norway has particular moral responsibilities due to its wealth, high and historic emissions, and so on, is harder to detect – but it is not impossible to find. The 2011 national budget states that, 'Today, the richest parts of the Earth's population cause so much stress on the environment and the resources that there is no room for others to increase their welfare without over-burdening the environments critical load' (MoF 2010–2011, p. 153).[7]

Despite such statements, this does not necessarily imply national action (that is, GHG emission reductions within Norway's borders). While the discourses identified by Hovden and Lindseth (2004, p. 66) are 'not mutually exclusive' since they 'share an overall concern with climate change and the view that action is needed', both discourses are related to the global approach but in different ways:

> both discourses actually use the global dimension as a central concept, but in very different ways: the NA discourse places emphasis on Norway as a responsible actor in the global arena, fulfilling its international obligations by reducing its GHG emissions; whereas the TG discourse refers to the global dimension in its emphasis on reducing global GHG emissions through a system that is internationally cost-effective. Thus, both discourses seek to appropriate 'the global' or the 'planetary' – terms which have long had a central place in progressive environmental politics and philosophy. (Hovden and Lindseth 2004, pp. 66–7)

There are some important nuances to consider. The global dimension in the TG can be divided into two different types of arguments. On the one hand, the consequential argument – what is the environmental effect of certain action? On the other hand, cost-efficiency arguments – where do we get the most out of our money? The first type of argument has been used to show that the effect of national action that increases national emissions in fact leads to a decrease in global emissions. One example is the argument that most of the increase in Norwegian GHG emissions come from (and will continue to come from) the oil and gas sector; but this gas is exported to Europe, making it possible for other countries to reduce their emissions by fuel-switching (from coal to gas), as for example in the United Kingdom. These arguments have in fact been used to *justify increased Norwegian national GHG emissions.* From this perspective Norway not only could, but *should,* increase its emissions! Before the Kyoto Protocol was negotiated in 1997, these arguments made some sense. However, after Kyoto, when Denmark and other European countries secured binding emissions targets, Norwegian national policies (and gas exports) arguably had no effect on emissions levels in Denmark as they are set by the internal distribution of emission reductions in the EU. Actions in Norway could, however, make GHG reductions cheaper in Denmark. If Denmark's fuel usage switches from coal to gas, they may need to do less in other sectors. Cost-efficient arguments have played a similar role:

> Cost-efficiency implies that the policy measures release activities that give as large as possible emission reductions for the resources applied. If one moves away from this, society has to give up unnecessarily much welfare in other areas to reach its environmental policy target. (Ministry of Environment (MoE), Report No. 34, 2006–2007 to the *Storting* (Parliament))

And further:

> Since reductions in GHG emissions has the same effect no matter where in the world they take place, climate change policies should give a large weight to global cost-efficiency. Measures in developing countries can give triple effect compared to expensive measures in rich countries. In addition to a larger climate effect per NOK, and a larger effect on the local environment, it can give a substantial development effect. (Ministry of Environment (MoE), Report No. 34, 2006–2007 to the *Storting*)

Arguments emphasizing cost-efficiency have therefore been used to assert that Norway *can* increase its domestic emissions within a sustainable development framework.

The main problem with Hovden and Lindseth's interpretation, however, is the location of the global level in the NA discourse. While stressing Norway's responsibilities for fulfilling its international obligations is a part of a global interpretation of climate change actions in NA, it is not in our opinion the most important. Thinking globally (TG) is not something that is, or has been, limited to the TG discourse. On the contrary, 'think globally, act locally' has long been a slogan for the environmental movement. Moreover, environmental space, for instance, is explicitly based on a notion of *global justice*. Thus, the national action prescribed is anchored in a distinct perception of global justice – that of equal emission rights on a per capita basis, often dubbed 'contraction and convergence'. This is based on historic and current emissions among the world's countries where Norway emits about 10 tonnes GHGs per capita, where the average is less than 4 tonnes, and where the sustainable level is less than 2 tonnes! For Norway, this would imply a 70–80 per cent reduction to reach an equal per capita share by 2050 within a 450 ppm scenario (NOU 2006, p. 27). The point here is that the NA discourse has a stronger global core based on the equity dimensions of sustainable development which are necessary to reconcile intra- and inter-generational justice. It should be noted that this is a dimension the 'future-oriented view' of sustainable development is unable to capture.

There are no easy answers as to how the global level should be included in the equation. The implications for sustainable development policies are contradictory. They depend on which national translation you advocate: consequential, cost-effective or global justice. Of these choices, global justice is closer to the core of sustainable development in the Brundtland vision. Given its major interest in oil and gas development, however, Norway has more or less tailor-made its climate change policies to oil and gas, favouring the first two types of argument. Emissions from energy industries witnessed an increase of 86.9 per cent between the years 1990 and 2006 and the increase 'is attributed primarily to the increased activity in the oil and gas extraction sector' (Norwegian Pollution Control Authority 2008, p. 77). In the Kyoto negotiations, Norway was part of the loose coalition of non-EU Annex I parties dubbed JUSSCANNZ.[8] They were united by anticipating 'greater difficulty than the EU in reducing emissions below 1990 levels' (Grubb et al. 1999, p. 34). This coalition managed to get a comprehensive coverage of greenhouse gases and the flexible mechanisms included in the Kyoto Protocol (Grubb et al. 1999). JUSSCANNZ later morphed into 'the Umbrella Group', an informal coalition that still comes together in international negotiations.[9]

The flexible mechanisms, also referred to as the Kyoto mechanisms, comprise: emissions trading (ET); joint implementation (JI); and the Clean Development Mechanism (CDM). These were designed to help Annex I parties cut the cost of meeting their emissions targets by taking advantage of opportunities to reduce emissions or increase greenhouse gas removals that cost less in other countries than at home.[10] Although the EU, China and the G77 managed to add the requirement that the Annex I parties must provide evidence that their use of the mechanisms is 'supplemental to domestic action' (which must constitute 'a significant element' of their efforts in meeting their commitments), both the comprehensive coverage of greenhouse gases and the Kyoto mechanisms secured the JUSSCANNZ countries (and others) flexibility in meeting their targets (Langhelle and Meadowcroft 2009, p. 247). Through the Kyoto Protocol, as well as in domestic politics, the consequentialist and cost-effective arguments were legitimized, and this is one reason why the national indicator for climate change is the Kyoto target.

The political controversy surrounding Norwegian climate change policies can be seen as a battle over *national translations of sustainable development*. This political cleavage in Norwegian politics has not only led to the resignation of a coalition government, but it has also largely hampered any serious attempt to implement strong sustainable development measures domestically. The national translation of sustainable development has made it possible for Norway to present itself as *sustainable* despite a 24.4 per cent increase in CO_2 emissions, and an 86.9 per cent increase in GHG emissions from the energy industries, between 1990 and 2006. Well done!

In their assessment of Norway's strategic sustainable development initiatives from 1989 to the 2007, Lafferty et al. (2007, p. 177) concluded that Norway's sustainable development profile is 'long on promise' and 'short on delivery', and that one major reason for this is the influence of a booming petroleum economy on distributive politics. An exceptional growth in public revenues due to oil and gas fosters intense political competition over the distribution of economic and welfare benefits – both among political parties and among governing coalitions – and so under-mines the political will to pursue a sustainable development agenda. Given the ability to use some of the surplus for development and environmental assistance, Norway stands as a sustainable development front-runner in international aid and international climate efforts while remaining a 'laggard' in sustainable production and consumption at home (Lafferty et al. 2007, p. 177).

In spite of new, ambitious objectives and despite the fact that Norway has a huge potential for renewable energy production (and export to Europe), there are few indications of more substantial policy changes. As far as energy is concerned, this reflects the situation of an ascendant petroleum energy system locked into a segmented policy regime where sustainable development indicators, the capital approach and climate change policies largely are tailored to protect the continued production of oil and gas in Norway. This is Norway's real sustainable development dilemma. In contrast to our neighbours (Sweden and Denmark), where the goal is to get rid of fossil fuels as soon as possible, this goal is politically impossible in Norway. Hence we can find a plausible explanation for the particular national translation of sustainable development in Norway.

7. CONCLUDING REMARKS: GIVING DIRECTION TOWARDS A SUSTAINABLE SOCIETY?

How then should one assess the Norwegian indicator set? As we argued earlier the indicators were intended to measure sustainable development conceptualized as non-declining welfare over time. They were also to take into account the environmental, social and economic dimensions of sustainability. And they were designed to have an influence on practical policy, be theory driven, and avoid weighted and aggregated indicators. They were also to maintain 'a sharp focus on matters that are or may be of great political and practical importance for policies to enhance the sustainability of future developments' (MoF 2005, p. 13). No doubt this understanding of sustainable development is that of non-declining welfare over time, with all its weaknesses. The indicators cover the environmental, social and economic dimensions of sustainability, but by avoiding weighted indicators the indicator set hides more than it reveals in terms of capturing sustainable development. Basically, it covers up the problem of climate change and the centrality of climate change in changing the course of development to a *sustainable* course. As such it does not contain a sharp focus on the matters that are of great political and practical importance for policies to enhance a sustainable development.

What then about its political influence? Has the indicator set influenced practical policy? From the fact that it has become part of the yearly national budget, and that the Ministry of Finance is behind it, one might argue that sustainable development has entered the centre stage of Norwegian politics. To some extent it has. However, there is a price. The state budget is now swamped with apparent references to sustainable development: 'sustainable growth' (pp. 14, 16), 'sustainable welfare state' (p. 80), 'sustainable growth in emerging markets' (pp. 115, 117), 'sustainable value creation' (p. 122), 'innovation and a sustainable Norway' (p. 126), 'sustainable competition in markets' (p. 134), and so on (MoF 2010–11).

The indicator set, however, is remarkably absent from the *important* political debates in Parliament. Climate change mitigation was heatedly debated in Parliament in 2007 and again in 2008. The strengthened policy focus in the form of the new policy strategy for climate change, adopted in 2008 as a political agreement among six of the seven parties currently represented in the Parliament, contributed to a new political momentum. With this national compromise the situation looked promising for substantial climate initiatives to emerge. If the promise to achieve two-thirds of the GHG emission reductions by 2020 at home is to be realized, Norway will have to implement stronger sustainability measures domestically. It remains to be seen whether the climate compromise in Parliament will stand the test of time. As of now the report to Parliament on how to achieve these targets has been delayed several times. Perhaps not surprisingly, however, these new initiatives are not explicitly linked to the national strategy for sustainable development.

As part of a process to revise and evaluate the sustainable development strategy in 2011, the Ministry of Finance organized meetings with representatives from academia, business and environmental NGOs, indicating some debate and discussion about the indicator set and the sustainable development strategy. However, the concept of sustainable development does not evoke enthusiasm, anger or substantial activity, either from politicians, the public administration, business or NGOs. There is currently limited active societal debate about sustainable development. Few, if any, representatives from civil society are providing any critique. Neither are they participating in any extensive dialogue with the Government on the sustainable development strategy. Maybe part of the reason is that the indicator set is unable to represent what really matters when it comes to realizing a sustainable development path. If this is the case, the real political influence of the indicator set is its ability to generate inaction rather than action. Thus, the indicator set has not managed to overcome the general impasse that currently characterizes Norway's sustainable development policies.

NOTES

1. Stiglitz et al. (2009) relate the source of perplexity to statisticians. It could easily be extended to other groups and politics in general.
2. For a critique of the 'future-oriented view', see Lafferty and Langhelle (1999).
3. There is actually a seventh thematic area not covered by the indicator set: Sami perspectives in environment and resource management (Brunvoll and Smith 2010, p. 9).
4. Author's italics.
5. Author's italics.
6. Norwegian GHG emissions dropped 5.4 per cent between 2008 and 2009, mainly due to the financial crisis. In 2010, they increased by 4.8 per cent (SSB 2011). GHG emissions in Norway, however, are expected to increase by almost 16 per cent by 2020 without any new measures (Ministry of Finance 2010–2011).
7. Author's translation.
8. JUSSCANNZ is an acronym derived from the following members in this informally organized association: Japan, United States, Switzerland, Canada, Australia, Norway and New Zealand (Depledge 2000). It started out as the JUSCANZ group, and expanded to JUSSCANNZ with the inclusion of Norway and Switzerland, while Switzerland 'frequently stood apart' (Grubb et al. 1999, p. 34)
9. The Umbrella Group is described in the following manner on the UNFCCC webpage: '. . . a loose coalition of non-EU developed countries which formed following the adoption of the Kyoto Protocol.' Although there is no formal list, the group is usually made up of Australia, Canada, Iceland, Japan, New Zealand, Norway, the Russian Federation, Ukraine and the US. The Umbrella Group evolved from the JUSSCANNZ group. Accessed 20 September 2011 at http://unfccc.int/parties_and_observers/parties/negotiating_groups/items/2714.php.
10. These mechanisms are described by UNFCCC in the following terms: under joint implementation, an Annex I Party may implement a project that reduces emissions (e.g. an energy efficiency scheme) or increases removals by sinks (e.g. a reforestation project) in the territory of another Annex I Party, and count the resulting emission reduction units (ERUs) against its own target. While the term 'joint implementation' does not appear in Arcticle 6 of the Protocol where this mechanism is defined, it is often used as convenient shorthand. In practice, joint implementation projects are most likely to take place in EITs, where there tends to be more scope for cutting emissions at low cost. . . . Under the clean development mechanism (CDM), Annex I Parties may implement projects in non-Annex I Parties that reduce emissions and use the resulting certified emission reductions (CERs) to help meet their own targets. The CDM also aims to help non-Annex I Parties achieve sustainable development and contribute to the ultimate objective of the Convention. . . . Under emissions trading, an Annex I Party may transfer some of the emissions under its assigned amount, known as assigned amount units (AAUs), to another Annex I Party that finds it relatively more difficult to meet its emissions target. See http://unfccc.int/kyoto_protocol/mechanisms/items/1673.php, accessed 18 September 2011.

REFERENCES

Adams, W. (1990), *Green Development. Environment and Sustainability in the Third World*, London: Routledge.

Asheim, G. (1999), 'Economic analysis of sustainability', in W.M. Lafferty and O. Langhelle (eds), *Towards Sustainable Development. On the Goals of Development – and the Conditions of Sustainability*, London: Macmillan, pp. 156–72.

Beckerman, W. (1994), '"Sustainable development": is it a useful concept?', *Environmental Values*, **3** (3), 191–209.

Beckerman, W. (1995), 'How would you like your sustainability, sir? Weak or strong? A reply to my critics', *Environmental Values*, **4** (1), 169–79.

Brunvoll, F., M. Greaker, S. Homstvedt, M. Kittilsen and T. Smith (2008), *Et bærekraftig samfunn? Indikatorer for bærekraftig utvikling 2008*, Rapport 2008: 25, Oslo,: SSB (Statistics Norway).

Brunvoll, F. and T. Smith (eds) (2010), *På rett vei?: Indikatorer for bærekraftig utvikling 2010*, Oslo: SSB

Common, M. (1996), 'Beckerman and his critics on strong and weak sustainability: confusing concepts and conditions', *Environmental Values*, **5** (1), 83–8.

Daly, H. (1995), 'On Wilfred Beckerman's critique of sustainable development', *Environmental Values*, **4** (1), 49–57.

Danielson, A., C. Hägg, H. Lindahl, L. Lundberg, J. Sonnegård and J. Enyimu (2007), *En Peer-review av Norges politik för hållbar utveckling*, Rapport, accessed 20 September 2011 at www.regjeringen.no/nb/dep/fin/tema/Barekraftig_utvikl ing/peer-review-av-norges-politikk-om-barekr.html?id=469840.

Depledge, J. (2000), 'Tracing the origins of the Kyoto Protocol: an article-by-article textual history', FCCC/TP/2000/2.

Dobson, A. (1998), *Justice and the Environment: Conceptions of Environmental Sustainability and Theories of Distributive Justice*, Oxford: Oxford University Press.

Dryzek, J. (1997), *The Politics of the Earth: Environmental Discourses*, Oxford: Oxford University Press.

Grubb, M., C. Vrolijk and D. Brack (1999), *The Kyoto Protocol: A Guide and Assessment*, London: Earthscan.

Holland, A. (1999), 'Sustainability: should we start from here?', in A. Dobson (ed.), *Fairness and Futurity: Essays on Environmental Sustainability and Social Justice*, Oxford: Oxford University Press, pp. 46–68.

Hovden, E. and G. Lindseth (2004), 'Discourses in Norwegian climate policy: national action or thinking globally?', *Political Studies*, **52** (3), 63–81.

Jacobs, M. (1995), 'Sustainable development, capital substitution and economic humility: a response to Beckerman', *Environmental Values*, **4** (1), 57–68.

Jacobs, M. (1999), 'Sustainable development as a contested concept', in A. Dobson (ed.), *Fairness and Futurity: Essays on Environmental Sustainability and Social Justice*, Oxford: Oxford University Press.

Kinley, K. (2006), keynote speech at 'Climate Change and Sustainable Development: An International Workshop to Strengthen Research and Understanding', New Delhi, 7 April 2006, accessed 20 September 2011 at http:// unfccc.int/files/press/news_room/statements/application/pdf/ 060407kinley.pdf.

Lafferty, W. (1996), 'The politics of sustainable development: Global norms for national implementation', *Environmental Politics*, **5** (2), 185–208.

Lafferty, W. and O. Langhelle (eds) (1999), *Towards Sustainable Development: On the Goals of Development – and the Conditions of Sustainability*, London: Macmillan.

Lafferty, W., J. Knudsen and O. Mosvold Larsen (2007), 'Pursuing sustainable development in Norway: the challenge of living up to Brundtland at home', *European Environment*, **17** (3), 177–88.

Langhelle, O. (1999), 'Sustainable development: Exploring the ethics of *Our Common Future*', *International Political Science Review*, **20** (2), 129–49.

Langhelle, O. (2000a), 'Sustainable development and social justice: Expanding the Rawlsian framework of global justice', *Environmental Values* **9** (2000), 295–323.

Langhelle, O. (2000b), 'Why ecological modernisation and sustainable development should not be conflated', *Journal of Environmental Policy and Planning*, **2** (4), 303–22.

Langhelle, O. and J. Meadowcroft (2009), 'CCS in comparative perspective', in J. Meadowcroft and O. Langhelle (eds), *Caching the Carbon. The Politics and Policy of Carbon Capture and Storage*, Cheltenham, UK and Northampton, MA, USA: Edward Elgar.

Malnes, R. (1990), *The Environment and Duties to Future Generations*, Lysaker, Norway: Fridtjof Nansen Institute.

Ministry of Environment (MoE) (2006–7), *Norsk klimapolitikk*, Rapport No. 34.

Ministry of Finance (MoF) (2005), *Indicators for Policies to Enhance Sustainable Development*. Oslo: MoF, accessed 20 September 2011 at www.regjeringen.no/upload/kilde/fin/bro/2005/0001/ddd/pdfv/246109-indicators.pdf.

Ministry of Finance (MoF) (2010–11), *Nasjonalbudsjettet 2011*, Rapport No. 2.

Norton, B. (1999), 'Ecology and opportunity: intergenerational equity and sustainable options', in A. Dobson (ed.), *Fairness and Futurity: Essays on Environmental Sustainability and Social Justice*, Oxford: Oxford University Press, pp. 118–50.

Norwegian Pollution Control Authority (SFT) (2008), *National Inventory Report: Greenhouse Gas Emissions 1990–2006 Reported According to the UNFCCC Reporting Guidelines*, Oslo: SFT.

Norges offentlige utredninger (NOU) (2005), *Enkle signaler i en kompleks verden. Forslag til et nasjonalt indikatorsett for bærekraftig utvikling.* Oslo: Statens forvaltningstjeneste. Informasjonsforvaltning, NOU 2005: 5.

NOU (2006), *Et klimavennlig Norge*, Informasjonsforvaltning, NOU 2006: 18, Oslo: Statens forvaltningstjeneste.

Organisation for Economic Co-operation and Development (OECD) (1993), *OECD Core Set of Indicators for Environmental Performance Reviews,* OECD Environment monographs no. 83, Paris: OECD.

OECD (1997), *OECD Environmental Performance Reviews – A Practical Introduction*, OCED/GD/GD(97)35, Paris: OECD.

Serafy, S. (1996), 'In defence of weak sustainability: a response to Beckerman', *Environmental Values*, **5** (1), 75–81.

Skolimowski, H. (1995), 'In defense of sustainable development', *Environmental Values*, **4** (1), 69–70.

Statistisk sentralbyrå (SSB) (2008), *Naturressurser og miljø 2008*, Oslo: SSB.

SSB (2011), *Kraftig oppgang i klimagassutslippene*, accessed 20 September 2011 at www.ssb.no/klimagassn/.

Stiglitz, J., A. Sen and J-P. Fitoussi (2009), *Report by the Commission on the Measurement of Economic Performance and Social Progress*, accessed 21 September 2011 at www.stiglitz-sen-fitoussi.fr.

United Nations (2008), *Measuring Sustainable Development. Report of the Joint UNECE/OECD/Eurostat Working Group on Statistics for Sustainable Development.* New York and Geneva: United Nations.

World Commission on Environment and Development (WCED) (1987), *Our Common Future*, Oxford: Oxford University Press.

10. Breaking the impasse on global environmental protection

Miranda A. Schreurs

The United Nations Conference on Sustainable Development (Rio+20) in June 2012 marked several important anniversaries. It has been 40 years since the United Nations Conference on the Human Environment (UNCHE) was held in Stockholm, 20 years since the UN Conference on Environment and Development (UNCED) was convened in Rio de Janeiro in 1992, and 10 years since the World Summit on Sustainable Development (WSSD) took place in Johannesburg in 2002. It is an appropriate time to reflect on what has been accomplished, what remains neglected, where the barriers to action lie, and what can be done to overcome obstacles to progress on addressing pressing sustainability challenges.

At this juncture it is clear that at the international level, as well as within many national jurisdictions, only halting progress is being made at fulfilling the numerous sustainable development and environmental objectives that have been set in the past. Globally, the environment is in an increasingly precarious state.

Rather than this reality galvanizing states into action, fatigue appears to be setting in with relation to the creation of new international environmental agreements and the implementation of several existing ones. The formation of environmental regimes was at the core of international political activities for several decades and there are now several hundred international environmental agreements. Yet, there has been frustratingly slow progress in relation to numerous pressing international environmental problems – including climate change, biodiversity loss, deforestation, ocean pollution and fisheries depletion, among others.

The remarkably unhurried pace at which international climate negotiations have progressed and our inability to date to put a stop to biodiversity loss are matters of great concern. The continued, and in some cases increasingly rapid, degradation and destruction of vital ecosystem services suggests there are serious inadequacies with existing global environmental governance structures and processes. Given the many serious threats facing the planet, and their potential impacts on human health and modern economic systems, why is it that global efforts to develop solutions encounter so much difficulty? The very mixed picture in terms of progress raises important questions regarding what can be done to improve governance of the global commons. Clearly, the international negotiations are not keeping pace with the seriousness of the problems they are expected to address. What can be done to improve governance for sustainability?

This chapter does not set out to define success or failure in regime formation and implementation, or to explain why some environmental problems have been addressed more successfully through international regimes than others, but rather to consider what alternative paths of activity are starting to be taken by actors who have lost patience with the international negotiations or who seek to influence them in the direction of greater sustainability.

While strong international agreements are to be hoped for, in cases where progress is slow or outcomes are disappointing, many actors are choosing to pursue parallel paths of action, presumably in the hope that others will follow suit and eventually improve the chances for successful international outcomes. Especially in highly complex global environmental cases such as biodiversity preservation and climate change, multiple strategies at multiple levels of government and society appear to be necessary.

1. INTERNATIONAL ENVIRONMENTAL PROTECTION AND SIGNS OF PROGRESS

It is not that there are no signs of progress. Forty years of national and global environmental efforts have resulted in considerable environmental learning and some performance improvements. There are various areas, at least in some parts of the world, where environmental conditions have improved, as for example with air and water pollution or the control of certain highly toxic chemicals. International environmental negotiations have been important in raising awareness and strengthening norms for protective and preventive action. There has been considerable scientific advancement in our understanding of the pressures facing the planet and a shift from broad, general statements to more concrete, measurable and verifiable goals. Global environmental negotiations have resulted in much institution-building and policy activity

There has also been a noticeable shift in the scale of problems at the focus of attention, from an early more narrow focus on industrial pollution and its environmental and human consequences, to a broader focus on trans-boundary and international environmental risks, including climate change, biodiversity loss, the destruction of marine fisheries and resource depletion. In addition, the concept of sustainable development has been promoted as a means of creating awareness of the need for integrating environmental and societal protections into economic development in such a way that intra- and inter-generational equity are also achieved.

Perhaps the most widely cited example of a successful international environmental agreement is the Montreal Protocol on Substances that Deplete the Ozone Layer. The use of various ozone-depleting chemicals has been largely phased out due to the Montreal Protocol. Chlorofluorocarbons (CFCs) that were widely used as refrigerants in refrigerators, automobiles and air conditioners, for the cleaning of semi-conductors and precision parts, in aerosol sprays, and in foam agents, have been replaced by other chemical substances that are non-ozone-depleting (Parson 2003). NASA observations suggest that due to the accumulation in the atmosphere of these long-lived chemicals (CFCs have lifespans of tens to hundreds of years) that were emitted over decades, the ozone 'hole' is still a serious problem and in 2011 reached a new record in size (NASA 2011), but the expectation is that with time the ozone layer will eventually begin to repair itself.

Another area where some signs of improvement are to be found in an otherwise frightening situation is with the loss of forested areas to agricultural and human settlements. In the 1990s, there was an estimated net loss of over 8.3 million hectares of forested land per year. The net rate of deforestation, although still 'alarming' according to the United Nations Food and Agricultural Organization, is down to about 5.2 million hectare per annum in the 2000–10 period. This is partly due to declines in deforestation in Brazil and Indonesia (where deforestation was most widespread in the 1990s), and large-scale tree-planting efforts in China, India, the United States and Vietnam. The net loss of forested area in the first decade of the 2000s equated to an area about the size of Costa Rica (UN News Centre 2010).

Some progress has also been achieved in terms of establishing protected areas. The percentage of land globally under some form of protected status has grown to 13 per cent, higher than the goal set down in the Biodiversity Convention of having 10 per cent of all ecological regions under protection by 2010. Still problematic, however, is that only about 5.8 per cent is under strict protection for biological diversity (Jenkins and Joppa 2009).

Signs of Concern

There are without doubt various signs of progress in terms of dealing with specific environmental matters. Still, the overall picture is worrisome. As the Millennium Ecosystem Assessment report that was released in 2005 points out, humans are rapidly degrading and destroying the ecological systems that are the basis for our species' long-term well-being and survival. Land is being converted for agricultural and other purposes at increasingly rapid rates, threatening global biodiversity. As a result of human activities, terrestrial species are going extinct at a rate that is as much as 1000 times background (historical) rates. An estimated 10–30 per cent of mammals, birds and amphibians are threatened with extinction. This is on top of the many species that have already been lost. Pollution of the oceans and human over-exploitation has destroyed large areas of coral reefs and depleted global fish stocks. And, greenhouse gas emissions are accumulating in the atmosphere at rates that threaten the planet with rapid increases in average global temperatures and the oceans with unnaturally high rates of acidification (MEA 2005).

When we consider where we are in dealing with rising greenhouse gas emissions, species loss and ecological degradation, it becomes clear that international efforts to address these challenges remain insufficient. And, with populations still growing rapidly in many parts of the world, these pressures will only be exacerbated. It is estimated that there are now more than 7 billion people on the planet and that the figure could reach 9 billion by 2050. Many of the most basic of human needs – such as clean water and sanitation services – are still not available to millions of people. According to United Nations estimates, 1 billion people lack access to safe drinking water, the vast majority of all illnesses are tied to polluted water, and water-related diseases are a major factor in millions of unnecessary deaths (UN Department of Public Information 2005).

In many areas the pace of political and institutional change is inadequate to keep up with the scale of the problems. Twenty years of international efforts to deal with climate change and biodiversity loss, or to promote sustainable development through the formation of global agreements, have met with mixed levels of success or failure, depending on where one prefers to lay the stress. David Vogel has suggested that the most successful international environmental agreements are those that are regional in scope, specific in focus and clearly associated with cross-border pollution. Writing in the mid-1990s, he suggested as examples of relatively successful agreements: the Montreal Protocol, the Convention on Long Range Transboundary Air Pollution, the Mediterranean Action Plan, the International Convention for the Prevention of Pollution from Ships, and the Convention for the Prevention of Marine Pollution by Dumping from Ships and Aircraft, the Convention for the Prevention of Marine Pollution from Land-Based Sources, and the Convention on the Protection of the Marine Environment of the Baltic Sea Area. Less successful, he suggests, have been the Convention on International Trade in Endangered Species, the International Tropical Timber Agreement, the Bonn Convention on Migratory Species, and the Convention on Biological Diversity. These latter cases have all required parties to carry substantial internal costs (Vogel 1997). There are certainly other areas of international environmental policy-making that could be added to this list, including climate change, ocean pollution, forest preservation and nanomaterials, among others. As Elizabeth DeSombre stated: 'International environmental cooperation is hard and is getting harder' (2005, p. 86).

At the heart of the matter is that the international environmental negotiations and agreements have not been able to alter many of the fundamental power relationships and institutional structures, as well as the consumption-based lifestyles that are at the root cause of the most serious environmental challenges today.

Insufficient attention has been given to some of the key ideas that came out of the World Commission on Environment and Development (WCED, or Brundtland Commission). The Brundtland Commission defined sustainable development as 'development which meets the needs of current generations without compromising the ability of future generations to meet their own needs'. It is a concept that underlines the importance of protecting natural resources and the environment, without which economic and social conditions cannot improve and could deteriorate. As the WCED pointed out, however, this will require an integration of 'economic and ecological considerations in decision making . . . [and] a change in attitudes and objectives and in institutional arrangements at every level' (WCED 1987). This revolution in thinking and in practice has yet to take place despite four decades of global environmental negotiations.

2.   FOUR DECADES OF GLOBAL ENVIRONMENTAL NEGOTIATIONS

The 1972 United Nations Conference on the Human Environment (UNCHE, or Stockholm Conference) is often taken as a turning point in global political awareness of environmental matters. The conference focused much-needed attention on a broad range of environmental pressures facing the planet and on the impacts of industrial 'toxicity' on natural systems. The conference also drew attention to the international dimensions of pollution, with a particular focus on acid rain. The Declaration of the United Nations Conference on the Human Environment enshrined the right to economic and social development while also calling for the protection of nature for present and future generations. The signatories of the declaration agreed that 'the heritage of wildlife and its habitat is gravely imperiled' and called for the safeguarding of 'the natural resources of the earth, including the air, water, land, flora and fauna and especially representative samples of natural ecosystems, [. . .] for the benefit of present and future generations . . .'. The declaration also emphasized the importance of safeguarding against the future exhaustion of non-renewable resources of the earth and ensuring that benefits from their use are shared by all.

Certainly much progress was made after this time (primarily in wealthier countries) in improving air quality, reducing water pollution, banning or controlling the use of many toxic chemicals, and finding new, ecologically less hazardous ways to manufacture many products. Capacities for environmental governance at the national level were strengthened through the creation of national environmental administrations and basic environmental legislation, covering air and water pollution, toxic substances and nature conservation. At the international level, the United Nations Environment Programme was formed. Since this time, the range of actors in the environmental and sustainable development communities has grown steadily (Conca and Dabelko 2010) and NGOs have won a place for themselves in international negotiations (Willets 1996).

A new interest in solving environmental problems through large international and global environmental agreements also gained force. Numerous international environmental agreements were formed, including the Convention on International Trade in Endangered Species, the Long Range Transboundary Air Pollution Convention, the Montreal Protocol on Substances that Deplete the Ozone Layer, and the Basel Convention on the Control of Transboundary Movements of Hazardous Wastes. More regionally specific international agreements were also established.

Yet, basic economic growth models remained largely unchallenged. The Stockholm Conference's warnings about the need to protect the planet's natural resources against future exhaustion were a concept that few nations embraced in their domestic environmental laws. Although by this time the notion of the precautionary principle was beginning to find roots in academic debate as well as in some limited policy fields, economic 'growth-first' norms continued to dominate. Rather than fundamental changes to energy and production systems, incremental energy- and resource-efficiency gains were emphasized, along with end-of-the-pipe pollution control solutions.

The United Nations Conference on Environment and Development (Rio Conference)

By the time the United Nations Conference on Environment and Development convened in Rio de Janeiro, there was growing concern that in our rush to develop, the very future of the planet was being put at risk. International environmental agreements were considered important for setting common goals and standards and creating a level playing field. Particularly big on the agenda were the issues of climate change, biodiversity loss and (tropical) deforestation (Paellemaerts 1992). In addition, the need to integrate economic development with environmental protection and the promotion of social equality began to be addressed under the concept of sustainable development.

With the Cold War over and many countries transitioning from authoritarian to more democratic structures, there was a strong sense of new possibilities for deepened international cooperation. A new era of global governance seemed to have dawned. Following on the success of the Montreal Protocol under which developed and developing states agreed to phase out chlorofluorocarbons and other ozone-depleting substances, there was a strong sense of possibility in tackling the degradation of the global commons through global agreements.

UNCED concluded with the formation of the United Nations Framework Convention on Climate Change (UNFCCC), the Convention on Biological Diversity (CBD), the Convention to Combat Desertification, a set of Forestry Principles and Agenda 21, an action plan for sustainable development.

Objectives were introduced in relationship to each of these areas:

1. to stabilize 'greenhouse gases in the atmosphere at a level that would prevent dangerous anthropogenic interference with the climate system';
2. to ensure the 'conservation of biological diversity, the sustainable use of its components and the fair and equitable sharing of the benefits arising out of the utilization of genetic resources';
3. 'to combat desertification and mitigate the effects of drought in countries experiencing serious drought and/or desertification, particularly in Africa ...' (note: desertification refers to land degradation in semi-arid and sub-humid regions from climate change and human activities);
4. to establish a global partnership to meet the challenges of environment and development.

At the national and local levels, states began to draw up sustainable development action plans (Lafferty and Meadowcroft 2000), and a structure was introduced to arrange for annual negotiations under the Biodiversity and Climate Change Conventions.

The Convention on Biological Diversity

The Convention on Biological Diversity (CBD) was established to address the rapid extinction of plant and animal species as a result of human settlements, economic and agricultural activities, land-use change, pollution, poaching and other factors. It has three straightforward objectives: (i) the conservation of biological diversity; (ii) the sustainable use of its components; and (iii) the fair and equitable sharing of the benefits arising out of the utilization of genetic resources. A target established in 2002 to significantly slow the loss of biological diversity by 2010, however, has not been achieved. The causes include land conversion due to agricultural and population pressures, invasive species and climate change, among other pressures, such as hunting and poaching.

At the meeting of the Conference of the Parties to the CBD in Nagoya, Japan in 2010, several new targets were established as part of a strategic plan for the decade through 2020. The 20 non-binding targets established include raising awareness about biodiversity loss, integrating biodiversity values into national and local development and poverty reduction strategies, removing subsidies harmful to biodiversity, and the setting of measurable targets. The rate of loss of natural habitats is to be at least halved, and the degradation and fragmentation of habitats significantly reduced. Fish and invertebrate stocks and areas under agriculture, aquaculture and forestry are to be managed and harvested sustainably. Pollution is to be brought down to levels that are not detrimental to ecosystem function and biodiversity. Nature reserves are to be expanded to cover 17 per cent of global land area (compared with 10–15 per cent today) and 10 per cent of marine areas (compared with just over 1 per cent today), and at least 15 per cent of degraded ecosystems are to be restored (CBD 2010). Countries are expected to draw up national plans related to these targets. Agreement was also reached in a Nagoya Protocol for rules on how countries should share benefits derived from genetic resources. Despite inadequate funding and a failure to meet initial biodiversity loss reduction goals, there has been less political acrimony in relation to the biodiversity negotiations than has been the case for climate change. Critical will be finding ways to make sure that the strategic goals are tied to concrete action plans, that monitoring and verification processes are in fact put into place, and that countries are held accountable in some fashion for non-compliance.

The Conference of the Parties to the CBD in Nagoya ended on a relatively positive note and with the hope that the international community might be able to achieve its 2020 targets. In contrast, the Conference of the Parties to the UNFCCC in Durban, South Africa ended with many questions as to where the climate negotiations are really headed.

Climate Change, the Kyoto Protocol and the Durban Platform

Global greenhouse gas emissions are rising rapidly. The concentration of greenhouse gas emissions in the atmosphere is estimated to have been about 280 parts per million (ppm) at the beginning of the Industrial Revolution. In 1990 they were at about 350 ppm. By 2012 they had risen to over 390 ppm (CO_2Now.org 2012). The Intergovernmental Panel on Climate Change (IPCC) warns that increases in the concentration of greenhouse gases raises the likelihood of irreversible change in the climate system as well as the chances of extreme weather events, including floods, droughts and temperature extremes. A major concern with rising global temperatures is that fresh water that is stored in ice – in the Arctic and Antarctic regions and in glaciers – will melt, raising sea levels and reducing the availability of fresh water. The IPCC suggests that tipping points are more likely to be reached if greenhouse gas concentrations go much beyond 450 ppm, a trajectory the global community is on and could hit sometime in mid-century if decisive political action is not taken.

Yet, the international climate negotiations that have been going on since preparations began for UNCED in the early 1990s have reached something of an impasse. At that conference the world's leaders agreed to the United Nations Framework Convention on Climate Change. Article 2 of the UNFCCC called for a 'stabilization of greenhouse gas concentrations in the atmosphere at a level that would prevent dangerous anthropogenic interference with the climate system' and set in motion annual meetings of the parties to the convention with the goal of establishing an international agreement to address rising greenhouse gas emissions. It took five more years before the Kyoto Protocol was negotiated in 1997, and another eight years before it came into force. As originally conceived, the Kyoto Protocol was supposed to cut the greenhouse gas emissions of the advanced industrialized states by 5.2 per cent of 1990 levels by 2012. But the United States pulled out in 2001 and Canada announced its intentions to exit from the agreement in December 2011. The decision by the United States to refrain from ratifying the agreement was an indication of a deep political divide that has persisted for the better part of the past two decades over climate change science and how (and whether) to try to mitigate greenhouse gas emissions. Opponents of the Kyoto Protocol argued that the agreement was unfair as it did not require developing countries to take action to stem the growth in their emissions. Thus, even at its best, the Kyoto Protocol was sorely restricted in terms of its potential impact due to the unwillingness of the United States, the largest greenhouse gas emitter among industrialized states, to join (Harrison and Sundstrom 2010). The protocol suffered another late blow when, just after the international climate negotiations in Durban, South Africa, Canada announced its intentions to formally withdraw from the agreement. With its carbon dioxide emissions soaring, Canada had no real chance of meeting its Kyoto Protocol emission reduction requirements. The international community also has no real recourse to sanctions to punish Canada for its failure to fulfil its 1997 pledge.

The Kyoto Protocol has been an important vehicle for the European Union to push domestic greenhouse gas emission targets and to strengthen relationships with developing countries on climate change through use of the Kyoto Protocol's flexibility mechanisms and, in particular, the Clean Development Mechanism. The EU as a whole has seen a substantial drop in emissions (although emissions at the end of 2009 were considerably higher in Ireland, Spain, Portugal and Greece than they were in 1990) and should easily be able to meet its Kyoto Protocol reduction commitments (–8 per cent of 1990 levels by 2012) (Würzel and Connelly 2011). However, the EU has had trouble convincing other states to agree to a second (post-2012) commitment period under the Kyoto Protocol. At the Durban climate negotiations, the EU was able to obtain some support for a second Kyoto Protocol commitment period, a crucial step in terms of keeping China and India involved in the negotiations. But Japan and Russia both made it clear that they have no intention of taking on further commitments under the Kyoto Protocol. Thus, while the Kyoto Protocol was kept alive in Durban, few countries outside of Europe have agreed to set new legally binding emission reduction targets. On the somewhat brighter side, the Kyoto Protocol is expected eventually to be superseded by an as-of-yet-still-non-extant alternative agreement. In Durban, agreement was reached among both developed and developing countries to work on a new global agreement (the Durban Platform) that is supposed to be negotiated by 2015 and to come into effect by 2020. But the contents of the agreement are uncertain and whether key states will in the end agree to ratify a new accord remains an open question. The climate negotiations cannot be dubbed a total failure, as the door to further discussions remains open and some progress was made on a Green Climate Fund to aid developing countries to cope with climate change, and on the establishment of a mechanism for protection of forests (REDD+). But given the seriousness of the climate change problem and the rate at which global emissions are rising, the snail's pace at which the international community is moving on a global climate agreement is worrying.

The strong hope at the beginning of the 1990s that an international climate agreement would be reached that would set into motion a coordinated global effort to reduce greenhouse gas emissions has been replaced by frustration and scepticism. The international climate negotiations remain important for the role they play in developing and diffusing scientific information, and in providing a forum for large and small states, developed and developing countries, civil society groups and those that are most likely to be heavily impacted by climate change to express their positions and views. The climate negotiations can also place a certain pressure on national governments to act, as at least for a concentrated period of time, global attention is focused on what actions they are taking. And there has been some other progress that can be linked closely to the agreement. More than 3850 Clean Development Mechanism projects were registered under the Kyoto Protocol as of early 2012 (UNFCCC 2012). These projects have reduced the business-as-usual growth in greenhouse gas emissions in China and India to a small extent, and a CDM levy helps to finance climate adaptation projects in developing countries. The European Union as a whole is on track to meet its greenhouse gas emission reduction goals, and some countries – such as Germany and Great Britain – have far exceeded emission reduction requirements expected of them.

Yet achieving consensus among some 190 states on the path to move forward, the pace of activities, and the differentiated responsibilities to be taken by states, is a daunting task that has proven to be bigger than the negotiators have known how to deal with (Victor 2001; Christiansen and Kellow 2002). Given that the concept of national sovereignty remains so strong, and that in the national politics of many states primacy is still given to economic growth models that are based on industrial and energy structures that formed decades or centuries ago, a shifting array of naysayers has managed to block substantial progress.

Moreover, there are other difficulties that are exacerbating the problem. An unintended consequence of the effort to protect the ozone layer through the Montreal Protocol is that some of the substitute chemicals (HFCs, PFCs and SF_6) that were introduced to replace CFCs are potent greenhouse gases that have global warming potentials hundreds to thousands of times those of CO_2. The Montreal Protocol was a success in terms of protecting the ozone layer. It brings with it, however, new challenges in relation to climate change. Efforts are mounting to bring attention to the importance of controlling these chemicals internationally (Lopez and Orsini 2011) and to developing potential replacements (Becken et al. 2011). But resistance to banning their use among some states remains strong.

The important question is what can be done to break through these various impasses.

3.   GREENING DEVELOPMENT

A fundamental obstacle to progress on sustainable development is a focus on economic growth models and indicators that do not include environmental considerations. Economic growth is premised on the availability of resources that can be exploited. As environmental degradation progresses, however, the basis for economic growth diminishes. The greening of growth and development is a critical step on the way to greater sustainability.

Removing Subsidies for Polluting Industries

One important way to improve the chances of movement towards more green and sustainable economic and energy structures and a successful global agreement is the removal of subsidies – real and hidden – for polluting industries. Subsidies cannot be justified for industries that are large greenhouse gas emitters.

In its 2010 *World Energy Outlook*, the International Energy Agency reported that fossil fuels receive six times the level of subsidies as renewable energies ($409 billion in 2010 compared with $66 billion for biofuels, wind and solar). These subsidies to the fossil fuel industry promote wasteful consumption, discourage investment in energy infrastructure, disproportionately benefit the rich, and distort markets and create barriers to clean energy investment (IEA 2010). Nuclear energy is also heavily subsidized. The Union of Concerned Scientists has calculated that if the legacy subsidies (all of the subsidies the industry has received over its history) are considered, they amount to 7 cents per kilowatt-hour, 'an amount equal to about 140 percent of the average wholesale price of power from 1960 to 2008, making the subsidies more valuable than the power produced by nuclear plants over that period. Without these subsidies, the industry would have faced a very different market reality – one in which many reactors would never have been built . . .' (UCS 2011). Clearly, there is an imbalance here that favours conventional industries over more-sustainable, renewable energies. This imbalance needs to be addressed.

Where state support is needed is for more research and development related to renewable energies and energy-efficiency technologies and related infrastructure – technologies that are congruent with sustainable development goals. While there has been much critique of the subsidies being used to support renewable energies, the renewable energy revolution that has started in recent years would not have been possible without this initial support. As the technology learning curve improves, the costs of renewable energies are declining and should eventually achieve grid parity. Positive incentives for the use of renewable resources and renewable energies should also be encouraged through feed-in-tariff and quota schemes, at least until renewables are at a point where they can compete against industries that have long benefited from such subsidies themselves.

Ecological Taxation, Green Procurement and Green Growth

A strong case can also be made for requiring green public procurement. Governments are typically the largest consumers of energy and resources. With the introduction of green purchasing requirements for energy, products and resources, governments can reduce their environmental footprints and lead the way for industries and consumers to follow. Sustainability requirements can also be included in all government-supported projects. Publicly funded construction, for example, should pay attention not just to short-term economic costs, but also to the sustainability of the construction materials used and to the implications of the building materials used for long-term energy and resource demand. Practices through which contracts are awarded to the lowest cost bidder, regardless of the sustainability of the projects and its long-term energy and resource costs, make little economic or environmental sense.

Tax burdens should also be shifted so that luxury and polluting consumption is more heavily taxed. Carbon taxes are a good example. Climate-friendly transportation could be supported through such taxes. Energy-efficiency improvements in housing could be encouraged through tax incentives financed through carbon taxes. More needs to be done to challenge existing economic structures and consumption-oriented lifestyles that pay insufficient heed to environmental constraints. Stronger interventions will be needed to shift societies in the direction of environmental good governance and sustainable development.

Many of these ideas can be linked to the concept of 'green growth', a major theme of the Rio+20 gathering. Governments and economic actors need to be persuaded that long-term well-being is linked to economic development that is energy- and resource-efficient and protective of biodiversity. Although there is considerable awareness of the health and environmental consequences of pollution, in many parts of the world there is still a strong belief that environmental protection can only be achieved *after* economies develop. This way of thinking needs to be altered. More industrialized countries have an obligation to be first movers, shifting away from the many unsustainable economic structures and practices of the past to cleaner, more-resource-respecting economic processes. They also need to significantly strengthen partnerships that can facilitate action in developing countries where development and environmental protection must come hand in hand.

Polycentric Governance with Ambitious Goals

Beyond these economic and investment considerations, more needs to be done to think about governance structures for sustainable development. David Victor, a long-time critic of the Kyoto Protocol process, argues that diplomats have failed to recognize that climate change is an inherently different problem than other environmental problems and that their focus on global targets and timetables is misguided. He argues instead for focusing on a smaller club – one made up of the most important emitters that would be expected to make contingent offers ('I'll do this, if you do that') (Victor 2011). Victor's focus remains at the national level and can itself be criticized for not giving sufficient voice to those who will be most heavily impacted by climate change. Yet, it does have merit to the extent that it directs attention to finding ways to move forward and make progress among smaller groups of countries. One could argue that this is in fact what the European Union itself has achieved. The European Union has set for itself energy-efficiency and renewable-energy targets that require cooperation by all member states and affiliated nations.

Climate change, and issues of sustainability more generally, are problems that require action at multiple levels of government: international, national, regional (prefectural, provincial, across communities) and local, as well as vertical and horizontal integration (Lafferty and Meadowcroft 2000; Lafferty 2004). Compared with the attention that has been given to international and national activities, however, until recently relatively limited attention has been paid to the role of urban and regional governments in combating global climate change (Bulkeley and Betsill 2003; Schreurs 2008, 2010).

Elinor Ostrom has argued that a more 'polycentric governance approach' to dealing with climate change appears necessary and possible. She suggests that a polycentric approach would work at various levels with monitoring by local, regional and national actors. In collective-action problems characterized by conflict, a polycentric approach offers the potential to pursue experimental efforts at multiple levels. These small- to medium-scale governance systems can be linked together through information networks and monitoring across and between levels. In particular, she points to the potential of strengthening the many smaller-scale efforts under way to mitigate climate change. She suggests the importance of finding ways to support the development of such a polycentric system in order to begin the process of reducing greenhouse gases and laying a strong foundation for a global agreement down the road (Ostrom 2012).

Towards Low-carbon Energy Systems

It may well be that the best chance for the international climate negotiations is by altering how alternative energy systems are viewed and breaking the grip of traditionally dominant energy players, as has been suggested by William Lafferty and Audun Ruud. The promotion of renewable energy in Europe has come to be seen as a policy that is not only good for climate change but also for jobs, social cohesion and energy security (Lafferty and Ruud 2008). As new coalitions form around these more climate-friendly energy systems, national policy debates can change. Of course, it must be recognized that this is still a very difficult challenge that faces much resistance from large conventional energy concerns as well as local opposition to wind parks and electricity grids 'in my backyard'.

Germany is perhaps the most formidable example today of a country that has politically accepted the need for a transition to a sustainable energy future. In the early 1990s, Germany had only about 3 per cent of its electricity from renewables. By 2012, this figure had climbed to about 20 per cent. What changed is that as early efforts at promoting renewables paid off, an increasingly powerful community of actors supportive of more sustainable energy structures formed. By the time the Energy and Climate Package of 2010 was formulated by the conservative government of Angela Merkel, a basic cross-party consensus had formed on the importance of tackling climate change and promoting renewable energy development (even though in 2010 Merkel backed an unpopular decision to lengthen the running lifetime of Germany's nuclear power plants, a decision that was then reversed after the Fukushima nuclear accident). Germany has basically set out to break both its dependence on traditional fossil fuels and on nuclear energy through the promotion of renewable energies and energy efficiency. By 2020, the plan is to reduce greenhouse gas emissions by 40 per cent of 1990 levels (as of 2010, emissions were 25 per cent below) and by 80–95 per cent by 2050. This is to be done through sharp improvements in energy efficiency and a strong expansion in renewable energies (35–40 per cent of electricity is to be from renewables by 2020 and 80 per cent by 2050). These figures are to be achieved while simultaneously phasing out nuclear energy. By being a pioneer among manufacturing economies in promoting new renewables, Germany is setting out to establish an energy system that will be both low carbon and resource-sustainable. This is one of the biggest experiments currently under way towards shifting a manufacturing economy away from heavily polluting fossil fuels and nuclear energy towards renewable forms of energy.

To the extent this model succeeds, it could well spread to other regions of Europe and elsewhere, and so serve as a powerful motor of change towards sustainability. Japan, for example, has been paying close attention to the German model as it tries to determine how to respond to the Fukushima nuclear disaster. While similar developments are not yet evident at the federal level in the United States, they can be seen at the state level, where states such as California and New York have embraced relatively ambitious renewable energy and climate change programmes.

Local Leadership and Experimentation

Ambitious efforts can be found among local communities as well. In fact, it is at the sub-national level that many of the most exciting developments are occurring. Many cities and municipalities in Europe, North America and increasingly now in Asia and Latin America have started to introduce sustainability and climate action plans. Indeed, there seems to be a rapid diffusion of activity among local communities with an interest in being leaders in these fields. This is visible both among major metropolitan centres (such as Berlin, New York, Seattle and Tokyo) as well as countless medium and smaller-sized cities and towns.

There are even a growing number of towns and regions that have established targets to become 100 per cent renewable energy communities (for example Scotland, the Cook Islands, and San Francisco have considered plans for achieving 100 per cent renewables by 2020). Others have already achieved this goal (for example Dardesheim, Germany; Samsø, Sweden; and Güssing, Austria).[1] If these activities are noticed by others, they can have multiplier effects. Various international networks have been established for just this purpose. In 2005 the Mayor of Seattle adopted a climate action plan committing the city to reduce its greenhouse gas emissions by 7 per cent of 1990 levels by 2012, 30 per cent by 2024 and 80 per cent by 2050 (http://www.seattle.gov/climate/). He then went out to challenge other mayors in the United States to do the same, launching the US Mayors' Climate Protection Agreement (http://www.seattle.gov/mayor/climate/). More than 1000 mayors have signed the US Mayors' Climate Protection Agreement. In other OECD countries, similar developments are taking place. In Europe, in February 2009, 400 cities agreed to a Covenant of Mayors' Initiative on climate change, pledging to go beyond the EU's 20 per cent greenhouse gas reduction goal by 2020 relative to 1990 levels through the implementation of a Sustainable Energy Action Plan (http://ec.europa.eu/energy/sustainable/doc/covenant_en.pdf). Kyoto Mayor

Yorikane Masumoto decided to take his city's efforts to the international stage by launching the World Mayors' Conference on Climate Change. The inaugural conference was held in Montreal, Canada in 2005 (http://www.iclei.org/index.php?id=7199).

For many years action on climate change was stalled by concerns about the costs associated with the introduction of climate measures. Perspectives are beginning to change – at least in some places – as it becomes increasingly clear that being 'green' can help cities to be more economically competitive. As these new ways of thinking take off and multiply, strengthening the coalitions of actors behind them, there is an increased chance that more national governments will be willing to take on climate goals and commit to international action. Structures and policies that facilitate and support such grassroots initiatives are highly important.

The Need for More Quantifiable and Measurable Goals and Systematic Monitoring

Yet another important lesson of the past several decades of international environmental negotiations is to combine the setting of sustainability goals and targets with improved information systems, and monitoring and verification schemes. Lack of data is often a barrier to understanding the extent of problems and can complicate efforts to monitor progress. Where targets exist, and data are made available to the public, non-governmental organizations and civil society actors are empowered in their efforts to monitor governmental, industrial and societal performance. This is part of what makes the Millennium Development Goals or the Millennium Environmental Assessment report so important and lends hope that the 20 goals for 2020 under the Biodiversity Strategic Plan may stimulate greater action.

Nevertheless, much more needs to be done to understand where the planet's ecological limits are – points beyond which tipping points could be reached (for example, with irreversible climate change, ecological collapse due to biodiversity loss, fisheries collapse due to overfishing, or mineral exhaustion due to excessive extraction and wasteful use), and what can be done to reduce the possibility of coming close to such dangerous limits (Rockström et al. 2009). Very troubling is the continued excessive exploitation of many resources and the stresses being placed on fragile ecological systems. Much as occurred with the overfishing of Atlantic cod that led to a sudden and potentially permanent collapse of this species, at the rate at which biological diversity is being lost there is concern not only that specific species may disappear but also that entire ecosystems could collapse. Rising greenhouse gas emissions could exacerbate this problem if average global temperatures tip the climatic system out of balance, further stressing ecological systems.

Looking Towards the Future

It is not only in relation to climate change that polycentric approaches may be useful, but also in relation to many other sustainability challenges. There are other issues that could become environmental or health concerns, although the scientific evidence remains uncertain, such as is the case with nanomaterials (SRU 2011). In 2008, a horizon-scanning effort by British environmental experts identified 25 potential problem areas for British biodiversity, including increasing demand for biofuels, geo-engineering to mitigate the effects of climate change, ocean acidification, changes in freshwater flows, decline in societal engagement with nature, and adoption of monetary valuation as a key criterion in conservation decision-making (Sutherland et al. 2008). Similar exercises should be carried out in relation to other regions of the world and in relation to different kinds of problems.

Much as was started with the Millennium Development Goals, a wider and more ambitious set of goals needs to be set for the future. They should be tied to an understanding of the ecological limits facing the planet. They should include short-, medium- and long-term time horizons. They should also examine areas of inaction. Although human creativity has made it possible for us to correct many mistakes of the past – such as in relation to the introduction of controls on emissions from stationary sources of air pollution and the monitoring and control of toxic chemicals, many problems still go largely unnoticed and unaddressed, such as the massive 'plastic patches' that are forming in the world's oceans or the highly radioactive nuclear waste that throughout the world remains in temporary storage facilities. There are also still no binding international agreements for the protection of coral reefs or forests.[2]

In another 20 years, when people look back at Rio+20, the hope is that they will be able to say that a turning point was reached and new, more-sustainable economic and energy structures began to be put in place.

4. CONCLUSION

International environmental agreements remain important for raising global awareness, strengthening environmental norms, and achieving some degree of consensus among states on paths of action to be followed. Achieving cooperation in the international climate negotiations, as well as in other international environmental negotiations, has proven difficult.

Furthering sustainable development will require a stronger emphasis on the greening of economic structures and the removal of incentives that support polluting and ecologically destructive industries. Many of the global environmental problems facing the planet today – ranging from toxic chemical pollution, to plastics in the environment, to climate change – are tied to the ways in which goods are valued and the extent to which externalities are incorporated into economic pricing. Shifting economies more strongly in the direction of green development is essential. This will require making information easily accessible about the sustainability of public investment and resource use and the development of measurable and verifiable sustainability targets. All of these actions must occur at multiple levels of government.

Most importantly, a more polycentric focus – one that encourages local and regional innovation for sustainable development and that supports horizontal and vertical connections among actors – is necessary. Some of the most innovative developments in the direction of sustainability today are coming from states and local government that see economic potential in the greening of energy and resource infrastructures.

NOTES

1. Overview information can be found at Ren 21, Institute for Sustainable Energy Policy, ICLEI Local Governments for Sustainability, 'Global Status Report on Local Renewable Energy Policies,' May 2011, http://www.ren21.net/Portals/97/documents/Publications/REN21_Local_Renewables_Policies_2011.pdf. See also the Eurosolar website: http://www.eurosolar.de/en/index.php?option=com_content&task=view&id=519&Itemid=8
2. Cases of non-regimes are examined in Radaslov Dimitrov (2006), *Science and International Environmental Policy: Regimes and Nonregimes in Global Governance*, Lanham, MD: Rowman & Littlefield.

REFERENCES

Becken, K., D. de Graaf, C. Elsner, G. Hoffmann, F. Krüger, K. Martens, W. Plehn and R. Sartorins (2011), 'Avoiding fluorinated greenhouse gases: prospects for phasing out', accessed at www.umweltdaten.de/publikationen/fpdf-l/3977.pdf.

Bulkeley, H. and M.M. Betsill (2003), *Cities and Climate Change: Urban Sustainability and Global Environmental Governance*, New York: Routledge.

Christiansen, S. and A. Kellow (2002), *International Environmental Policy: Interests and the Failure of the Kyoto Process*, Cheltenham, UK and Northampton, MA, USA: Edward Elgar.

Conca, K. and G.D. Dabelko (2010), *Green Planet Blues: Four Decades of Global Environmental Politics*, Boulder, CO: Westview.

Convention on Biological Diversity (CBD) (2010), COP 10 Decision X/2, Strategic Plan for Biodiversity 2011–2020, accessed at www.cbd.int/decision/cop/?id=12268.

CO_2Now.org (2012), accessed at http://co2now.org/.

DeSombre, E.R. (2005), 'The evolution of international environmental cooperation', *International Environmental Law and International Relations*, 1 (1–2), 75–87.

Dimitrov, R. (2006), *Science and International Environmental Policy: Regimes and Nonregimes in Global Governance*, Lanham, MD: Rowman & Littlefield.

Harrison, K. and L. McIntosh Sundstrom (2010), *Global Commons, Domestic Decisions: The Comparative Politics of Climate Change*, Cambridge, MA: MIT Press.

International Energy Agency (IEA) (2010), *World Energy Outlook 2010: Executive Summary*, Paris: OECD/IEA.

Jenkens, C.N. and L. Joppa (2009), *Expansion of the Global Terrestrial Protected Area System*, Durham, NC: Duke University.

Lafferty, W.M. (ed.) (2004), *Governance for Sustainable Development: The Challenge of Adapting Form to Function*, Cheltenham, UK and Northampton, MA, USA: Edward Elgar.

Lafferty, W.M. and J. Meadowcroft (2000), *Implementing Sustainable Development: Strategies and Initiatives in High Consumption Societies*, Oxford: Oxford University Press.

Lafferty, W.M. and A. Ruud (2008), *Promoting Sustainable Electricity in Europe: Challenging the Path Dependence of Dominant Energy Systems*, Cheltenham, UK and Northampton, MA, USA: Edward Elgar.

Lopez, M.J. and M. Orsini (2011), Workshop Report on 'Climate Change: Reduction of Non CO2 Emissions', Directorate-General for Internal Policies, Brussels, 28 June 2011, accessed at www.europarl.europa.eu/document/activities/cont/201109/20110923ATT27350/20110923ATT27350EN.pdf.

Millennium Ecosystem Assessment (MEA) (2005), accessed at www.maweb.org/en/index.aspx.

(National Aeronautics and Space Administration (NASA) (2011), '2011: the Year of Two Ozone Holes', accessed at www.theozonehole.com/2011two.htm.

Ostrom, E. (2012), 'Nested externalities and polycentric institutions: must we wait for global solutions to climate change before taking actions at other scales?', *Economic Theory*, **49** (2), 353–69.

Paellemaerts, M. (1992), 'International environmental law from Stockholm to Rio: back to the future', *Review of European Community & International Environmental Law*, 1 (3), 254–66.

Parson, E. (2003), *Protecting the Ozone Layer: Science and Strategy*, Oxford: Oxford University Press.

Rockström, J., W. Stefan, K. Noone, A. Persson, S. Chapin, E. Lambin, T. Leuton, M. Scheffer, C. Folke, J.J. Schellnhaber, B. Nykvist. C.A. de Wit, T. Hughes, S. van der Leeuw, H. Rodke, S. Sörin, P.K. Synder, R. Costanza, U. Svedin, M. Falkenmark, L. Karlberg, R.W. Corell, V.J. Fabry, J. Hansen, B. Walker, D. Liverman, K. Richardson, P. Crutzen and J. Foley (2009), 'Planetary boundaries: exploring the safe operating space for humanity', *Ecology and Society*, **14** (2), Article 32.

Sachverständigenrat für Umweltfragen (SRU) (2011), Vorsorge Strategien für Nanomaterialien, accessed at www.umweltrat.de/SharedDocs/Downloads/DE/02_Sondergutachten/2011_09_SG_Vorsorgestrategien%20für%20Nanomaterialien.pdf?__blob=publicationFile.

Schreurs, M.A. (2008), 'From the bottom up: local and subnational climate change politics', *Journal of Environment and Development*, **17** (4), 343–55.

Schreurs, M.A. (2010) 'Multi-level governance and global climate change in East Asia', *Asian Economic Policy Review*, **5** (1), 88–105.

Sutherland, W.J., M. Bailey, I. Bainbridge, T. Brereton, J. Dick, J. Drewitt, N. Dulvy, N. Dusic, R. Freckleton, K. Gaston, P. Gilder, R. Green, L. Heathwaite, S. Johnson, D. Macdonald, R. Mitchell, D. Osborn, R. Owen, J. Pretty, S. Prior, H. Prosser, H. Pullin, P. Rose, A. Stott, T. Tew, C. Thomas, D. Thompson, J. Vickery, M. Walker, C. Walmsley, S. Warrington, A. Watkinson, R. Williams, R. Woodroffe and H. Woodroof (2008), 'Future novel threats and opportunities facing UK biodiversity identified by horizon scanning', *Journal of Applied Ecology*, **45** (3), 821–33.

Union of Concerned Scientists (UCS) (2011), 'Nuclear power still not viable without subsidies', executive summary, accessed at www.ucsusa.org/assets/documents/nuclear_power/nuclear_subsidies_summary.pdf.

United Nations Department of Public Information, Secretariat of UN Water (2005), 'Water for Life Decade, 2005–2015', accessed at www.un.org/waterforlifedecade/pdf/waterforlifebklt-e.pdf.

United Nations Framework Convention on Climate Change (UNFCCC) (2012), 'Clean development mechanism', accessed at http://cdm.unfccc.int/

UN News Centre (2010), 'Rate of deforestation in decline but rate remains alarming, UN agency says', accessed at www.un.org/apps/news/story.asp?NewsID=34195.

Victor, D. (2001), *The Collapse of the Kyoto Protocol and the Struggle to Slow Global Warming*, Princeton, NJ: Princeton University Press.

Victor, D. (2011), *Global Warming Gridlock: Creating More Effective Strategies for Protecting the Planet*, Cambridge: Cambridge University Press.

Vogel, D. (1997), 'Trading up and governing across: transnational governance and environmental protection', *Journal of European Public Policy*, **4** (4), 556–71.

Willets, P. (1996) 'From Stockholm to Rio and beyond: the impact of the environmental movement on the United Nations Consultative Arrangements for NGOs', *Review of International Studies*, **22**, 57–80.

World Commission on Environment and Development (WCED) (1987), 'Towards sustainable development', Chapter 2 in *Our Common Future*, accessed at www.un-documents.net/ocf-02.htm.

Würzel, R. and J. Connelly (2011), *The European Union as a Leader in International Climate Change Politics*, Abingdon and New York: Routledge.

11. Governance by diffusion: exploring a new mechanism of international policy coordination

Per-Olof Busch and Helge Jörgens

International policy coordination, understood as the mutual adjustment of the interests, goals and actions of collective actors in the international system, is a key aspect of the scholarly debate on global governance. Basically, this debate centres on the potential, restriction and impact of coordination among independent actors in the absence of a centralized political authority (Jachtenfuchs 2003; Zürn 1998; Rosenau 1995; Rosenau and Czempiel 1992). So far most theoretical approaches to the study of international relations focus on one or another form of centralized top–down coordination (see, for example, Keohane 1984; Abbott et al. 2000; Chayes et al. 1998). By contrast, other theoretically conceivable and empirically observable forms of de-centralized or horizontal policy coordination have received surprisingly little attention in the international relations literature. This holds especially true for processes of cross-national policy diffusion where information on innovative policies is communicated internationally, leading states to adopt these policies voluntarily and without expecting any kind of quid pro quo (Busch et al. 2005; Jörgens 2004). Coordination, in this case, does not result from international agreement, but emerges from the mutual adjustment of autonomous states to each other's policy decisions. Although there is a growing body of literature examining processes of policy diffusion (Simmons et al. 2008; Holzinger et al. 2007), the governance potential of these diffusion processes is still widely ignored (exceptions are Kern 2000; Jörgens 2004; Busch and Jörgens 2007).

In this chapter we seek to add a new perspective to the growing body of diffusion research by exploring systematically the aptitude of diffusion as a distinct mode of international policy coordination, its functioning and its relative importance compared with other, more centralized steering mechanisms.[1] Even before the spectacular failure of the world climate summit in Copenhagen in 2009, we can observe a rapidly growing scholarly as well as practical interest in alternative forms of international policy coordination that go beyond multilateral cooperation or environmental 'summitry' (Sabel and Zeitlin 2010; Aldy and Stavins 2009). Against this background, and by systematically exploring the empirical link between policy diffusion and international governance, we argue that paying greater attention to the governance potential of diffusion processes can help policy-makers to move 'beyond the impasse' of formal negotiations and develop alternative or supplementary forms of international environmental policy coordination that could be used more consciously in the future.

In the next section we define the concept of policy diffusion and distinguish diffusion from other modes of international environmental policy coordination, namely cooperation and coercion. In Section 3 we demonstrate empirically how interdependent, but not centrally coordinated, policy adoptions can add up to produce regulatory patterns that are similar to the patterns caused by multilateral cooperation or bilateral coercion. In the fourth section we take a closer look at the microfoundations of diffusion processes and ask the following questions: how do ideas travel in the international system? What motivates state actors to take up these ideas and emulate the policies of other countries? What are the structural and situational factors that promote or hamper the speed or extent of international diffusion processes? Can we identify specific features of a policy that increase or reduce its ability to diffuse?

Based on this exploration, Section 5 explores the potential of policy diffusion as a distinct mode of global governance. It asks whether, how and to what extent different actors in the international system (nation-states, trans-national networks, international organizations or the European Union) can actively make use of diffusion processes to address problems of international policy coordination. By asking whether and how diffusion processes can be influenced, we bridge the gap between the empirical observation that policy coordination can emerge unexpectedly from unilateral decisions of de-centralized actors, on the one hand, and the practical search for alternative modes of governance in problem areas where the conditions for hierarchical or cooperative problem-solving are not given, on the other. The article ends with a summary of the potential and limits of what we term governance by diffusion.

1.   WHAT IS POLICY DIFFUSION?

We define policy diffusion as a process by which information on policy innovation is communicated in the international system and adopted voluntarily and unilaterally by an increasing number of countries over time (see Busch and Jörgens 2010, p. 32). Contrary to bilateral or multilateral forms of policy coordination, reciprocity plays no role in diffusion processes. Individual states take over the policies of other states unilaterally, unconditionally and without expecting other states to do the same. By stressing communication – rather than cooperation or coercion – as the basic mechanism by which policy innovations are transferred internationally, we follow the general social-scientific use that understands diffusion as 'the process in which an innovation is communicated through certain channels over time among the members of a social system' (Rogers 2003). From a governance perspective, diffusion thus represents a horizontal mode of international policy coordination that is located somewhere between the traditional dichotomy of top–down explanations, which understand national policy change as a result of external coercion or international harmonization, and bottom–up explanations, which attribute policy change primarily to national factors:

> Top-down explanations discuss the advance of regulatory reforms as a response of national policy makers to exogenous (and often common) pressures from various international sources or national policy communities [. . .]. Bottom-up explanations examine the advance or stagnation of reforms as the outcome of domestic balances of power and specific national styles. [. . .] The horizontal approach to change treats the decision to adopt regulatory reform as an 'interdependent' decision that is taken within a group of actors who closely observe each other. The observation of regulatory reform in one sector increases the probability of regulatory reforms being adopted [. . .] in the same sector in another country. (Levi-Faur 2005, pp. 25–6)

Diffusion and Policy Coordination

Distinguishing between top–down, bottom–up and horizontal modes of cross-national policy coordination paves the way for an understanding of policy diffusion as a distinct mechanism of global governance and international policy coordination. In this vein, diffusion can be conceived as a special type of policy coordination beyond institutionalized cooperation. As a conceptual bridge between comparative politics and international relations, it sheds light on the phenomenon of horizontal, non-cooperative coordination among interdependent nation-states in the international system that has been largely neglected up to now. The lack of a suitable technical term to describe this type of policy coordination indicates a blind spot, both in comparative politics and international relations. The diffusion concept as we use it – understood as a sequential pattern of non-compulsory introductions of similar or identical policies, in the course of which the prior decisions of one or more states influence the subsequent decisions of others – could fill this terminological and conceptual gap.

Until now, political science has explored such forms of policy coordination only marginally. The mechanism of 'partisan mutual adjustment' described by Charles Lindblom (1965, p. 3) arguably comes closest. Lindblom argued 'people can coordinate with each other without anyone's coordinating them, without a dominant common purpose, and without rules that fully prescribe their relations to each other' (Lindblom 1965, p. 3). Against this backdrop, he distinguishes a total of 12 forms of coordination by mutual adjustment which are formulated in a sufficiently abstract way to be transferred to the field of international politics. However, only the first three mechanisms which Lindblom subsumes under the heading of 'adaptive adjustment' and 'in which a decision maker simply adapts to decisions around him, that is, makes those decisions that he can make without first enlisting, as in negotiation, a response from another decision maker', are of interest for the conceptual categorization of policy diffusion as a mechanism of international policy coordination (Lindblom 1965, p. 33).

In this perspective, coordination is achieved by the fact that national governments observe the decisions of other governments and react to these unilaterally, without expecting other states to do the same, without centrally given rules and without setting goals for the development of the overall system. Policy diffusion corresponds largely to this basic logic of 'partisan mutual adjustment', but constitutes a special case insofar as it comprises only imitative behaviour. Thus, diffusion comprises all those cases of 'adaptive adjustment' that show a homogenizing effect.

In the cognate disciplines of sociology and economics, de-centralized forms of coordination have received more attention, both theoretically and empirically, than in political science. This is most apparent in economics where markets are assumed to be the main governance mechanism while hierarchical coordination is taken into consideration only in cases of market failure. In sociology, de-centralized forms of coordination also have a long tradition. As early as 1890, Gabriel de Tarde published the book *The Laws of Imitation*, which posited innovation and imitation as elementary social acts, thereby defining society as the result of imitative behaviour at the individual level (de Tarde 1903). By assuming that society produced and reproduced itself, its norms and institutions, only through the repeated aggregation of many individual acts of imitation, de Tarde developed a strong alternative to Durkheim's concept of social facts.

Like Lindblom's notion of de-centralized mutual adjustment in political science, de Tarde's theory of societal constitution by imitation was soon relegated to the background of sociological theory. How can this common disregard of de-centralized and non-cooperative forms of coordination in the social science literature be explained? The core of the rejection of these concepts becomes clear in Emile Durkheim's criticism of de Tarde's diffusion theory. Durkheim argues that de Tardes' approach 'is no theory, but merely a summary of that what observation tells us' and that imitation can never constitute the essence of social phenomena (Durkheim 1991, p. 112). In the more recent international relations debate a similar argument was brought forward against the idea of horizontal policy coordination articulated in the concept of trans-national and trans-governmental relations (Keohane and Nye 1972). As Katzenstein et al. (1998, pp. 659–63) argue in their historical overview of the field of international political economy, horizontal policy coordination in pluralistic actor constellations had indeed moved, for a short time, into the centre of scholarly attention, but was quickly replaced by international regime theory which focused predominantly on the 'results of formal interstate agreements' (Keohane and Nye 1989, p. 258). The reason for the rejection of this research perspective, which – despite repeated attempts to resuscitate it (Risse-Kappen 1995) – to this day is of rather marginal importance, cannot be found in the absence of empirical references to the actual existence of horizontal coordination. It is found in the theoretical and methodical implications of such an approach: 'Transnational relations posited a world composed of many different actors with different interests and capabilities. Such a model can provide a rich description. But the operationalization of cause and effect relationships is complex because it is difficult to specify interests and capabilities ex ante. The larger the number of actors, the greater the diversity of their resources (ideas, money, access, organization); and the wider the number of possible alliances, the more difficult such specification becomes, especially if there are interaction effects among different groups' (Katzenstein et al. 1998, p. 659).

Instead of investigating systematically the potential of decentralized and non-cooperative forms of governance, which are in practice ubiquitous, a narrow focus on collective decision-making and central governance has so far prevailed in the literature (from the early social contract theories to sociological theories of society, pluralism and ultimately modern international relations theory) which tends to marginalize a whole class of frequently observed phenomena for theoretical and methodical reasons. Diffusion research in political science offers a chance to investigate more systematically how international order can emerge from horizontal interactions among decentralized but interdependent actors, in the absence of central coordination, direction or planning. Due to the continuous 'diffusion' of diffusion research, this approach is now gaining influence in comparative politics and international relations (see, for example, Levi-Faur and Jordana 2005; Simmons et al. 2008). In the following we will show empirically how diffusion processes can bring about a degree of policy coordination, which is comparable to that achieved by negotiation or coercion. Then, the central bases of diffusion research are briefly outlined.

3. DIFFUSION AS A DISTINCT MODE OF INTERNATIONAL ENVIRONMENTAL POLICY COORDINATION – EMPIRICAL EXAMPLES

We have argued from a theoretical perspective not only that deliberately achieved coordination is politically relevant and in need of explanation, but also that we have to pay closer attention to those instances where policies are coordinated without any of the involved actors having intended this coordination from the start or having made it the condition of their respective action. In this section we use two empirical examples from the area of environmental politics – the global spread of environmental framework laws and of national environmental ministries – to show that this type of emergent coordination is not only a theoretical option, but actually takes place, and that it entails a degree of coordination that is comparable in its function and effect to centrally negotiated international arrangements or hierarchical imposition. The examples, which are only briefly outlined here, are based on an extensive research project on the diffusion of environmental policy innovations in the international system (Tews and Jänicke 2005). They are described elsewhere in more detail (Busch and Jörgens 2010, 2005a). They show that diffusion processes can contribute to international environmental policy coordination and environmental governance much as do international harmonization by multilateral agreements or even supranational European Union law.

Environmental Framework Laws

Environmental framework laws are general environmental laws, which establish overarching rules for several areas of environmental regulation (for example air pollution control, water pollution control, soil protection, nature conservation). They differ from specialized environmental laws which have their focus on single environmental media or problem areas (for example waste laws, clean air acts or soil conservation laws). In their general form environmental framework laws lay down the basic principles and purposes of national environmental policy, regulate the competences and duties of administrative authorities as well as determine

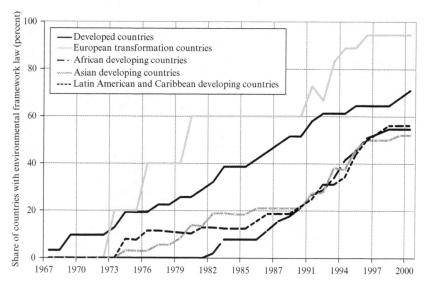

Source: Authors' data.

Figure 11.1   Global proliferation of environmental framework laws in selected world regions

environmental policy instruments. In their particular details they contain concrete regulations for different areas of environmental protection. The first environmental framework laws emerged at the end of the 1960s in Sweden, the United States and Japan. By 2000 roughly 70 per cent of the highly developed industrial countries, more than 90 per cent of the Central and Eastern European transformation countries (see Figure 11.1) and 110 countries worldwide (see Figure 11.2) had established environmental framework laws. In Germany an aggregation of media-specific environmental laws into a comprehensive environmental code has been discussed since the 1970s; nevertheless, the implementation of this plan has failed up to now because of constitutional barriers.

How can this rapid and far-reaching spread of environmental framework laws be explained? An explanation exclusively based on national factors such as electoral preferences, the influence of interest groups or ecological problem pressure would not do justice to the great temporal proximity of the introductions in a large number of very different countries. At the same time, there are no binding international rules that could explain the remarkable pattern of spread, in particular since the beginning of the 1990s. Our investigation shows that in the 1970s

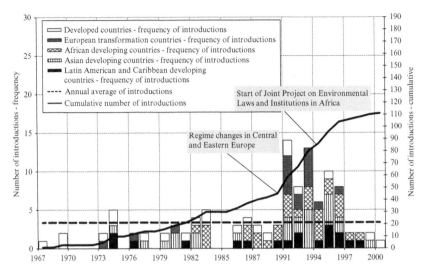

Source: Authors' data.

Figure 11.2   Worldwide proliferation of environmental framework laws

and 1980s horizontal imitation among individual states played the most important role for the international spread of this policy innovation. In the 1990s a number of international organizations, partially in direct collaboration with single nation-states as for example Germany or the Netherlands, started to spread information about this policy innovation. Their activities ranged from organizing international conferences and supplying information about international 'best practice' in the area of environmental legislation to sending policy advisers to developing countries and in some cases even to financial support for legislative projects. In Eastern Europe, Latin America, Africa and Asia, this led to a rapid increase in the number of national environmental framework laws (see Figure 11.1).

In Western industrial countries the spread slowed down at the beginning of the 1990s. This can be explained, on the one hand, by the high degree of saturation with environmental framework laws that had already been reached. On the other hand this has also been the result of institutional path dependencies. The majority of industrialized countries have a historically developed set of specialized environmental laws and regulations whose consolidation required a significantly bigger coordination effort than the creation of an integrated environmental law in states that were only beginning to develop their legal basis for environmental protection or which – like the central and eastern European states – went through a fundamental political and juridical transformation process. Additionally, institutional barriers such as the constitutional distribution of competences between the central government and the federal states in Germany could also prevent a consolidation of existing environmental laws in spite of political majorities in favour of such a policy change (Busch and Jörgens 2005a, pp. 94–8).[1]

National Ministries of the Environment

Since end of the 1960s the creation of national ministries of the environment has been closely connected with the establishment of environmental protection as an independent policy area. Great Britain set up a national ministry of the environment in 1970 and was the first country, worldwide, to do so. In the following three decades this policy innovation has rapidly spread around the world. By 2000, national ministries of the environment existed in almost all Western industrialized countries, in all Eastern European countries and in more than 100 countries worldwide (see Figure 11.3). Although the environmental ministries of different countries differ with regard to their personnel and financial resources, the qualification and motivation of their staff, and their influence in the political process, the worldwide spread of this department in various governments brought about a huge expansion and strengthening of national – and in their sum also international – environmental protection capacities (Jörgens 1996; Weidner and Jänicke 2002; Meyer et al. 1997).

What are the causes of this spread of ministries of the environment? Our investigation of the spread of environmental ministries shows that domestic factors such as electoral preferences, the influence of interest groups or ecological problem pressure were of low importance at the time of the creation of environmental ministries. Paradoxically, the few governments that actually had to react to internal pressure (in particular Japan and the United States) refrained from establishing an environmental ministry until very recently (in the case of the US even until today), and instead started out by creating specialized environmental agencies responsible for overseeing the implementation of environmental laws and regulations. The creation of national ministries of the environment was not the result of binding international arrangements, nor is there evidence that countries were forced externally to set up national environmental ministries. A purely accidental and isolated creation of such institutions is rather improbable in view of the remarkable accumulation of ministry foundations at the beginning of the 1970s, in the middle of the 1980s and in the beginning of the 1990s.

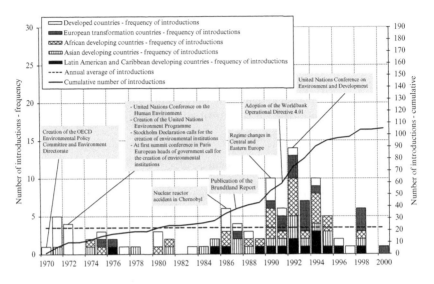

Source: Authors' data.

Figure 11.3 Worldwide proliferation of ministries of the environment

Instead, our analysis shows that mutual observation, reinforced by increasing informational activities of international organizations, has triggered cross-national imitation and learning processes. In addition, an internationally recognized norm, which evolved in the 1960s and 1970s, had turned the protection of the natural environment into a central component of governmental activity. At least in Western industrial countries, environmental protection has been seen as a token of modernity and good governance since the beginning of the 1970s and governmental commitment in this area was never fundamentally called into question (Jörgens 1996; Meyer et al. 1997). Against this backdrop, states often used the creation of national environmental ministries to increase the legitimacy of their domestic political institutions, whereas the failure to adequately institutionalize this new task increasingly placed governments under internal and external pressure. Thus, in the absence of internationally binding rules, the most important mechanism of spread for national environmental ministries was the communication- and norm-based diffusion within international actor networks (Busch and Jörgens 2005a, pp. 64–9, 79–88).

Diffusion, Cooperation and Coercion Compared: Laws on Access to Environmental Information and Environmental Impact Assessment

Our examples show that multilateral agreements or coercive imposition are by no means a necessary pre-condition for the international spread of policies and institutional arrangements. Policy innovations can spread rapidly and among a large number of countries merely through voluntary and information-based diffusion processes. The degree of international policy coordination achieved in this manner becomes even more apparent if we compare these examples of policy diffusion with similar cases of international harmonization or imposed policy adoption. In the following discussion we briefly present the international spread of laws on access to environmental information, which occurred primarily through legal harmonization as well as the spread of environmental impact assessments, which primarily resulted from external imposition through World Bank conditionality.

Environmental information laws grant citizens access to environmentally relevant information held by state authorities. Their proliferation (see Figure 11.4) shows a pattern very similar to our previous examples. However, behind this pattern we find a different set of mechanisms that caused this policy innovation to spread throughout the OECD and Eastern Europe. After a long phase of slow spread, in the course of which only around one-quarter of the countries examined laid down rules for the access to environmental information, two legal acts – the Council Directive on Free Access to Environmental Information (EEC/90/313) that came into force in 1990 and the Aarhus Convention adopted in 1998 – significantly accelerated the spread of this policy innovation (see Figure 11.4). Thus, by 2000, multilateral cooperation and subsequent legal harmonization had produced very similar results to the non-compulsory diffusion of environmental ministries and environmental framework laws.

Environmental impact assessments are ex ante evaluations of the possible environmental consequences of public or private infrastructure projects. Their global proliferation also follows a pattern similar to that of environmental framework laws and environmental ministries (see Figure 11.5). However, in contrast to the former, it is based on a combination of legal harmonization and external imposition. While in Europe most national adoptions were directly caused by Council Directive 85/337/ EEC, which came into force in 1985, many Eastern European, African and Latin American countries were heavily influenced in their national policy choices by a decision of the World Bank from 1991 (Operational Directive 4.01) which made World Bank loans conditional upon the realization of environmental impact assessments. A large part of the national adoptions

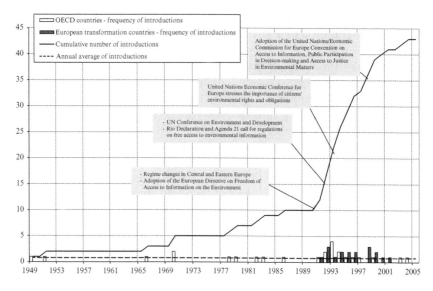

Source: Authors' data.

Figure 11.4   Proliferation of laws on access to environmental information in Western industrial countries and Eastern European countries

of environmental impact assessments can therefore be traced back to the mechanisms of legal harmonization and financial conditionality.

Our comparison of the international spread of different environmental policy innovations illustrates that policy diffusion, defined as the unilateral and voluntary adoption of policy innovations which are communicated in the international system, can function as a distinct mode of international policy coordination whose results are not necessarily inferior to those of cooperative decision-making in international institutions or coercive imposition by a hegemonic actor.

Whether diffusion processes, varying under different conditions and with different actors, can be used as a deliberate and purposeful governance mode (governance by diffusion) is the subject of the following sections. Section 4 describes in more detail the patterns, mechanisms and determinants of international diffusion processes. Against this background section 5 asks whether and how diffusion processes can be deliberately influenced by different actors in the international system.

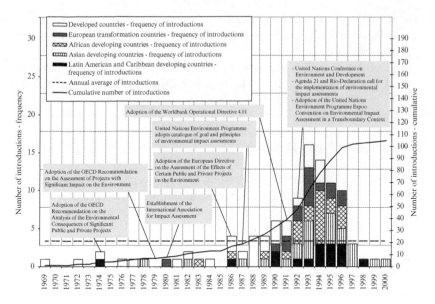

Source: Authors' data.

Figure 11.5   Worldwide proliferation of environmental impact assessments

4.   PATTERNS, MECHANISMS AND DETERMINANTS OF POLICY DIFFUSION

As the examples in the previous section have shown, policy diffusion is a multilayered process that is fed by various sub-mechanisms such as imitation, learning, competition, benchmarking or legitimacy-seeking. Moreover, information about policy innovation can spread through different communication channels. It can be transferred directly from one state to another – as in the case of the diffusion of environmental framework laws in the 1970s and 1980s. Alternatively, policy models can be taken up by international organizations and then made available to a larger number of countries simultaneously – as in the case of environmental ministries and environmental framework laws in the 1990s. The motives of states and governments to adopt particular policy innovations that have been communicated in the international system also vary considerably. In our examples, these motives range from the (boundedly) rational adoption of policy innovations judged as effective elsewhere (for example, the integration of sectoral environmental laws in an environmental framework law)

all the way up to the scripted imitation of acts widely judged as appropriate or legitimate (for example, the establishment of national ministries of
the environment).

The purpose of this section is to give a brief overview of the different
causal mechanisms through which policy diffusion may occur as well
as the intervening factors that affect the speed and scope of diffusion
processes.

Mechanisms of Policy Diffusion

Mechanisms are 'recurring processes which link certain causes to certain
effects' (Mayntz 2002, p. 24, authors' translation). They are also seen as
'the causal pathway, process or intermediate variable by which a causal
factor of theoretical interest is thought to affect an outcome' (Gerring
2008, p. 163). Examining the mechanisms of policy adoption helps us
to understand how knowledge about the policies of one country is converted into another country's decision to adopt similar policies. A large
number of diffusion mechanisms have been identified in the literature,
but these can be grouped into four generic categories: (1) (boundedly)
rational learning; (2) symbolic imitation; (3) norm-based action; and (4)
competition (for a similar categorization, see Braun and Gilardi 2006).

In the first case of (boundedly) rational learning, national decision-
makers search across boundaries for effective solutions to domestic problems. The previous policy choices of states which had been confronted with
comparable problems then offer valuable clues for their own decisions
(Rose 1991). Especially in situations in which the complexity of problems
and the amount of information relevant for decision-making exceed the
capacities of national decision-makers to process this information, they
tend to base their actions on a small set of abstract decision rules and criteria which are applicable to many different situations (Simon 1957). Or
as Simmons and Elkins have put it: 'Policymakers may be capable, at best,
of something akin to a boundedly rational search for policy guidance'
(Simmons and Elkins 2003, p. 282). A pivotal decision rule, in this respect,
is the analogy. Here, decisions-makers draw on decisions taken in comparable situations in other jurisdictions or at an earlier point in time (Walker
1969, p. 889). In complex decision situations, time-pressed policy-makers
are therefore more likely to copy policies already carried out somewhere
else than to invent new programmes (Karch 2008).

The second group, symbolic imitation, comprises the different ways
in which policy innovations are adopted in order to gain national and
international legitimacy. Policy innovations which are highly visible
and which represent widely recognized values are particularly suited for

symbolic imitation (Braun and Gilardi 2006). In the area of environmental policy, this mechanism played a central role, for instance, in the diffusion of ministries of the environment, but also in the spread of sustainable development strategies and the introduction of constitutional clauses on environmental protection (Busch and Jörgens 2005a; on the diffusion of sustainable development strategies, see also Jörgens 2004).

The third group of diffusion mechanisms comprises, on the one hand, processes of norm-based socialization that played an important role, for instance, during the integration of Central and Eastern European countries into the community of Western states (Checkel 2005). On the other hand, processes of normative suasion, for example by international organizations or transnational actor networks, fall into this category (Keck and Sikkink 1998). This group of mechanisms also comprises the scripted execution of a behaviour judged as appropriate (March and Olsen 1998), as for example in the case of the establishment of ministries of the environment or the adoption of environmental laws in Central and Eastern Europe after 1990 (Busch and Jörgens 2005a).

The fourth group comprises several mechanisms based on competition. In the case of economic competition, states act strategically in order to improve their international competitiveness. Mostly this competition is conceived as a race to the bottom, where states alternately lower national standards until a common minimum is reached (Holzinger and Knill 2005). A second mechanism in this group is political competition. Here states struggle to become pioneers or early adopters of a policy innovation so that they can influence international policy developments in accordance with their domestic regulatory traditions and institutional structures, thereby minimizing future political and economic adjustment costs (Héritier et al. 1994). In the environmental policy field such processes of diffusion by political competition are found above all in issue areas relevant to the Single European Market (for example packaging waste laws, see Gehring 1997; Haverland 2000). Finally, this group includes a mechanism of social competition referred to as 'structural equivalence' (Burt 1987). Structural equivalence describes a similar relation of two persons to a third one. To hold this relation stable, these persons observe each other mutually and imitate the behaviour of each other (Tews 2005, p. 32).

Intervening Factors

Empirical studies show that the identification of different diffusion mechanisms is insufficient to explain diverging diffusion patterns. An intervening variable that can explain why some policy innovations spread very quickly, while others are introduced only gradually, is the specific properties of a policy innovation (Kern et al. 2001). Theodore Lowi (Lowi 1972), for example, has argued that regulative and distributive programmes are easier to introduce than redistributive ones. Another issue is that the structure of the policy problem in question may facilitate or hamper the diffusion of policies and programmes (Jänicke and Volkery 2001) – for example, whether the problem is immediately visible and discernible or whether it constitutes a creeping problem that is hidden from perception. Another issue is whether there is a simple technical add-on solution for the problem or whether its solution requires a correction of established political or institutional paths. Our research shows that environmental laws that address widely visible environmental problems such as, for example, air or water pollution, spread much faster than laws which concern more 'invisible' problems, such as, for example soil degradation (Busch and Jörgens 2005a, p. 132).

While the problem structure and the specific properties of policy innovations can explain differences in the speed of diffusion, they fail to explain why some states are regularly found among the pioneers or early adopters of a policy innovation, while others are always among the latecomers. This is why diffusion research has identified the national political and administrative as well as the economic and scientific capacities as important determinants of a country's ability to innovate (Jänicke and Weidner 1997). This research's assumption is that states with stronger capacities are more capable than others of transforming information about political innovations elsewhere into actual decisions (Walker 1969). However, the empirical observation that the United States belongs either to the pioneers of a new policy innovation or refrains altogether from its introduction (Binder 2005) points to the fact that abundant domestic capacities may not always facilitate the adoption of foreign models, but can also constitute an obstacle to their introduction. Moreover, empirical studies also show that insufficient political and scientific capacities may force states to adopt external models rather than develop their own solutions, especially in knowledge-intensive policy areas (Hoberg 1991). In summary, it appears that national political and institutional capacities constitute important intervening factors that help to explain why some countries are more inclined to draw lessons from foreign policies than others. The actual effect of domestic capacities, however, may vary from situation to situation and can only be adequately assessed by means of qualitative case studies and deep process tracing.

Finally, the domestic political context of the adopting state, in particular its stable political institutions, act as a filter that may be open for certain policy innovations while being resistant to others. Historical institutionalism with its focus on institutional path dependencies has made this point (Steinmo et al. 1992). More recently, research on the Europeanization of domestic policies has taken up and further developed this argument (Börzel and Risse 2003). The unsuccessful attempt to introduce an environmental framework law in Germany in 1999 (and again in 2008) due to the federal government's lack of constitutional competencies in the areas of water and nature protection may illustrate this filter effect of domestic institutions.

Summing up this section, we can say that the mechanisms by which external policy models are adopted domestically determine whether a specific policy innovation proliferates at all. The special characteristics of a policy innovation, by contrast, primarily have an effect on the speed at which an innovation spreads. Finally, the domestic political-institutional context of the adopting state determines whether individual countries adopt a particular policy innovation, and if so, at what point in time (Jänicke et al. 2005).

5. 'GOVERNANCE BY DIFFUSION': POTENTIAL AND LIMITS

The case studies in section 3 of this chapter demonstrated that decentralized diffusion processes, based on communication and mutual observation among interdependent states, can have coordination effects that are comparable with those of multilateral cooperation and subsequent legal harmonization. Based on our examples, and the discussion of the determinants of policy diffusion in the previous sections, we can argue plausibly that these indirect governance effects occur not only with regard to 'easy' cases, that is, policies or institutions that are highly compatible with different domestic institutional contexts and that are unlikely to raise strong opposition from the governments or influential interest groups of potential adopting countries, but also with regard to more complex policy innovations. Environmental framework laws, for example, were adopted voluntarily by a large number of countries although this required – at least in the affluent Western democracies – a massive restructuring of the existing legal system in the environmental field. Thus, it can be argued that successful environmental governance through processes of voluntary and de-centralized policy diffusion is not restricted to those policy innovations that, due to their inherent characteristics, trigger only limited resistance. By contrast, diffusion could well be a promising governance mode, *especially* in those cases where intergovernmental cooperation is difficult. In those cases, successful diffusion may help to pave the way for a subsequent legal harmonization.

However, the fact that processes of cross-national policy diffusion have coordination effects in the international system does not automatically imply that this governance potential can be actively used to solve global policy problems. In the rest of this chapter we therefore explore whether and how national governments or international organizations can deliberately influence diffusion processes and thus make use of policy diffusion as a means of international governance.

Potential Starting Points for Using Diffusion Processes as a Mode of Governance

(i)   Creating and enhancing channels of cross-national communication

The scope and the speed of diffusion processes are strongly influenced by the existence of an effective communication infrastructure among national governments. Consequently, a starting point in any effort to influence and utilize the dynamics of policy diffusion would be to strengthen and institutionalize the communication flows among national governments or their policy-relevant sub-units. However, unlike in the 1960s and 1970s, today an impressive and well-functioning infrastructure of international organizations is in place in the environmental field as well as in many other policy areas. These international organizations provide important communication channels that can help new policy ideas and empirical examples of best practice be communicated quickly to governments throughout the world. Therefore, attempts to strengthen and institutionalize cross-national communication flows nowadays have to focus primarily on the creation of highly specialized communication networks, such as issue specific international commissions or committees. These kinds of specialized committees within larger international organizations could allow faster and more targeted cross-national information flows in particular issue areas. In the field of environmental policy, governments as well as international organizations increasingly make use of such issue-specific expert networks to spread information about successful policies or examples of best practice. The successful diffusion of national environmental policy plans and sustainable development strategies in the early 1990s, for example, cannot be understood without reference to the important role of the International Network of Green Planners, an issue-specific network that was created with the explicit aim of disseminating the idea of green planning (Jörgens 2004). Similarly, information on the establishment and design of national eco-labelling schemes was disseminated within the Global Ecolabelling Network (Kern and Kissling-Näf 2005). In the EU, specialized committees where representatives of the member states meet, exchange information and mutually observe each other's policies are already an integral part of the Open Method of Coordination (Nedergaard 2007).

Besides these issue-specific networks, whose main function is to institutionalize the exchange of policy-relevant information among the members of national environmental administrations, other less official networks, such as epistemic communities or transnational advocacy networks, which often are in close contact with representatives from national governments and provide them with information on policy alternatives, also help to enhance policy-relevant information flows. Encouraging the creation of such transnational networks and supporting their operations therefore can be another important step in the creation of an issue-specific international communication infrastructure.

(ii) Generating information

The existence of communication channels alone does not determine in any way the type of information that is communicated within them. A second, complementary option for externally influencing and steering diffusion processes is therefore to provide or alter the information that is transferred internationally. In particular, larger international organizations with ample research capacities are able to act as independent sources of information. Unlike nation-states, which are assumed to place their own national interests above the interests of international society, international organizations obtain their authority precisely from their assumed impartiality. As a consequence, they are generally seen as reliable sources of information in the international discourse (Busch 2009). As Barnett and Finnemore (2004) show, contemporary international organizations constitute actors in their own right which are – at least partially – able to autonomously shape international agendas, set rules of appropriate state behaviour, generate knowledge as well as to develop and disseminate models for best practice in a wide range of policy areas. The range of possibilities for international organizations to feed and shape cross-national information flows in specific issue areas is very broad, and ranges from regular reporting and evaluation of member states' policies to the selection and dissemination of generalized models of effective or appropriate state behaviour.

(iii) Improving the 'diffusability' of policy models

As organizational studies have shown, policy innovations spread faster if they are removed from a particular national or temporal context and transformed into an abstract model that is compatible with different politico-institutional conditions (DiMaggio and Powell 1983, pp. 155–6). David Strang and colleagues refer to such abstract models as 'theorized models'

(Strang and Meyer 1993; Strang and Soule 1998, p. 277). International organizations as well as transnational actors have long since begun to transform real-world examples of best practice into generalized blueprints and policy recommendations. Rather than promoting a particular, context-laden national policy, they identify the essential elements of this new approach and summarize them under a new heading. Increasing the diffusability of policy innovations by making them less context sensitive thus constitutes a third way of externally influencing cross-national processes of policy diffusion.

(iv)   Using 'peers' to accelerate the diffusion of policy innovations

The mere knowledge of a policy innovation is usually not sufficient to ensure that a country actually adopts it. What may be more important is the particular way in which a government learns about new policy alternatives. Diffusion research has shown that communication or mutual observation among peers is much more likely to lead to behavioural changes than information obtained from a less valued source (Tews 2005, p. 32). More specifically, Rogers argues that:

> [t]he trial of a new idea by a peer can substitute, at least in part, for the individual's trial of an innovation [. . .]. This 'trial by others' provides a vicarious trial for an individual. Change agents often seek to speed up the innovation-decision process for individuals by sponsoring demonstrations of a new idea in a social system. A demonstration can be quite effective in speeding up the diffusion process, especially if the demonstrator is an opinion leader. (Rogers 2003, p. 177)

These peer dynamics can be used in various ways. First, they point once again to the importance of so-called peer reviews, which have been successfully used by international organizations, in particular by the OECD (Lehtonen 2005). Second, by initiating regional pilot projects, other countries within a cultural or regional peer group can be stimulated to adopt similar policies. Third, even in situations where collective action is needed to solve cross-boundary problems, the peer dynamics described above make a strong case for unilateral action by individual nation-states – especially by international opinion leaders – to incite other governments to follow suit. This last option is what Lindblom has called 'coordination by prior decision' (Lindblom 1965, pp. 80–83). It has been successfully put into practice, for example, by the Netherlands in its effort to universalize its strategic approach to environmental planning (Jörgens 2004).

(v)   Increasing transparency

Studies on international regimes have demonstrated that the effectiveness of a regime increases with the degree to which it makes the behaviour of states transparent. Basically, regime theory assumes that states are more willing to comply with international rules if they can be sure that other states do the same and that free-riding is discouraged (Mitchell 1998). Although in diffusion processes states do not make the introduction of a policy conditional on other countries doing the same, information on how other states react to commonly experienced problems may nevertheless increase a state's willingness to adopt widespread policy models. On the one hand, transparency may affect the payoffs of domestic policy adoptions. If states consider adopting a policy in order to gain international legitimacy or improve their international reputation, a high degree of visibility of state action in the issue area concerned becomes a crucial precondition for their adopting it. On the other hand, transparency may have an accelerating effect on international dynamics referred to by the notions of critical mass or tipping points (Finnemore and Sikkink 1998). Adopting a certain programme or creating a particular institution becomes the appropriate thing to do only if policy-makers are aware that this is exactly what their peers in other countries are doing.

(vi)   Strengthening domestic capacities

Some scholars have raised the possibility of strengthening domestic capacities for adopting policy innovations as a means to accelerate cross-national diffusion processes (Kern 2000, pp. 46–7). Similarly, case studies show that a lack of domestic capacities constitutes a major obstacle to the voluntary adoption of policy innovations (Busch and Jörgens 2005a). The accelerating effect of financial incentives has been systematically demonstrated by Welch and Thompson (1980) in a study on the spread of 57 policies across the United States. The study finds that federal grants in aid have an accelerating effect on the diffusion of policy innovations. Another way of strengthening domestic capacities for the adoption of new policies is through the transfer of political, legal or technological know-how.

(vii) Seizing opportunities

Our empirical analysis showed that the spread of environmental ministries – and, as a matter of fact, many other environmental policy innovations (Busch and Jörgens 2005b) – accelerated dramatically in the aftermath of the collapse of Communist regimes in Eastern Europe. This observation suggests that under certain conditions unforeseen events can strongly affect the diffusion of policy innovations. Although by definition such events cannot be brought about deliberately, policy entrepreneurs can try to seize the opportunities provided by them to promote their own political values and programmes. For example, in the case of former Communist regimes in Central and Eastern Europe, the process of regime transformation was accompanied by great uncertainty on the part of the new governments as to what should be considered appropriate political behaviour. In this situation international environmental non-governmental organizations as well as international organizations were able to infuse these transitional political systems with much needed values and orientations. A case in point here is the Rio Conference in 1992, which provided high-level orientation to the emerging democracies and thus triggered an unprecedented peak in the worldwide adoption of environmental policy innovations (Busch and Jörgens 2005b).

Obstacles and Limits to Governance by Diffusion

However, our empirical cases also provide some evidence that the approach to governance by diffusion outlined above has its limits and therefore should be treated as a complement to, rather than a substitute for, the predominant governance approach, that is, international policy coordination through intergovernmental cooperation. In this section we will therefore briefly point out some possible obstacles and limits that may confront attempts deliberately to influence the cross-national diffusion of policy innovations.

A first obstacle that may limit the range of issue areas where diffusion can constitute a promising mode of policy coordination is the time dimension. It seems logical that binding international agreements can prompt a more immediate reaction by the targeted governments than transnational information flows. As a result, we can assume that governance by diffusion is less useful in cases where an immediate response to imminent danger is needed than in cases where policy change may come about more gradually.

A second obstacle that could limit the range of issue areas where diffusion constitutes an adequate governance mode is path dependence. As the case of environmental framework laws in some Western industrialized countries shows, policy innovations in domains with deeply embedded regulatory traditions are less likely to diffuse through international communication flows than other, more recent policies. In a similar vein, redistributive policies such as eco-taxes or policies addressing wicked or persistent problems (Jänicke and Volkery 2001) – that is, problems that are hard to solve due to a problem structure that is difficult to place on political agendas or that lack straightforward technological solutions – are unlikely to spread through diffusion. A typical example of such a wicked or persistent problem is soil contamination, a policy area that is characterized by the extremely low visibility of environmental degradation and, at the same time, a near complete lack of technological solutions (Kern et al. 2000). Policy entrepreneurs therefore should be particularly careful in relying on diffusion as a mode of international policy coordination in cases that are characterized by long and incremental regulatory traditions or by wicked problem structures.

A more general problem of diffusion-based policy coordination is that diffusion processes themselves tend to create path dependencies. This is problematic particularly in cases where different functionally equivalent policy alternatives spread in parallel. In these cases different political or technological paths may be established that complicate future attempts to harmonize national regulations. The parallel spread of feed-in tariffs and green certificate systems for renewable electricity is a case in point where a diffusion-driven process and a cooperation-driven proliferation process interfered with each other (Busch and Jörgens 2011). Another example can be found in the spread of eco-labels, where the early diffusion of this policy led to the establishment of different national eco-labelling systems whose product categories and certification criteria were largely incompatible. Today, the path dependencies that were created in this way constitute a serious obstacle to the international harmonization of green product labelling (Kern and Kissling-Näf 2005).

Finally, there is room for doubt whether the policy innovations that diffuse internationally always constitute the most adequate response to pressing international policy problems. In particular symbolic policies, which increase a government's legitimacy both internally and externally without generating high implementation costs, can be expected to diffuse rapidly without solving any problems. However, in the environmental field this danger is limited as even the most symbolic policy adoptions, that is, the creation of national environmental ministries or the formulation of environmental strategies, clearly increase the domestic capacity for dealing with environmental problems (Weidner and Jänicke 2002). Moreover, most symbolic policies can be easily added to existing regulatory systems and therefore normally do not negatively affect a country's regulatory capacity.

6. CONCLUSION

In this chapter we have shown that individual but interdependent acts of unilateral and voluntary policy adoption often add up to a substantial degree of international policy coordination, which is comparable with the effects of direct multilateral cooperation or the coercive exercise of hegemonic power. Moreover, we argue that – under certain circumstances – processes of policy diffusion can be deliberately influenced by internationally operating policy entrepreneurs, such as international organizations, trans-national actor networks or individual nation-states. These findings have theoretical as well as practical implications. From a theoretical perspective, our study shows that policy diffusion should receive more attention as an explanatory concept in the study of international relations and comparative politics. In particular, it should receive more attention as a possible cause of global order in the absence of direct intergovernmental cooperation. In practical terms, conceiving of diffusion processes as a potential source of global order can open new options for global governance beyond the traditional realm of inter-governmentalism. Especially in areas where inter-governmental agreements are hard to conclude or where international organizations lack the competencies to legislate, improving the conditions for the diffusion of new ideas and concepts can be a promising alternative that in many cases may be more than just a second-best solution and that may very well take global environmental policy coordination beyond the current impasse of multilateral treaty negotiations.

NOTES

1. We thank William M. Lafferty, Oluf Langhelle and James Meadowcroft for their valuable comments on an earlier version of this chapter. The data used in the case studies was collected in the research project, 'The diffusion of environmental policy innovations as an aspect of the globalization of environmental policy', conducted at the Environmental Policy Research Centre of the Free University Berlin and financed by the German Volkswagen Foundation (Tews and Jänicke 2005).
2. After a reform of the federal organization of the German state in 2006, which partly expanded the federal government's legislative competencies, a second attempt was made to replace various specialized laws with a comprehensive environmental code. This time, however, conflicts between different government departments eventually led to the abandonment of the project.

REFERENCES

Abbott, K., R. Keohane, A. Moravcsik, A.-M. Slaughter and D. Snidal (2000), 'The concept of legalization', *International Organization*, **54** (3), 401–19.

Aldy, J. and R. Stavins (eds) (2009), *Post-Kyoto International Climate Policy: Implementing Architectures for Agreement*, Cambridge: Cambridge University Press.

Barnett, M. and M. Finnemore (2004), *Rules for the World: International Organizations in Global Politics*, Ithaca, NY: Cornell University Press.

Binder, M. (2005), 'Umweltpolitische Basisinnovationen im Industriel-ändervergleich. Ein grafisch-statistischer Überblick', in Kerstin Tews and Martin Jänicke (eds), *Die Diffusion umweltpolitischer Innovationen im internationalen System*, Wiesbaden, Germany: VS Verlag für Sozialwissenschaften, pp. 195–231.

Börzel, T. and T. Risse (2003), 'Conceptualizing the domestic impact of Europe', in Kevin Featherstone and Claudio M. Radaelli (eds), *The Politics of Europeanization*, Oxford: Oxford University Press, pp. 57–80.

Braun, D. and F. Gilardi (2006), 'Taking "Galton's problem" seriously. Towards a theory of policy diffusion', *Journal of Theoretical Politics*, **18** (3), 298–322.

Burt, R. (1987), 'Social contagion and innovation: cohesion versus structural equivalence', *American Journal of Sociology*, **92** (6), 1287–1335.

Busch, P.-O. (2009), 'The OECD environment directorate: the art of persuasion and its limitations', in Frank Biermann and Bernd Siebenhüner (eds), *Managers of Global Change: The Influence of International Environmental Bureaucracies*, Cambridge, MA: MIT Press, pp. 75–99.

Busch, P.-O. and H. Jörgens (2005a), 'Globale Ausbreitungsmuster umweltpolitischer Institutionen', in Kerstin Tews and Martin Jänicke (eds), *Die Diffusion umweltpolitischer Innovationen im internationalen System*, Wiesbaden, Germany: VS Verlag für Sozialwissenschaften, pp. 55–193.

Busch, P.-O. and H. Jörgens (2005b), 'International patterns of environmental policy change and convergence', *European Environment*, **15** (2), 80–101.

Busch, P.-O. and H. Jörgens (2007), 'Dezentrale Politikkoordination im internationalen System – Ursachen, Mechanismen und Wirkungen der internationalen Diffusion politischer Innovationen', in Katharina Holzinger, Helge Jörgens and Christoph Knill (eds), *Transfer, Diffusion und Konvergenz von Politiken*, Wiesbaden, Germany: VS Verlag für Sozialwissenschaften, pp. 56–84.

Busch, P.-O. and H. Jörgens (2010), 'Governance by diffusion. International environmental policy coordination in the era of globalization', dissertation, Berlin.

Busch, P.-O. and H. Jörgens (2011), 'The diffusion of renewable energy policies in Europe: potential and pitfalls of an alternative Europeanisation mechanism', in Francesc Morata and Israel Solorio (eds), *European Energy Policy. The Environmental Dimension*, Barcelona, Spain: University Institute for European Studies, pp. 97–123.

Busch, P.-O., H. Jörgens and K. Tews (2005), 'The global diffusion of regulatory instruments: the making of a new international environmental regime', *ANNALS of the American Academy of Political and Social Science*, **598** (1), 146–67.

Chayes, A., A. Chayes and R. Mitchell (1998), 'Managing compliance: a comparative perspective', in Edith B. Weiss and Harold K. Jacobson (eds), *Engaging Countries. Strengthening Compliance with International Environmental Accords*, Cambridge, MA: MIT Press, pp. 39–62.

Checkel, J. (2005), 'International institutions and socialization in Europe: introduction and framework', *International Organization*, **59** (4), 801–26.

De Tarde, G. (1903), *The Laws of Imitation*, New York: Henry Holt and Company.

DiMaggio, P. and W. Powell (1983), 'The iron cage revisited. Institutional isomorphism and collective rationality in the organizational field', *American Sociological Review*, **48** (2), 147–60.

Durkheim, É. (1991), *Die Regeln der soziologischen Methode*, Frankfurt, Germany: Suhrkamp.

Finnemore, M. and K. Sikkink (1998), 'International norm dynamics and political change', *International Organization*, **52** (4), 887–917.

Gehring, T. (1997), 'Governing in nested institutions: environmental policy in the European Union and the case of packaging waste', *Journal of European Public Policy*, **4** (3), 337–54.

Gerring, J. (2008), 'Review article: the mechanismic worldview: thinking inside the box', *British Journal of Political Science*, **38** (1), 161–79.

Haverland, M. (2000), 'National adaptation to European integration: the importance of institutional veto points', *Journal of Public Policy*, **20** (1), 83–103.

Héritier, A., C. Knill, S. Mingers and M. Becka (1994), *Die Veränderung von Staatlichkeit in Europa*, Opladen, Germany: Leske + Budrich.

Hoberg, G. (1991), 'Sleeping with an elephant: the American influence on Canadian environmental regulation', *Journal of Public Policy*, **11** (1), 107–31.

Holzinger, K. and C. Knill (2005), 'Causes and conditions of cross-national policy convergence', *Journal of European Public Policy*, **12** (5), 775–96.

Holzinger, K., H. Jörgens and C. Knill (eds) (2007), *Transfer, Diffusion und Konvergenz von Politiken*, Wiesbaden, Germany: VS Verlag für Sozialwissenschaften.

Jachtenfuchs, M. (2003), 'Regieren jenseits der Staatlichkeit', in Gunther Hellmann, Klaus-Dieter Wolf and Michael Zürn (eds), *Die neuen internationalen Beziehungen. Forschungsstand und Perspektiven in Deutschland*, Baden-Baden, Germany: Nomos, pp. 495–518.

Jänicke, M. and A. Volkery (2001), 'Persistente Probleme des Umweltschutzes', *Natur und Kultur*, **2**(2), 45–59.

Jänicke, M. and H. Weidner (eds) (1997), *National Environmental Policies: A Comparative Study of Capacity-Building*, Berlin: Springer.

Jänicke, M., H. Jörgens and K. Tews (2005), 'Einleitung: Zur Untersuchung der Diffusion umweltpolitischer Innovationen', in Kerstin Tews and Martin Jänicke (eds), *Die Diffusion umweltpolitischer Innovationen im internationalen System*, Wiesbaden, Germany: VS Verlag für Sozialwissenschaften, pp. 19–23.

Jörgens, H. (1996), 'Die Institutionalisierung von Umweltpolitik im internationalen Vergleich', in Martin Jänicke (ed.), *Umweltpolitik der Industrieländer. Entwicklung – Bilanz – Erfolgsbedingungen*, Berlin: Edition Sigma, pp. 59–112.

Jörgens, H. (2004), 'Governance by diffusion: implementing global norms through cross-national imitation and learning', in William M. Lafferty (ed.), *Governance for Sustainable Development: The Challenge of Adapting Form to Function*, Cheltenham, UK and Northampton, MA, USA: Edward Elgar, pp. 246–83.

Karch, A. (2008), 'Diffusion mechanisms and the policymaking process', paper prepared for presentation at the 2008 Annual Meeting of the American Political Science Association, 28–31 August, Boston, MA.

Katzenstein, P., R. Keohane and S. Krasner (1998), 'International organization and the study of world politics', *International Organization* **52** (4), 645–85.

Keck, M. and K. Sikkink (1998), *Activists Beyond Borders: Advocacy Networks in International Politics*, Ithaca, NY: Cornell University Press.

Keohane, R. (1984), *After Hegemony: Cooperation and Discord in the World Political Economy*, Princeton, NJ: Princeton University Press.

Keohane, R. and J. Nye (eds) (1972), *Transnational Relations and World Politics*, Cambridge, MA: Harvard University Press.

Keohane, R. and J. Nye (1989), *Power and Interdependence*, Glenview, IL: Scott, Foreman.

Kern, K. (2000), *Die Diffusion von Politikinnovationen: Umweltpolitische*

Innovationen im Mehrebenensystem der USA, Opladen, Germany: Leske + Budrich.

Kern, K. and I. Kissling-Näf (2005), 'Politikkonvergenz und Politikdiffusion durch Regierungs- und Nichtregierungsorganisationen: Ein internationaler Vergleich von Umweltzeichen', in Kerstin Tews and Martin Jänicke (eds), *Die Diffusion umweltpolitischer Innovationen im internationalen System*, Wiesbaden, Germany: VS Verlag für Sozialwissenschaften, pp. 301–51.

Kern, K., H. Jörgens and M. Jänicke (2000), 'Die Diffusion umweltpolitischer Innovationen. Ein Beitrag zur Globalisierung von Umweltpolitik', *Zeitschrift für Umweltpolitik & Umweltrecht*, **23** (4), 507–46.

Kern, K., H. Jörgens and M. Jänicke (2001), 'The diffusion of environmental policy innovations: a contribution to the globalisation of environmental policy', WZB discussion paper FS II 01-302, Berlin..

Lehtonen, M. (2005), 'OECD environmental performance review programme: accountability (f)or learning?', *Evaluation*, **11**, 169–88.

Levi-Faur, D. (2005), 'The global diffusion of regulatory capitalism', *ANNALS of the American Academy of Political and Social Science*, **598** (1), 12–32.

Levi-Faur, D. and J. Jordana (2005), 'Conclusion: regulatory capitalism: policy irritants and convergent divergence', *ANNALS of the American Academy of Political and Social Science*, **598** (1), 191–7.

Lindblom, C. (1965), *The Intelligence of Democracy: Decision Making Through Mutual Adjustment*, New York: Free Press.

Lowi, T. (1972), 'Four systems of policy, politics, and choice', *Public Administration Review*, **22**, 298–310.

March, J. and J. Olsen (1998), 'The institutional dynamics of international political orders', *International Organization*, **52** (4), 943–69.

Mayntz, R. (2002), 'Zur Theoriefähigkeit makro-sozialer Analysen', in Renate Mayntz (ed.), *Akteure – Mechanismen – Modelle. Zur Theoriefähigkeit makro-sozialer Analysen*, Frankfurt, Germany: Campus, pp. 7–43.

Meyer, J., D. Frank, A. Hironaka, E. Schofer and N. Tuma (1997), 'The structuring of a world environmental regime, 1870–1990', *International Organization*, **51** (4), 623–51.

Mitchell, R. (1998), 'Sources of transparency: information systems in international regimes', *International Studies Quarterly*, **42** (1), 109–30.

Nedergaard, P. (2007), 'Maximizing policy learning in international committees: An analysis of the European Open Method of Coordination (OMC) Committees', *Scandinavian Political Studies*, **30** (4), 521–46.

Risse-Kappen, T. (ed.) (1995), *Bringing Transnational Relations Back In: Non-State Actors, Domestic Structures, and International Institutions*, Cambridge: Cambridge University Press.

Rogers, E. (2003), *Diffusion of Innovations*, New York: Simon and Schuster.

Rose, R. (1991), 'What is lesson-drawing?', *Journal of Public Policy*, **11** (1), 3–30.

Rosenau, J. (1995), 'Governance in the twenty-first century', *Global Governance*, **1** (1), 13–43.

Rosenau, J. and E.-O. Czempiel (eds) (1992), *Governance Without Government: Order and Change in World Politics*, Cambridge: Cambridge University Press.

Sabel, C. and J. Zeitlin (eds) (2010), *Experimentalist Governance in the European Union: Towards a New Architecture*, Oxford: Oxford University Press.

Simmons, B. and Z. Elkins (2003), 'Globalization and policy diffusion: Explaining three decades of liberalization', in Miles Kahler and David A. Lake (eds),

Governance in a Global Economy: Political Authority in Transition, Princeton, NJ: Princeton University Press, pp. 275–304.

Simmons, B., F. Dobbin and G. Garrett (eds) (2008), *The Global Diffusion of Markets and Democracy*, Cambridge: Cambridge University Press.

Simon, H. (1957), *Administrative Behavior: A Study of Decision-Making Processes in Administrative Organizations*, New York: Free Press.

Steinmo, S., K. Thelen and F. Longstreeth (eds) (1992), *Structuring Politics: Historical Institutionalism in Comparative Analysis*, Cambridge: Cambridge University Press.

Strang, D. and J. Meyer (1993), 'Institutional conditions for diffusion', *Theory and Society*, **22** (4), 487–511.

Strang, D. and S. Soule (1998), 'Diffusion in organizations and social movements: from hybrid corn to poison pills', *Annual Review of Sociology*, **24**, 265–90.

Tews, K. (2005), 'Die Diffusion umweltpolitischer Innovationen: Eckpunkte eines Analysemodells', in Kerstin Tews and Martin Jänicke (eds), *Die Diffusion umweltpolitischer Innovationen im internationalen System*, Wiesbaden, Germany: VS Verlag für Sozialwissenschaften, pp. 25–54.

Tews, K. and M. Jänicke (Hrsg.) (2005), *Die Diffusion umweltpolitischer Innovationen im internationalen System*, Wiesbaden, Germany: VS Verlag für Sozialwissenschaften.

Walker, J. (1969), 'The diffusion of innovations among the American states', *American Political Science Review*, **63** (3), 880–99.

Weidner, H. and M. Jänicke (2002), 'Summary: environmental capacity building in a converging world', in Helmut Weidner and Martin Jänicke (eds), *Capacity Building in National Environmental Policy: A Comparative Study of 17 Countries*, Berlin: Springer, pp. 409–43.

Welch, S. and K. Thompson (1980), 'The impact of federal incentives on state policy innovation', *American Journal of Political Science*, **24** (4), 715–29.

Zürn, M. (1998), *Regieren jenseits des Nationalstaats. Globalisierung und Denationalisierung als Chance*, Frankfurt, Germany: Suhrkamp.

12. Climate change, the common good and the promotion of sustainable development

Susan Baker

The aim of this chapter is to use the notion of the 'common good' to ground an environmental ethic that will help underpin our responses to global environmental change, particularly climate change.[1] Given the need to engage in collective action in the face of our climate crisis, combined with the often politically fragile, hesitant and, to date, ineffective nature of such collective action, it becomes important to find ways to ground such action on strong normative principles. Furthermore, many of the actions that are taken arise out of a concern to promote national self-interest, which often has little in common with a state's declaratory commitment to promote sustainable development. To help break the impasse on collective action to protect our common future, we turn to the development of an environmental ethic based on the notion of the common good.

The attempt to apply normative principles to practical problems brings us to issues of applied ethics. When we adopt the notion of the common good as a normative principle this then forms a moral standard that regulates right and wrong conduct in relation to how we – international agencies and organizations, governments, society and the individual – both mitigate and adapt to global climate change.[2] The onus is on us to develop these normative principles because we have the power of reasoning and we have both the capacity and the obligation to act as ethical beings. As we will argue, however, this power does not make humans the primary subjects of ethical deliberations and moral behaviour.

We draw upon the idea of the common good because it has a long pedigree in both ethics and in political philosophy, where the promotion of the common good is seen both as a function of the just state and as an underpinning to democracy. Indeed, one understanding of democracy is that it is a kind of political constitution, wherein elected government acts as an agent for the people, with responsibility to make and enforce laws that promote the common good of citizens (Freeman 2007, p. 212).

This chapter provides an additional way to help further the commitment to the promotion of sustainable development, so central to the theme of this book. It is important to specify what we understand by sustainable development from the onset, and especially given the variety of approaches taken to sustainable development in both theory and in policy practice. We take it that promoting sustainable development is a social and political project that builds on recognition that we live in an ecological system that is characterized by two features: the planetary resources within that system are finite, and the ecosystem itself is delicately balanced. This balance can and is being disturbed by human behaviour. Within this context of limitations and balance, the promotion of sustainable development aims at realizing models of development that reduce both the resource intensity of production (sustainable production) and the levels of consumption in the developed world (sustainable consumption), thereby creating the conditions necessary for ecologically legitimate development, particularly in developing nations. In policy practice, this means that efforts to promote sustainable development are about finding ways to realize principles of inter- and intra-generational equity, especially through establishing appropriate governance institutions and arrangements (Baker 2006; Lafferty 2004; Meadowcroft 2007). This interpretation is in line with the claim, implicit in the writings of many of the contributors to this volume, that from the perspective of sustainable development, environmental issues such as those relating to climate change are quintessentially issues of an ethical nature, often with strong distributional dimensions, especially when viewed from a global perspective.

My initial interest in the notion of the common good arose from the belief that global environmental change threatens the common fate of *humankind*, now and into the future. Climate change in particular will disrupt ecosystem services, such as nutrient cycles, crop pollination and decomposition of wastes, and will lead to the spread of disease, and increase the prevalence of flooding of human settlements. As such, addressing climate change is about preserving the life chances of present and future generations. As far back as 1987, the Brundtland Report articulated the environmental challenge as that of safeguarding *our common future* (WCED 1987). Later, the Rio Earth Summit called for global efforts to deal with the environmental crisis because it threatened the common fate of humanity.

However, as international efforts to address climate change falter and as individual states move to act in their own best interests, the sense of the common nature of the problem of climate change is receding further into the background. Furthermore, as states seek to ensure that they are not put at competitive or political disadvantages by climate change, efforts are increasingly focusing on adaptation rather than on mitigation measures. In this context there is real danger that climate change policy may in fact move society further away from, rather than closer to, the promotion of sustainable development, deepening the existing policy impasses on this matter.

Given that the developed world has greater ability to draw down capital, technological and political resources to enable it to adapt, the potential for further deepening of inequalities grows. With this comes additional potential for fracturing any sense of the commonality of the predicament now facing human society. We are also concerned that the emphasis on addressing climate change through technological innovation, for example in the energy and transport sectors, will fuel traditional models of economic growth, which we argue is incompatible with a commitment to promote sustainable development (Baker 2006). Energy policy is particularly problematic here, in that many states now seek to reduce their carbon emissions by making greater reliance upon nuclear power, a policy that displaces environmental problems, in particular those dealing with nuclear waste and decommissioning, onwards to future generations. This breaches one of the key normative principles of sustainable development, that of inter-generational equity.

If climate change adaptation strategies move society further away from the promotion of sustainable development, it is increasingly likely that measures will provide only short-term relief. This is because by not addressing the underlying causes of climate change these actions will provide *no* means of assuring that climate disruption will not continue and that further ecosystem disruptions, of a yet unknown nature, may also occur. We argue therefore that the problem of climate change calls for us to find ways to build an economic system that allows humans to live within the carrying capacity of the planet's ecosystem and to build social, political and cultural values and norms that facilitate and support this system. From this perspective, addressing climate change as an ethical problem can potentially provide new grounds to both strengthen and legitimize the political, social and individual *will to act* and thereby help to overcome the policy impasse that we now face with respect to the willingness to adopt effective public policy to promote sustainable development in the face of global environmental change.

As an investigation into normative ethics, this chapter is interested in establishing moral principles (to determine which actions are right) and virtues (to decide which states of character are morally good). As such, it is interested in moral rules that have direct implications for human behaviour and ways of life, and what the institutions that support them should be like. Philosophical inquiries into this matter have tended to focus on either the social context or the authority from whence moral values (that is, moral principles and virtues) are derived. Traditionally, the response is either that moral values are human conventions, which are rooted in place and time, or that moral values ultimately depend on an omnipotent and good God. Depending on the answer given, ideas of the common good are seen as either formed in the social realm, so they become related to theories of virtue or they become determined by the natural law. In this chapter, we start from a different approach, placing the base for moral values in the ecological world, a realm different from the social and human, but which falls short of the divine domain. We remain neutral, however, in this chapter as to whether our notion of the common good can in turn be referred upwards to a further theological rationale.

We argue that the ecosystem and the natural environment that unfolds within it together provide the context within which moral values are to be established and to which decisions about moral principles and virtues need to refer. The common good, in this scheme, while it may relate in impor-tant ways to the social and/or spiritual dimensions, is also crucially linked with the good of the environment and the ecosystem. This is because we hold that the preservation of life, and of human fulfilment, is dependent on the maintenance of a healthy environment and on the maintenance of ecosystem functioning and services – what we call the maintenance of ecological integrity. Beyond this, we also hold that a healthy environment and functioning ecosystem are values in and of themselves. As such, this chapter is written around what might be loosely called a green theory of value (see Barry 1999; Goodin 1992; Kassiola 2002).

Our explorations of the ethical dimensions of climate change policy addresses ethical considerations in the context of liberal political thought. We do this because the concern of this volume, implicit or otherwise, is to address problems in relation to how to ensure effective governance for sustainable development in political systems where matters in relation to the conduct of social actors and institutions are determined by principles embedded in notions of rights. A focus on rights invariably raises the complex issue as to the relative weight to be given to the moral claims of individuals, on the one hand, and to those of society, on the other. This provides a very fertile ground on which to debate matters of the common good as they relate to balancing the good of the individual with that of the good of society. Furthermore, matters in relation to rights are often mentioned in the literature on sustainable development. Meadowcroft, for example, argues that at the heart of commitment to the promotion of sustainable development lie calls for changes to existing rights and entitle-ments and established distributions of power (Meadowcroft 2001, p. 182). Acterberg has also argued that society has to construct 'a shared public basis' on which to ground the legitimacy and acceptance of restrictions and corrections that are necessitated by commitment to the promotion of sustainable development (Acterberg 1993). However, discussions have tended to focus on how best to *exercise* rights, be they for present or future generations, human or other species (see, for example, the work of Dobson 1998), neglecting the thornier issue of how to balance entitlements to, with restrictions on, rights.

This chapter is structured as follows. It begins with an elaboration of the notion of the common good, providing a brief outline of early developments in theory, and then turns attention to the seminal work of Rawls. The limitations of Rawls' treatment of the common good, particularly given the centrality he affords to rights, are explored. We then seek to develop a notion of the common good that extends beyond the human domain. The promotion of sustainable development through public policy actions based on a notion of the common good, but which displaces the centrality of rights, turns attention to public reason and democratic deliberation. In our conclusion we explore how the notion of the common good can help us go beyond the current impasse and find a new will to implement effective collective efforts to promote sustainable development.

1. THE NOTION OF THE COMMON GOOD

The term the 'common good' is known by several other names, including the 'international public good', the 'good of the whole' and the 'good for all persons'. The term has a long history, underpinned by scholarship that extends back to Greek philosophy. Much of this scholarship lies within theology and, as an ethical and moral imperative, the common good is central to the tenets of many religious faiths. For example, the notion of the common good is particularly well developed in Catholic social teaching (Dorr 1983; O'Brien and Shannon 1992; Stiltner 1999; Hollenbach 2002). More recently, the World Council of Churches' publications on *Christian Social and Economic Ethics in World Perspective* have stressed this notion. Beyond this, the term is now emerging, albeit in only a tentative way, as an ethical norm for assessing national policies and the effect of globalization on people's lives. This is particularly the case within development studies. The United Nations Human Development Reports, for example, affirm the importance of the common good in the face of a global economy that is marked by unprecedented prosperity alongside devastating poverty (O'Connor 2002). The idea of the common good is also increasingly identifiable with the progressive left in contemporary American politics. Appeals to the common good have also surfaced in discussions of corporate social responsibilities. However, despite these early signs of a return to favour, the usefulness of the notion of the common good as a tool to help mount an effective policy response to sustainable development, and in the context of climate change, remains largely unexplored.

Development of the Notion of the Common Good

The notion of the common good originated with Plato, Aristotle and Cicero. Aristotle used the concept as a basis for his distinction between 'right' constitutions, which are in the common interest, and 'wrong' constitutions, which are in the interest of the ruler. However, it is the work of Thomas Aquinas that has provided the bedrock upon which most scholarship on the common good, as developed in Western moral and political philosophy, rests.

Aquinas's treatment of the common good of the universe runs parallel to his discussions of the common good of citizens that constitute a particular society. He sees the common good (*bonum commune*) as a basic principle in the way God governs the universe and in the way a king rules a kingdom. He claimed that God created living and nonliving entities in an orderly relationship to one another, achieving their internal common good, that is, the well functioning of the universe (Kempshall 1999). Both seek the good of the many over the good of the one. In addition, creatures and humans cooperate with one another for the good of the whole because they are related to God as their Creator. At the root of this appetite for the common good is the natural inclination each creature has for God – who is the absolute common good of all creatures (Shaefer 2005, pp. 22–3). Aquinas believed that the entire universe of interconnected parts achieves its purpose through the functioning of all parts in relation to one another, in ways that are appropriate to what he sees as the innate characteristics of each part. This created common good is the good of the whole order of beings – functioning in appropriate, relational ways to sustain themselves as intended by God, towards whom they aim. God, in this view, is the uncreated common good of the entire universe (Schaefer 2005). Aquinas argued not only that creatures cooperate in securing the common good but that they do this within a hierarchical 'chain of being'. Entities that have a higher grade of goodness, in particular humans, have a greater appetite for the common good and are inclined to seek to do good for others far removed from themselves.

While Aquinas's notion of the common good provides an ecological principle to underpin his ethical system, his notion is also embedded in cosmology. Inherent in his writings is the belief that creatures are related to one another, to the universe as a totality and ultimately to God. In this scheme, the physical world become a means through which what he sees as God's goodness, wisdom, power and other attributes can be contemplated. It is hardly appropriate for our purposes to develop a notion of the common good using the views of medieval theology that sees the diverse constituents of the world (such as nature, ecosystems, biodiversity and humans) as having been created as specific types, ordered hierarchically in relation to one another, so as to function according to a divine plan, and where the goodness of creatures and the goodness of the world – including ideas of the common good – arise only by virtue of the fact that God created and ordered this great chain of being.

However, while Aquinas's medieval cosmology has limited appeal, his work has strongly influenced subsequent understandings of the common good as it relates to political authority. Aquinas's belief that the realization of the common good is the end purpose of law and government has come to underpin the notion that the promotion of the common good is fundamental to the workings of the political order. Among early liberal theorists, as developed from Locke in the eighteenth century, there is much agreement that the end or aim of government should be to promote the common good. This is generally seen to require acceptance of the individual's basic rights in society. However, although allowing a thin notion of the common good, early theories of liberalism were narrow, focusing on personal freedom and political equality. A key concern was to ensure that individuals were not forced to support some specific notion of the common good (for example, a specific religious doctrine), violating the freedom of those who do not share in that goal. There was a critique of 'paternalism', the interference of a state or an individual with another person, against their will, and defended or motivated by a claim that the person interfered with will be better off or protected (Dworkin 2010) from tyranny or even oppression. As such, nothing strikes terror into the heart of classical liberals more than the proposition that the common good forms the basis of justice, in other words, that our system of rights is derivative of, and conditioned by, the common good (Simhony 2005).

However, as liberal theory developed, an array of different positions arose, including in relation to such central matters as the nature of society, the nature of the self and the relative weight to be given to the rights and claims of the individual and of society. Green and Hobhouse, for example, both tried to reconcile the two by arguing that the common good necessarily included the good of both society and the individuals (Gaus 2001, pp. 19–20). Hobhouse in particular helped to develop a liberal stance that supported an interventionist role for the state in mediating the inequalities arising from the development of the market economy, especially through the provision of basic social welfare. He also advocated social obligation, public duty and social reform (see Meadowcroft 1994). Green presented an analysis of a right, which aimed at providing the conditions for the development of personality but which was derived from the common good. However, Green's attempts to reconcile moral individualism with the morality of the collective good did not settle the dispute between those who stressed individual rights, and those who insisted that liberalism can only be grounded on appeals to collective welfare. Debates continued into the twentieth century and, as Gaus has argued: 'A history of twentieth-century liberal theory would have much to say about the various defences of moral individualism, criticisms by more collective or communal liberals, as well as attempts to reconcile the two' (Gaus 2001, p. 19).

The decade of the 1990s in particular saw liberalism in search of new ways to overcome the criticism that it was overly individualistic. Attention was turned to addressing how we can be social creatures, members of cultures and raised in various traditions, while also being autonomous choosers who employ our liberty to construct lives of our own (Gaus 2001, pp. 17–18). As such, liberal theory began to recognize that no liberal society can include an unlimited variety of possible life plans – the liberal state can be neutral among a range of actual choices, but not neutral among *all conceivable choices* (Downing and Thigpen 1993). Rawls did much to move attention away from the focus on the individual to focus on principles of justice as they relate to society as a whole, including its institutions. Attention is given to the works of Rawls in this chapter because of the crucial influence he has had on the development of twentieth-century liberal thinking and of political philosophy more generally.

2.   RAWLS: JUSTICE, RIGHTS AND THE COMMON GOOD

Drawing upon social contract theory, particularly as espoused by Rousseau, Rawls developed the idea of 'constitutional democracy', which is based on the key principles of equality, freedom, social cooperation and justice (Rawls 1999). For Rawls the primary aim of democratic legislation is not to promote individuals' happiness, but rather individuals' freedom and the common good for all citizens: 'Government is assumed to aim at the common good, that is at maintaining conditions and achieving objectives that are similarly to everyone's advantage' (Rawls 1999, p. 205). Rawls followed Rousseau in that, for him, just social conditions and institutions (a just political constitution, legal procedures, economic norms, just property system, and so on) are seen to benefit all reasonable and rational citizens. He argued that a desirable feature of democracy is that the political constraints of justice that regulate our conduct should be freely acceptable to us as equal citizens from a fair position. In his notion of justice as 'fairness', Rawls placed strong emphasis on the requirement of justice of all the basic institutions of society. Rawls held that if the convention of democracy is to promote the common good, and if justice is the common good, the primary purpose and role of democratic government is to promote justice (Freeman 2007, p. 217). Rawls gave centrality to notions of justice in his writings, rather than to the common good *per se*.

Rawls's conception of justice is built around the ideal of free and equal moral persons, co-operating on the basis of reciprocity and mutual respect (Freeman 2007, pp. 216–17). The primary role for just institutions is to provide the conditions for realizing this ideal of citizens as free, equal and independent. However, democratic citizens also have objective interest in maintaining the conditions for their freedom and equality, that is, they develop and exercise moral powers. Given their sense of justice, free and equal citizens normally want to pursue personal aims in ways consistent with just institutions and the common good. In other words, Rawls holds that we have a higher-order interest in preserving our equal status and self-respect as free citizens and in maintaining the moral powers that enable us to take part in social cooperation.

Rawls' theory of justice is closely linked to his complex theory of rights, which is based on two key principles of justice:

1. Each person has an equal claim to a fully adequate scheme of equal basic rights and liberties, which scheme is compatible with the same scheme for all; and in this scheme the equal political liberties, and only those liberties, are to be guaranteed their fair value.
2. Social and economic inequalities are to satisfy two conditions: first, they are to be attached to positions and offices open to all under conditions of fair equality of opportunity; and second, they are to be to the greatest benefit of the least advantaged members of society (Rawls 1993, pp. 5–6).

Importantly, the first principle, about equal rights and liberties, has priority over the second and is a principle of strict equality. This applies to the constitutional structures and the guarantees of the political and legal system. In relation to the second principle, matters are somewhat more complex. The second principle relates to the operation of the social and economic system, including policies in relation to redistribution, social security, education, and so on, and give space for permissible inequality. Such matters, for example issues in relation to property rights, are not values in themselves and cannot act as the foundation of the justice of institutions. The first part of the second principle, about fair equality of opportunity, has priority over the second part, the so-called difference principle. While his position allows inequalities, which might arise for example from effort or work (or what was later described by so-called luck egalitarians as option luck), Rawls nonetheless places limits on the inequalities that may arise, in that people are only entitled to the rewards from their efforts under the rules of a just system (Nagel 2008, p. 68).

Rawls, however, differs from other liberals, such as Mill, in that his concept of rights is not instrumental. For Rawls, individual rights are not good because of the results they will bring about, but are good in themselves. He thus presents a deontological stance, that is, the right is understood to be prior to the good.

It is in the context of his basic principles of justice and rights that Rawls' theory of the common good can be understood. This theory contains three interrelated elements. First, in a well-ordered society, where each carries out his or her life plan to the fullest extent possible, the citizens together in an aggregate and participatory sense 'realise their common or matching nature' as a shared or common good (Keys 2006, p. 35). Of course, various constraints act on people's lives, such as limitations of time and talent, so that each individual can develop only a small fraction of his or her latent potentialities. However, in a well-ordered, basically just society, the citizens will see themselves as benefiting from the flourishing of all the other members. Second, citizens will come together also in affirming the two principles of justice and the social and civic institutions supporting then. Finally, Rawls holds that all citizens come to regard participation in the political life of their well-ordered society as a good in and of itself. Shared common ends and practices thus become not instrumentally valuable, but good in themselves (Keys 2006, pp. 35–6).

Although presenting a contractual foundation for the common good, similar to that found in other writers such as Rousseau, his theoretical base is nonetheless individualistic (Keys 2006, p. 37). This is because the strict priority of individual rights and liberties, over the reduction of social and economic inequalities, is at the core of his position. At its base is the idea that the individual engages in this rational endeavour because it assists the individual in attaining his or her own ends. Redistribution to the benefit of the least advantaged is unacceptable on its own, being just only if it proceeded from social arrangements that facilitate the exercise of basic liberties (Freeden 1996, p. 230). Thus, his position errs on the side of providing the strongest defence of individual rights against collective decision-making. For liberal thinking, rights form the linchpin around which discussions of the common good turn.

Rawls' stance has been criticized by many, including Sandel, who presents a model of society based on belief in a deeper human com-monality or inter-subjectivity than what Rawls' model of the self will allow (Sandel 1982). Sandel argues that the notion of community among humans must enter into the very constitution of our identities (Keys 2006). Sandel's notion of constitutive community presents an understanding of the human self or moral agent that locates the identity of the moral subject more fundamentally in commonality than in individuality. Sandel argues that only when the self is conceived of as community is it capable of engag-ing in the moral reflections that are needed to discern our common ends or common good. While Sandel's account gives priority to community, for Rawls it is the 'individuated' human agent for whom the virtue of (deonto-logical) justice is primary (Keys 2006, pp. 42–4).

Similarly, and despite his strong commitment to the belief that inequali-ties in life are social evils bearing on the justice of a society, we take issue with Rawls. We accept Rawls' position that holds that matters in relation to the operation of the social and economic system are not the foundation or the value that grounds the justice of institutions. However, we accept the position for reasons that are different from those offered by Rawls. Rawls appeals to a higher set of values; that is, he grounds the justice of a system on matters in relation to rights. We, on the other hand, wish to move beyond a position that gives priority to rights, and instead ground the justice of institutions on whether, and to what extent, they maintain ecological integrity. Here the maintenance of ecological integrity is a higher principle. Our conception of the common good incorporates an ecological dimension – the principle that collective action can only be construed to promote the good in so far as it supports the maintenance of the ecological basis of life (such as ecosystem function and the provi-sion of ecosystem services). The ecological system is of a different order of magnitude to the social and economic system, in that the latter is a human construct, whereas the former provides the necessary conditions within which the latter can unfold. As such it has to take precedence over and above other considerations. Thus, the common good, as understood here, is given precedent over and above *rights*. Ecological factors or, to be more precise, the consequences of irrational environmental behaviour, as is discussed in the following section, are such that they propel the priority of the good over the right.

As stated earlier, we are interested in using the idea of the common good not just to address the common fate of humankind, but the common fate of all living entities as well as addressing matters in relation to the main-tenance of a healthy environment and ecosystem. Contemporary liberal political values now include preserving the natural order to further the good of ourselves and of future generations. Rawls, for example, would support promoting biological and medical knowledge by fostering species of animals and plants, and protecting the beauties of nature for purposes of public recreation and 'the pleasures of a deeper understanding of the world' (Rawls 2005, p. 245, as quoted in Freeman 2007, p. 389). While this position recognizes that human life, whether operating at the individual or social levels, is embedded in an ecological system that provides the context, as well as the conditions, for human flourishing, this thinking is limited. It is grounded on an anthropocentric rationale that protects nature because of its value, material or otherwise, to humans. In contrast, the prioritization of the human is called into question from our position, which holds that all living organisms form a complex web of inter-dependency and are embedded in a natural system within which humans do not hold a central place.

In the same way that positing too sharp a distinction between the public and the private spheres is inadequate, if we wish to take fully into account the reciprocal interrelationship that exists between the self and society, we now wish to turn to criticize the view that posits too sharp a distinction between the self and society, on the one hand, and nature, on the other. This brings us to present a transactional view of nature where the self, society and nature are seen as constituting and being constituted by the others (see Evanoff 2005). Using this approach, we argue that the self is formed and reformed in and through constant interaction with both its social and natural environments. Social environments, for their part, function through the individuals that comprise them and the natural environments that sustain them. Natural environments can also be seen as both making certain forms of life and society possible, while in turn being modified by the forms of life and society that are actually created. Nature is in a constantly changing, dynamic relationship with humans. Just as human beings are embedded in the natural world, and are shaped by it, nature too is continuously shaped by our interactions with our environment. This relationship can be beneficial or harmful to humans, just as humans can interact in ways that support or disrupt natural eco-cycles and systems, deplete natural resources, and diminish plant and animal biodiversity. However, humans are not the centre of this relationship, because a good, healthy, viable environment can exist without any human society. Drawing upon, but also extending the classic Aristotelian notion of the common good, we argue that good societies cannot be produced in the absence of good, natural environments, but we are mindful that we can have a good, healthy, viable environment without any human society.

This view of nature can be used to infuse the notion of the common good with an awareness of the interrelationships that exist among the self, society and nature. With this recognition comes the realization that any aim of society to promote the common good has to embrace not just the needs of humanity, but also that of other life forms as well as the maintenance of ecosystem processes. Here the promotion of the common good of humanity is intrinsically bound up with the continuing unfolding of nature and the natural world. This does not imply, however, that human endeavours have necessarily to be given precedence within that process – the decision to do so is the outcome of the adoption of a particular ideological stance.

However, this is only part of our position. As well as extending the notion of the common good to take account of all living entities and to take account of the ecosystem itself, we do not wish to do this because of human needs, for example, for ecosystem services to maintain life. This is because we see the maintenance of a healthy environment and functioning ecosystem as a good in itself, otherwise we will be grounding the notion of the common good on a fragmented view of nature that prioritizes the benefits people obtain from ecosystems. Here we draw upon the well-developed arguments within environmental ethics in support of the view that nature has *intrinsic* value over and above consideration of what the wealth of nature and the ecosystem can provide in services to humankind (see Attfield 1991).

This stance allows us to take further issue with Rawls. Rawls, like other liberals, holds that a just state should refrain from trying to impose on its members a single conception of the ends and meaning of life. In this sense, he believes that a just society should adopt an attitude of toleration and the expectation of reasonable pluralism, and should leave people free to pursue their ultimate aims, provided they do not interfere with the other requirements of justice (Nagel 2008, p. 73). However, for our purposes, this neutrality is not strong enough, in that we argue for the need to impose an overarching conception of the aims of the good life if we are to protect the base upon which future life can unfold. Rawls says that the principles of right are prior to the conception of the good. However, we argue that the good, as it relates to the overarching requirement to preserve ecological integrity, is prior to the system of rights.

Asserting the primacy of the ecological also has an impact upon the concept of the common good. It is also of importance for the conception of, or the primacy given to, rights. It means that many 'common goods' are ruled out because they might compromise ecological integrity. To put the matter another way, we use the criterion of ecological integrity to judge whether actions promote the common good. By prioritizing the primacy of the ecological, it follows that the good comes before the right. This accepted, we can criticize Rawls on two grounds: first, that his conception of the good ignores the ecological dimension and, second, that the ecological dimension cannot simply be added on to his conceptualization of the good, because once the ecological dimension is taken into account, the good has to take primacy over the right.

This position directly parallels Dryzek's argument in respect to ecological rationality. Rationality is commonly understood to relate to different forms, such as functional (the inherent functioning of a system), substantive (whether it is appropriate to the achievement of a given goal), procedural (how an individual or organization thinks through a problem or course of action) or technical and economic (means for efficient achievement of a goal) forms. To this Dryzek adds 'ecological rationality', arguing that ecosystems have their own rationality. He claims that 'in the absence of human interest, ecological rationality may be recognized in terms of an ecosystem's provision of life support to itself' (Dryzek 1987, p. 44). He argues that ecological rationality is a fundamental form of reasoning, more fundamental than other forms of rationality that drive economic or political or technical decision-making:

> The preservation and promotion of the integrity of the ecological and material underpinning of society – ecological rationality – should take priority over competing forms of reason in collective choices with an impact on that integrity. (Dryzek 1987, pp. 58–9)

For Dryzek ecological rationality has absolute priority over other forms of reason because failure to address ecological considerations, including failure to ensure that policies do not disrupt ecosystem functioning and services, will result over time in the elimination of the other forms. It would hardly be rational if the use of ecological resources had the consequences of exhausting these resources and thus the basis for other rationalities.

The development of the concept of ecological rationality by Dryzek has helped to inform our thinking about rationality in collective action. While Rawls calls for a more classic understanding of rationality, and Habermas discusses how both procedural and substantive rationality might be reunited in the context of environmental politics and deliberative democracy, Dryzek argues for the potential of ecological rationality to act as a tool for the reform of our political and administrative structures and the rejuvenation of our politics (Baber and Bartlett 1999).

Dryzek holds that the application of other forms of rationality to public policy-making, decoupled from reasonableness and ecological context, is a faulty guide to sound governance. We wish to develop this argument further by exploring the implications of Dryzek's position for societal governance, including and in relation to social responses to global environmental change. Giving priority to ecological rationality requires moving from a focus on personal, or individuals' means and ends, to a collective focus. It also means bringing an ethical dimension into the discussion, thus shifting emphasis from the material to the relational. There is nothing new in this, because before modernity, the concept of rationality always had ethical overtones. A rational person, or society, was one that showed allegiance to a standard of values that transcended the instrumental or economic (Baber and Bartlett 1999, p. 3). Here we merely give new voice to those older notions.

This means that we are not able to shy away from the rather difficult matter of discussing the conditions under which restrictions on the freedom of people to pursue their ultimate aims may need to be imposed, and how democratic society is to confront this problem while still retaining its democratic nature. Yet, and as was said above, while the matter of restrictions is implicit in many discussions on sustainable development, particularly those relating to consumption, this matter has remained the elephant in the room of green theorizing. Nevertheless we wish to confront it here.

We argue that it is not merely a matter of devising a list of rights that we wish to see restricted, although we could think of many such – the right to drive a gas-guzzling automobile, or to plant non-native species in one's own garden, or to produce and sell non-repairable household goods. However, devising such a list does not get us very far, not least because in practice in any democratic society it is difficult to think of any area of social or economic life where there are not some forms of acceptable restrictions already in place. This includes restrictions on the type of fuel one is allowed to put in a car (even if it is gas-guzzling), prohibitions on growing plants classified as invasive alien species in one's garden (such as Japanese knotweed) or on producing and selling certain products, or to certain groups, such as selling fireworks to children. Collective life would indeed prove impossible if we had unfettered individual rights. Rawls and other liberals would accept that rights are not absolute, and that in a just society, individual rights are limited by the need to accord equal rights to others, and to avoid harm or ill to others. However, at root, these restrictions are legitimized by virtue of the fact that the individual's continuous participation in such a society is a rational endeavour in that it helps the individual to attain his or her own ends. The strict priority of individual rights and liberties, including when it comes to matters of distribution to address social, environmental or economic inequalities, is at the core of this position. Thus, it errs on the side of providing the strongest defence of individual rights against collective decision-making. As said above, for liberal thinking, rights form the linchpin around which discussions of the common good are lashed. In contrast, rather than adding to the list of actions, products or behaviours that we would wish to see restricted, we would prefer to re-orientate the principles that underpin collective life away from prioritization of the individual good to giving centrality to the common good. The consequence of this is that many more rights could be curtailed, over and above those that can be curtailed (either in practice or by further additions) on purely liberal grounds.

Taking this stance, we accept that we do not live in a society (be it understood at the local, regional, national or international levels) which shares or is united in its devotion to a common conception of the good. Moreover, we acknowledge that maintaining orthodoxy has always required oppression, because harmonious agreement over fundamental values does not maintain itself naturally (Nagel 2008, p. 83). It is to this we now briefly turn.

3.   PROMOTING SUSTAINABLE DEVELOPMENT ON THE BASIS OF THE COMMON GOOD

Our discussion of the common good has now to turn to the vexed issue of how to ground the legitimacy and authority of the common good. The notion of the common good as developed in past scholarship rests its legitimacy on the authority of the Church or on political authority. Traditionally, these two forms of authority have been given lead roles as *determinants* of the common good, acting as the authority with the power to determine what amounts to the common good for their constituents. However, in the contemporary period and across Western society as a whole, the authority of the Church is no longer seen as legitimate in this respect. Similarly, the authority of the state cannot be seen as necessarily and in all cases co-determinant with the common good of its people.

Liberal theory is well aware of this problem of legitimacy. For Rousseau, for example, public reason provided the means for citizens to reflect upon measures that advance the common good. Similarly, Rawls argued that because the liberal state has to be neutral, in that it cannot identify itself with the promotion of any particular values, there is need for public rational discourse about the proper functioning of the liberal state (Gaus 2001, p. 24). Public reason in Rawls provides the terms of political debate and justification for the use of coercive political power among free and equal citizens (Freeman 2007, p. 414). However, Rawls envisages that the difference principle, which requires society to maximize the share that goes to the least advantaged, will act as the primary principle to guide the deliberations of democratic citizens as they debate the common good (Freeman 2007, p. 100). However, we differ from liberal thinking in that we prioritize a different, non-anthropocentric principle to drive those engagements.

In democratic society, the nature of the political, social and individual actions – laws, policies and governance processes – that need to be under-taken to promote sustainable development are determined not in advance by theory, but worked out and negotiated in practice by and through political processes (Lafferty and Meadowcroft 2000). In contemporary green theorizing, the process of legitimization of environmental policy is increasingly seen as requiring a deliberative turn (Meadowcroft 2001). The term deliberative democracy is used within a school of political theory that assumes that genuinely representative public participation in decision-making has the potential to produce policy decisions that are more just and more rational (effective and efficient) than actually existing represent-ative mechanisms (Baber 2004, p. 332). For environmental theorists, delib-eration, particularly when this brings enhanced civil society participation in policy-making and governance processes, are seen to give opportunity to engage with the development and implementation of policies based on the promotion of sustainable development that are relevant and appropri-ate to particular societies and contexts and that consequently stand greater chance of success. We support this turn to deliberative democracy, not least because it may get us past accusations of 'perfectionism' – that is, commitment to a particular contested idea of the ends of life and insistence that it is the proper role of a political community to guide its members in that direction by coercion, education, the exclusion of other options, and control of the cultural environmental (Nagel 2008, p. 73). It can also help to revive the notion that public discourse might allow citizens to act out of a sense of abiding public spirit, a spirit that was so important to early democratic theorists.

Further attention needs to be given to this matter, however, not least in terms of debating how deliberative democracy can promote the common good over and above individual rights. We hope that we have at least pointed thinking in that direction.

4. CONCLUSION

The need for collective action to address our common problem of climate change and to ensure our sustainable futures calls for renewed actions on several fronts, as is evidenced by the various contributions in this book. In this chapter, we have explored one way in which we might move forward on this matter. In so doing, we have attempted to confront directly the fact that if we are to take actions to promote our sustainable futures, this cannot be done in ways that prioritize the good of all. There are conflict-ing interests at stake. The unsustainable patterns of resource use that exist in high-consumption societies will have to be changed, including through reductions in consumption and changes in production. At the same time the legitimate development aspirations of the poor and the marginalized will have to be promoted. Thus, dealing with global environmental change, including climate change, requires restrictions on the behaviour of some alongside the opening up of new life opportunities for others. In short, transition to more sustainable economic, social and political models of development will see some groups lose while others benefit from that change. In this context, we argue, there is need to open up a new debate on the validity of the liberal project which rests ultimately on the centrality of rights, rooted in the individual, for legitimizing political action.

While political philosophy, especially that developed by Rawls, has addressed the complex issue of how to balance individual and public goods, rights remain the linchpin around which the public and personal good revolve. Rights discourse highlights the particular, irreducible claims of individuals over and against one another and against unjustifiable encroachments from society as a whole and from its governments (Keys 2006, p. 9). Rawls' deontological liberalism is premised on the priority of rights and hence of justice, over the good. This chapter hopefully has called into question the focus on the centrality of rights, right-based proceduralism as well as a deontological liberalism. If responsible environmental behaviour is grounded on a strong ethics of the common good, this shifts focus away from individual rights, even where individuals are understood to have some form of community engagement, to an opposite priority: where the maintenance of ecosystem integrity and the future of life on the planet become the guiding principle for actions, even when this means that rights are displaced by obligations to other life forms and to the natural systems that sustain them.

Discussions on the common good have tended to assume that humans are the primary subjects of ethical deliberations and of moral behaviour, although green theory does discuss the extension of rights to certain animals. Our notion of the common good has, however, extended our understanding of reciprocity from the self to society, and from society to the natural environment within which all life forms progress and develop. This idea of the common good helps us to realize that society cannot proceed on the basis that social organizations, institutions and processes should be geared towards securing effective human opportunities, but that we have also to take account of the reciprocal nature of the relationship between human beings and the wider environmental and ecological contexts within which they are embedded. From this perspective, liberal democracy can be seen as inherently unsupportive of the norm of sustainable development because it takes human interests as the measure of all values (see Mathews 1991 for discussion on links between environmentalism and democracy). Many environmental political theorists have argued that discursive democracy creates a situation in which interests other than one's own are called into mind, including the interests of nature, other species and of future generations (Attfield 1991; Goodin 1996; Dobson 1996). While a great deal of attention has been given in this literature to identifying the conditions that facilitate discursive and participatory practices, there remains a lack of solid grounds for asserting that the use of such deliberative practices leads to a broader, ecologically sounder, perspective on interests. To promote our sustainable future, it is not sufficient that deliberation merely brings reason, fairness, inclusiveness and equality into play, but that it takes place in the presence of a broadly shared notion of the common good. Such deliberations have to be subject to the 'critical tribunal' of ecological rationality (Ekersley 1999, pp. 65–76). We propose that grounding deliberations in the public sphere on an ethic of the common good, as understood in this chapter, can serve to underpin the claims that a deliberative turn in democratic practices can help to promote a more sustainable future. While those supporting the deliberative turn *hope* that deliberative processes can produce consensus – and change minds through reasoned argument (Baber 2004, p. 339) – we give substance to these aspirations by providing a shared, environmental value to underpin this process.

In this sense we hope to have, at least in part, answered the call to provide deliberative democracy with a 'moral, conceptual, and affective framework' (Valdez 2001, p. 353). In taking the notion of the common good, central in Christian theological and moral traditions, and developing a modern, secular and ecological notion of the common good, we hope to produce something 'close to the kind of solidarity that religion engenders without the divisiveness that religion can create' (Baber 2004, p. 341).

The idea of the common good as developed herein can contribute to overcoming the gap between, on the one hand, the widespread declaratory intent made by both international and national organizations, institutions and actors to promote sustainable development and, on the other, the development of a more effective engagement with policy. Stress on the common good can provide us with an ethics of environmental responsibility that can be used to ground collective action and provide a new political *will to act*. We also argue that the notion of the common good can provide an organizing principle for collective action. In addition, the idea of the common good as developed in this chapter can help ground the legitimacy of restrictions that have to be put on human behaviours in order to promote our sustainable futures. We argue that a right-based liberalism provides a fundamentally inadequate basis for addressing the challenges faced by global environmental change. Over time, a renewed discourse on the common good could also serve to re-articulate the discourse so that behavioural changes are seen less in terms of restrictions and more in terms of *contributions* to our collective future. This brings to mind the concern of Bennett that in the disenchanted world – a world populated by individuals who are sensitive about their personal rights and dominated by reason and alienation – ethics has become a code to which one is obligated rather than a source of affective commitment (Bennett 2001). If we come to accept the principle of the common good and we carve out space in public discourse and deliberations to elaborate on this principle, rights can become derivative of, and conditional upon, their contribution to the good of the community, understood both in social and natural terms. Finally, the commitment to the common good can remind us of the need to address environmental change in ways that are in keeping with the normative principles of sustainable development, as discussed in the opening sections of this chapter.

We are mindful that our aim is not to provide what Berlin calls 'the final solution' of the ultimate reconciliation of values. We are not seeking an all-purpose tool that would allow us consciously to control society, but rather to develop a normative principle that can be used to ground democratic deliberations in pursuit of sustainable development. Here we provide a way to link the relationship between nature and the polity, by integrating a primary commitment to the common good with a dedication to the promotion of sustainable development. In engaging in these deliberations, we need to be aware that in order to promote sustainable development, the good of the individual or indeed of society cannot always be directly prioritized in these deliberations. Liberalism is closely associated with Enlightenment thinking, and we have called into question key principles of liberalism as they relate to both the insistence on rights and the centrality given to the rational endeavours of citizens living in good standing to overcoming nature and control her destiny. In questioning this endeavour, we are making what may appear to be an uncomfortable assertion, namely that in promoting the common good as a base for our sustainable futures we will preclude certain values and human behaviours that are currently cherished in our liberal political order. But, to paraphrase Bohman (1996), in the face of global environmental change, setting loose the beast of collective will is a risky necessity.

NOTES

1.　I am particularly grateful for the detailed comments provided by the volume editors. Without their careful guidance this chapter might not have been written.

2. A simplified distinction is made here between 'morals' and 'ethics'. 'Morals' is here used to define personal character, while 'ethics' stress a social system in which those morals are applied. In other words, ethics points to standards or codes of behaviour expected by the group to which the individual belongs. This could be national ethics, social ethics, company ethics, professional ethics or even family ethics.

REFERENCES

Acterberg, W. (1993), 'Can liberal democracy survive the environmental crisis? Sustainability, liberal neutrality and overlapping consensus', in A. Dobson and P. Lucardie (eds), *The Politics of Nature: Explorations in Green Political Theory*, London: Routledge, pp. 62–81.

Attfield, R. (1991), *The Ethics of Environmental Concern*, 2nd edn, Athens, GA: University of Georgia Press.

Baber, W. (2004), 'Ecology and democratic governance: towards a deliberative model of environmental politics', *The Social Science Journal*, 41, 331–46.

Baber, W.F. and Bartlett, R.V. (1999), 'From rationality to reasonableness in environmental administration', *Journal of Management History*, 5 (1), 55–67.

Baker, S. (2006), *Sustainable Development*, London: Routledge.

Barry, J. (1999), *Rethinking Green Politics: Nature, Virtue and Progress*, London: Sage.

Bennett, J. (2001), *The Enchantment of Modern Life*, Princeton, NJ: Princeton University Press.

Bohman, J. (1996), *Public Deliberations: Pluralism, Complexity, and Democracy*, Cambridge, MA: MIT Press.

Dobson, A. (1996), 'Democratizing green theory: preconditions and principles', in B. Doherty and M. de Gues (eds), *Democracy and Green Political Theory: Sustainability, Rights and Citizenship*, London: Routledge, pp. 132–48.

Dobson, A. (1998), *Justice and the Environment: Conceptions of Environmental Sustainability and Dimensions of Social Justice*, Oxford: Oxford University Press.

Dorr, D. (1983), *Options for the Poor: A Hundred Years of Vatican Social Teaching*, New York: Maryknoll Institute.

Dowling, L. and R. Thigpen (1993), 'Virtue and the common good in liberal theory', *The Journal of Politics*, 55 (4), 1046–59.

Dryzek, R. (1987), *Rational Ecology: Environment and Political Economy*, Oxford: Blackwell.

Dworkin, G. (2010), 'Paternalism', *The Stanford Encyclopedia of Philosophy*, Summer edn, edited by Edward N. Zalta, accessed at http://plato.stanford.edu/archives/sum2010/entries/paternalism.

Ekersley, R. (1999), 'The failed promise of critical theory', in C. Merchant (ed.), *Ecology*, New York: Humanity Books, pp. 65–76.

Evanoff, R. (2005), 'Reconciling self, society, and nature in environmental ethics', *Capitalism Nature Socialism*, 16 (3), 107–14.

Freeden, M. (1996), *Ideologies and Political Theory: A Conceptual Approach*, Oxford: Clarendon Press.

Freeman, S. (2007), *Rawls*, London: Routledge.

Gaus, G. (2001), 'Ideological dominance through philosophical confusion:

liberalism in the twentieth century', in M. Freeden (ed.), *Reassessing Political Ideologies: The Durability of Dissent*, London: Routledge, pp. 13–34.

Goodin, R. (1992), *Green Political Theory*, Cambridge and Cambridge, MA: Polity Press/Blackwell.

Goodin, R. (1996), 'Enfranchising the Earth, and its alternatives', *Political Studies*, **XLIV**, 835–49.

Hollenbach, D. (2002), *The Common Good and Christian Ethics*, Cambridge: Cambridge University Press.

Kassiola, J. (ed.) (2002), *Explorations in Environmental Political Theory: Thinking About What We Value*, Armonk, NY: M.E. Sharpe.

Kempshall, M. S. (1999), *The Common Good in Late Medieval Political Thought*, Oxford: Oxford University Press.

Keys, M. (2006), *Aquinas, Aristotle and the Promise of the Common Good*, Cambridge: Cambridge University Press.

Lafferty W. (ed.) (2004), *Governance for Sustainable Development: The Challenge of Adapting Form to Function*, Cheltenham, UK and Northampton, MA, USA: Edward Elgar.

Lafferty, W. and J. Meadowcroft (2000), 'Introduction', in W. Lafferty and J. Meadowcroft (eds), *Implementing Sustainable Development: Strategies and Initiatives in High Consumption Societies*, Oxford: Oxford University Press, pp. 1–22.

Mathews, F. (1991), 'Democracy and the ecological crisis', *Legal Services Bulletin*, **16** (4), pp. 157–9.

Meadowcroft, J. (ed.) (1994), *L.T. Hobhouse: Liberalism and Other Writings*, Cambridge: Cambridge University Press.

Meadowcroft, J. (2001), 'Green political perspectives at the dawn of the twenty-first century', in M. Freeden (ed.), *Reassessing Political Ideologies: The Durability of Dissent*, London: Routledge, pp. 175–92.

Meadowcroft, J. (2007), 'Who is in charge here? Governance for sustainable development in a complex world', *Environmental Policy and Planning*, **9** (3–4), 193–212.

Nagel, T. (2008), 'Rawls and liberalism', in S. Freeman (ed.), *The Cambridge Companion to Rawls*, 7th edn, Cambridge: Cambridge University Press, pp. 62–85.

National Conference of (US) Catholic Bishops (1986), *Economic Justice for All: Pastoral Letter on Catholic Social Teaching and the U.S. Economy*, Washington, DC: United States Catholic Conference.

O'Brien, D.J. and T. Shannon (1992), *Catholic Social Thought: The Documentary Heritage*, New York: Maryknoll Institute.

O'Connor, J. (2002), 'Making the case for the common good in a global economy: the United Nations human development reports 1990–2001', *Journal of Religious Ethics*, **3** (1), 157–73.

Rawls, J. (1993), *Political Liberalism*, New York: Columbia University Press.

Rawls, J. (1999), *A Theory of Justice*, revised edn, Cambridge, MA: Harvard University Press.

Rawls, J. (2005), *Political Liberalism*, expanded edn, New York: Columbia University Press.

Sandel, M. (1982), *Liberalism and the Limits of Justice*, Cambridge, MA: Cambridge University Press.

Schaefer, J. (2005), 'Valuing earth intrinsically and instrumentally: a theological framework for environmental ethics', *Theological Studies*, **66** (4), 783–814.

Simhony, A. (2005), 'A liberalism of the common good: some recent studies of T.H. Green's moral and political theory', *British Journal of Politics and International Relations*, **7**, 126–44.

Stiltner, B. (1999), *Religion and the Common Good*, Lanham, MD: Rowman & Littlefield.

Valdez, J. (2001), *Deliberative Democracy: Political Legitimacy and Self-Determination in Multicultural Societies*, Boulder, CO: Westview Press.

World Commission on Environment and Development (WCED) (1987), *Our Common Future*, Oxford: Oxford University Press.

13. Pushing the boundaries: governance for sustainable development and a politics of limits

James Meadowcroft

This chapter is concerned with ideas about limits and their centrality to sustainable development. It explores the possibility of constructing a 'politics of limits' – a political orientation that sets environmental limits at the core of societal deliberation and action. The suggestion is that while sustainable development cannot be reduced to a politics of limits, the successful emergence of such a political orientation is necessary to break the impasse that currently bedevils efforts to achieve a more consequent engagement with sustainability. Yet even as a 'politics of limits' appears essential, it is also problematic. And this also requires consideration.

The discussion is organized into five sections that examine: the place of limits in arguments over the environment and sustainable development; contemporary interest in environmental limits; limits and politics more generally; the construction of a new 'politics of limits'; and, finally, some difficulties associated with this approach.

1. ENVIRONMENTAL ARGUMENT AND ENVIRONMENTAL LIMITS

Limits have always played a role in environmental argument. In the most obvious sense environmental pressures become apparent as specific thresholds are passed: with excess hunting, game becomes scarce; as more sewage is dumped into a river, the water becomes unsafe to drink; and as pollutants from fossil fuel combustion increase, so urban air quality declines. Moreover, solutions to environmental problems typically involve the collective enforcement of limits: restricting hunting; regulating the discharge of waste to water; curtailing smokestack emissions; and so on. Consequently, arguments about where natural limits lie and where legal limits should be imposed are at the core of contemporary environmental politics.

Consider two iconic representations of environmental concern: *The Limits to Growth*, a report prepared for the Club of Rome in 1972 (Meadows et al. 1972); and *Our Common Future*, issued 15 years later by the World Commission on Environment and Development (WCED 1987).

The basic message of *The Limits to Growth* was that exponential expansion of human civilization could not continue indefinitely. On a finite planet the scale of the human presence could not increase without end – one day growth would have to stop. The report focused on five key elements: population, industrialization, food production, pollution and the consumption of non-renewable natural resources. Adopting a systems approach, the authors used an early computer model to simulate future societal developments. The authors' conclusions were stark:

> If the present growth trends in world population, industrialization, pollution, food production, and resource depletion continue unchanged, the limits to growth on this planet will be reached sometime within the next one hundred years. The most probable result will be a rather sudden and uncontrollable decline in both population and industrial capacity. (Meadows et al. 1972, p. 23)

To avoid such overshoot and subsequent societal collapse, humankind needed to learn to live within the Earth's limits. The challenge was to initiate an orderly transition towards a sustainable state of global equilibrium characterized by stable levels of population and physical capital. In such a steady-state society, technological and social progress could continue. Indeed, 'any human activity' that did 'not require a large flow of irreplaceable resources or produce severe environmental degradation might continue to grow indefinitely' (Meadows et al. 1972, p. 175). But the scale of the overall human presence would be deliberately limited and the resultant pressures on the biosphere capped.

Key features of the authors' discussion included:

- framing the problem in terms of 'limits to growth', that is environmental and resource limits to the continued expansion of human societies (especially population and industrial capital, with their associated material requirements – land, raw materials and waste assimilation);
- emphasis on the urgency of the situation, the relative proximity of limits and the danger of overshoot and collapse;
- criticism of 'technical solutions' and blind faith that technological innovation will always provide answers;

- deliberate endorsement of 'a self-imposed restriction on growth', with the notion of a gradual transition to an 'equilibrium' or 'steady-state' society.

The Limits to Growth generated considerable debate, with critics accusing its authors of underestimating the human potential for innovation and neglecting the critical role of markets and the price mechanism in driving the search for new technologies and resources (Nordhaus 1974). Symbolic of this controversy was the famous Ehrlich/Simon wager over the price of industrial commodities. Ecologist Paul Ehrlich bet that over time the prices of five metals (copper, chromium, nickel, tin and tungsten) would rise (due to higher demand and impending resource scarcities) while economist Julian Simon maintained that prices would fall (because even if demand rose, substitutes would be found). Ehrlich had to pay out, as the prices of all five metals fell between 1980 and 1990. Much was made of Simon's victory, but the evolution of metal prices over a decade appears to be a poor proxy for environmental limits. There is a substantial cyclical component to metals prices (moving with the ups and downs of the world economy) and linkages to other commodity prices (such as oil). Subsequent analysis shows the payout to have been highly dependent on the start and end years of the wager. Moreover, it has since become clear that limits relating to the environment's capacities to absorb waste (for example greenhouse gases) bite at the global level more rapidly than do resource constraints.

Environmental limits play a more equivocal role in *Our Common Future*. There 'sustainable development' was famously defined as 'development that meets the needs of the present without compromising the ability of future generations to meet their own needs' (WCED 1987, p. 43). The Commission went on to explain that sustainable development contained:

> within it two key concepts: the concept of needs, in particular the essential needs of the world's poor, to which overriding priority should be given; and the idea of limitations imposed by the state of technology and social organization on the environment's ability to meet present and future needs.

Limits are therefore a critical element in the definition of sustainable development: but emphasis is placed not so much on the fixed carrying capacity of the biosphere, as on the shortcomings in technology and social organization that restrict the environment's potential to support human activities. A little later the authors explain:

> Growth has no set limits in terms of population or resource use beyond which lies ecological disaster. Different limits hold for the use of energy, materials, water and land. Many of these will manifest themselves in the form of rising

costs and diminishing returns rather than in the form of any sudden loss of a resource base. The accumulation of knowledge and the development of technology can enhance the carrying capacity of the resource base. But ultimate limits there are, and sustainability requires that long before these are reached, the world must ensure equitable access to the constrained resource and reorient technological efforts to relive the pressure. (WCED 1987, p. 45)

So while the authors distanced themselves from simplistic notions of a single or absolute environmental limit and emphasized the dynamism of technology and social practices, they also acknowledged the existence of 'ultimate limits' and stressed the importance of keeping the global development trajectory within the bounds of ecological possibility.

The WCED deliberately focused attention on 'development' – a process of societal advance relating to living standards, health, education, culture, science and so on. Since development was not merely about material consumption, it was a process to which all societies could aspire, and which was in principle open ended. Sustainable development was development that paid due consideration to environmental issues and equity. Economic growth was important for sustainable development, especially for poorer countries that could not meet the basic needs of their populations. 'Elsewhere' economic growth could be consistent with sustainable development 'provided the content of growth reflects the broad principles of sustainability'. Thus sustainable development required 'a change in the content of growth, to make it less-material and energy intensive and more equitable in its impact' (WCED 1987, p. 52). Moreover, the report argued that:

> many of us live beyond the world's ecological means, for instance in our patterns of energy use. Perceived needs are socially and culturally determined, and sustainable development requires the promotion of values that encourage consumption standards that are within the bounds of the ecological possible and to which all can reasonably aspire. (WCED 1987, p. 44)

It has been traditional to juxtapose these two documents, with *The Limits to Growth* seen as the more pessimistic, predicated on a choice *between* environment and economy, while *Our Common Future* suggested that continued economic advance and environmental protection could go hand in hand. Certainly, the WCED was not 'anti-growth': indeed, the report called for 'a new era of growth' that would end a decade of economic stagnation in the poor countries. It did not talk of a transition to a 'steady state' economy and generally sought to transform the argument over the desirability of growth into one over the character of authentic 'development'.[1] Some political forces that found *The Limits to Growth* distasteful could live with *Our Common Future*. But there are also deep affinities between the two perspectives: both argued that economic growth was not an end in itself and that emphasis should be placed not just on material consumption, but also on the higher products of human civilization. Both documents recognized a need for greater material production to raise living standards in poor countries, and both pointed to some form of 'absolute' ecological limits that had to be respected to avoid catastrophe.

If one looks more broadly at the development of environmental argument since the birth of the modern movement in the 1960s, it is possible to identify four basic ways in which limits are invoked:

Limits as Ecological Constraints, as 'External' Limits on Human Activity

The first sort of limit is grounded in the physical character of natural systems. It makes an appearance in debates over emission standards, ecological carrying capacity, critical loads, sustainable yields and most famously limits to growth. The underlying idea is that biophysical boundaries matter. Such limits can be conceptualized with respect to harvest rates for biological materials; the capacity of environmental media to assimilate pollutants; the safe levels of human exposure to toxic substances; and ecosystem tolerance of disruption. In the simplest sense this is about recognizing specific thresholds. In a more sophisticated presentation natural systems are understood to operate within defined (although sometimes flexible and hard to identify) parameters. Up to a certain point disturbances can be accommodated: natural processes absorb the disruption and perturbations are dampened. But beyond that point the biological/ecological/natural system cannot repair itself, consequences are felt more widely, and significant change ensues. In political discussion the emphasis may be placed either on the biophysical frontier that acts as a limit (for example, carrying capacity or sensitivity of the Earth's climate system) or on the human activity that will be frustrated (the existing development trajectory, continuing economic growth): but in each case the underlying limit is 'natural'. It is a limit that is enforced ultimately by nature over and against human will. Of course, it may be possible temporarily to move 'beyond the limit', to exceed the critical load or to expand economic activity beyond what the environment can support: but then ecological consequences will follow, consequences that may undermine the human activities that breached the limits.

Limits to the Human Capacity to Manipulate Nature (and Society)

A second invocation of limits draws attention not to the bounded capacity of the environment that surrounds (and ultimately sustains) us, but rather to the fallibility of humans; the imperfection of our knowledge; the weaknesses of our institutions; and the failings of our technologies. And because our understanding and our creations are *necessarily* limited we should be wary of overambitious projects to subdue nature, to bend all natural systems to our purposes or to comprehensively manage the biosphere. Here emphasis is placed on the limits of human cognitive capacities, on our inability reliably to anticipate the future and on the repeated failure of our attempts to manage biological systems as if they were engineered systems (Gunderson and Holling 2002). At the extreme, discussion of these sorts of limits may be associated with a critique of the 'hubristic' and 'mechanistic worldview' of modern science and a repudiation of 'the Enlightenment Project'. But it is in any case focused on the unavoidable limits to human knowledge of complex eco-social systems and the difficulties of managing under conditions of uncertainty. In policy terms this form of limits points to the importance of governance approaches that emphasize precaution. In a broader sense it is an appeal to humility. There is an obvious link to traditional conservative worries about the ambition of social reformers (who exaggerate our capacity to manipulate society or remake humankind), but this affinity is developed in different ways in varied strands of environmental argument.

Limits to the Potential of the Materialistic Development Model to Satisfy Human Needs

The third appeal to limits relates to the incapacity of modern materialistic/consumer society to satisfy human needs. The focus here is upon the futility of the endless quest for enhanced material satisfactions. The argument is that contemporary developed societies have long since passed the point where further material affluence increases well-being. Indeed, by over-consuming we are actively harming our health and happiness. Reference is made to critiques of gross domestic product (GDP) as an indicator of societal welfare and to studies that show that after a certain point higher incomes do not translate into greater happiness. Such arguments can reference the declining marginal utility of income, and engage with debates about what makes life worth living. Typically emphasis is placed on the value of increased time for family and social activities, leisure, education and civic engagement, and perhaps spiritual pursuits rather than greater material consumption. Additionally a contrast is drawn between the over-consumption of the affluent and the under-consumption of the poor still struggling to meet their basic needs. Here limits are associated with balance. Thus an end to consumer society and materialist culture is seen not as an unfortunate consequence of environmental scarcity, but as a welcome movement towards a more meaningful way of life.

Limits as Self-restraint

The fourth form of limits trades on the idea of *self*-restraint in our interactions with the environment. The perspective is that humans can consciously *choose* to alter their behaviour to preserve environmental values. The focus is on humans as active subjects as thinking and self-aware agents capable of making deliberate choices and of consciously modifying the way they individually and collectively interact with their surroundings. The grounding for such restraint can be self-interested: based on recognition that bio-physical limits exist (and/or that our capacities to control nature and anticipate events are limited; and/or that over-consumption is bad for us). But it may also be associated with moral self-binding, where we limit our actions in order to discharge moral responsibilities to others: for example, by conserving the environment for fellow citizens (in current or future generations), or to accommodate increasing consumption in poor countries, or for the benefit of non-human nature. These could be described as 'ethical limits' to human conduct with respect to the environment: limits that we *should* enforce upon ourselves. The key here is the exercise of individual and/or collective self-restraint – avoiding doing what otherwise one might do, in order to protect some environmental value. Such self-limitation is therefore about value choice: about changing behaviour to promote certain environmental ends. Self-limitation can be approached at the individual or the collective level: applying to the conduct of individuals, families, groups, communities, towns, regions, states and ultimately humankind as a whole. Social practices of concern can be affected by individual choice (selection of consumer products, avoiding car use to help the climate), collective action (by environmental groups or business) or political intervention (regulation, state expenditure).

The understanding of limits involved within each of these four dimensions can be appreciated by considering their extreme antitheses: perspectives untroubled by such limits. In the first place, there is the image of a bountiful (rather than a bounded) earth that can satisfy growing demands for resources and waste sinks – if not indefinitely – at least far into the future. Second, there is the vision of a masterful and resourceful humanity that has the potential to develop technologies of production and control to manipulate the ecology to meet evolving societal needs. Third, there is a view of progress based on continuous material transformation and acquisition: where individual and collective consumption can grow without cease to satisfy expanding desires. Finally, there is a view that repudiates collectively imposed restrictions on appropriations from nature as unnecessary – representing an unwarranted extension of government meddling, an unjustified infringement on liberty, or pointless self-denial (because other societies will ultimately exploit whatever resources we refrain from using today).

Elements from the four understandings of limits described above are interwoven into environmental argument. By combining different kinds of claims in relation to each of them, very different political perspectives can emerge. Much turns upon the scale at which limits are understood – do they refer to local or regional phenomena, to specific media, substances, or processes, and to particular activities and institutions? Or are they invoked more broadly, at a macro level, concerning system-wide, societal or global effects? The appeal to limits may be implicit rather than explicit: for environmental advocates often find it fruitful to emphasize the positive consequences of societal action – what is to be conserved or enabled, rather than what is to be forgone. This is particularly true at the macro scale, when limits might appear to impinge on established ways of life, general patterns of economic activity and the interests of powerful actors.

2.   CONCERN WITH LIMITS TODAY

Over the past few years interest in environmental limits has become increasingly manifest. Scientific reports have highlighted growing pressures on the planet, including: the destabilization of the climate system; loss of biodiversity; overexploitation of water resources; and the declining health of the oceans (IPCC 2008; Millennium Ecosystem Assessment 2005). In each case, research has pointed to the finite nature of the biosphere, the accelerating pace of human-induced change and the risks of crossing critical thresholds. For example, a recent piece in *Nature* attempts to provide a scientific foundation for defining the critical biophysical limits confronting humanity. In 'Planetary boundaries: exploring the safe operating space for humanity', Rockström and collaborators (2009) identify nine problem areas: climate change; ocean acidification; stratospheric ozone depletion; interference with biochemical nitrogen and phosphorus cycles; global freshwater use; land system change; the rate at which biodiversity is being lost; chemical pollution; and atmospheric aerosol loading. For some of these they suggest provisional quantitative limits (for example: climate change, less than 350 ppm or 1 Wm^{-2} radiative forcing; global freshwater use, less than 4000 km^3 of abstractions per year; global biodiversity loss, less than 10 species per million per year). But in other areas (for example, chemical pollution or atmospheric aerosol loading) they argue science does not yet allow us to formulate precise limits, although we know that in principle these must exist.

Another illustration of this preoccupation with limits is the increasing interest in 'ecological footprint' analysis. Pioneered by William Rees and Mathis Wackernagel in the mid-1990s, the ecological footprint is an attempt to evaluate the biological resources required to support the production/consumption patterns of existing human societies (Wackernagel and Rees 1996; Rees 2000). This can then be compared with available biocapacity to determine the extent to which a community is living within its ecological means. Over the past decade the environmental footprint has been taken up by government bodies, business and the environmental movement and applied to countries, cities, households and even individuals. This scalability and the powerful metaphor of measuring the human footprint on the planet have contributed to its success. Sometimes the results are presented in terms of the number of Earths that would be required to support humankind, were everyone to live like the citizens of a particular country. For example, it is claimed that 4.3 Earths would be needed if we all lived like the average Canadian. Globally, footprint analysis suggests that by 1980 the total human footprint already had surpassed the existing planetary biocapacity.

Popular media have also taken up this issue of limits. Consider, for example, recent *Scientific American* articles about environmental limits: including 'Population and sustainability: can we avoid limiting the number of people?' (Engelman 2009), 'Boundaries for a healthy planet' (Foley et al. 2010) and 'How much is left: the limits of Earth's resources?' (Zemi Media 2010). Over the past decade there has been renewed discussion of the advantages and costs of economic growth, and of the tools used to assess social welfare. One high-profile contribution has come from the Commission on the Measurement of Economic Performance and Social Progress established by Nicolas Sarkozy, the former French president (Stiglitz et al. 2009). The Commission argued for new approaches to assess social welfare and sustainability in light of economic developments and environmental crises.

There has also been a rash of publications by more radical economic writers suggesting that, in rich countries at least, it is time to move beyond economic growth. Consider, for example, Peter Victor's *Managing Without Growth* (2008); Tim Jackson's *Prosperity Without Growth* (2009); and the New Economics Foundation's *Growth Isn't Possible* (2010). These works revitalize the tradition of steady-state economics associated with thinkers such as Herman Daly (Daly 1977), arguing that we are reaching the limits of economic growth and must now consider alternative development pathways.

A number of political factors have encouraged this renewed interest in ecological limits. First, there is the problem of climate change. While ozone depletion was in some respects the first truly *global* environmental problem, climate change raises the issue of environmental limits – in this case the quantity of GHGs that humans can release to the atmosphere without serious ecological disruption – in a way that much more directly challenges existing societal practices. Fossil energy has fuelled the rise of industrial civilization. Twenty years after the issue was formally recognized as an international problem with the signing of the UN Framework Convention on Climate Change (1992), societies are just beginning to appreciate what the emissions reduction challenge really entails. Second, there is the general experience with environmental policy over the past four decades. On the one hand, policy initiatives in developed countries have been relatively successful in reducing conventional air and water pollution, protecting public health and expanding protected areas. On the other hand, continued growth in population and material consumption in both developed and developing countries means that the total environmental burden imposed by humankind on the Earth continues to increase. In other words, environmental efficiency gains are being swamped by absolute growth. Third, volatile oil prices and the stagnation of conventional oil production has led to concerns about peak oil and increased dependence on oil imported from politically unstable regions. So for the first time since the 1970s there is talk about what to do when oil runs out. Fourth, the dramatic economic expansion of large and rapidly developing countries (especially China and India) has raised issues about competition for scarce resources and the environmental consequences of extending 'Northern' lifestyles across the planet. Finally, there is the increased 'interrelatedness' of global problems, including the economy, food supplies, energy production and consumption, environment, water use and so on. Consider the recent backlash against biofuels, which were at first heralded as a solution to climate change (as well as a solution to worries about energy security and rural development) and then were berated for driving up food prices and accelerating environmental damage (especially corn-based ethanol, through water and agri-chemical requirements, as well as debatable GHG credentials).

Yet if the last few years have seen an increased discussion of environmental limits, they have also witnessed an interesting juxtaposition. Governments in developed countries continue to deal with fallout from the financial collapse of 2008–09, including: high unemployment and falling government tax receipts related to slow economic growth; painful deficit reduction measures; and concerns over debt and default. A return to higher rates of economic growth appears central to the solution of these economic woes. Yet more economic growth also looks set to deliver additional environmental burdens and ultimately threatens to breach further environmental limits.

Those with an interest in promoting environmental protection have gravitated around two poles in their response: on the one hand, there is a call for green growth and, on the other, there is an appeal to end the era of economic growth. The first current is reflected in recent Organisation for Economic Co-operation and Development (OECD) and United Nations Environment Programme (UNEP) publications (OECD 2011a, 2011b; UNEP 2011). The idea is to change the character of growth, to invest in green infrastructure, expand green jobs and the green economy. For example, in the United Kingdom Nicholas Stern, author of the influential *Stern Review of the Economics of Climate Change* in 2006, has called on government to encourage a surge of investment for a low-carbon transition. This is what might be described as the official or mainstream environmental approach. The underlying idea is to decouple environmental burdens from economic activity: so even as the economy grows, overall environmental pressures will fall (OECD 2001). To be clear, what is implied here is an *absolute* decoupling (and not just a relative decoupling, where the efficiency with which environmental resources are consumed increases, but so too does the absolute environmental burden). The second current argues that the time has come to end the growth economy: first in the rich countries and, over coming decades, also in the developing world. Economists such as Victor and Jackson urge a gradual transition away from growth, while more radical proponents call for 'de-growth' – the shrinking of Western economies back within frontiers the planet can tolerate.

The debate between 'green growth' and 'end growth' turns in large part on beliefs about three inter-related questions: (1) the extent to which decoupling of economic activity from environmental burdens is actually possible; (2) the depth of the changes to the existing economic system required to resolve environmental issues; and (3) the understanding of the approach that will be most helpful in shifting current practices.

For green growth advocates, the potential for decoupling is significant, the transformation of existing economic practices can be achieved incrementally, and attention should be focused on the environmental ills to be corrected rather than on an abstract repudiation of growth. For the growth critics, absolute decoupling on the scale required is impossible, the economic system requires fundamental transformation, and it is necessary to target growth economics explicitly.

The differences between these perspectives raise profound questions about the nature of economic activity and eco-social interactions that cannot be pursued in detail here. For our purposes it is sufficient to note that limits actually play an important role in *both* perspectives. For the growth critics this is more obvious: to avoid broaching environmental limits we must wean ourselves off economic growth, first in rich countries and ultimately worldwide. Yet it is true also for the proponents of green growth: to avoid broaching environmental limits we must switch from a traditional economic model to green growth – that is to say, economic growth that is compatible with a lowering of absolute environmental burdens. So, provided the requirement for absolute decoupling is taken seriously by the green growth proponents, both perspectives require a profound change to established patterns of economic activity. Imposing a 'consensus' across the two groups (with which neither would be entirely happy), we could say that there is agreement: *that economic growth based on the continuous expansion of damaging appropriations from nature needs to draw to a close. Thus what might be termed the era of 'extensive' economic growth (that relies on increasing environmentally destructive resource inputs and waste generation to achieve greater economic output) must be brought to an end.* Of course, the consequences of such a change would be understood differently by the two currents: for the growth critics it would lead to a gradual winding down of economic growth (as all growth would ultimately fall into this extensive category), while for green growth proponents it could open the door to a new era of (non-environmentally destructive) economic expansion.

3.   POLITICS AND LIMITS

At first glance the idea of developing a 'politics of limits' might appear unpromising. Many analysts have documented the difficulties which democratic political systems experience in managing environmental problems (Lafferty and Meadowcroft 1996). Environmental problems are manifest on spatial and temporal scales that fit poorly with the routines of democratic politics. Impacts may cross borders and accumulate slowly over time. Issues may require specialist scientific assessments and include major uncertainties. Strict limits are notoriously hard to define. Remedial action always disturbs established interests and patterns of behaviour. And those ultimately affected by environmental disruption may have no representation in current deliberations. Such 'absent constituencies' include citizens of other nations, future generations and non-human nature.

Moreover, contemporary institutions are linked to a development trajectory *predicated* on extensive economic growth of the kind we now need to leave behind. Indeed, there has been something of an implicit bargain over the past century: Western political systems involve private owner-ship of productive assets and market-mediated exchange, representative democracy, the welfare state and continuously increasing material outputs and standards of living (Gough and Meadowcroft 2011). It is not an exaggeration to say that social stability rests on a foundation of growing material consumption. Over time there have been vast environmental efficiency gains, but these are over-run consistently by rises in absolute consumption. And pity the politician who fails to preside over an economy that is achieving healthy economic growth.

It is important to note, however, that politics and limits (although perhaps not yet environmental limits) do have an underlying affinity. To a large extent politics – and more particularly the state as a public power – is concerned with the adjudication and enforcement of limits. After all, every 'right' (including a right to property) represents an entitlement for the right-holder but a limit on everyone else. Indeed, political theory has always been concerned with limits, and classic arguments have related to the appropriate size of the political community, the boundaries of politi-cal obligation, and limits to individual and collective freedom. Consider Aristotle's famous discussion on the dimension of the polis (Aristotle 1945), Christian political thinking about the limits of temporal author-ity (Dyson 2002), Locke's 'enough and as good left behind' arguments about property (Locke 1998), Kant and Hegel's debate over the existence of international society (Hegel 1991; Kant 1991), and so on. If we under-stand politics as 'who gets what, when, where and how' (Lasswell 1936), it is clear that limits to political action, authority and processes become central.

Moreover, the state has always been involved in struggles over defining and enforcing limits. Most obviously states are confined to specific por-tions of the world's surface: they are territorially bounded, and despite abstract claims of 'sovereignty' what states can do is limited, both practi-cally and by the progressive development of international law. Above all, over the past several hundred years, political and constitutional battles within states largely have focused on circumscribing the arbitrary power of political authorities (through the establishment of the rule of law, responsible government, the separation of powers, federalism and so on). States uphold individual and collective rights by maintaining systems of law and such systems limit individual and collective freedom in certain domains so that a more meaningful system of freedoms and other enti-tlements can be enjoyed by all citizens (Hobhouse 1994; Rawls 1971). Moreover, political democracy is only possible if there are common rules of the game – concerning the conduct of fair elections – respected by all parties. In other words, political *limits* make democracy possible.

Legal rules structure the operation of the economy and influence its impacts on the environment. Reference has already been made to property rights, but limits are also placed on the activities which business can undertake and the sorts of contracts that will be enforced by the state. Regulations about minimum wages and working conditions, the operation of industrial facilities, preparation of financial statements, consumer protection, and so on, limit the conditions in which market competition takes place. Anti-monopoly, 'fair competition' and market access rules, as well as incentives and the tax system, influence economic activity. Indeed, literally thousands of regulations structure what is and is not permitted – not just on the economic front but in every aspect of social interaction. Many constraints on behaviour towards the environment are already in existence (emissions controls, protected areas, and so on) – but on the whole these do not relate directly to large-scale environmental limits, especially global limits, where the scale of human activity now threatens the long-term viability of important ecological processes.

So from this perspective talk about 'limits' is not introducing something entirely alien into political life, but rather about expanding the sorts of considerations that must be accommodated and the kinds of issues that politics and the state must consider when deciding about collective action.

4.   TOWARDS A NEW POLITICS OF LIMITS?

So, what might a politics of *environmental limits* actually entail? There is no one way to answer this question. Since the 1960s environmental thinkers have struggled to define the contours of a green society and they have come up with rather different ideas about what this might imply. In parliaments, green parties have advanced varied agendas that link environmental protection with other social causes. The enactment of environmental regulation by governments has imposed certain constraints on environmental conduct. Yet for all this we are only starting to get an idea of what a politics of limits would actually imply.

To be clear when talking about 'a politics of' limits in this way, the intention is to capture something essential about the character of political argument, structure and process. It is to indicate concerns that lie at the centre of public debate, that underpin political action and government activity. In its initial manifestations, a politics of limits could be articulated by specific groups or coalitions, but over time it would become embedded in policies and institutions, and it would ultimately colour the overall character of political interaction. Although a detailed elaboration of such a politics cannot be attempted here, it is possible to suggest some of its most general characteristics.

First, a politics of limits would place concern with social/ecological interactions at the centre of political life. The problem of meeting evolving human needs while protecting local and global ecosystems would be at the heart of political argument and a core preoccupation of government. Here environmental limits would in the first instance be related to material impacts – the way human activities touch the natural world and the environment affects societal welfare. Thus a physical understanding of limits, as generated *by the interaction between human activities and environmental systems and processes*, would ground such a politics. After all, in the ecological domain it is *physical phenomena* that matter, not abstract categories, human intentions or financial statistics. Yet defining these limits in ways that make sense to science and that can be translated into the context of societal decision-making, as well as determining the ways in which existing practices and institutions should be adjusted, are far from trivial and will constitute much of the actual content of a politics of limits.

Why is defining such environmental limits so challenging? In the first place, it is because of the *complexity* of eco/social interactions: society and ecology interact on many different levels in a variety of different ways, so there are many potential 'limits' operative in different domains and at different spatial and temporal scales. Second, there are pervasive *uncertainties* that make it hard to identify relevant limits and to specify at which point they will become operative. Our understanding of ecosystems, social systems and ecosystem/social system coupling is bounded: we have not identified all important causal pathways, let alone understood their interconnections and feedback processes. And in many cases we will only be certain where a threshold lies after it has been crossed. Third, there is an irreducibly *normative* character to limit identifying exercises, which involves decisions about the significance of thresholds and the distribution of risks. Science may provide a quantitative evaluation of (a), what degree of human intervention is (b), how likely to provoke (c), a specific change in environmental conditions. But whether this is an 'environmental limit' of significance to societal development depends also on judgements about the meaning of such a change. For example, the loss of X per cent of a species' habitat may create a Y per cent likelihood of its extinction: but is this a limit with which we should be concerned? The consequences of different levels of pressure on ecosystems vary, and different patterns of human adjustment are possible. So environmental limits rarely appear clear cut, but seem more a question of degree. It is always possible to argue that the real limit is not *here*, but *there*. All of these difficulties are present in large-scale problems such as climate change or biodiversity loss. The physical processes are complex and rife with uncertainty and there can be no purely scientific procedure to determine safe climate change or an acceptable rate of species loss. This does not mean that environmental limits do not exist, lack scientific foundation, or are arbitrary. It does mean that while science is essential to establish the physical processes underpinning environmental limits, the definition of these limits requires normative choice and political argument.

In summary, material interactions remain the essential starting point for conceptualizing a politics of limits. The focus is on physical impacts associated with the human presence, which ultimately depend upon the size of the population and nature of the technologies, the patterns of resource use and waste generation, of societal production and consumption. For example, the greenhouse gas emissions contributing to climate change are largely energy related and they can be understood as a product of human numbers, energy use per person and the carbon content of that energy. This suggests that if we are serious about controlling greenhouse gas emissions, we must affect at least one (or preferably all) of these: (1) *population* – influencing births/deaths/migrations; (2) *energy use per person* – changing technologies and lifestyles; and (3) the *carbon intensity of energy* – switching to low-carbon energy sources or avoiding carbon emissions from fossil sources (for example, by employing carbon capture and storage). Discussion of each of these elements and of the different ways action on these fronts could be combined would figure in a politics of limits.

One advantage of starting with physical processes is that it partially sidesteps unfruitful arguments about growth in the abstract, and a pro-/anti-economic growth dichotomy. The growth about which we should be concerned is in the first place growth in *material impacts* that relate to environmental limits: and here the growth problem (that is, the problem of the continuing increase of these impacts) must be addressed. Human societies cannot go on pressing against limited ecosystems without disastrous consequences. But the relationship between the growth of *specific material impacts* and economic growth writ large is not straightforward. Generally, economic growth has meant greater material impacts. However, all material impacts are not of the same significance (some are more directly related to proximate and critical limits). And we have sometimes experienced GDP growth that is absolutely decoupled (at least in particular countries and certain periods) from specific environmental impacts. Problematizing economic growth is an essential part of a politics of limits, because the growth economy of today is driving us beyond environmental limits. However, a general opposition to economic growth is not, as the assessment of economic growth must depend upon its qualities and the context in which it occurs.

A difficulty with general discussions of growth is the constant confusion about whether we are talking about a growth in financial turnover or in material flows: the two are linked, but in variable ways. Economists continue to discuss the nature, sources and measurement of economic growth. There is increasing recognition that beyond a certain point, conventionally measured GDP growth is not well correlated with advances in social welfare. Over the long term, economic growth rates in developed countries have declined (and are today modest compared with those in rapidly developing countries such as China), but at 2–3 per cent a year on average they still result in a doubling of economic activity every few decades. As we have seen, under current conditions this results in a worrying increase in absolute environmental burdens. However, modern social structures are predicated on such growth and its periodic interruption (in recessions, depressions, and so on) results in untold hardship. Again this suggests that rather than focusing on the aggregate economic growth rate – and assuming it to be either entirely welfare-promoting or environment-destroying – we should be concerned in the first instance with the material impacts (on the environment *and* on social welfare) of specific policies, projects and practices.

The concern with growth can mislead in another way: for in many respects human societies are *already* breaching environmental limits. It is not just that further growth in material impacts will get us into trouble (although of course it will), but that existing patterns of activity (for example, releasing GHGs at current rates) are already beyond the limits. This is another way of saying that absolute reductions in environmental burdens from economic activity (whether that activity is growing, stable or shrinking) must be pursued until the total environmental pressures associated with a particular biophysical limit are within, scientifically founded but socially determined, tolerance levels.

In addition to the external physical understanding of limits discussed above, a politics of limits would also accommodate limitations in the *human capacity* to consciously manage the ecosphere, economic/social interactions and our own collective development. That is not to say societies would abandon such management efforts! But rather that these would be predicated upon a recognition that they could only ever be partially successful. Here a politics of limits would acknowledge the inevitability of incomplete understandings, focus on management in conditions of radical uncertainty, and be cautious with proposals for large-scale biophysical and socio-political engineering.

Moreover, a politics of limits could not avoid engaging with the materialist orientation of *current societal development* models. So far governments have been extremely reluctant to approach this issue. However, a turn away from a society of expansive material consumption (with planned obsolescence, the deliberate manipulation of material desires, and so on) appears unavoidable. Conceptions of entitlement and needs would need to be redefined and to be subject to political contestation and to regulation.

Finally, a politics of limits would place self-limitation at the centre of political argument: self-limitation both for self-interested and other-interested reasons and at both the individual and collective levels. Thus each of the four understandings of limits described earlier would be operative, but their particular place would be politically constructed and subject to continuing contestation.

Second, in functional terms, a politics of limits would require:

- *A public ideology* – that can underpin political respect for environmental limits: this includes acknowledging limits and the need to live within them; an ecologically sensitive perspective on human ends; and some recognition of responsibility for environmental 'stewardship' (Barry 1999).
- *Continuing public debate* – around the character of environmental limits and the approaches to accommodate and/or avoid them. Limits are multiple and over time the biosphere, knowledge of economic and social interactions, technologies and understandings of societal needs evolve: so there can be no one-shot institutional design or political bargain that deals with environmental limits once and for all.
- *An effective public power* – that can regulate economic and social interactions, and can conduct an array of related activities, including: support for scientific research on natural and social systems and their interactions; measuring and monitoring; forecasting and planning; mechanisms for policy delivery and review; and public discussion and decisions about priorities.
- A political *coalition* – that supports giving life to such a politics of limits.

Third, a politics of limits would need to be a politics of *opportunity* and of individual and collective *self-realization*. In the Western political tradition, limits are justified by the benefits they confer: limits on the individual's freedom to do what he or she wills are required to secure rights and collective self-government; limits to the powers of the executive are necessary to secure the rule of law; limits to the powers of majorities are necessary to secure the rights of minorities; and so on. So too with the recognition of environmental limits: they can serve as a foundation for higher forms of social life, thus opening up new possibilities in other dimensions of individual and social attainment. This is where *sustainable development* comes into play – for it is not just about respecting environmental limits, but also about transforming development: the path of societal advance – in a word 'progress', and finding a creative way forward for human societies to meet their needs and flourish.

Fourth, a politics of limits would necessarily represent *a politics of transition*, as societal institutions are adjusted over many generations to come to terms with environmental limits. This contradicts ecological visions that see the switch from an industrial to an ecological society as a single qualitative leap. Precisely because ecological limits are multiple, and emerge from societal as well as scientific understanding, the process of adjusting to them will extend into the distant future. While the transition to a low-carbon emission society that is today discussed as a response to climate change presents an enormous challenge, it would not constitute the end of adjustment. The social economy we have inherited from the twentieth century has proven (relatively) good at securing *extensive* economic growth – growth that depends on the continuous expansion of appropriations from nature and is linked with a rising human population and ever greater material consumption. The challenge is to transform economic, social and political institutions so that our economy can deliver without threatening environmental limits. This is likely to involve changes not just to environmental policy narrowly conceived, but also to the institutional conditions framing economic activity as a whole: the balance between private and social provision; the delineation of incentives; the rules governing property rights and corporate behaviour; and the terms of international trade. It may imply a transformation of social welfare systems, the redistribution of paid employment, a redefinition of consumption and so on. *Squeezing out extensive growth* will take time as economies must adjust to seeking welfare gains, employment and profits in areas that do not increase critical environmental burdens. To talk of de-materializing welfare satisfaction is too crude – because material flows are not equal, and those that seriously impact the environment must be addressed most urgently. But in essence it is true that we must 'walk more lightly upon the planet' and to the extent that there are more of us, living longer, we must learn to walk more lightly still. Indeed, it is only by making strenuous efforts to achieve absolute decoupling that we will actually learn what is and is not possible. In this regard previous experience is of limited help; after all, it is not that decoupling has been tried and failed, *but rather that no one has yet tried very hard.*

Finally, this would need to be a *non-exclusionary form of politics*, in the sense that there would be no idea that a politics of limits is the be all and end all of politics. On the contrary, it is just one consideration that affects, but does not subsume, others (Meadowcroft 2005). In other words, adjusting social development to natural limits is a necessary step in human advance, but it does not tell us everything about the human story and what human societies and individuals may yet accomplish.

It should therefore be clear that the starting point for a politics of limits must be serious reflection and open political discussion about the elements propelling human society beyond environmental limits, and about possible lines of adjustment required to address these dilemmas. This means that issues such as the quality (and quantity) of economic growth, the scale and character of production and consumption, and population levels, growth rates and migration – topics that largely have been marginalized in arguments about sustainable development so far – must be introduced into mainstream political discourse. Visions of endless material expansion and norms of unreflexive growth must be challenged. And argument should focus on the options, alternatives and trade-offs required to make recognition of environmental limits consequent.

5. A LIMIT TO LIMITS?

There are of course many potential difficulties with the political vision roughly sketched out above. Let us focus on four common worries about this sort of limits talk. Two of these engage with the *desirability* of a politics of limits and two with its *feasibility*:

- *A politics of environmental limits might unduly circumscribe human ambition.* The concern here is that such a political vision would be defensive, uninspiring and inward looking. It could constitute a recipe for societal stagnation, choking off social dynamism and innovation. The suggestion is that by promoting an acceptance of environmental limits one might encourage a complacent and defeatist attitude of 'settling with what we have' and stifle the wellsprings of human creativity. It is argued that population growth and economic expansion generally have been associated with progress and increased well-being. The pressure to feed and to meet the needs of an expanding civilization encourages innovation. So on this reading the result of 'a politics of limits' would be to extinguish progress, mortgage the future of our civilization and ultimately to open the way for the expansion of other societies that had no such (self-limiting) compunction.

- *A politics of environmental limits could be exploited to legitimate inequity.* The idea here is that the powerful could exploit claims about environmental scarcity to justify austerity for the majority while maintaining privileges for the elite. Thus environmental injustices would be layered on top of existing inequalities. Ultimately politics could become a zero-sum game with a brutal struggle for what remains. So a politics of limits could serve as a cover for those wishing to preserve existing national and/or international inequalities.

- *A politics of environmental limits will not work because the real problem is capitalism.* This argument is that there is little point discussing a politics of limits because capitalist accumulation drives environmentally destructive economic growth. As long as the existing economic system remains – with its emphasis on short-term profits, the commodification of the social and ecological worlds and the accumulation of capital – a materially extensive growth economy will persist. To orient the societal economy in a different direction one would *first* need to do away with the capitalist drive for profits, accumulation and continuously expanding markets.

- *A politics of environmental limits will not work because voters will never go for it.* The suggestion here is that voters will never accept the restrictions on personal consumption (house size, cars, consumer goods), and the limits on family size and immigration, or any of the other onerous elements a politics of limits might imply. Thus it is just not possible. A democratic electorate would never opt for austerity and restricted choice. There will always be political forces that are willing to offer voters an easy solution, and at critical junctures these will triumph at the polls.

Each of these objections points to a significant concern about a politics of limits: that an exaggerated focus on environmental limits could stifle creativity or justify grave inequalities or that it represents a pipe dream because of the blocking effects of underlying economic or political structures. A full discussion of the many issues raised by these points cannot be provided here, but we can at least indicate some of the lines replies could take:

1. With respect to *stagnation* there is no compelling reason why a society that recognized environmental limits would eschew dynamism and progress. On the contrary, encouraging innovation – in technology, but also in social practices and organization – would be essential to learning to 'live within' environmental limits. The vision is not one of

a static society existing in balance with an unchanging nature (a community frozen as it were, just before its growth would extend beyond sustainability limits). Rather it is one of a dynamic society that continues a positive development trajectory, but which avoids avenues that breach environmental limits. Of course, realizing such a vision in practice remains the challenge.

2. With respect to the justification of *inequity* and the maintenance of injustice, here again there appears no necessary connection between the recognition of environmental limits and the abandonment of social justice. A politics of environmental limits would not mean that per capita welfare would fall (although the environmental consequences of material production and consumption practices would be on a downward track). Far from ignoring distributive issues, a politics of limits would be deeply entangled in arguments about equity: for conservation of the environment is related to the protection of those most vulnerable to the impacts of environmental degradation (through lost livelihoods, deteriorating health, and so on) – the poor and disadvantaged, future generations and non-human nature. As well, the distributive impacts of remedial measures would be central to defining the appropriate response to environmental limits. Indeed, it is not the recognition of limits, but rather the current denial of environmental limits, that generates inequity: the resulting environment burdens are disproportionately borne by the poor; the promise of ever rising material expansion and trickle-down benefits distracts from redistributive measures. And the nightmare scenario where political life comes to resemble 'lifeboat ethics' is surely much more likely if we do *not* take up the struggle today to shape a positive vision of living within environmental limits.

3. With respect to the 'it is all about capitalism' argument, a lot depends on how capitalism is understood, what is to replace it, and how this change is to come about. Abolishing private ownership of major productive assets would not automatically stop extensive growth. Nor does there seem to be any reason in *principle* why an economy involving private ownership of productive assets and wage labour cannot be maintained within environmental frontiers (although this issue continues to be debated). Whether this can *actually* be achieved remains to be seen in practice. Certainly we need a social economy that looks very different from the one we know today, and many of the rules of the game would have to change before a politics of limits could become a reality. However, if we wait for the end of capitalism to address environmental limits, we may wait a long time. Surely building a politics of limits is one way to get the process of reform under way.

4. With respect to the *pathologies of democratic decision*, critics may be premature in writing off the capacity of representative democracies to make hard choices, and to preside over the transformation of established patterns of living (production, consumption and reproduction). This argument assumes that electors will be asked to vote for a less appealing future (one with restricted material opportunities, a more intrusive public power, higher taxes and fewer jobs, diminished personal liberty and so on). Of course, environmentalists would present the alternative differently: offering voters a better future, where living standards can be maintained over the long run, where citizens can live more meaningful lives, societal benefits are more widely shared, and new opportunities can be opened up by restrictions on environmentally corrosive practices. But this is, in any case, not a one-shot electoral choice: rather it will involve iterative decisions at many levels (local, regional, national and trans-national) spread over many decades. Thus it does not seem impossible that over time democratic electorates might edge closer to a politics of limits. But forging the political coalitions and transition pathways required for such movement remains the most significant political challenge of the contemporary era.

6. CONCLUSION

This chapter has explored the way limits have appeared in discourses of the environment and sustainable development. It has suggested that the impasse in governance for sustainability is related to a failure to acknowledge the significance of environmental limits. We have now had 40 years of modern environmental policy and two decades of discussion regarding sustainable development. In many developed countries politicians and business leaders are more than happy to talk about sustainability, environmental protection and the challenge of ensuring long-term social prosperity. However, they are also content to pass over those two awkward concepts highlighted in the original WCED discussion of sustainable development – *needs* and *limits* – which emphasized the priority of meeting the basic needs of the poor and the reality of environmental limits. As long as policy tries to slide around these issues, it is likely to face an impasse. This is not to say that there will be no progress in addressing environmental problems, but that gains in environmental efficiency will tend to be overshadowed by other difficulties.

 There is a parallel here with William Lafferty's well-known discussion of environmental policy integration (2004), where he argues that in certain contexts 'integration' *must* imply a principled priority is given to the environment. In other words, it is not possible to take sustainable development seriously if on every occasion the trade-offs favour economic and social objectives and the environment is never trumps. On certain important issues the environment must come first. And this is akin to affirming that societies must take environmental limits seriously.

REFERENCES

Aristotle (1945), *The Politics*, translated by Benjamin Jowett, Oxford: Oxford University Press.
Barry, J. (1999), *Rethinking Green Politics: Nature, Virtue and Progress*, London: Sage.
Daly, H. (1977), *Steady State Economics*, New York: Freeman and Company.
Dyson, R. (ed.) (2002), *St Thomas Aquinas Political Writings*, translated by R. Dyson, Cambridge: Cambridge University Press.
Engelman, R. (2009), 'Population and sustainability: can we avoid limiting the number of people?', *Scientific American*, accessed at www.scientificamerican. com/article.cfm?id=population-and-sustainability.
Foley, J., G. Daily, R. Howarth, D. Vaccari, A. Morris, E. Lambin, S. Doney, P. Gleick and D. Fahey et al. (2010), 'Boundaries for a healthy planet', accessed at www.scientificamerican.com/article.cfm?id=boundaries-for-a-healthy-planet.
Gough, I. and J. Meadowcroft (2011), 'Decarbonising the welfare state', in J. Dryzek, R. Norgaard and D. Schlosberg (eds), *The Oxford Handbook of Climate Change and Society*, London: Oxford University Press, pp. 490–503.
Gunderson, L. and C. Holling (eds) (2002), *Panarchy: Understanding Transformations in Human and Natural Systems*, Washington, DC: Island Press.
Hegel, G. (1991), *Elements of the Philosophy of Right*, edited by A. Wood, translated by H. Nisbet, Cambridge: Cambridge University Press.
Hobhouse, L. (1994), *Hobhouse: Liberalism and Other Writings*, edited by J. Meadowcroft, Cambridge: Cambridge University Press.
Intergovernmental Panel on Climate Change (IPCC) (2008), *Climate Change 2007: Synthesis Report*, Geneva: Intergovernmental Panel on Climate Change.
Jackson, T. (2009), *Prosperity without Growth*, London: Earthscan.
Kant, I. (1991), *Political Writings*, edited by H. Reiss, translated by H. Nisbet, Cambridge: Cambridge University Press.
Lafferty, W. (2004), 'From environmental protection to sustainable development: the challenge of decoupling through sectoral integration', in W. Lafferty (ed.), *Governance for Sustainable Development: The Challenge of Adapting Form to Function*, Cheltenham, UK and Northampton, MA: Edward Elgar.
Lafferty, W. and J. Meadowcroft (eds) (1996), *Democracy and the Environment: Problems and Prospects*, Cheltenham, UK and Northampton, MA: Edward Elgar.
Lasswell, H. (1936), *Politics: Who gets What, When, How*, New York: Smith.
Locke, J. (1998), *Two Treatises of Government*, 3rd edn, edited by P. Laslett, Cambridge: Cambridge University Press.
Meadowcroft, J. (2005), 'From welfare state to ecostate?', in J. Barry and

R. Eckersley (eds), *The State and the Global Ecological Crisis*, Cambridge, MA: MIT Press, pp. 3–23.

Meadows, D., D. Meadows, J. Randers and W. Behrens III (1972), *The Limits to Growth*, London: Pan Books.

Millennium Ecosystem Assessment (2005), *Ecosystems and Human Well Being: A Synthesis*, Washington, DC: Island Press.

New Economics Foundation (2010), *Growth Isn't Possible: Why We Need a New Economic Direction*, London: New Economics Foundation.

Nordhaus, W. (1974), 'Resources as a constraint on growth', *American Economic Review*, **64** (2), 22–6.

Organisation for Economic Co-operation and Development (OECD) (2001), *OECD Environmental Strategy for the First Decade of the 21st Century*, Paris: OECD.

OECD (2011a), *Towards Green Growth*, Paris: OECD.

OECD (2011b), *Towards Green Growth: Monitoring Progress OECD Indicators*, Paris: OECD.

Rees, W. (2000), 'Eco-footprint analysis: merits and brickbats', *Ecological Economics*, **32** (3), 371–4.

Rawls, J. (1971), *A Theory of Justice*, Cambridge, MA: Belknap Press.

Rockström, J., W. Steffen, K. Noone, Å. Persson, F. Chapin III, E. Lambin, T. Lenton et al. (2009), 'A safe operating space for humanity', *Nature*, **461**, 472–5.

Stiglitz, J., A. Sen and J.-P. Fitoussi (2009), *Report of the Commission on the Measurement of Economic Performance and Social Progress*, Paris.

United Nations Environment Programme (UNEP) (2011), *Towards a Green Economy: Pathways to Sustainable Development and Poverty Eradication*, Nairobi: United Nations Environment Programme.

Victor, P. (2008), *Managing Without Growth: Slower by Design, Not Disaster*, Cheltenham, UK and Northampton, MA: Edward Elgar.

Wackernagel, M. and W. Rees (1996), *Our Ecological Footprint: Reducing Human Impact on the Earth*, Gabriola Island, CA: New Society Publishers.

World Commission on Environment and Development (WCED) (1987), *Our Common Future*, World Commission on Environment and Development, Oxford: Oxford University Press.

Zemi Media (2010), 'How much is left? The limits of Earth's resources, made interactive', *Scientific American*, accessed at www.scientificamerican.com/article.cfm?id=interactive-how-much-is-left#.

14. Governance for sustainable development: the impasse of dysfunctional democracy

William M. Lafferty

Whether and how the marriage of polyarchal democracy to market-capitalism can be made more favourable to the further democratization of polyarchy is a profoundly difficult question for which there are no easy answers, and certainly no brief ones. The relation between a country's democratic political system and its nondemocratic economic system has presented a formidable and persistent challenge to democratic goals and practices throughout the twentieth century. *That challenge will surely continue in the twenty-first century*

R. Dahl, *On Democracy,* 1998, p. 179

The theme of the Oslo Symposium, for which the draft chapters of the present work were written, was the crucial issue of addressing the general impasse which had arisen with respect to the implementation of the international accords agreed at the Rio Earth Summit in 1992. The theme was selected to mark the conclusion by the Research Council of Norway of the Programme for Research and Documentation for a Sustainable Society (ProSus), a 'strategic programme' supported by the Council during the period 1995–2009. As Director of ProSus throughout this period, I was honoured to celebrate my own 'age of retirement' at the symposium, and to participate in the discussion of the papers prepared for the event. By way of providing a conclusion to the present volume, I have been asked by the editors to give my summary assessment of what I see as the major reason for the impasse encountered in the pursuit of sustainable development (SD) implementation. Given the very specific evaluative mandate of the ProSus programme, this was a most reasonable – though clearly challenging – request. My nomination for 'most fundamental impasse' is the nature of the Western model of political decision-making itself: a model I choose to profile (following the work of Schumpeter, Dahl and numerous successors) as 'competitive democracy'.

I return to the nature and implications of the model below, but would first like to briefly profile the different perspectives on problems and possible solutions to the SD impasse as focused by the contributions to the present volume. The authors invited to the Oslo Symposium are all experts in different national and policy-specific areas. It was up to them to highlight aspects of SD implementation that they felt showed promise of overcoming the impasse. Their contributions thus constitute an independent checklist of diverse initiatives on different SD-related goals at different levels of governance. As such, the contributions provide a rich variety of governing mechanisms and policies for pursuing the Rio and Johannesburg agendas within the existing norms and procedures of the Western democratic model. My task is then to argue that while incremental and context-dependent progress is better than no progress at all, it is neither effective enough in practice nor conceptually adequate as theory to achieve the paradigm shift stipulated by the SD programme.

Hence the nub of my own contribution. While the contributors to the Oslo Symposium document and analyse several ploys for realizing SD strategies, my critical task is to assess the potential of such ploys within the values and practices of existing democratic norms. Whereas most of the contributions highlight and analyse different aspects of the overall agenda (alternative energy, water management, biodiversity, climate change) within and across different levels of governance and different modes of descriptive versus normative discourse, my challenge is to probe deeper into the conceptual essence of the SD idea itself. What are the most essential ethical premises of the SD idea? Which crucial functional prerequisites can be derived from these premises? How does the dominant model of Western competitive democracy – viewed in the context of the argument as the most essential common mode of decision-making for achieving SD goals – fit with the normative functionality underlying the goals?

These are big questions indeed – the type of challenge perhaps that can only be contemplated at the juncture of a major career passage, having been nourished by a long season in the vineyard of normative-empirical research. Given the current international climate for pursuing sustainable development, however – 25 years after the articulation of *Our Common Future* – the need for such a debate is more pressing than ever. Both the Brundtland Commission and the Rio Earth Summit were defining events in the history of international cooperation for a just and sustainable world order. Given the timing and demands imposed on both events, it is not surprising that the relationship between democratic form and SD function was not raised. This has, however, led to an atmosphere where political scientists, with very few exceptions, have simply shunned debate on the issue. Over the years the only general response I have received to my own position is that: 'Well, democracy may have its problems with respect to environmental protection, but the overall record is much better than for dictatorships.'

Given that I have never maintained the opposite, we are clearly talking about an issue that lends itself to serious miscommunication. I greatly welcome, therefore, the opportunity to once again address the subject of democratic dysfunctionality vis-à-vis the SD agenda, and thank my colleagues at the Oslo Symposium for providing such an excellent platform for the effort.

1.   ANCHORING DEMOCRACY: THE COHEN PERSUASION

Acknowledging that the idea of democracy has clearly proved to be an 'essentially contestable concept' (Connolly 1974) we must start by staking out our 'home turf'. Of the numerous possible references to the topic that might be chosen, I have yet to come across a generic approach that is more pithily satisfying than that of Carl Cohen in his classic work *Democracy* from 1971.[1] There are three elements from Cohen's approach which are of particular relevance in the present context: his core definition; a stylized model of the elements of democracy; and his differentiation of three criteria for a general assessment of the nature and quality of participation.

Cohen defines democracy as follows: 'Democracy is that system of community government in which, by and large, the members of a community participate, directly or indirectly, in the making of decisions which affect them all' (1971, p. 7). Three aspects of this definition are particularly important for the 'form versus function' debate (see Lafferty 2004, ch. 1).

First, the definition focuses explicitly on the activity of making decisions. Democracy is one of many possible forms for both 'constituting' and 'steering' human activity. It thus sets standards and identifies institutions for a specific mode of structuring social reality.

Second, the definition applies to any 'community', by which Cohen means a group of individuals with a common self-identity (as to membership of the community) and a common purpose. A community in this sense need not be a *political* community per se – an association identifiable by common 'citizenship'. Whether and how 'democracy' applies to a community is thus a contingent question as to whether participation in community decision-making has been 'democratized' to any extent. One can, in other words, both apply democratic norms and learn much about the functioning of democracy from democratized associations, whether in schools, workplaces, industries, voluntary associations, and so on.

Third, the generic decision-making instrument for a democratic community is *participation, directly* or *indirectly* by the *members* of the community in *decisions which affect them all*. This criterion specifies both a delimitation as to membership and 'affectedness' and a potential qualification as to the degree of participation itself. Whereas the first aspect allows for variation in entitlement to participate, the second involves a potential for variation in the degree of actual involvement and decisiveness.

As we will see in the discussion below, all three of these 'generic' aspects of 'democracy' influence the way we view, analyse and apply the idea in both academic and practical discourses. They serve to delimit a specific understanding of the basic idea of democracy, laying a foundation for constructive dialogue as to what any ostensible (posited, purported) democratic system implies. Why Cohen chooses this approach as 'seminal' and 'generic' to the democratic idea is spelled out more completely in his work. My justification for choosing it as a conceptual point of departure for the present analysis is based on a conviction that the definition captures the etymological and semantic essence of the idea as it has been expressed and debated throughout the history of the Western world. If it is accepted that democracy is 'an idea in history' (Hagtvet and Lafferty, 1984) – an idea that must be constantly won for, and adapted to, new forms of 'community' – Cohen's understanding of the idea is at once correct, concise and constructive. It provides, in short, a fruitful standard for at least working with, if not resolving, the 'essential contestability' of the concept.

The second aspect of his approach that I want to introduce is my own attempt to capture Cohen's elaboration of the core idea in terms amenable to practical application and assessment. This effort is summarized in the very simple 'model' presented in Figure 14.1. Building directly on Cohen's conceptual elaboration, the aim here is to outline in interactive form the most important adjunct dimensions of democracy: that is, the key sub-concepts that Cohen views as major qualifying factors affecting the modes and workings of democracy in practice. As presented in Figure 14.1, these are: *logical preconditions, conditioners, instruments* and *outputs*. These reflect, I believe, many of the crucial issues that arise in debates on democracy. They serve to further stake out a conceptual space for clarifying the relationship between democratic 'forms' and community 'functions' and will be used towards this end in the form versus function discussion to follow.[2]

Finally, as a third perspective from Cohen's work, I want to introduce his differentiation between the *breadth, depth* and *range* of participatory decision-making. The first two of these dimensions refer respectively to the amount and quality of participation itself, while the third refers to the scope and decisiveness of the decision-making in question. It is Cohen's intention that the three dimensions be used as rough standards for democratic evaluation.

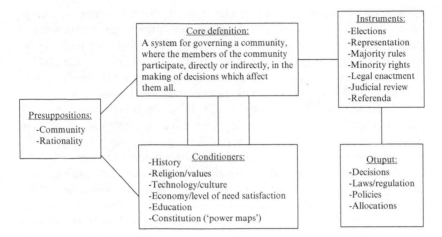

Source: Lafferty/ProSus/University of Oslo/04.11.2000 – Freely derived from Carl Cohen, Democracy (1971).

Figure 14.1 Democracy: a conceptual model

I have elaborated on these standards elsewhere (Lafferty 1983, 2002) and will not go into detail here. It can be pointed out in advance, however, that the three normative dimensions clearly imply difficult 'trade-offs' among the standards. One can, for example, maximize the breadth of participation through universal suffrage, granting all 'members' the right to take part in decision-making. But such a grant automatically involves a qualification of both 'depth' and 'range', since, for the large majority of members, it will be very difficult to take part deeply (taking serious responsibility for making a decision) across a broad range of issue areas. Likewise, the question of 'range' must be related to a discussion of *decisiveness*. Clearly, many issues in a community need to be decided ('constituted') more firmly and definitively than others, despite the fact that their point of departure is in parliamentary, majority-based decision-making. Democracy must not only be able to protect itself in a robust and long-term fashion, but it must also be able to 'fence off' selected issues particularly crucial to community welfare.

Cohen anticipates such trade-offs by making two further distinctions. He differentiates between *directive governance* and *administrative govern-ance* in relation to depth, and between *sovereign scope* and *effective scope* in relation to range. The distinctions are addressed to the opening in his definition for either direct or indirect participation, and are designed to avoid polemical discussions as to what is real versus illusory democracy.

Community members can, for example, be entitled to exercise sovereign control over an area, and do so by expressing preferences for alternative policy paths (directions), without necessarily exercising 'effective' control through 'administrative governance'. As we will see below, such distinctions are of crucial importance in determining appropriate levels of governance for effective decision-making in environmental issues.

Taken together, the three aspects of Cohen's approach provide significant conceptual tools for discussing normative expectations for different associations of interest-based actors. The logical presuppositions of the stylized model indicate that any specific discussion must begin by: (1) identifying the relevant interest(s) that shape community/associational identity; and (2) confirming a commitment to 'rational' decision-making procedures among those entitled to participate. Given that these logical premises exist, the relationship between democracy and any form of community activity then involves more detailed prescription and/or assessment of the degree to which the decision-making practice in question contributes (or not) to the effective realization of associational goals. In Cohen's own terms:

> So democracy, like most other affairs in the world of human society, is a matter of degree, and a matter of degree on many levels. The crucial questions to be answered in appraising democracy are not 'where is it?' and 'where is it not?' – but, where democracy is the professed aim and ideal, 'how broad and deep is it?' and 'upon what issues is it really operative?' (Cohen, 1971, p. 34)

The variation on this theme to be applied here is: given that virtually all nations of the world have formally subscribed to the goal of sustainable development – and that the goal is to be realized through democratic means – how well-suited are existing, and normatively dominant, democratic models and norms for actually achieving the goal? The progress of democracy has, since its inception and original codification in Athens, moved from the Greek polis; through Roman republics, Italian and Swiss city-states and European-American nation-states; through the emerging nations of the developing world and communist federations; to experiments with different forms of regional union around the globe. Decision-making procedures for both the League of Nations and the United Nations have also been anchored in democratic principles. Further, we have witnessed over the past half century and more a widespread tendency to attach democratic norms to a plethora of sub-national communities and associations, including neighbourhood democracy, workplace democracy, industrial democracy, public-sector democracy and even market democracy. And at each turning – each experiment in normative community steering – the interaction between the democratic idea and associational ambitions and practices has been characterized by heated debate and an enormous variety of hybrid associational experiments.

As indicated above, however, the hybrid under consideration here, democracy and sustainable development, has received little attention in academic discourse and even less in either the mass media or public debating forums.[3] In light of our research efforts, there are at least three major reasons for this particular impasse.

First, there is the massive inertia attached to the globalization of 'free-market' values in production, trade, consumption and general lifestyle images. Due to the decline of communism/socialism as a united counter-force to capitalism in the post-Rio period – peaking in the break-up of the previous Soviet Union and the installation of state-supported capitalism in China – there have been virtually no serious academic or political discussions of alternatives to the Western model of 'competitive', 'polyarchal' or 'market' democracy. The latter model, which already had existed as a market analogy for nearly two centuries, was virtually rechristened as symbolizing the 'end of history'. The economic parameters of free enterprise and market dynamics became the uncontested premises for national and global development, and 'liberal-pluralist-competitive democracy' was its 'natural' governing adjunct.

Second, the overarching goal from Rio, sustainable development, was from the start perceived (or at least portrayed) as a 'diffuse', 'overly complicated', 'woefully idealistic', 'social-democratic-ideological fudge'. It came from a typical United Nations Commission, steered by an unassailable commitment to bureaucratic compromise, and was simply incomprehensible, unsaleable and unworkable as a domestic political programme. The term itself, 'sustainable development', which was clearly delimited in the Brundtland Report, was quickly shortened to 'sustainability', opening the way for a complete evisceration of the basic idea. What the Brundtland Report had clearly differentiated as an 'alternative model of growth' became a general (and politically meaningless) case for sustainable this and sustainable that. Even those with a political responsibility for enacting SD commitments and programmes felt an embarrassed need to smile when touting the term openly to gatherings of ostensible stakeholders.[4]

The term – and the numerous specifics of (for example) *Our Common Future*, the Rio Earth Charter of Principles and Agenda 21 – have, of course, been dutifully codified and diffused. As clearly documented in the present volume (most particularly by Meadowcroft, and Busch and Jörgens), the generalized SD goals have been reworked into values, targets and indicators for national and regional strategies and action plans. Crucial issues related to priorities, policy instruments and unavoidable trade-offs have, however, been sorely neglected. And it is in relation to this neglect – the avowed 'wickedness' of the SD agenda as a programme initiative – that the lack of any serious debate as to democratic dysfunctionality is most glaring. The problem has simply been defined as an issue for democratic reform.

Third, there has been *a constant barrier related to the concept and understanding of 'democracy' itself.* No matter how many times one prefaces a presentation, an article or a panel discussion with a clear statement as to the goal of the exercise – a critique of *existing* democratic norms and procedures from *within* the boundaries of democratic discourse and democratization – it proves nearly impossible to convince an audience that the goal is not an anti-democratic, or at least non-democratic, solution. Even as one labours to press home the message that democratic structures can be designed in numerous forms to suit numerous functions, and that the 'toolbox of democratization' contains numerous and varied instruments, procedures and institutional forms, one nonetheless sees the eyes of an audience glossing over, attention wandering and comprehension declining. In short, it is no accident that reforms of existing democratic institutions – changes in electoral systems, for example – are notoriously hard to realize. Despite the widespread and well-documented fact that existing democracies vary considerably in the governing mechanisms at play within and across systems, and that democratization has been a major driver of progressive humanism, there appears to be an innate defence mechanism in place against the democratic revision of one's own system.

For all of these reasons, therefore, the attempt to raise an active and serious debate on the challenge of pursuing sustainable development within the dominant auspices of competitive democracy has been pretty much a non-starter. Hope springs eternal, however, in the guild of democracy craftsmen and given the timing of the current publication – 20 years after Rio and in the middle of an international economic crisis and major transition in global power relationships – I feel a pressing need to both restate and elaborate the case for democracy-SD revision.

2.   DEMOCRACY AND SUSTAINABLE DEVELOPMENT: COMING TO GRIPS WITH THE SD IMPASSE

Having earlier argued the need for a critical form versus function approach to the democracy-SD relationship, I will here use the basic analytic framework to further substantiate the relevance of the approach.[5] Whereas earlier works focused on key logical contradictions between competitive/liberal-pluralist democracy and the functional prerequisites of the SD principles and goals adopted at Rio, with the aim of reconciling the contradictions through specific types of democratic reform, here the purpose is to demonstrate the relevance of the approach for understanding the current impasse in SD implementation. This will be done in two steps: first, a brief overview of the form versus function argument as developed by the present author and his colleagues in ProSus; and second, an attempt to relate selected key aspects of the argument to the contributions in the present volume.

In an attempt to restate the argument as succinctly as possible, I will here relate the approach to three aspects of Cohen's generic approach to democracy: the two logical presuppositions, *community* and *rationality*; and the evaluative dimension of *range/decisiveness*. The contradictions between the existing dominant form of competitive or polyarchal democracy and the functional requirements of sustainable development can then be further illustrated. More broadly, the overview attempts to outline several critical questions. What is the general relevance of Cohen's approach for a stylized model of competitive democracy? How do his presuppositions and dimensions jibe with key prerequisites of the global SD programme as unanimously endorsed at Rio? How do the contradictions between existing democratic presuppositions and endorsed SD prerequisites function as *conditioners* of governance for sustainable development? And, finally, what can be done. What *instruments of democratic governance* can be brought to bear to facilitate a transition from competitive market democracy to cooperative ecological democracy?

Community

Whereas competitive democracy (CP) involves: (1) a notion of community based on historically defined administrative boundaries (villages, towns, cities, counties, nation-states, and so on); with (2) a notion of citizenship based on individual membership and the direct representation of interests, sustainable development (SD) involves: (1) a notion of community based on ecological interdependence (niches, habitats, ecosystems, regions, and so on); with (2) an expanded notion of citizenship that incorporates the interests of 'future generations', the 'the world's poor', and (possibly) the existential interests of other species.

As indicated above, for Cohen, any discussion of democracy presupposes a grouping of individuals that has developed a minimum degree of self-identity *as* a community or association. Why and how the sense of self-identity and common interest develops is a question of contextual dependence and empirical documentation. However, given that the discourse on the development of Western democracy originated with reference to a given Greek city-state (the polis, Athens), it is not surprising that the paradigmatic unit for democratic discourse became a community of individuals bound together by a common identity within a delimited spatial unit organized for self-governance. And virtually all variants of subsequent units where democracy has served as a set of self-governing principles have been similarly bounded political communities. The size and complexity of the units has varied tremendously over the centuries. But virtually all forms of polity today are identifiable in terms of varying degrees of political-legal-administrative responsibility for demarcated jurisdictions and their citizen populations. The business of democracy has, in other words, been carried out and assessed within communities constituted by the political function, with boundaries drawn on maps.

The international commitments of nation-states to the goals of sustainable development presuppose, however, a mode of trans-community inter-dependence and responsibility that is not bounded by political-geographical borders. Whether in the area of environmental degradation, climate change, biodiversity depletion or acute poverty and human destitution, the notion of separate legal communities with delimited spheres of responsibility raises definitive barriers against effective SD governance. We may enjoy the rights, responsibilities and overall benefits of democratic citizenship within delimited territorial units of varying scope and sovereignty, but the challenge of achieving sustainable development on a global scale poses new functional challenges for both community identity and community purpose (see, for example, Young 2006).

A similar contradiction emerges with respect to the basic premises of individual citizenship as a basis for political representation and democratic decision-making. In the context of Cohen's position, community membership is logically tied to *individual interests* and *direct representation*. Aggregating these interests into collective decisions is what Thompson (1970) refers to as the 'democratic objective': that is, that decision-making should reflect the aggregated preferences of *specific* individuals and interests passed upwards within the system. One of the most crucial differences between conservative and liberalist notions of this objective was the transition from so-called 'virtual representation' to 'direct representation': from a system where representatives were expected to make decisions *on behalf of* the *perceived interests* of their 'constituents' to a system where individual expressions of self-interest and choice are (ideally) aggregated and weighed into majoritarian preferences and outcomes.

And, interestingly enough, it is the *former* notion of both *attributed* and *indirect* interests that underlies the communitarian ideals of sustainable development. All of the core United Nations SD texts presuppose virtual community interests, whether as premises for the ecological survival of human communities themselves, the survival of animal species or to meet the morally justifiable 'essential needs of the world's poor' (WCED 1987; United Nations 1994). The challenge to Cohen's logic consists, in other words, of a prima facie expansion of the basis for community identity and the meaning of the 'all' who are both affected by, and entitled to, participatory decision-making. While the existing mosaic of political communities within and across nation-states understands community interests as a matter of fragmented sovereignty within states and transnational bargaining across states, the ideals of SD community interests rest on a functional need to transcend the traditional political mosaic by elevating crucial aspects of the *global community* (the range of affected interests) to new levels of moral entitlement and decisiveness.

In sum, the existing political units of Western competitive democracy have developed under specific, and relatively similar, historical conditions. We live in villages, townships, municipalities, counties and states with borders that, in most cases, were defined under pre-modern conditions for pre-modern purposes. Yet our identities and political responsibilities remain attached to the established administrative units. When we cross a border from one country to another or from one state to another, we leave (in varying degrees) our duties as citizen behind. But problems related to environment and ecosystems know no such borders. We live within ecological niches of varying scope and holistic inter-penetration. The concept of sustainable development presupposes that basic identities and responsibilities be shifted from time-worn and possibly dysfunctional administrative units – not (in the first instance) as a *replacement* for current allegiances, but as *a supplementary identity in the direction of an emerging ecological community and globally responsible citizenship*.

Rationality

Whereas CP involves a form of rational decision-making based on principles of: (1) freedom and equality before the law; (2) common sense and equality of opinion; and (3) pluralism and incremental majoritarian decisions, SD involves a need for: (1) goal-oriented redistributions of risk, gain and loss; (2) a stronger position for science and expertise; and (3) holistic integrated decisions.

Cohen's treatment of his second 'logical presupposition for democracy', rationality, is both brief (less than three pages) and relatively simplistic. The idea refers, he says, to three 'fundamental capacities that general participation in common affairs requires': '(1) the faculty of forming a plan or grasping a rule for judgment or action ... (2) the faculty of using that

rule, by applying it to particular cases, or following the plan of action …
[and] (3) the faculty of intellectual communication, of reasoning with one
another' (Cohen 1971, p. 54). In this sense, rationality is a sort of 'bottom
line' for *homo sapiens*, a set of minimum criteria for making and communicating 'sense' in the dialogical process of creating social reality with other
rational beings.

Cohen opens, however, a conceptual window of interest for the present
discussion. Pointing out that, even where the three faculties of the presupposition are realized in practice, 'they provide no assurance whatever
that democratic government will work smoothly, or that it is best of the
available alternatives' (1971, p. 57). Following up on this – clearly in
the interest of saying something more substantive on the issue – he then
adds:

> It remains to account for the fact that, even where its presuppositions are real-
> ized, democracy may not develop, or may develop and then fail, or may con-
> tinue meeting with only limited success. For such an explanation one must go
> beyond what democracy presupposes, inquiring carefully into the conditions of
> its operational success. (Cohen 1971, p. 57)

Cohen connects, in other words, the empirical role of 'conditions'
directly to the logical role of rationality as a 'presupposition' for democratic assessment. The implication is clear: rationality is just as much a
logical sine qua non for discussing the relevance of democracy as a standard for governance as is the idea of community. Even more so than in
the case of the latter, however, Cohen feels a need to signal at the outset
that the analytical 'cutting edge' of 'rationality' lies in the basic principles
guiding the faculty for 'forming a plan or grasping a rule for judgment or
action'.

It was in direct response to this need that we, at the inception of our
research on democracy and sustainable development, turned to the work
of John Dryzek. In his seminal book on *Rational Ecology* (published in the
same town and same year as *Our Common Future*), Dryzek (1987) makes a
comprehensive case for the distinctness and necessity of ecological rationality as a premise for collective decision-making. It is the type of book
that, once digested, changes one's perception radically on the nature and
functional potential of the rationality underlying competitive democracy.
The nature and reason for this change is explained more thoroughly in the
sources referenced. For purposes of the present volume, we can simply
restate several of the most important points.[6] They grasp and restate the
essence of 'ecological rationality' as an expanded and more substantive
variant of the basic 'discursive rationality' reflected in Cohen's list of
faculties:

1. Dryzek's point of departure for identifying ecological problems is the particular nature of ecosystems. These exhibit several distinct characteristics:

   a. *Interpenetration*: ecosystems are always embedded in other ecosystems. Though it is possible to identify borders of ecosystems for analytic reasons, it must always be remembered that there is considerable activity and exchange taking place at and across the borders.

   b. *Emergence*: ecosystem properties can never be circumscribed by knowledge of the components of the system alone. New properties and characteristics emerge from unpredictable interactions within the subsystem.

   c. *Homeostasis*: ecosystems are self-regulating, constantly adapting to both external and internal forces. This does not imply, however, that there is an identifiable purpose related to self-regulation. Overall, structural-functional adaptation takes place on a contingent, not a teleological, basis.

2. Human activity is viewed as taking place within (and being dependent on) these ecosystem characteristics. The relationship between human and natural systems gives rise to six types of ecological problems in this context:

   a. *Complexity*: ecosystems are, in their own right, extremely difficult to systematize and predict. This complexity is only made *more* intricate and unpredictable as a result of human societal activity.

   b. *Non-reducibility*: it is not possible to provide compensatory solutions to ecosystem disruption by manipulating one or more sub-components of the system. Partial instrumental interventions will invariably lead to unpredictable consequences.

   c. *Variability*: regardless of how similar ecosystems may appear, they will always vary in significant ways across both space and time. Differences in sociocultural forms compound this variability.

   d. *Uncertainty*: the total effect of all three ecosystem characteristics creates problems of severe unpredictability. Given the fact that intervention itself can contribute to uncertainty, it is often not even possible to delimit confidence intervals for probability estimates.

   e. *Collectiveness*: the interaction between human and ecological systems affects large numbers of actors, giving rise to problems of 'collective rationality'. What appears to be rational on an individual level is quite often irrational for *either* the social collectivity or ecosystem as a whole.

f.   *Spontaneity*: ecosystems have a tendency to right their own imbalances, a feature which human intervention often obscures or actively undermines. The problem arises as to how to understand and harness this particular characteristic without turning it against the ecosystem itself.

3.   Finally, there is an additional and highly relevant feature of Dryzek's understanding of ecological rationality: namely, that his position is avowedly anthropocentric. Interest is only focused on those aspects of ecosystems which 'provide the basic requirements for human life' (1987, p. 34). These include *productive needs*, *protection* (against harm) and *waste assimilation*. Dryzek stresses here that this focus is not meant to underestimate other aspects and functions of ecosystems (either aesthetic or biocentric values), but that the anthropocentric focus is necessary to be able to relate ecological rationality to other forms of functional rationality (whether economic, social, legal or political). He is in this respect more concerned with 'what ecosystems can do for humans, rather than with what ecosystems can do for themselves' (1987, p. 36). Obviously this is also a central focus for the notion of sustainable development with its underlying goal of satisfying basic human needs within the limits of nature.

For Dryzek it is the ecological rationality of 'social choice mechanisms' as these interact with natural systems and, in practice, lead to different 'ecological problems' that is the focus of analysis. In the present context this translates into an emphasis on the types of problems which the social-choice mechanisms of competitive democracy lead to and confront when trying to realize the UN programme for sustainable development, which specifically and very radically aims to incorporate ecological rationality. The challenge inherent in this confrontation – speaking the 'truth' of sustainable development to the 'powers' of competitive democracy (Wildavsky 1987) – is thus a task of creating *new communities* (*demos*) which aim to adapt existing social-choice mechanisms to a *new* (*ecological*) *rationality*.

It is also with direct reference to this task that we can identify the three more specific 'contradictions' outlined above. The three key premises of competitive-polyarchal democracy – freedom and equality before the law; common sense and equality of opinion; and pluralism and incremental majoritarian decisions – need to be offset in ecological democracy by: SD-directed redistributions of risk, gain and loss; a stronger position for science and expertise; and the making of holistic integrated decisions. In the earlier work, the following types of instrumental redress to these contradictions are proposed.

Reallocation of risk and responsibility in market relations

A keyword from Rio here is 'sustainable production and consumption'. Most essentially this involves a combination of: (1) stronger regulatory guidelines as to the 'carrying capacity' of natural life-support systems *for* a 'free'-market economy, with (2) a more focused emphasis on 'cooperative management regimes' within the different sectors. While the former strengthens the legal basis for what is acceptable in terms of both resource extraction and the over-burdening of sinks, the latter provides a more cooperative basis for how such restrictions can be most effectively implemented in practice.

Democratized science

There is perhaps no other area where the need for ecological rationality and a new model of ecological democracy should be more easily acknowledged than here. As argued earlier, the ethical status of the SD programme has rested strongly on the analyses and conclusions of natural scientists (Lafferty 1996b, 2001a). This was true for the earliest stages of the environmental movement and is even more true today in the areas of climate change and biodiversity depletion. Yet the compelling nature of scientific evidence as a basis for effective SD policy appears to be declining rather than increasing. Liberal-capitalist democrats are able to build on the intellectual traditions of Thomas Paine's classic work *Common Sense* (1776) to reinforce populist support in the media for climate-change scepticism. Two of the most central reforms advocated here have been: (1) a strengthening of national scientific councils for SD policy clearance; and (2) a more de-centralized use of 'consensus conferences' to substantiate and focus necessary action in crucial areas. Both of these governing instruments can also be supported by a much more active institutionalization of 'the precautionary principle' at all levels of government.

Holism and emergent properties

Finally, there is the overarching ecological challenge of holistic interdependence. Most concretely this challenges traditional democratic thinking at its federalist multilevel core. Tackling global interactions and interdependencies within a system inherently committed to de-centralization of power and state-local administrative *in*-dependence is probably the most difficult aspect of effective SD programming. And in this area, the best offering from the democratic toolbox is a combination of political-administrative prioritization, planning and goal-related implementation. As thoroughly documented by Meadowcroft (1997, 1999), the SD persuasion clearly implies a resurgence for democratic planning; a resurgence strongly demonstrated by the entire Rio process and its resulting declaration of principles, conventions and action plans. Though sorely neglected by the large majority of UN member states that unanimously adopted it, the combined Rio Earth Charter and Agenda 21 is a milestone in global commitment to planned and integrated change. And in the search for *some* attempt to take the commitment seriously in practice – the efforts of the European Union to integrate both the Charter and the Agenda into European soft law have been well documented by several contributors to the present volume.[7] In short, there is probably no more effective steering instrument available for developing this aspect of ecological democracy than an integrated multilevel focus on the implementation and monitoring of global sustainable development.

Range and Decisiveness

Whereas CP involves general standards of ongoing debate, dialogue, reflection and learning for virtually all sovereign decisions, SD involves a need for relatively prompt, decisive and robust decisions in selected high-priority areas of action (environmental degradation, ecological disruption, the elimination of poverty).

The commitment of competitive democracy to the benefits of debate and reflective learning is one of the most 'sacred' of the polyarchal values. The prototypical images of the Athenian Assembly, the Roman Forum, or the American Constitutional Convention all serve to establish free and open discussion as the essence and point of departure for democratic practice – and not just liberal-pluralist democratic practice. The notion of 'participatory learning' through discussion and trial-and-error govern-ance has been a crucial value of the idealist, participationist and discursive turns in modern progressive democratic reform. But just as 'love is not enough' to secure either healthy personalities or healthy relationships (Bettleheim 1950: Kellerman 2009), participation is not enough to secure a healthy, just and sustainable planet. Competitive dialogue, debate and interactive learning cannot be unconditionally limited in an ostensible democracy, but they definitely *can* be supplemented by democratically sanctioned limits and goal-related prescriptions. Just as democracy must introduce legal restrictions on behaviour and speech deemed threaten-ing for the very existence of democracy itself (Cohen 1971), so too can it introduce constitutional and other legal 'rules of the road' to steer social choice mechanisms and societal development itself in more sustainable directions.

If there is one lesson that emerges more and more clearly from long-term analyses of governmental attempts to implement sustainable devel-opment, it is that competitive party politics works systematically against substantial and robust SD progress (Lafferty et al. 2007). More than any other single variable in the search for barriers to effective SD governance, the OECD has designated a 'lack of political will' as the most crucial factor (OECD 2001a, 2001b, 2002a, 2002b). And, as I will argue below, there is potentially no more effective way to strengthen the political will for sustainable development than to strengthen the legal status of goal-oriented principles for SD implementation. The time has clearly come, in other words, for a 'constitutional turn' in the conflict between the rationality inherent in polyarchal political 'forms' and the rationality necessary to achieve functional sustainable development.

3. DEMOCRATIC FORM VERSUS FUNCTION IN THE PRESENT VOLUME

Given that the aim of the both the Oslo Symposium and the present volume is to confront the 'impasse' in efforts to promote sustainable development in Western-style democracies, in what way, if at all, do the individual contributions touch on the issue as here outlined? Is, in other words, the challenge of democratic 'form' being out of kilter with sustainable-development 'function' salient in the work of leading scholars in the general policy area focused on by the Symposium? And, if not directly in focus, what points of implicit relevance for a more-focused debate in the future can be derived? Finally, whether addressed directly, implicitly or not at all, what does a reading of the different contributions tell us about the difficulties facing both an academic and practical transition towards a more effective implementation of the Rio SD programme?

Two caveats on this exercise must, however, be immediately stated. First it must be clearly understood that the invited participants were not specifically asked to address the issue of democratic form versus SD function at all. My attempt to glean insights and possible lessons from the contributions should, therefore, not be seen as a critique. That I find more or less relevance for *my own ex-post problematization of the relationship in question* is not something that the authors of the chapters could have anticipated. Nor should the degrees of relevance attributed by me have any substantive bearing on the relevance and applicability of the contributions to *other* major issues related to the SD impasse.

Second, the exigencies of providing a most kindly requested 'afterword' to the present volume do not allow for detailed treatment of all the contributions. My overview must, therefore, be quintessentially 'Whiggish': that is, it must be blatantly selective from my own point of view and interests. Just as the traditional Whig wrote political history from the vantage of a particular party, I too must pen my comments from the vantage of my own 'pet peeve' vis-à-vis the SD impasse: the inherent dysfunctionality of the competitive-democracy persuasion. It is, in short, my peeve and my read which underlie the assessment and should be understood in this light.

Of the contributions to the Oslo Symposium here published, two can be seen as directly concerned with the nature, scope and transformative potential of *ecological*, as opposed to *'political-administrative' communities*: the contributions by Narodoslawsky and Coenen/Bressers. Both of these analyses demonstrate the need, as well as the obvious empirical usefulness, of operating with concepts of community identity and common interest that transcend the normal political boundaries. In the case of Narodoslawsky, the transcendence involves generating commonalities of *regional interests* associated with the underlying premises for the technological and commercial exploitation of renewable energy sources. Equally important from the point of view of democratic reform, however, the analysis avoids an open-ended endorsement of 'small-is-beautiful' regionalism. To the contrary, the chapter concludes by stressing a clear need for further political-science analysis to develop governing mechanisms for integrating more self-contained eco-energy regions into national, transnational and eventually global domains for authoritative decision-making.

For Coenen and Bressers, on the other hand, the issue of community interests and rationality is more implicit, since it is completely natural for them to use broader geographic/ecological units of analysis (watersheds, river basins, and so on) as natural units of analysis for water management. Their goal is to explore the dilemmas that arise in the name of more integrated water management. They demonstrate that, while current sectoral approaches clearly cannot provide effective SD solutions, more recent attempts to define and operationalize 'new water management' also generate significant new modes of complexity and conflict. Once again, the implication for democratic reform seems to be that, while the 'old' methods are clearly incompatible with SD goals and outcomes, there are no 'quick fixes' within overarching decision-making structures that have long been conditioned by competitive interest-based politics.

Of the remaining ten chapters, six focus on issues that directly reflect problems related to *the rationality of existing modes of governance* for sustainable development. Five of the six studies have, moreover, three relevant features in common (excluding the chapter by Busch and Jörgens). First, they touch on issues of *multilevel governance* – the challenge of coordinating and reconciling steering initiatives across differing domains of both designated and effective sovereignty; second, they are all concerned with different aspects of *participation*, by both citizens and non-governmental organizations; and, third, they all focus on *distinctive individual issues within the SD programme* – nature conservation/biodiversity for Eckerberg and different aspects of climate change for Aall, Lundqvist, Bomberg and Schreurs. In the following I will try to highlight, in the briefest possible terms, the relevance of these features for the contradictions in form and function outlined above.

With respect to multilevel governance, the five studies designated all provide significant insights into the challenge of working towards SD goals across local, national, regional and international political domains. While Eckerberg, Aall and Lundqvist focus mostly on the within-nation context, Bomberg and Schreurs are most concerned with conditions affecting climate-change politics at the national (state) and supra-national (federal) levels. The first three studies emphasize the potential of local communities in Norway and Sweden to promote the SD sub-programmes within existing central-local divisions of powers and responsibility. Though differing in analytic and empirical focus, all three studies find evidence for both positive and negative implementation results. What is important here, however, is that they all problematize the difficulties front-running local communities have in achieving lasting SD results without active support – in most cases purely financial – from the central government. Largely due to the strong impact of the Local Agenda 21 initiative in the immediate post-Rio period, local communities in Scandinavia generally jumped the gun on SD implementation, often far surpassing national efforts at meaningful attempts to come to grips with the Rio agenda. A very general conclusion from all three studies, however, is that: (1) the local initiatives were in fact kick-started by central programmes and funding; (2) there was relatively little integration with, and follow-up from, the central authorities; and (3) the local initiatives demonstrated relatively little staying power once the national support was terminated.

From the point of view of democracy and SD, the studies thus indicate a major constitutional and practical incompatibility between shared national and local commitments to externally prescribed SD goals, and the extant democratic structures and rules of the game necessary to effectively realize the commitments in tandem. In this sense the studies also clearly illustrate in a most specific way the difficulties pointed out by Narodoslawsky for trying to promote and literally capitalize eco-regional initiatives within existing modes of governance. Lundqvist in particular points to a need for: more effective trans-community eco-cooperation; more strongly focused legalistic policy instruments; and more effective governing mechanisms for profiling and resolving trade-offs between the economic, social and environmental goals of local communities.

Both Bomberg and Schreurs also focus on the differing institutional conditions that structure the potential of pro-SD actors to push for change at higher levels of decision-making, in both the European Union and United States. Bomberg in particular identifies the institutional norms and political practices that function to constrain different organizational ploys for combating climate-changing emissions (framing, alliance-building and mobilization). She lists these as adverserialism, fragmentation and partisanship – all, in my view, standard adjuncts of the competitive-democracy model. That both Bomberg and Schreurs also view the structuring conditions for climate-change policy as more progressive (pro-Rio/pro-Kyoto) in Europe than in the United States can also be associated with the much stronger position accorded to not only competitive democracy but market democracy in America. In short, the studies indicate that while the spirit of Rio is demonstrably willing in the domains analysed, the 'flesh' of existing democratic politics is weak.

As for the second common theme across the studies – an emphasis on increased and expanded participation as both a general 'good' for legitimizing SD values, and a very specific 'good' for promoting 'social learning' and more effective implementation – I will be both briefer and more judgemental. Without going into specifics as to how this most essential aspect of Cohen's definition of democracy is treated in the designated studies, I will simply state that, in general, a pro-participation stance is usually perceived as a sine qua non of effective SD implementation, and that none of the five contributions under review here offer notable exceptions to the norm. Indeed, I myself am cited as a strong advocate of the importance of participation as a necessary governing tool for effecting the SD transition. So I willingly take my place in the dock and turn the proceedings over to my retired alter ego.

As already indicated in the previous section, the point is both very simple and very crucial. Love – in the form of an open-ended commitment to participation as the ultimate democratic principle – is 'not enough' when it comes to the environment and sustainable development. While there are some good reasons for promoting broader and deeper participation (Cohen's terms) as positive for SD implementation, there are also several good reasons for raising warning flags. Among the contributions to the present volume, we find both tendencies. Eckerberg and Aall, for example, are clearly positive to both participation and decentralization in their assessments, while Mullally and Meadowcroft are much more guarded. In my view the issue comes down to the validity of the functional requirements for SD goals and outcomes raised by the contradictions presented in the preceding section. While there can be much to gain by stressing the participatory ideals of competitive democracy in relation to both social learning and the broader mobilization of actors deemed necessary to achieve implementation, there is also much to worry about with respect to what Meadowcroft treats extensively as the 'politics of limits'.

As I will return to this question, as absolutely central to my conclusion below, I will rest my case here and move on to the third theme I want to raise with respect to the democracy-SD impasse: the issue of *range and decisiveness*. As I read the experience of international attempts to implement the Rio accords over the past 20 years, it is the dysfunction-ality of competitive democracy with respect to the transformative, and increasingly urgent, goals of the SD project that underlies the impasse. Expanding the range of a competitive party politics, steeped in the path-dependency of intra-national conflicts of interest over the economic and social 'goods' of the welfare state, to the global and largely idealistic goals of Rio, has been a 'stretch too far'. Competitive democracy has developed as a symbiotic meta-system for social choice and allocation throughout the transition from pre-industrial through industrial to post-industrial politics, but the basic premises of the model have not been functionally benign for sustainable development.

Effective Monitoring of SD Progress

Four of the contributions to the volume present analyses which, in my view, support this interpretation, but they do so in a relatively circum-spect manner. They raise numerous issues related to the impasse, but are clearly more circumspect and judicious with respect to implications of the impasse for the compatibility of current democratic practices than I. No problem. As stated above it is 'my peeve'. The analyses in question skate, however, so closely up to the critical border I have staked out – and are so crucial for the general impasse problem in doing so – that I want to high-light just a single point from each. Others can then decide on which side of the border the ice is thinnest.

From the contribution by Langhelle and Ruud I want to highlight the importance of their critical assessment of the Norwegian monitoring system for progress on sustainable development. Clearly, such a system is an integral part of determining the degree to which the Norwegian Strategy for Sustainable Development (RMoFA 2002; RMoF 2005) is evaluated, revised and (in theory) implemented. When responsibility for the strategy was transferred to the Ministry of Finance in 2003, most pro-ponents of SD in Norway viewed this as very positive. Sustainable devel-opment would, from then on, it was thought, be directly incorporated into national financial and budgetary decisions.

As it turned out, however, the ministry treated their responsibility for SD as simply another aspect of the normal budgetary process. Major focus was placed on the development of a new set of Indicators for Sustainable Development with the resulting indicator set expressly designed to focus different measures of capital (economic, social, environmental). There was, however, very little indication of priorities, benchmarks or guidelines as to the different types of capital. Further, the indicators chosen are very static. They serve to indicate incremental changes in the 16 measures focused upon, with very little direct relevance for the crucial question of 'decoupling' and virtually no serious mention of either critical limits or the precautionary principle. All suggestions to include more dynamic indicators of, for example, decoupling (as introduced in the United Kingdom), went unheeded.

The entire exercise, and its subsequent application (as summarized by Langhelle and Ruud), thus indicates a state of inertia in the system that reflects established socioeconomic methodology and departmental practice. Neither the indicators nor the inclusion of the SD strategy itself in the national budget has had any serious impact on either public debate or policy implementation. The prerogatives of competitive party politics, in constant search of budgetary allocations in support of party-friendly special interests, function to dissuade effective governance for sustainable development.

Transcending Context and Contingency

Mullally's chapter on the Irish experience with SD implementation is replete with crucial insights and probing questions as to several of the key factors contributing to the SD impasse. The analysis is comprehensive and well documented on a number of issues. But what emerges most clearly for the present discussion is the way in which contextual features of the established decision-making system interact with contingent developments to effectively undermine the best of national SD intentions.

In terms of national decision-making, Ireland was particularly well prepared for taking strong initial steps in the post-Rio period for a 'partnership' approach to SD values and goals. The history of Ireland after the partial resolution of the struggle for independence from Great Britain in 1922 led to a strong 'communitarian' orientation in the new 26-county state. This was clearly manifest in both the original Free-State Constitution of 1922, but even more so in the new constitution of the Republic of Ireland in 1937. Orchestrated from the start by Eamon de Valera, the constitutional imagery stressed familial values and cooperative goals in economic, social and cultural life. This laid the foundation for strong institutions based on the 'social partnership' during the post-war period, a mode of national social choice that was firmly in place upon the arrival of the Rio Accords. Mullally's analysis illustrates clearly how this entrenchment initially structured in a most positive way the formulation of a national strategy for SD, as well as how it subsequently raised its own 'path-dependent' barriers to effective implementation.

The chapter complements this analysis with parallel perspectives on the particular trajectory of Ireland's by-now classic boom-bust economic development. In little more than a decade, Ireland's imagery has somersaulted from Celtic Tiger to Battered Alley Cat. The vaunted social partnership between government, business and labour self-destructed in a blaze of internecine criticism, and the values and goals of sustainable development vanished in the smoke. Both 'business as usual' and 'politics as usual' proved totally incapable of effectively addressing the Rio agenda, and the ensuing 'politics of crisis' has as yet provided little hope for a revival.

Mullally's detailed analysis of the attempt to promote more sustainable outcomes at the local level (through both Local Agenda 21 and the subsequent introduction of city and county development boards – CDBs) also reveals similar results with respect to inconsistencies and contradictions related to poorly focused and poorly integrated policy instruments. All in all, therefore, the experience of the Irish attempt to conceptualize, plan and govern for sustainable development provides solid evidence for why the core governing impetus for effective SD implementation must undertake the task in a much more serious 'constitutional' and 'directive' manner if traditional modes of parliamentary politics and social partnership are to succeed. Though clearly depressing for some, one of Mullally's many conclusions warrants repetition in the service of democratic reform:

> We might also conclude that deliberation is also a necessary, but not sufficient, condition of governance for sustainable development. ... Participation in reforming practices and structures that fall far short of realizing fundamental change, undermines rather than reinforces societal capacity.

In short, the biases and path dependency of the governing 'media' in Ireland, conducted as both business and politics as usual, clearly indicate that the 'message' of sustainable development, as so well comprehended and embraced in Ireland, requires *significantly different democratic media* to succeed.

The Ethics of More Authoritative Governance

In her very timely, challenging and typically 'brave' contribution to the volume, Susan Baker takes head on a key normative issue related to what democratic reform for sustainable development entails. As one of the first political scientists to directly address the issue of governance for SD (1996; Baker et al. 1997), Baker is particularly well prepared for probing the difficult question of basic ethical principles. Her mode of explication here is to focus on the age-old concept of the 'common good'. She does so moreover by creatively confronting what she portrays as a dominant liberal consensus on the primacy of individual rights (in its most 'social form' as developed by John Rawls), with the work of John Dryzek on 'ecological rationality' and social choice. Her crucial premise is that 'good societies cannot be produced in the absence of good natural environments', and that the latter is both understandable and *potentially consensual* as 'ecological integrity'.

The feature of Baker's presentation that is most crucial for the democracy-SD issue raised here is her direct confrontation of what she refers to as 'the elephant in the room' and the 'vexed question': namely, 'the conditions under which restrictions on the freedom of people to pursue their ultimate aims may need to be imposed and how democratic society is to confront this problem while still retaining its democratic nature'.

What is unique about Baker's presentation is the way she openly begins by taking a very principled stand on the contention that human rationality does not in and of itself imply that humans are 'the primary subjects of ethical deliberations and moral behaviour'. It is this premise that leads her to embrace the principle of ecological integrity as a normative standard that is *somehow* transcendent of collective processes and individual rights and preferences. The basic ambivalence of the position is, as I view it, inherent in the use of the term 'subjects' above. Are we talking about subjects in the sense of a conscious mind vis-à-vis objective reality (the essence of homo sapiens) or in the sense of being a 'subject to authority'?

As it turns out the issue proves crucial for Baker's argument, as she, on the one hand, embraces ecological integrity as an overarching principle for the public good while, on the other, concludes that deliberative democracy is probably the only way to satisfactorily legitimize the principle. Her analysis lays bare the crucial normative dilemma in question, and admirably encourages thereby others to sharpen their *own* understandings of an ecological versus a liberal common good. She herself appears to land on the side of deliberative democracy, but acknowledges in the end that 'setting loose the beast of collective will is a risky necessity'. Just how risky, however, remains an open question – risky perhaps within a context of deliberative democracy that assumes that deliberations will become more and more ecologically 'correct', but equally risky in a context of a global consensus on a necessary programme for sustainable development? Or, even more acutely, in the context of a scientific consensus on the nature of 'ecological integrity' in relation to climate change? More 'vexed questions' which – building further on Baker's tussle with the common good – will be addressed below.

Democratic Reform for a 'Politics of Limits'

Finally there is what I view as the most comprehensive and specific contribution to the democracy-SD impasse of the volume, James Meadowcroft's chapter on the 'politics of limits'. In typical Meadowcroft fashion, the contribution addresses *the* critical issues of the SD impasse in a reflective cut-to-the-quick essayistic style. The richness of the explication and analysis of the limits problematic within the SD discourse is impossible to capture in only a few paragraphs. Suffice it to say that it outlines an agenda for further discussion that is sorely needed, and that is indeed pregnant with implications and possibilities for the crucial question as to 'where do we go from here?' That I again choose to be both selective and cryptic in exploiting the contribution for my own problematic is solely justified by the ease through which the reader can confirm the 'limits' of my choice.

As I read Meadowcroft his position provides a perfect bridge between Baker's more general normative-theoretic approach and my own attempt to focus the impasse discussion on the specifics of democratic dysfunctionality. Whereas Baker argues for associating the common good with the notion of ecological integrity, and for both justifying and operationalizing the latter through deliberative democracy, Meadowcroft convincingly outlines what this probably involves for practical politics. In an essential ideological sense, he goes back to what he terms the 'two awkward concepts' of the Brundtland Report – needs and limits – and demonstrates how the inter-dependence between the two is *the* core feature of the SD programme. Satisfying the 'essential needs of the world's poor' can only be achieved – within an ethical framework for preserving natural life-support systems – by accepting and constituting a 'politics of limits'. Steering development in accord with an overarching principle of ecological integrity must thus address *both* the material limits of the global carrying capacity of nature, and the social limits on survival and 'essential-need' satisfaction inherent in global inequality.

It is by way of addressing this issue in greater detail that Meadowcroft provides five general characteristics of a new politics of limits. In the first of these characteristics – the manner by which a politics of limits 'would place concern with social/ecological interactions at the centre of political life' – he elaborates on several aspects of ecological rationality as endorsed by both Dryzek and Baker. Most important in my view here is that Meadowcroft moves the discussion away from a discussion of growth versus no growth, towards a more complex assessment of the factors affecting 'material interactions' among populations, resource bases, technologies and culturally determined levels of consumption in specific settings. In addition to clarifying the basic notion of ecological limits, moreover, he goes on to discuss four additional 'requirements' for a politics of limits. Each of these points opens new avenues for further discussions of specific norms, procedures and governing mechanisms by which a focus on limits could improve the effectiveness of SD implementation.

Meadowcroft also raises, however, four potential difficulties with his projective outline of a politics of limits. Two of his concerns here touch on possible negative outcomes of a general sort. A politics of limits might: (1) 'unduly circumscribe human ambition' (by choking off 'social dynamism and innovation'); and/or (2) 'be exploited to legitimate inequality' (by making politics a zero-sum game 'with a brutal struggle for what remains'). As Meadowcroft himself provides good arguments for why these types of potential problem need not arise, I will let them lie here. It is the remaining two problems which interest me most: (3) 'that a politics of environmental limits will not work because the real problem is capitalism'; and (4) that it will not work 'because voters will never go for it'. The first concern rounds us back to the problem identified by Robert Dahl in the citation prefacing the present chapter; and the second goes directly to the crux of my peeve with competitive democracy – the need to reform the model in a more authoritative direction with respect to the functional requirements of sustainable development. Meadowcroft's brief treatment of the two issues thus provides a fruitful bridge to my own conclusions.

4.   SPEAKING POWER TO TRUTH

When Aaron Wildavsky promulgated the phrase 'speaking truth to power' with his book of the same name (Wildavsky 1987), his mission was to strengthen the status of policy analysis within political science and governance. He tried, as he said, to strike a balance between 'dogma and scepticism' in policy analysis by stressing implementation as a challenge for learning and adaptation in realizing the goals of governmental programmes. In an 'aspiring democracy' he said:

> the truth we speak is partial. There is always more than one version of the truth and we can be most certain that the latest statement isn't it. This is not only democracy's truth, it is also democracy's dogma. (1987, p. 404)

Wildavsky passed away in 1993, but two years after his death a final work appeared (edited by his colleague Arnold Meltsner) entitled *But is it TRUE?: A Citizen's Guide to Environmental Health and Safety Issues* (Wildavsky 1995). In this work, Wildavsky turns clearly towards scepticism, giving voice (particularly in the area of environmental policy) to what today would qualify as hard-core doubt as to either the validity or legitimacy of mainstream research on climate change.

By reversing Wildavsky's phrase to 'speaking power to truth', I want to signal two principal (and principled) conclusions from my own experience in the field of SD policy analysis: first, that the truth underlying the commitment to sustainable development is of a particularly strong ethical nature; and, second, that the power necessary to realize this particular policy truth has in fact been undermined by a misconstrued application of democratic dogma.

The Ethics of SD-related 'Truth'

As for the first conclusion let me start by making explicit an ethical conviction that underlies much of what is said above in the discussion of the 'contradictions' between competitive and ecological democracy. In an earlier article (Lafferty 1996b, 2000a referred to above), I made the argument that the 'moral pressure' underlying the SD programme could be grounded by two separate understandings of ethics: a 'realist' natural-law-based approach and a 'consensual' democracy-based approach. Without going into detail as to the conceptual nature of these approaches, or as to why I view them as particularly strong sources for policy adoption and implementation, let me simply restate what was said earlier: (1) that the realist orientation is based on the normative weight of scientific results in the area of human-induced disruption of 'ecological integrity', as well as the leading role taken by natural scientists in supporting the SD agenda; and (2) that the 'consensualist' orientation is based on the exceptional endorsement by the international community of nations (within the UN system) of the SD programme.

My claim, in other words, is that the 'truth' underlying the goal of sustainable development (as the 'common good', if you will) is quite massively supported by the two dominant ethical theories of modern rationalism. The values, goals, strategies and action plans of the programme are thus about as good as it gets when it comes to answering the question: 'Why are member states of the United Nations, their leaders and citizens morally obligated to pursue the SD agenda as quickly and effectively as possible?'

So much for the truth of the programme: the moral pressure necessary – though widely acknowledged by policy analysts to be lacking – behind 'political will'. And here the crucial aspect of the 'impasse' appears to be the dominant *competing truth* – vis-à-vis both ecological integrity and global developmental justice – the value system of free market (liberalist) capitalism. It is the alternative ethics of this system, with respect to both natural-science realism and United Nations' consensualism, that emerges as 'policy trump' in trade-off after trade-off where crucial decisions as to ecological integrity and global justice are taken. This, I believe, is not a contention, but a well-documented conclusion from empirical studies of the record of SD implementation. It is thus not surprising that capitalism is listed by Meadowcroft as a crucial barrier against a politics of limits, or that Robert Dahl identifies market capitalism and its consequences as a major challenge to polyarchy.

Alternative 'Powers' for More Effective SD Governing

Which leads us to 'power'. Given that the SD programme may involve a particularly truthful set of values and goals, how can democratic power be brought to bear in an effective, goal-related manner? While Baker raises the hope that discursive democracy might lead to a strong and more effective commitment to ecological integrity, Meadowcroft raises a number of empirically based doubts as to whether democratic voters ever will go for it. Robert Dahl also gives voice to similar concerns, viewing capitalism as a 'nondemocratic economic system' that poses 'a formidable and persistent challenge to democratic goals and practices throughout the twentieth century', a challenge that 'will surely continue in the twenty-first century'. Clearly, the speaking of democratic power to the truth of sustainable development requires a new and more authoritative voice if the SD policy discourse is to move beyond the current impasse.

Both Dahl and Meadowcroft follow up with initial attempts to confront the challenge of the impasse. Their confrontations with Baker's 'vexed issue' are, however, characterized by the deep-seated ambivalence towards criticism of democracy mentioned earlier. They both acknowledge that governance according to liberal-capitalist principles creates serious problems for democracy in general (Dahl's thrust), and for the pursuit of sustainable development in particular (Meadowcroft's thrust). Neither gives voice, however, to any specific procedural or institutional reform that might move us beyond the impasse.

For Dahl the major challenge is to try to redress the negative impacts on equality fostered by capitalism in the hope that if only greater equality can be realized within democratic decision-making the end results will be better all round. He does not address the questionability of the premise such a view rests on: namely, that greater equality of decision-making resources and fairer electoral procedures will result in positive outcomes for global sustainability. Whereas this clearly *might* be true for both citizen-based and interest-group politics 'as usual', it has demonstrably proved to be *not* true for the politics of sustainable development. Here the nod goes clearly to Dryzek and Baker. Governing by competitive representative democracy to achieve goals that are at best embraced by environmental activists and their idealist organizations does not guarantee outcomes that reflect either ecological rationality or global justice.

As for Meadowcroft, he clearly recognizes the latter dilemma as crucial to the SD impasse and has written a great deal on the topic. Yet even he seems to have difficulty in accepting the prospect of more authoritative steering through functionally specific democratic reforms. As I understand his concluding comments here on the 'pathologies' of democratic decision-making, he entertains the possibility that existing modes of competitive representative politics could develop to transcend the acknowledged barriers. His projected time-span is, however, long ('over many decades') and will require 'iterative decisions at many levels (local, national and trans-national)'. In this context, 'democratic electorates might edge closer to a politics of limits', but 'forging the political coalitions and transition pathways required for such movement remains the most significant political challenge of the contemporary era'.

Both Dahl and Meadowcroft appear therefore to place their hopes for a more effectual and consequent politics for sustainable development in improvements in what Cohen identifies as the *conditions* for democracy (Figure 14.1). For Dahl, this implies an across-the-board and relatively general endorsement of greater equality in political resources. Meadwocroft is also concerned with greater equality in political influence, but he also stresses the possibility of altering other conditions – basic values of consumption and lifestyles, technological innovation and new alliances among pro-SD interest groups – through interactive policy learning and (more implicitly) the gradual diffusion of 'best-practice' (as documented here by Busch and Jörgens). Neither of these key thinkers seem to feel, in other words, that it is the nature of the basic *presuppositions* of the competitive-democracy model (its modes of 'community' and 'rationality') that needs revision, nor do they stress a need for amending these presuppositions, and their reflection in constitutional conditions, through a more goal-related use of legal instruments.

5. CONCLUSION: STRENGTHENING DECISIVENESS FOR SD OUTCOMES

It is from here that my own position takes its point of departure. Without wishing to sacrifice any of the basic rights of polyarchy, or to change the institutional procedures for corporate-pluralist decision-making as manifest in Northern European democratic states, my strong feeling is that the governing norms inherent in these systems must be supplemented by democratic reforms that are functionally designed to better realize SD commitments. Several such reforms have been put forth in the earlier works mentioned above and several more could clearly be gleaned from the growing green-state and ecological-democracy literature. In concluding this postscript, however, I would like to redraw attention to a key governing mechanism for sustainable development: the ProSus 'benchmarks' for both prescribing and assessing environmental policy integration (EPI). The EPI concept and the benchmarks themselves are thoroughly elaborated, and applied, elsewhere.[8] Here I would like to more pointedly relate the steering mechanism to the discussion of democracy above. In what way could a more consequential focus on the general notion of EPI speak 'power' to the 'truth' of SD as a highly prioritized 'social choice'? How can we significantly strengthen the political will which so many international, regional and national organizations acknowledge as *the* crucial missing link in SD implementation and which both Dahl and Meadowcroft highlight in their respective critiques of existing democratic practices?

Altering the Presuppositions

First it seems to me essential that if we are to move from strong ethical endorsement of the SD programme to more effectual implementation through SD principles we must directly address the *presuppositions of ecological democracy*. This is a task that impinges on the generically essential feature of democracy as developed by Cohen: its participatory nature as a mode of governance. The presuppositions of *community* and *rationality* underlie and circumscribe the most essential constituting features of any given manifestation of 'democracy' in practice. And if, as we have seen, these features are embedded in a given understanding of community (historically determined administratively bounded populations) and a given understanding of rationality (a competitive game to determine 'who governs?'), the 'deep structure' of the system in question exerts a fundamental meta-influence on the practices and outcomes of the decision-making process. In the face of consensual demands for more effective action to achieve SD, such a deep structure must be addressed by active governing for change. It cannot be left to a hope of 'social policy learning' over time.

Does this imply 'top–down' steering? Yes. Does it imply 'undemocratic' steering? No. To mention only two types of policy initiatives that directly impinge on the nature of the presuppositions: (1) constant, ongoing discussions in most Western democracies as to reforming the boundaries of existing 'communities'; and (2) constant, ongoing discussions as to the guiding principles for public-educational institutions at all levels of learning, from kindergarten to graduate school. The ability of governing authorities, through legislation and administrative regulation, to significantly affect these presuppositions in the direction of 'ecological' rather than 'service and allocatory' communities and towards prioritizing and promoting 'ecological rationality' rather than 'competitive majoritarian rationality' in designated areas are decidedly present. The political will to become more forceful in these policy areas is no different instrumentally from the political will that already structures, controls and sanctions numerous types of 'good' and 'bad' behaviour.

Introducing New Democratic Instruments

Second, there is the question of securing the SD benefits achieved by a reworking of the presuppositions for more *consequential outputs and outcomes to realize SD goals.* The road to perdition is notoriously paved with good intentions and, given the pliable and fickle nature of human intentions, SD must be secured and channelled to not only produce new outputs (in the form of policies and programmes), but also new outcomes (in the form of demonstrable long-term results). We must move from new presuppositions to the introduction of new and more determinative *democratic instruments.* The *range* of democratic governance must be circumscribed. It must be openly acknowledged that the principles and instruments necessary to guarantee and maintain the *sovereign range* of democracy are not (and in truth never have been) identical to the principles and instruments necessary to achieve an effective *administrative range* of democracy. It is here that the EPI mechanisms come into play, as they are designed to provide a specific mode of democratically sanctioned sub-governance for a more consequent application of ecological rationality and SD goals. Three general characteristics of this more 'authoritative' design are: (1) greater legalism and regulation; (2) greater caution as to risk; and (3) strengthened advocacy in monitoring implementation.

The common feature of all three of these characteristics is that they specifically deviate from not only normal administrative practice within existing 'competitive-democracy' governments, but also from dominant thinking within the pro-SD lobby. The turn towards more authoritative governing for sustainable development is thus at odds with both the move towards greater reliance on 'free-market' principles and economic steering instruments that has dominated American and European governments for the past several decades, and the ongoing dominance of de-centralization, increased stakeholder participation, 'partnerships' and other variants of 'deliberative democracy' that have dominated SD politics since their inception at Rio. Not of course that either market-related instruments or stakeholder involvement are not important for SD implementation: just that they have had their day in the SD sun; have not been able to ward off the impending darkness; and have increasingly become as much a part of the problem as of the solution. Not so much for what they stand for in the way of greater NGO involvement and influence, but for how the overall SD discourse has become increasingly mired down in 'process' rather than 'product' (see Chapter 12 by Lafferty and Coenen in Lafferty 2001b).

A need for returning to the blessings of law and regulation is in this view totally necessary for overcoming the impasse in SD implementation. Just as goal-directed regulation always has been a feature of democratic governments in time of crisis and threat, so too is it now demonstrably necessary to move the SD agenda. Ideally this could come in the form of much stronger constitutional guarantees for the protection of different aspects of ecological rationality, the rights of future generations and the rights of the world's poor to 'essential-need' satisfaction. The process of changing constitutions is, however, notoriously time-consuming in most liberal-pluralist democracies, so that the necessary legalism in question will probably have to come from existing legislative procedures. Either way, the crucial aspect is to impose greater determinism in areas of critical importance for protecting and sustaining natural life-support systems, as well as eliminating the cultural, social, economic and political barriers to eliminating essential-need poverty. As stressed by both Baker and Meadowcroft here, democratic states impose all kinds of serious across-the-political-spectrum and long-term restrictions on citizens, businesses and markets in general. There is therefore no principled hindrance on using the 'democratic toolbox' to impose stronger and more effective pro-SD regulations.

The moral authority for such regulation must, however, be both well founded and widely embraced. It is here that the role of research, science and risk must come to bear. The SD agenda is in many ways unique to democratic decision-making. It actively seeks legitimacy in and through classic participatory, citizen-based norms. Yet major aspects of its prioritized policy list are almost totally dependent on scientific research and expert opinion. The demands generated for action and change in the name of either 'ecological rationality' or the changing parameters of morally unacceptable poverty on a world basis are not traditional economic or social demands from specific affected groups within a given community. As clearly illuminated by Meadowcroft, a politics of limits, in all its manifold relevance for sustainable development, is a very different type of politics indeed.

And the challenge of ascertaining a consensual point of departure for why and how SD-related change *must* be enacted – in the face of what can only be described as dire consequences for either the health of the planet or the life chances of the world's poor – is *not* an amenable task for competitive politics as usual. In fact it often involves finding an action solution at the opposite end of the decision-making continuum from the competitive model. Whereas the essence of polyarchy is often associated with the majority principle and the right of the winning side in electoral contests to pursue *their* version of the 'truth' in any given policy area, the essence of ecological/SD democracy is, in critical areas, to make the *right* decision vis-à-vis system-threatening developments. Science and expert opinion must in other words be given a position of 'principled priority' in decisions affecting critical states of conditions deemed essential for human survival. The institutional status of scientific advisory councils and the way by which scientifically based assessments of risk are channelled into and weighted in SD-related policy decisions are thus crucial issues for democratic reform.[9] Discussions and debates as to the use of 'consensus conferences' and different modes of institutionalizing the 'precautionary principle' (as specifically related to the SD discourse) are also of pressing importance.[10]

Strengthening Advocacy Monitoring

Finally, a third aspect of the benchmarks which reinforce the self-binding of specific SD issues to 'strong-law regulation' is the introduction of *advocacy monitoring of the implementation process*. By 'advocacy monitoring' I mean a form of public auditing, an ongoing systematic evaluation by professional public servants of the follow-through on SD decisions. As the record of implementation since Rio clearly indicates for virtually all polyarchal regimes, the gap between rhetorical policy 'outputs' and realized 'policy outcomes' is considerable. For the most SD-conscious regimes, the rhetorical commitment to the goals of Rio and Johannesburg have been highly impressive: a rhetorical output of charters, principles, strategies and action plans. Yet through the normal give-and-take of competitive party politics and regimes of shifting ideological persuasion, the follow-up – even by acknowledged front-runners such as Sweden, Norway, the Netherlands and the United Kingdom – has become an increasing embarrassment for responsible public administrators. Confronted with the hands-on task of 'speaking truth to power', they have increasingly understood that the varying powers of shifting regimes make a mockery of purported overarching truths.

This problem too is no newcomer to students of democratic

effectiveness. In most issue areas, however, conflicts over the trade-off between maintaining ingrown administrative procedures for adapting to alternating democratic mandates and the achievement of long-term policy goals have been decided in favour of the former. There are of course exceptions: commitments to national security; persistent threats to public health; major investments in infrastructure for economic development; putting a man on the moon. There have, however, been virtually *no* exceptions for sustainable development: neither the prevention of human-induced climate change, the decimation of biodiversity, the depletion and contamination of vital resources (water, air, forests) or the eradication of life-stunting poverty. They all proceed pretty much apace with the imbalance between rhetoric and achievement becoming more and more a fact of 'political reality'.

Methods for constraining the workings of competitive politics are clearly available in the democratic toolbox. Three types of reform, all with existing precedents, are: (1) strengthening the SD mandate for institutionalized public auditing of the implementation of legislatively sanctioned policies (for example, the separate Department for Performance Auditing within the Office of the Auditor General of Norway);[11] (2) the establishment of a separate Commissioner of Sustainable Development, with a mandate to present recurring policy and strategy reviews to parliament (with both the Canadian and Swedish experiences to build on, but with even stronger 'constitutional shields' against politically motivated changes of the mandate);[12] and (3) the establishment of a separate 'Ombudsman for Sustainable Development', with strong ongoing advocacy powers in support of ecological integrity, generational justice and the elimination of essential-need poverty.[13]

Realizing Moral Decisiveness

> Yes, imagine it; wish it; *will* it even – but *do* it?
> No, I can't understand it.
>
> Henrik Ibsen, Peer Gynt, Act 3, Scene 1

For Ibsen's Peer Gynt – as for all of Peer's descendants among environmental politicians in today's Western democracies – to imagine, wish for and even express a political will for sustainable development is one thing: but to actually *do it* – to find the means within the generic scope of democratic theory to actually *realize* change – is clearly a challenge beyond competitive politics as usual. The irony of applying the quote to the impasse on climate change is, however, even more biting. The 'it' that Peer is referring to is an act of self-mutilation by an accidentally observed farm boy. As Peer watches from afar, the lad severs his own finger with a sickle to avoid conscription. What more appropriate imagery could be evoked to capture the actions of politicians who, in the face of massive scientific evidence, emasculate climate-change agreements to avoid responsibility for emission-cutting costs? No, Peer; it can't be understood.

But that is where we stand at this juncture in the relatively short and relatively inconsequential history of SD implementation. The integrated programme for change outlined above – a programme for strengthening the community basis, policy rationale and decisiveness of democratic governance for sustainable development – is empirically based, logically coherent and interactively cumulative in effect. While each aspect of the reform is in accord with generic democratic norms, the overall advantage in 'authoritative determination' within the range of SD principles and goals would be exceptional – just the type of exceptionality that a transformative shift towards a sustainable and more just global community requires.

Yet we should have no illusions. The 'truth' of sustainable development as an ultimate common good is clearly less actively endorsed today than it was during the period 1972–92 (from Stockholm to Rio). The first publication issued under my leadership of 'The Project for an Alternative Future' (the forerunner to ProSus) was entitled *Ikke Bare Si Det, Men Gjøre Det!* (*Don't Just Say It, But Do It!* – Stenseth and Hertzberg 1992). Twenty years after this amazingly foresightful collection of 33 essays on the topic of sustainable development, there is one essay of particular importance for the position outlined here. The Norwegian economic historian (and earlier Chair of the Norwegian Committee for the Nobel Peace Prize) Francis Sejersted used the Marxist-structuralist term 'systemic coercion' (*systemtvang*) to explain the deep-seated intransigence of environmental problems (Sejersted 1992). How, he asked, can we overcome the systemic coercion that seems to block both economic and political attempts to bring about change? Does the answer possibly lie in a more conscious effort to change the cultural and technological bases of the 'coercion' in question?

Another leading thinker on SD issues, Erik Damman – founder of the organization 'The Future in Our Hands' (*Alternativ Framtid*) – was asked to conclude the book with an afterword. His choice of title was 'Is the change that is necessary, possible?' (Damman 1992). Damman referred back to Sejersted's use of the systemic coercion concept, endorsed it, placed it in a context of globalization and offered several possible ways out of the growing tendency for national and local communities to 'have to' bend and adapt to economic, growth-driven imperatives. Also, his 'solutions' were mainly outlined in terms of informational, technological, cultural and ideological transformation.

I choose to conclude with 20-year-old citations from these two highly respected public intellectuals for three reasons: (1) they defined the challenge of promoting sustainable development in a way that strongly affected my own understanding and motivation in the area of trying to determine 'What works, where, when and how?' to achieve SD goals; (2) neither of the two, in their joint concern for systemic coercion and the many suggestions put forth to overcome the problem, raised the prospect of democratic reform; and (3) virtually all of their suggestions for making possible what 'had to be done' to overcome the coercion have been subsequently elaborated upon theoretically, and promulgated ideologically, *without* significant progress in overcoming the multifaceted inertia that was in place after Rio, after Johannesburg and after Rio +20.

Thus I conclude with the earlier cited testimony to Marshall McLuhan. 'The medium is the message', and the message is the systemic coercion (perhaps we should say 'path dependency') of competitive democracy as a 'medium' for resolving the impasse on sustainable development. I have no illusions that this message will be taken any more seriously by the political representatives of competitive democracy today than was done by their predecessors 20 years ago. It is, however, a *different* message; it goes to the core problem of the impasse and – perhaps most decisive in the long run, though hardly very consoling in the short run – it is in line with a *most* robust 'law' of societal dynamics: form (ultimately) follows function!

NOTES

1. The position presented here builds most directly on the following works in English: Lafferty (1996a, 2000b, 2001a, 2002, 2004) and Lafferty and Meadowcroft (1996). It also draws heavily, in Norwegian, on Hagtvet and Lafferty (1984).
2. It is important to stress here that the model in Figure 14.1, while building directly on Cohen's concepts, is my own construction.
3. Most of the early 'pioneers' in analyses of 'democracy and the environment' were contributors to an earlier volume by Lafferty and Meadowcroft (1996). Since then, several important works addressed to this particular 'pairing' have been published.
4. The generalizations in this section are well documented in several publications. See, for example: Lafferty and Meadowcroft (1996, 2000); Lafferty et al. (1997, 2002); Lafferty and Langhelle (1999); Lafferty (1996b, 2004).
5. The most relevant publications in English are Chapters 1 and 12 of Lafferty and Meadowcroft (1996); Lafferty (1996a, 1996b, 1997, 2000b, 2001a, 2002); the concluding chapter of Lafferty and Meadowcroft (2000); and Chapter 11 of Lafferty (2004). The approach has also been presented and discussed at numerous international meetings, conferences and workshops throughout the period 1995–2009. The three aspects of Cohen's work applied here – *community*, *rationality* and *range/decisiveness* – are directly derived from these sources.
6. The summary builds most directly on Lafferty (2000b).
7. See in particular the numerous works of Susan Baker, Elisabeth Bomberg and Helge Jörgens and their colleagues. Note further the exceptional efforts of the European Sustainable Development Network (ESDN): (as accessed 14 November 2011: http://

www.sd-network.eu/), and the work by the European Commission in cooperation with EuroStat on monitoring both strategic SD initiatives and SD indicators in the EU (EC 2009).

8. The key sources here (of which there are many) are most specifically documented, analysed, debated and pragmatically developed in the following texts: Lenschow (2002); Lafferty and Hovden (2003); Jordan and Liefferink (2004); EEA (2005a, 2005b); Nilsson (2005); Nilsson and Ekerberg (2007); Jordan and Lenschow (2008); and Knudsen (2009). Reference must also be made to the large number of books, papers, reports, and so on, produced within the EU-supported Coordinated Action on Environmental Policy Integration and Multi-level Governance (EPIGOV): available online at the website of the Ecologic Institute: (as accessed 18 November 2011: http://ecologic.eu/projekte/epigov/). The 'benchmarks' themselves are most specifically elaborated in Chapter 7 of Lafferty (2004) and have been applied as evaluation standards in Hovden and Torjussen (2002); Lafferty et al. (2005); Lafferty et al. (2007); and Knudsen (2009).

9. The record and impact of the Netherlands Scientific Council for Government Policy is illustrative of the function in question. The Council was officially established in 1974 with the following mandate: 'The Council shall: (1) supply for Government Policy scientifically sound information on developments which may affect society in the long term and draw timely attention to anomalies and bottlenecks to be anticipated; (2) provide a scientific structure which the Government could use when establishing priorities and which would ensure that a consistent policy is pursued; (3) with respect to studies undertaken in the sphere of research on future developments and long-term planning in both public and private sectors, make recommendations on the elimination of structural inadequacies, the furtherance of specific studies and the improvement of communication and coordination.' The Council has produced hundreds of cutting-edge reports on areas of crucial significance for SD policy. (See www.wrr.nl/english/index.jsp, as accessed 16 November 2011).

10. Note that there are at least two popular usages of the 'consensus conference' idea: one that stresses the need for involving a broad spectrum of stakeholders in projected policy areas (widely used in Denmark, the UK and the Netherlands for example); and another devoted solely to producing consensus among a given community of scientists as to the best knowledge available for a given state of affairs, and the probable consequences of proposed policy interventions (as defined and employed by, for example, the National Institutes of Health in the United States (ee http://consensus.nih.gov/aboutcdp.htm, as accessed 16 November 2011). With respect to the debate on applying risk analysis and the precautionary principle to SD-related decision-making, see for example: O'Brien (2000); EEA (2002); O'Riordan et al. (2001); de Sadeleer (2002, 2007); Fisher et al. (2006); and Zander (2010).

11. An updated version of 'The Guidelines for Performance Auditing' is available at the website of the Office of the Auditor General, www.riksrevisjonen.no/en/Methodology/PerformanceAuditing/Pages/PerformanceAuditing.aspx (as accessed 23 November 2011). The following questions are deemed 'pertinent' to the conduct of performance audits: (1) Are resources being used to address issues that are in compliance with the decisions and intentions of the Storting? (goal achievement); (2) Is the use of resources and concomitant instruments effective in relation to the goals formulated by the Storting in the relevant area?; (3) Are regulations laid down by the Storting being complied with?; (4) Are the policy instruments, management tools and regulations effective and appropriate for a follow-up of the decisions and intentions of the Storting?; (5) Has the Government supplied the Storting with sufficient documentation to facilitate an appropriate decision?; (6) Are applicable environmental policies being implemented so that principles for sustainable development and appropriate management of natural resources are being complied with?

12. The mandate, activities and reports of the Commissioner are available at the website of the Office of the Auditor General of Canada, www.oag-bvg.gc.ca/internet/English/cesd_fs_e_921.html (as accessed 15 November 2011).

13. To our knowledge there are currently no specific mandates for ombudsmen for sustainable development in effect at the national level. The EU mandate for the European Ombudsman does, however, include responsibility for the environment, and the current occupant of the position, P. Nikiforos Diamandouros, presented earlier this year an excellent overview of the functions (and administrative ambitions!) of the office, www.ombudsman.europa.eu/en/activities/speech.faces/en/10558/html.bookmark (as accessed 18 November 2011). The difference between an ombudsman and a commissioner of sustainable development is not always clear across different political systems. In general, however, it appears that an ombudsman's function is more proactive and receptive of incoming 'complaints' on an ongoing basis, while a commissioner is usually more evaluative and documentary on a recurring periodic basis. Norway today boasts six different ombudsmen offices at the national level: for the public administration; equality and anti-discrimination; children; the armed forces; non-military civil service (as an alternative to military service); and patients. There is, however, no ombudsman for the environment or sustainable development, despite the existence of Article 110b of the Norwegian Constitution that states (since 1992 – the year of Rio) that: 'Every person has a right to an environment that is conducive to health and to a natural environment whose productivity and diversity are maintained. Natural resources should be managed on the basis of comprehensive long-term considerations whereby this right will be safeguarded for future generations as well.' (English version available at the website of the Norwegian Storting, www.stortinget.no/en/In-English/About-the-Storting/The-Constitution/The-Constitution/, as accessed 22 November 2011). See also the excellent comparative overview of the Office of Ombudsman in Europe by Kucsko-Stadlmayer (2008).

REFERENCES

Baker, S. (1996), 'Environmental policy in the European Union: institutional dilemmas and democratic practice', in W.M. Lafferty and J. Meadowcroft (eds), *Democracy and the Environment: Problems and Prospects*, Cheltenham, UK and Brookfield, VT, US: Edward Elgar.

Baker, S., M. Kousis, D. Richardson and S. Young (eds) (1997), *The Politics of Sustainable Development: Theory, Policy and Practice within the European Union*, London: Routledge.

Bettleheim, B. (1950), *Love is Not Enough: The Treatment of Emotionally Disturbed Children*, Glencoe, IL: The Free Press.

Cohen, C. (1971), *Democracy*, New York: The Free Press.

Connolly, W.E. (1974), *The Terms of Political Discourse*, Oxford: Basil Blackwell Ltd.

Dahl, R. (1998), *On Democracy*, New Haven, CT and London: Yale University Press.

Damman, E. (1992), 'Er den nødvendige forandring mulig?' ['Is the change that is necessary, possible?'], in N.C. Stenseth and K. Hertzberg (eds), *Ikke Bare Si Det, Men Gjøre Det!: Om Bærekraftig Utvikling*, Oslo: Universitetesforlaget, pp. 371–6.

de Sadeleer, N. (2002), *Environmental Principles from Political Slogans to Legal Rules*, Oxford: Oxford University Press.

de Sadeleer, N. (2007), *Implementing the Precautionary Principle: Approaches from the Nordic Countries, the EU and USA*, London: Earthscan.

Dryzek, J. (1987), *Rational Ecology: Environment and Political Economy*, Oxford: Basil Blackwell Ltd.

EC (European Commission) (2009), *Sustainable Development in the European Union: 2009 Monitoring Report of the EU Sustainable Development Strategy*, Luxembourg: Office for Official Publications of the European Communities.

EEA (European Environment Agency) (2002), *Late Lessons from Early Warnings: The Precautionary Principle 1896–2000*, environmental issue report, No. 22, Copenhagen: 2001, accessed 20 November 2011 at www.eea.europa.eu/publications/environmental_issue_report_2001_22/Issue_Report_No_22.pdf.

EEA (2005a), *Environmental Policy Integration in Europe: State of Play and an Evaluative Framework*, technical report no. 2/2005, Copenhagen: European Environment Agency.

EEA (2005b), *Environmental Policy Integration in Europe: Administrative Culture and Practices*, technical report no. 5/2005, Copenhagen: European Environment Agency.

Fisher, E., J. Jones and R. von Schomberg (eds) (2006), *Implementing the Precautionary Principle: Perspectives and Prospects*, Cheltenham, UK and Northhampton, MA, USA: Edward Elgar.

Hagtvet, B. and W.M. Lafferty (eds) (1984), *Demokrati og Demokratisering* [*Democracy and Democratization*], Oslo: Aschehoug Forlag.

Hovden, E. and S. Torjussen (2002), 'Environmental policy integration in Norway', in W.M. Lafferty, M. Nordskag and H.A. Aakre (eds), *Realizing Rio in Norway: Evaluative Studies of Sustainable Development*, Oslo: ProSus, pp. 21–42.

Jordan, A. and A. Lenschow (eds) (2008), *Innovation in Environmental Policy?: Integrating the Environment for Sustainable Development*, Cheltenham, UK and Northampton, MA, USA: Edward Elgar.

Jordan, A. and D. Liefferink (eds) (2004), *Environmental Policy in Europe: The Europeanization of National Environmental Policy*, London: Routledge.

Kellerman, H. (2009), *Love is Not Enough: Making Your Marriage Work*, Santa Barbara, CA and Oxford: ABC-CLIO.

Knudsen, J. (2009), *Environmental Policy Integration and Energy: Conceptual Clarification and Comparative Analysis of Standards and Mechanisms*, PhD dissertation, Centre for Clean Technology and Environmental Policy (CSTM), University of Twente, Enschede, the Netherlands.

Kucsko-Stadlmayer, G. (ed.) (2008), *European Ombudsman-Institutions: A Comparative Legal Analysis Regarding the Multifaceted Realisation of an Idea*, Vienna and New York: Springer Verlag.

Lafferty, W.M. (1983), 'Deltakelse og demokrati: momenter i en uendelig dialog' ['Participation and democracy: moments in a never-ending dialogue'], in T. Bergh (ed.) *Deltakerdemokratiet* [*Participatory Democracy*], Oslo: University Press, pp. 30–50.

Lafferty, W.M. (1996a), 'Democracy in an ecological state', paper presented to the Conference on the Ecological State, EU Concerted Action on 'The Ecological State: Towards a New Generation of Policies and Institutions', 28 November–1 December, Seville, Spain.

Lafferty, W.M. (1996b), 'The politics of sustainable development: problems and prospects after Rio', *Environmental Politics*, **5**, 185–208.

Lafferty, W.M. (1997), 'Democratic governance and sustainable development: Inherent conflicts and potential reforms', paper presented to the IPSA Roundtable on *Division of Powers as a Challenge in Contemporary Democracies*, 4–5 March, Rio de Janeiro, Brazil, pp. 1–24.

Lafferty, W.M. (2000a), 'The politics of sustainable development', in John Dryzek (ed.), *Debating the Earth*, Oxford and New York: Oxford University Press, pp. 360–95.

Lafferty, W.M. (2000b), 'Democratic parameters for regional sustainable development: the need for a new demos with a new rationality', paper presented to the ENSURE/SUSTAIN Symposium on 'Making Regional Sustainable Development Visible', Schloss Seggau, 13–15 November, Leipzig, Austria, pp. 1–31.

Lafferty, W.M. (2001a), 'Democracy and ecological rationality: new trials for an old ceremony', in G. Lachapelle and J. Trent (eds), *Globalization, Governance and Identity: The Emergence of New Partnerships*, Montreal, QC: University of Montreal Press, pp. 39–65.

Lafferty, W.M. (ed.) (2001b), *Sustainable Communities in Europe*, London and Sterling, VA: Earthscan.

Lafferty, W.M. (2002), 'Varieties of democratic experience: normative criteria for cross-national assessments of citizenship', in Dieter Fuchs, Edeltraud Roller and Bernard Wessels (eds), *Bürger und Demokratie in Ost und West: Studien zur politischen Kultur und xum politischen Prozess*, Festschrift for Hans-Dieter Klingemann, Weisbaden, Germany: Westdeutscher Verland, pp. 50–72.

Lafferty, W.M. (ed.) (2004), *Governance for Sustainable Development: The Challenge of Adapting Form to Function*, Cheltenham, UK and Northampton, MA, USA: Edward Elgar.

Lafferty, W.M. and E. Hovden (2003), 'Environmental policy integration: towards an analytical framework', *Environmental Politics*, **12** (3), 1–22.

Lafferty, W.M. and O.S. Langhelle (eds) (1999), *Towards Sustainable Development: On the Goals of Development – and the Conditions of Sustainability*, London: Macmillan Press.

Lafferty, W.M. and J. Meadowcroft (eds) (1996), *Democracy and the Environment: Problems and Prospects*, Cheltenham, UK and Brookfield, VT: Edward Elgar.

Lafferty, W.M. and J. Meadowcroft (eds) (2000), *Implementing Sustainable Development: Strategies and Initiatives in High Consumption Societies*, Oxford and New York: Oxford University Press.

Lafferty, W.M., O.S. Langhelle, P. Mugaas and M.H. Ruge (eds) (1997), *Rio + 5: Norges Oppfølging av FN-konferansen om Miljø og Utvikling*, Oslo: Tano Aschehoug.

Lafferty, W.M., M. Nordskag and H.A. Aakre (eds) (2002), *Realizing Rio in Norway: Evaluative Studies of Sustainable Development*, Oslo: ProSus.

Lafferty, W.M., A. Ruud and O.M. Larsen (2005), 'Environmental policy integration: how will we know it when we see it? The case of green innovation policy in Norway', in *Governance of Innovation Systems: Case Studies in Cross-Sectoral Policy*, Paris: OECD, pp. 221–44.

Lafferty, W.M., J. Knudsen and O.M. Larsen (2007), 'Pursuing sustainable development in Norway: the challenge of living up to Brundtland at home', *European Environment*, **17**, 177–88.

Lenschow, A. (2002), *Environmental Policy Integration: Greening Sectoral Policies in Europe*, London: Earthscan.

Meadowcroft, J. (1997), 'Planning, democracy and the challenge of sustainable development', *International Political Science Review*, **18**, 167–90.

Meadowcroft, J. (1999), 'The politics of sustainable development: emergent arenas and challenges for political science', *International Political Science Review*, **20**, 219–37.

Nilsson, M. (2005), *Connecting Reason to Power, Assessments, Learning, and Environmental Policy Integration in Swedish Energy Policy*, PhD dissertation, Faculty of Technology, Policy and Management, University of Delft, submitted 12 September, Stockholm: Stockholm Environment Institute.

Nilsson, M. and K. Eckerberg (eds) (2007), *Environmental Policy Integration in Practice*, London: Earthscan.

O'Brien, M. (2000), *Making Better Environmental Decisions: An Alternative to Risk Assessments*, Cambridge, MA and London: The MIT Press.

OECD (Organisation for Economic Co-operation and Development) (2001a), *Policies to Enhance Sustainable Development*, Paris: OECD.

OECD (2001b), *Sustainable Development: Critical Issues*, Paris: OECD.

OECD (2002a), *Governance for Sustainable Development: Five OECD Case Studies*, Paris: OECD.

OECD (2002b), *Sustainable Development Strategies: A Resource Book*, London and Sterling, VA: Earthscan in cooperation with OECD and UNDP.

O'Riordan, T., J. Cameron and A. Jordan (2001), *Reinterpreting the Precautionary Principle*, London: Cameron May.

Paine, T. (1776 [1986]), *Common Sense*, London: Penguin Classics.

RMoFA (Royal Ministry of Foreign Affairs) (2002), *National Strategy of Sustainable Development*, Oslo: RMoFA, accessed 5 December 2011 at www. regjeringen.no/upload/kilde/ud/bro/2003/0013/ddd/pdfv/171847-nsbu.pdf.

RMoF (2005), *Indicators for Policies to Enhance Sustainable Development*, Oslo: Royal Ministry of Finance, accessed 5 December 2011 at www.regjeringen.no/ upload/kilde/fin/bro/2005/0001/ddd/pdfv/246109-indicators.pdf.

Sejersted, F. (1992), 'Fra den truende natur til den truende teknologi' ['From threatening nature to threatening technology'], in N.C. Stenseth and K. Hertzberg (eds), *Ikke Bare Si Det, Men Gjøre Det!: Om Bærekraftig Utvikling*, Oslo: Universitetesforlaget, pp. 57–64.

Stenseth, N.C and K. Hertzberg (eds) (1992), *Ikke Bare Si Det, Men Gjøre Det! Om Bærekraftig Utvikling* [*Don't Just Say It, But Do It! On Sustainable Development*], Oslo: Unviersitetsforlaget.

Thompson, D.F. (1970), *The Democratic Citizen: Social Science and Democratic Theory in the Twentieth Century*, Cambridge: Cambridge University Press.

United Nations (1994), *Earth Summit Agenda 21: The United Nations Programme of Action from Rio*, New York: United Nations Department of Public Information.

WCED (World Commission on Environment and Development) (1987), *Our Common Future*, New York and Oxford: Oxford University Press.

Wildavsky, A. (1987), *Speaking Truth to Power: The Art and Craft of Policy Analysis* (second edn, 2002), New Brunswick, NJ and London: Transaction Publishers.

Wildavsky, A. (1995), *But is it True? A Citizen's Guide to Environmental Health and Safety Issues*, Cambridge, MA and London: Harvard University Press.

Young, O. (2006), 'Vertical interplay among scale-dependent environmental and resource regimes', *Ecology and Society*, **11** (1), 27, accessed 5 December 2011 at www.ecologyandsociety.org/vol11/iss1/art27/.

Zander, J. (2010), *The Application of the Precautionary Principle in Practice: Comparative Perspectives*, Cambridge: Cambridge University Press.

Index